Learning in likely places

Varieties of apprenticeship in Japan

Likely places of learning in Japan include folkcraft village pottery workshops, the clubhouses of female shellfish divers, traditional theaters, and the neighborhood public bath. The education of potters, divers, actors, and other novices generates identity within their specific communities of practice. In this collection of nineteen case studies of situated learning in such likely places, the contributors take apprenticeship as a fundamental model of experiential education in authentic arenas of cultural practice. Together, the essays demonstrate a rich variety of Japanese pedagogical arrangements and learning patterns, both historical and contemporary.

The volume seeks to displace the current focus on school achievement in Japan with a broader understanding of the social context of knowledge acquisition. An examination of learners as apprentices is applied to diverse segments of Japanese society. Although, for example, a female shellfish diver and an autodidact economist have no master, their conventions of learning are better compared to apprenticeship than to schooling because they must learn without being explicitly taught. Learning patterns similar to those developed in the workshop, clubhouse, or theater can be found throughout Japanese society. Medical residents and auto mechanics share with potters and actors an introduction to their professional craft through forms of apprenticeship.

These cases demonstrate both the power of formal apprenticeship and the diversity of learning arrangements and patterns in Japan that transmit traditions of art, craft, work, and community. All cases respond to the call for a new focus on "situated learning," an educational anthropology of the social relations and meanings of educational process. The authors include anthropologists, art historians, humanists, educational specialists, and an economic historian. Six cases are accounts of personal learning experiences in settings of Japanese practice.

John Singleton is an educational anthropologist and Professor Emeritus of Education and Anthropology, University of Pittsburgh. In 1997 he received the George and Louise Spindler Award for outstanding contributions to educational anthropology. His previous books are *Nichū: A Japanese School* (lectures on applied anthropology in China) and *Yingyong Renleixue.*

Learning in doing: Social, cognitive, and computational perspectives

General Editors
ROY PEA, *SRI International, Center for Technology in Learning*
JOHN SEELY BROWN, *Xerox Palo Alto Research Center*
JAN HAWKINS, *Center for Children and Technology, New York*

Computation and Human Experience
PHILIP E. AGRE

The Computer as Medium
PETER BOGH ANDERSEN, BERIT HOLMQVIST, and JENS F. JENSEN (eds.)

Understanding Practice: Perspectives on Activity and Context
SETH CHAIKLIN and JEAN LAVE (eds.)

Situated Cognition: On Human Knowledge and Computer Representations
WILLIAM J. CLANCEY

Cognition and Tool Use: The Blacksmith at Work
CHARLES M. KELLER and JANET DIXON KELLER

Situated Learning: Legitimate Peripheral Participation
JEAN LAVE and ETIENNE WENGER

Sociocultural Psychology: Theory and Practice of Doing and Knowing
LAURA M. W. MARTIN, KATHERINE NELSON, and ETHEL TOBACH (eds.)

The Construction Zone: Working for Cognitive Change in School
DENIS NEWMAN, PEG GRIFFIN, and MICHAEL COLE

Street Mathematics and School Mathematics
TEREZINHA NUNES, DAVID WILLIAM CARRAHER, and
ANALUCIA DIAS SCHLIEMANN

Distributed Cognitions: Psychological and Educational Considerations
GAVRIEL SALOMON (ed.)

Plans and Situated Actions:
The Problem of Human–Machine Communication
LUCY A. SUCHMAN

Mind and Social Practice: Selected Writings by Sylvia Scribner
ETHEL TOBACH, RACHEL JOFFEE FALMAGNE, MARY B. PARLEE,
LAURA M. W. MARTIN, and AGGIE KAPELMAN (eds.)

Sociocultural Studies of Mind
JAMES V. WERTSCH, PABLO DEL RIO, and AMELIA ALVAREZ (eds.)

Communities of Practice: Learning, Meaning, and Identity
ETIENNE WENGER

Learning in likely places

Varieties of apprenticeship in Japan

Edited by
JOHN SINGLETON

CAMBRIDGE
UNIVERSITY PRESS

PUBLISHED BY THE PRESS SYNDICATE OF THE UNIVERSITY OF CAMBRIDGE
The Pitt Building, Trumpington Street, Cambridge CB2 1RP, United Kingdom

CAMBRIDGE UNIVERSITY PRESS
The Edinburgh Building, Cambridge CB2 2RU, UK http://www.cup.cam.ac.uk
40 West 20th Street, New York, NY 10011-4211, USA http://www.cup.org
10 Stamford Road, Oakleigh, Melbourne 3166, Australia

First published 1998

Printed in the United States of America

Typeset in Ehrhardt 11/13 pt. in AMS-TEX [FH]

Library of Congress Cataloging in Publication Data

Learning in likely places : varieties of apprenticeship in Japan /
edited by John Singleton.

p. cm. – (Learning in doing)

ISBN 0-521-48012-4 (hc)

1. Experiential learning – Japan – Case studies. 2. Transfer of
training – Japan – Case studies. 3. Educational anthropology – Japan –
Case studies. 4. Apprentices – Japan – Case studies. I. Singleton,
John Calhoun. II. Series.
LB1059.L33 1998
371.3′8 – dc21 97-25904
CIP

*A catalog record for this book is available from
the British Library.*

ISBN 0 521 48012 4 hardback

Contents

Contributors

Scott Clark, Associate Professor of Anthropology, Rose-Hulman Institute of Technology, 5500 Wabash Avenue, Terre Haute, IN 47803

Millie Creighton, Associate Professor of Anthropology, University of British Columbia, Vancouver, B.C., Canada V6T 2B2

Gary DeCoker, Associate Professor of Education, Ohio Wesleyan University, Delaware, OH 43015

Bill Haase, Potter, 843 Hawk Mountain Road, Kempton, PA 19529

Sarah Hersh, Assistant Professor of Violin and Viola, The Crane School of Music, State University of New York–Potsdam, Potsdam, NY 13676

Jacquetta F. Hill, Professor of Education and Anthropology, University of Illinois, Urbana, IL 61801

Brenda G. Jordan, Research Associate, History of Art and Architecture, University of Pittsburgh, Pittsburgh, PA 15260

William W. Kelly, Professor of Anthropology, Yale University, New Haven, CT 06520-8277

Jill Kleinberg, Associate Professor of International Management, School of Business, University of Kansas, Lawrence, KS 66045

Susan O. Long, Associate Professor of Anthropology, John Carroll University, University Heights, OH 44118

Maureen W. McClure, Associate Professor of Administrative and Policy Studies, School of Education, University of Pittsburgh, Pittsburgh, PA 15260

Kathryn Ellen Madono, Doctoral Candidate in Education, University of Pittsburgh, Pittsburgh, PA 15260

Saburo Morita, Professor of Cultural Anthropology, Konan University, Kobe, Japan 658

Lois Peak, Project Officer, National Center for Education Statistics, U.S. Department of Education, Washington, DC 20208

David W. Plath, Professor of Anthropology and East Asian Languages and Cultures, University of Illinois, Urbana, IL 61801

J. Thomas Rimer, Professor of East Asian Languages and Literatures, University of Pittsburgh, Pittsburgh, PA 15260

Jonah Salz, Associate Professor of Comparative Theatre, Faculty of Intercultural Communication, Ryukoku University, Seta, Shiga 520-21, Japan

John Singleton, Professor Emeritus of Education and Anthropology, University of Pittsburgh, Pittsburgh, PA 15260

Richard J. Smethurst, Professor of History, University of Pittsburgh, Pittsburgh, PA 15260

Robert J. Smith, Goldwin Smith Professor Emeritus of Anthropology, Cornell University, Ithaca, NY 14853

Stephen R. Smith, Associate Professor of Anthropology, Department of Sociology, Wittenberg University, Springfield, Ohio 45501

Series foreword

This series for Cambridge University Press is becoming widely known as an international forum for studies of situated learning and cognition.

Innovative contributions from anthropology; cognitive, developmental, and cultural psychology; computer science; education; and social theory are providing theory and research that seeks new ways of understanding the social, historical, and contextual nature of the learning, thinking, and practice that emerges from human activity. The empirical settings of these research inquiries range from the classroom, to the workplace, to the high-technology office, to learning in the streets and in other communities of practice.

The situated nature of learning and remembering through activity is a central fact. It may appear obvious that human minds develop in social situations, and that they come to appropriate the tools that culture provides to support and extend their sphere of activity and communicative competencies. But cognitive theories of knowledge representation and learning alone have not provided sufficient insight into these relationships.

This series was born of the conviction that new and exciting interdisciplinary syntheses are under way, as scholars and practitioners from diverse fields seek to develop theory and empirical investigations adequate for characterizing the complex relations of social and mental life, and for understanding successful learning wherever it occurs. The series invites contributions that advance our understanding of these seminal issues.

Roy Pea
John Seely Brown
Jan Hawkins

Series foreword

Preface

What started out to be a book about apprenticeship in Japan turned out to be a book about learning in "likely places." In retrospect, we wonder how it could have turned out any other way. Apprenticeship in Japanese arts and crafts is inherently fascinating, and the explicit institutions of Japanese learning – from *iemoto* (lineage "schools") to private academies – abound in rich profusion and are culturally honored.

Once the word got around – primarily in anthropological circles of Japanese studies – that we were working on Japanese apprenticeship, new cases came forward. Better yet, we quickly expanded into cross-disciplinary collaboration with colleagues in art history, drama, economic history, and comparative education. We also found first-person accounts of significant learning experiences in Japanese calligraphy, folkcraft pottery, weaving, violin teaching, and Zen practice.

The constraints of what we meant by "apprenticeship" were expanded by reference to experiential learning – in places like the public bath, the neighborhood garage, the local festival, the hospital, professional baseball, and a weaving workshop for urban housewives. Our humanist colleagues led us into traditional Japanese drama and fine arts.

Each case led to particular insights. The addition of an accomplished autodidact to the exemplars of "situated learning," for instance, made a general point about the importance of looking at learning before teaching. We all learned about the diversity of Japanese learning arrangements.

In all of this, we were aided by an explicit Japanese cultural attachment to intensive learning practice. But it is in the anthropology of education that we achieve, at least implicitly, a disciplined coherence for this book. Jean Lave and Etienne Wenger's seminal theoretical suggestion of "situated learning" was our disciplinary reference in thinking through what we could say about the social and cultural processes of learning from our local Japanese studies. David Plath extended our contemplation with an explicit conception of the physical embodiment of learning, evidenced by the calluses of experience. It is presented here as an epilogue.

At an invitational workshop in Pittsburgh, April 22–25, 1993, we were able to assemble eighteen authors and their case study drafts of learning in Japan – the basis for this volume. The workshop, "Apprenticeship Education in Japan," was sponsored by the University of Pittsburgh through the Asian Studies Program, the Japan Studies Council, and the National Resource Center for East Asian Studies. Special funding also came from the Japan Iron and Steel Foundation, Mitsubishi, and Sumitomo Endowments of the University, and grants came from the Toshiba International Foundation and the NKK Corporation. L. Keith Brown, Jonathan Wolff, and Dianne Dakis of the Asian Studies Program, together with their staff and special assistant Frank Dressler, as well as colleagues in the Japan Studies Council, gave indispensable assistance and gracious encouragement. The Mai Thai restaurant also facilitated our celebration of the Pittsburgh workshop scholarly camaraderie with distinctive ethnic style.

Workshop colleagues who are not included in the table of contents, but who stimulated us immeasurably, were Sharon Traweek and Richard Florida. Other authors came into the fold after the workshop – Robert J. Smith, Jonah Salz, and William W. Kelly.

Subsequent presentations of selected cases in symposia at annual meetings of the Association for Asian Studies (1994) and the American Anthropological Association (1995) have been useful in gauging the significance of our work. Millie Creighton and Jacquetta Hill deserve credit as the prime movers of these presentations.

As it stands, our most compelling call to attention is the drama of our local stories of learning in Japan – and about the appropriation of cultural learning practices for individual and institutional purposes in widely varying social contexts. If we are appreciated for our short stories, alone, I will consider that a generous reception.

John Singleton

Introduction

Situated learning in Japan: Our educational analysis

John Singleton

Classic accounts of induction into Japanese art, craft, religion, and work have had imaginative resonance in many parts of the world. They derive authority from the authors' encounters with culturally different systems of Japanese knowledge. The experience of foreign observers and participants in these practices has led to an important, but as yet unanthologized, literature on local learning in Japan.[1] Dramatic accounts draw strength from their contradictions of our implicit assumptions about learning. They suggest culturally specific theories of learning, ways in which people explain education in Japanese social and cultural contexts.

Eugen Herrigel, for instance, described his arduous induction into the art of archery (1953). As a German philosophy professor in Japan, he wanted to learn about Zen mysticism. Friends he approached for an introduction said "that it was quite hopeless for a European to attempt to penetrate into this realm of spiritual life . . . unless he began by learning one of the Japanese arts associated with Zen" (p. 17). The book, *Zen in the Art of Archery,* describes his years of often frustrating experience with an archery master.[2] Herrigel came to realize the importance attached to mastering highly precise practice exercise forms (*kata*), such as the way in which one would draw the bow, practiced without even releasing an arrow.

> It is this mastery of form that the Japanese method of instruction seeks to inculcate. Practice, repetition, and repetition of the repeated with ever increasing intensity are its distinctive features for long stretches of the way. (p. 44)

Herrigel finally experienced a "direct transference of the spirit" (p. 50) from the master to the student. Character development of the learner was an unstated, but pervasive, goal of training in the art.

The case studies presented here extend this literature on local learning in Japan while they incorporate what we have learned from Herrigel and others. Potters, painters, and auto mechanics, too, practice their *kata.* We aim to demonstrate the rich variety of pedagogical arrangements and learning patterns both historical and contemporary for transmitting dynamic traditions. An interest in cultural transmission and acquisition (see Wolcott 1991), as well as a fascination for Japanese local culture, led us into a description of learning in likely places. The cases are written by Japan studies specialists and people, like Herrigel, who have been immersed in Japanese educational practices. For educational research, these cases are an extension of the idea of "situated learning" (Lave and Wenger 1991).

"Situated learning" is a deceptively simple theory, taking apprenticeship as a fundamental model of experiential education in authentic arenas of practice. Education is treated as an identity (cf. Goodenough 1961) and community-creating process within specific communities of practitioners. Seeing apprenticeship and education as "legitimate peripheral participation" emphasizes the ways in which people are drawn into, and develop social competence within, communities of practice.

Lave and Wenger (1991:65–85) defined "situated learning" by citing five paradigmatic cases of apprenticeship: (1) young tailor apprentices of Monrovia, Libera, learning to sew, cut, and design suits; (2) Yucatec Mayan mothers of Mexico, more informally acquiring the role of recognized midwives; (3) U.S. Navy quartermasters learning their seamanship at sea; (4) apprentice butchers in American supermarkets, not so effectively inducted into the butchering trade; and (5) new members of Alcoholics Anonymous, learning to take on the lifelong identity of nondrinking "alcoholics." Our Japanese cases should engage this conception of situated learning.

Much as Kuhn (1970) described "academic disciplines" and Becker (1982) conceived of "art worlds," the paradigmatic cases of situated learning exist in particular "communities of practice" that share knowledge, identities, values, techniques, and a focus on masterly role performance. Becker described an "art world" as a community or network of people who produce, consume, and communicate around an art tradition. Kuhn described an academic discipline as a "time-tested and group-licensed way of seeing" (1970:189).[3]

> Scientific knowledge, like language, is intrinsically the common property of a group or else nothing at all. To understand it we shall need to know the special characteristics of the groups that create and use it. (Kuhn 1970:210)

A "community of practice" must be seen in the same way, defined by its social patterns and organization. Some may think of it as more of a "network" than a community because there are no implications of geographic proximity, just significant social interaction and communication.

Art worlds and scientific disciplines establish a community of identity. These illustrations are not intended, however, to award artistic authenticity or scientific authority to communities of practice but rather to suggest that knowledge and technology are inseparable from social practice. Ethnographic descriptions and other local accounts are therefore appropriate means for approaching educational and community practice.

In associating practice with situated learning, we are shifting between

> a view according to which cognitive processes (and thus learning) are primary and a view according to which social practice is the primary, generative phenomenon, and learning is one of its characteristics .... Legitimate peripheral participation is proposed as a descriptor of engagement in social practice that entails learning as an integral constituent. (Lave and Wenger 1991:34–35)

But what is this "practice"? It is at once both productive activity (including engagement in an occupation or profession) and a learning activity, a repetitive and systematic exercise to acquire a skill. It is here that there are specific Japanese conceptions of practice as exercise that do not emphasize the acquisition of skill or proficiency, and that do not "presuppose a specific talent ... [or] call for a special training" (von Durckheim 1962:34–35). Practice becomes a way of continuing self-discipline.

> At first, of course, intense alertness, a firm untiring will and great perseverance are needed to repeat the same thing again and again until finally the skill is perfected. But practice in the real sense begins only when technique as such has been mastered, for only then can the aspirant perceive to what extent self pride and the desire to shine, as well as fear of failure, obstruct his path. (pp. 42–43)

It is the theory of situated learning that has encouraged us to assemble our cases from local Japanese communities of practice, both contemporary and historical. These cases demonstrate the power of formal apprenticeship learning and the diversity of learning arrangements and patterns that transmit traditions of art, craft, work, and community in Japan. This is not a claim for Japanese exceptionalism;[4] Japan has no monopoly on the pedagogies and learning patterns described here. There is, however, an explicit historical appreciation for these practices in many local Japanese settings.

In this book, we point to likely places of learning outside of school in Japan. Rich cultural traditions of learning are examined in their local contexts in order to go beyond the now familiar Japanese public school mathematics classroom. These traditions lead to an appreciation of learning patterns that have been overshadowed by a "modern" single-minded focus on cognitive school achievement in Japan and elsewhere.[5]

Artisanal apprenticeship in traditional arts, crafts, and drama, as well as in modern occupations, organizes culturally explicit patterns of learning in Japan. Craft apprentices are educated in workshops where they identify with the skills, roles, and ideology of a master. Artists, actors, and practitioners of the martial arts, as well as tea ceremony and flower arrangement specialists, are guided, and certified, by long-honored traditions of learning, incorporated in hereditary "schools" that use the vocabulary of Japanese family descent (*iemoto*). Children are incorporated into the social community in less explicitly educational settings (e.g., the public bath or local festivals). Sport, work, and religion, too, are the products of other forms of community socialization in places less explicitly structured for education.

By describing how people learn in these likely places of education, we aim to deschool our conceptions of education and gain a greater understanding of the Japanese cultural displays of persistence and enthusiasm in learning for life. Our case studies provide the substance for a comparative analysis of situated learning in Japan and should enlarge our appreciation for the diversity of educational practice there. Learning is often energized by reference to Japanese historical traditions that have been adapted to modern work and creative production, but other traditions are also invented and adapted from diverse sources; modern knowledge and practice from other societies is incorporated into contemporary Japanese culture.

We all begin with an emphasis on the connection between settings of learning and what is learned. This view comes naturally to cultural anthropologists, and to our scholarly allies in Japanese studies, as we seek to describe learning in the local settings with which we are familiar in Japan. Rich traditions of knowledge, performance, and learning in Japan provide provocative materials for an anthropologically biased analysis of Japanese cultural acquisition.

Origins of the book

The idea of this book began as a comparison of learning among female abalone shellfish divers, known as *ama* (Plath and Hill 1987), and mostly male folkcraft potters (Singleton 1989a) in rural Japanese communities. Potters and divers would seem to have little in common, except as they are considred exotics in Japanese tourist travel promotions. Their work careers are, however, viable segments of the Japanese post-industrial economy, generating highly valued products. Consumption of their products is, indeed, an indicator of refined taste in the larger society. The producers manage to earn a comfortable, and sometimes prosperous, modern livelihood in practicing their crafts, while symbolizing for their countrymen the nostalgia of a preindustrial way of life. There is, here, an ironic contrast between the symbolic meanings and actual lifestyles in such craft careers.

At first, we thought of all learners in these diverse crafts as participating in a common model of apprenticeship. The skills practiced in their careers are generally unschooled but highly developed through practice. When one inquires about their craft learning, we are told that fathers do not teach the sons who will be their potter successors and that mothers do not teach their daughters who might be interested in following their family occupation as divers. Persistent practice and dedication to the craft in the context of production provides the opportunity to learn.

But our comparison forced us to recognize differences in learning and pedagogical practice. There is a sharp contrast between the formal relations of master and disciple (*deshi,* a common term for apprentice) in a potters' workshop and the social relations of novice and experienced divers in the coastal fishing reefs. Potters relate to masters; *ama* do not. There is an explicit language of apprenticeship and specific models for acquiring the craft skills of pottery, whereas divers enter the coastal waters informally and learn, as they pursue their career, from their peers in the clubhouse of their small diving teams and from their partnership with boatmen.

Beyond their educational and career differences, however, potters and divers are persistent in learning their complex crafts and in improving performance with age, and they are continually imaginative in exploiting (and conserving) the resources with which they work. Their work relies on highly complex technologies, acquired with difficulty through practice. Neither model for learning is like a school; there is no focus upon didactic teaching and telling. Novices do not gather with a teacher who will tell them what they need to know or construct tests of their knowledge independent of their practice of the craft. Although children may grow up in a working household, their acquisition of the craft technology seems to begin with their adult decision to enter the family business.

As Hill, Plath, and Singleton initiated this comparison of potter and diver learning, we utilized situated learning and avoided metaphors of schools, classrooms, and white rats learning to run mazes. We were drawn to Lave's use of her studies of apprenticeship (1977, 1982; Lave and Wenger 1991) and to other ethnographic accounts of apprenticeship in different times and places (e.g., Coy 1989; Goody 1982).

We found a number of colleagues who were intrigued by the educational questions raised when we stopped treating educational process in Japan as "something like school." Thus we expanded our cases of Japanese learning into the transmission of traditional arts, religion, and the sense of community, as well as adding other examples of craft apprenticeship, learning in other social frames, and creative appropriations of cultural learning practices in nontraditional settings.

Education in the fine arts, craft apprenticeship, informal career and community education, or cultural appropriations did not follow a single pedagogical pattern (e.g., eschewing didactic instruction), but all of our cases developed new and intriguing implications when analyzed as situated learning and when compared with the expectations of traditional apprenticeship.

At an invitational workshop in Pittsburgh in April 1993,[6] we were able to assemble the original authors and their case studies of learning in Japan – the basis for this volume. We first thought of it as a workshop on apprenticeship in Japan, but it was soon apparent that we needed a different term to designate our common educational interests. As we sought a title, Scott Clark suggested provocatively that we describe this as "learning in likely places."

In this view of learning, the school is an unlikely case. It helps us to decenter entrenched assumptions about educational process, especially the implication that education can be effectively decontextualized and contained within schools. This title allows us to use our cases to liberate learning from schooling, and it acknowledges the wide variety of places where, and ways in which, learning occurs.

Our cases and papers are divided into four sections that address not only apprenticeship and socialization in work and community in Japanese education but also the long traditions of learning in the traditional arts and the ways in which pedagogical patterns and cultural knowledge have been appropriated to new purposes in and out of Japan. The sections are:

- *Part I* – Actors, artists, and calligraphers: Learning in the traditional arts
- *Part II* – Potters, weavers, mechanics, doctors, and violinists: Learning in artisanal apprenticeship
- *Part III* – Work and community socialization: Diversity in learning arrangements
- *Part IV* – Appropriations of cultural practice

A final paper (see Plath), which inaugurated our workshop in Pittsburgh, has been included as an epilogue that pushes further away from cognitive constructions of knowledge and knowledge embedded in social practice to point at that knowledge which is embedded in the body.

I. Actors, artists, and calligraphers: Learning in the traditional arts

The first section, beyond this introduction, is devoted to cases of longstanding learning traditions in the traditional arts of Japan. The social locations of these cases in the transmission of longstanding art traditions include the lineage schools (*iemoto*) that formally certified artistic achievement, professional families of actors and artists, and a "new religion" that incorporates art into religious practice.

The *iemoto* system, described by Robert Smith, is well known as a uniquely Japanese organization for the maintenance of culturally specific fine arts traditions. *Iemoto* refers ambiguously to both a household-like organization and to the head of that organization. Smith describes the ways in which fictive family relationships modeled on the Japanese household are used selectively for the organization of traditional arts (and trades). Licensing of adepts and teachers, maintained as a monopoly by a family, has been important in the performing arts, but Smith also interjects the unforgettable example of a *sashimi* fish-slicing school *iemoto* whose current head had to give up his first career as a rock-and-roll musician. Highly effective in providing continuity for longstanding artistic traditions, the *iemoto* organizations are formally organized communities of practice, characterized by a licensed authenticity in the arts they convey. As settings of learning, they differ in their focus upon professional succession and more diffuse avocational practice, as well as the extent to which they have become formal organizations of education.

A classic reference in Japanese thought about teaching and learning is Zeami's secret instructions to his successors, written over 500 years ago but only brought to public attention in this century. They contain prescriptions for the organization of experience over a professional lifetime which would lead a *nō* actor to masterful performance. Rimer points out that a critical element for Zeami is a lifelong search for mastery in the evolving experiences of performance: "The search for mastery never ceases." Zeami's treatises were not, however, intended for the performers. Even today, now that the secret treatises have been discovered and printed in modernized language, they have not been read by many professional *nō* actors. The written discussion of training practice is not relevant to the learner. Practice, not pedagogical discussion, is their path to learning.

In a similar tradition, Japanese fine artists were trained within the formal schools of painting. Jordan's description of Kyōsai's art education in the 1800s is a dramatic example of educational practice in a classical painter's atelier. Looked at from the learner's experience, Jordan shows the many possibilities for personal initiative and practice outside of the master's control – not just a passive acceptance of direction – in the education of a creative artist. The "copybook method" of teaching painting, copying exactly the master's copies of exemplary paintings, was the formal method of instruction. The ambitious learner was expected, however, literally to "steal the secrets"[7] of a painting technique. Seemingly constrained by a rigidified school of painting, Kyōsai became an eccentric artist. He acquired a wide variety of skills through his own initiative and invented a succession of personal styles in his career.

DeCoker develops a set of seven general characteristics of learning and teaching from his experience in traditional Japanese fine and martial arts classes. His classes were sponsored by Oomoto, a Japanese "new religion." In Oomoto, the practice of art is a spiritual quest. He compares his own learning with directions from ancient calligraphy texts on artistic practice and the principles of learning. Here, too, model forms are rigorously practiced. Learning is expected to be difficult. DeCoker suggests that a teacher is legitimated by his reputation for severity (*kibishii*).

Salz describes the initiation of child actors into the comic plays (*kyōgen*) associated with *nō* drama. Even today, Salz finds professional families in the traditional arts systematically incorporating their successors from an early age. The learning practice is much like that prescribed by Zeami.

Learning in the traditional fine arts, sometimes with the imprimatur of an *iemoto* school, sets a model for learning that can be seen again in less culturally prestigious artisanal apprenticeships of potters and mechanics.

II. Potters, weavers, mechanics, doctors, and violinists: Learning in artisanal apprenticeship

The second section of the book brings together cases of contemporary apprenticeship, beginning with the learning experiences of novice potters in folkcraft pottery villages, but extending to auto mechanics in a neighborhood garage, violin teachers, medical doctors, and modern housewives drawn into an intensive weaving workship during their vacations.

There are common expectations and differences between novices and masters in these settings. Often there is little formal sense of an explicit time to be served in this relationship other than an expectation of several years of apprenticeship in serious professional settings. All presume an individual commitment to a significant career of practice in the discipline or field. Even the vacationing housewives in a summer weaving workshop are treated like apprentices and expected to return regularly.

To appreciate the novice's experience in apprenticeship, an account of actual experience opens this section (see Haase, Chapter 6). That the novice was an American potter in a rural Japanese folkcraft pottery workshop made the author more aware of the general cultural assumptions of learning, especially when he was surprised by his master's expectations. He had to learn how to learn. Demonstrating his commitment to the craft and his master were problematic. Though the workshop was part of a community of practice, the novice was expected to limit his social life to interaction with the people of the master's shop.

Routine practice with basic wheel-thrown pottery forms in the workshop was the fundamental learning activity expected of a novice. Rote repetition of forms, whether in practice of the martial arts *kata* or turning out thousands of small sake cups for practice, is a common theme in these reports. But even before this begins, one must earn the right to observe and learn by doing the menial scutwork of the master and the workplace. All of this is a direct test of a would-be learner's motivation and persistence.

Workshop patterns of learning and production vary widely, and there are broad differences among masters, as evidenced in Mashiko, a large pottery town (see Singleton, Chapter 7). Different ideologies of pottery production, some associated with the modern *mingei* (folkcraft) movement, lead to different expectations of learners and their relations to their teachers. Apprenticeship takes many forms and leads to contrasting sets of expectations in this setting. Both personality and community shape the experiences to be encountered by novices.

Learning untaught expectations is not only a cross-cultural problem, which Haase experienced, but a pedagogical technique, as Madono discovered in the neighborhood auto repair garage (Chapter 8). It is part of embedded tutoring in the workplace. In the garage, Madono finds two contrasting patterns of mentor–novice relations among the employees, which she associates with bureaucratic regulation (like schooling) and artisanal craft (like apprenticeship). Individual workers seem to be disposed personally toward either regulatory or craft career specializations, which are identified with different patterns of social relations, control of labor, work practice, tool use, and ideas about learning. The success of the garage is dependent, however, on both patterns of practice, given its responsibility for automobile inspection as well as general repairs. Novices often learn in both ways. Bureaucrats and artisans work together while maintaining their separate career views.

Hersh and Peak (Chapter 9) have been apprentices with Suzuki Shinichi, creator of the internationally famous Suzuki method of violin teaching for young children (Peak 1986; Hersh 1995). Both his basic method of teaching and his specific organization of practice for his proteges, who will go out to teach his method, illustrate a kind of classical apprenticeship in the performing arts. Though he is a teacher of teachers, all of his interaction with his personal students is concerned with the improvement of their own violin performance. There is no discussion of pedagogy. Students discover that they must take the initiative if they wish to see children's violin classes in action. Ultimately, for both children and their teachers, individual spiritual development is the explicit goal of the master.

The postgraduate education of physicians in Japan is often confusing to Americans. Long (Chapter 10) explains that there is an apprenticeship model at work quite different from the American pattern of internships, which rotate a young doctor systematically through the different areas of hospital-based medical practice. Japanese doctors experience instead the responsibilities and benefits of apprenticeship to a professorial mentor and, in return, perform much of their mentor's research work. Although there is a clear beginning to their postgraduate medical education, there is no clearly marked ending. Much as young potter apprentices are expected after their training to work for the master, young doctors, too, often stay on for a year or two to "pay back" their professor.

Nevertheless, doctors share with potters, auto mechanics, and violin teachers apprenticeship-like patterns of introduction to their professional craft. They have similar choices to make about professional style and specialization, and they gain enhanced reputation through apprenticeship with prestigious mentors.

The weaver's workshop for urban women vacationers (see Creighton, Chapter 11) is another version of apprenticeship, with artisanal concern for experiential knowledge of the materials of production and many imaginative strategies to bring the women into an artisanal community of practice. Creighton's case is only one of an extensive range of avocational careers in Japan, as some people from all walks of life take up lifetime commitments to perfecting the practice of the fine, performing, domestic, and martial arts. Study of tea ceremony, alone, absorbs the learning energies of a very large group of people (cf. Anderson 1991). Creighton shows how avocational commitments can be generated through a kind of limited apprenticeship.

Another important aspect of Creighton's case is the strategy used by the workshop masters to discourage their students' dependence upon the mentors. They deliberately avoid a paternalistic responsibility for the women, refusing to take responsibility for their individual welfare. It is a dramatic demonstration of their expectation that the novices will learn to take care of each other.

While there is a general enthusiasm here for the local settings and educational experiences of craft apprenticeship, we can easily overlook the potential for pain, exploitation, political manipulation, and terror in the interpersonal relationships of learning, even in the likely places of craft and work.[8] The construction of trust between apprentice and master is, at best, fraught with ambiguity and other obstacles to their educational goals. Only a few of the cases here even suggest this possibility. We still need ethnographic reports, which would caution us to evaluate more carefully the varieties of apprenticeship learning that we celebrate.[9]

III. Work and community socialization: Diversity in learning arrangements

Four cases that diverge from traditional apprenticeship but which reinforce the analysis of educational process as situated learning form the fourth section. Female shellfish divers (see Hill and Plath, Chapter 12) and the autodidact (see Smethurst, Chapter 13) recognize no apprentice-like relationship of a novice with a master, but the conventions of learning are better understood by comparison with apprenticeship than schooling.

Hill and Plath call important attention to another characteristic of craft knowledge – that it is "moneyed." Conditions of knowledge transfer are strongly linked to the nature of marketing and distribution of the product of the craft. There is individual competition for recognition and reward.

This case also demonstrates how expertise in a sophisticated technology is developed – by continuing practice in a dangerous environment. The experts are the muscular senior women who have persisted in their trade.

Even academic knowledge can be mastered in nonacademic ways, as Smethurst shows. The autodidact is another case of situated learning. A modern government bureaucrat educated himself in economics to the point of very creative performance, without a university degree. Takahashi, as Finance Minister during the difficult 1930s, achieved successes that eluded his predecessor, a graduate of prestigious Tokyo University. Much like the potter's apprentice, he had to learn how to learn without didactic instruction.

Dependent on self-discipline and representing intense self-commitment, while learning to appropriate the knowledge of others, or "stealing their secrets," *ama* and autodidact are not unlike the eccentric painter (see Jordan, Chapter 3). They all display creative personal strategies for appropriating the skills and working knowledge required in their careers.

Children, too, are inducted into a "community of practice," not defined by artisanal skills but by general social competency, the ability to interact with unrelated people in their neighborhood community. Whether at the public bath (see Clark, Chapter 14) or in the local festivals (see Morita, Chapter 15), children experience the embedded social tutoring of public places and performances in their local community.

Clark, the acknowledged phrase maker of our workshop, coined the term "embedded tutoring" to describe the nondidactic but intentional instruction of many of our cases. This is a term we would like to add to discussions of education as "situated learning." Neither "legitimate peripheral participation" nor "didactic teaching" covers the numerous varieties of implicit pedagogical strategies in the social settings we describe.

Clark uses "embedded tutoring" to call attention to the educational effects of the public bath, socializing children into the community beyond immediate family and kin. His case suggests the need to look beyond explicit teaching and mentoring toward what is implicitly transmitted through social participation in all of the settings we describe.

IV. Appropriations of cultural practice

Finally we include four cases that focus on creative uses of cultural practice – knowledge, organizational forms, and patterns of pedagogy – in nontraditional settings. It is in these settings that we see both conscious and implicit appropriations of cultural practice to serve the purposes of learners in newly improvised settings – special sports coaching, self-help therapeutic groups, an American Zen commune, and an overseas office of a modern Japanese corporation.[10]

Kelly (see Chapter 16) describes the ways in which one talented baseball coach borrowed liberally from a number of traditional arts to enhance the batting skills of Sadaharu Oh, on his way to becoming the world home run king of professional baseball. The very practices that lead to continuity in traditional arts are used here for training relevant to the new martial art of Japanese baseball. The learner in this case was far more talented as a baseball player than his coach. The act of mentoring, however, showed pedagogical ingenuity in the appropriation of cultural forms for enhancing performance in a very different art.

Baseball in Japan is itself a culturally constructed appropriation, perplexing to Americans who do not recognize many of its practices. But so are Zen religious practice and Danshukai, an organizational adaptation of a successful U.S. educational form, Alcoholics Anonymous (AA). Cultural appropriation can go in both directions.

McClure (see Chapter 18) describes an American creation of a "Zen ashram" in the United States, which operates without benefit of native Japanese instruction. In their indigenous settings, Zen and AA include intensive education in identity change. They are examples of culturally specific intensive educational processes, with claims to global application. Zen is the driving force in Herrigel's (1953) intense learning of archery. Lave and Wenger (1991) use AA as their last paradigmatic example of situated learning, beyond conventional artisanal apprenticeship – centering on the transmission of a new identity through legitimate peripheral participation in a community of practice. In AA, one has to learn to be a lifelong "alcoholic." In Zen, one never loses the new sense of self gained through intensive practice.

Much as we might expect but rarely foresee, Smith (see Chapter 17) shows how AA in Japan has to be reinvented as Danshukai, its Japanese incarnation, contradicting many of the explicit rules held dear by the American membership. Not just Christian symbolism is abandoned; the anonymity of members is abandoned, and the AA emphasis on individual responsibility is transformed into familial responsibility for behavior.

In the American invention of a Zen ashram, McClure shows how Japanese (and Indian) mystical traditions are culturally restructured by Americans for American participants. Yet one can see elements of Japanese educational principles carried across cultural boundaries. Once again, art appreciation and practice become central to the religious quest (cf. DeCoker, Chapter 4). And there is a persistent commitment to practice.

Our last case (see Kleinberg, Chapter 19) is a successful adaptation of a Japanese business form for American employees in the United States.

In deliberate but unschoollike ways, the Japanese corporations have constructed workplaces that put Japanese and American assumptions about learning and work to the test of binational collaboration. Not always successful in their attempts to use American employees in Japanese ways, it is refreshing to have a closely detailed ethnographic description of interpersonal relationships and the construction of learning practices in one sales group.

Kleinberg cautions us, however, that this is an unusual case of success in the application of Japanese cultural principles for Americans in a corporate business organization. It took an intuitively creative Japanese manager to achieve this result, as well as bicultural interpreters. Not every employee was successfully inducted into the group. We learn much from Kleinberg's description of failure, the unteachable employee, in this otherwise successful adaptation of Japanese group process.

Epilogue

Plath argues for a conception of learning not only as socially embedded but as physically embodied. Just as the body is callused from specific experience, one accrues experiential education, what can be "known," in the body. This is how the marine divers (*ama*), who Plath studies, know their trade. It is not the cognitively explicit product we associate with didactic instruction. As his *ama* informant told him, with some exasperation when he pressed her to describe how she learned her trade, "*Sensei,* it's not like school." A common Japanese expression refers to such bodily learning as *karada de oboeru* (learning by the body). It is a phrase that is regularly applied to potters at the wheel, *ama* searching the reef for abalone, auto mechanics, and people explaining the significance of the practice forms (*kata*) of the martial arts.

Concluding perspectives on education in Japan

A school-centric educational discourse depends upon the classroom (and *juku,* private tutoring classes) for a fundamental conception of learning. We are here using apprenticeship, and other forms of education, to explore Japanese cultural theories of learning. There are in all of these cases two major characteristics worth pointing out.

There is, first of all, a powerful pedagogy that depends upon the observational skills of a motivated learner. It is the ability to respond to "teaching without teaching" and is personified in the learner or apprentice called a *minarai.* But it is the learner who has to puzzle out the ways in which unobtrusive observation and persistent stealth will be tolerated in particular places at particular times in such a way that the necessary skills and practices will become evident.

In the second place, there is a consistent respect for persistence in practice of the seemingly simple foundational forms (*kata*) associated with an art – the calligraphic strokes for a particular Chinese character (*kanji*); the small teacup (*guinomi*), which a novice potter is expected to practice 10,000 times; the internalization of dramatic texts in the traditional theater; or the constant repetition of "Twinkle, twinkle little star" by students in Suzuki method violin classes. Whereas these are practice forms for learning the art, they are also warm-up exercises to be used for a lifetime in the continuing refinement of artistic practice. As Zeami emphasized, the professional actor continues to learn throughout a career – to believe that one has achieved a perfect control is to lose the possibility of continuing art (see Rimer, Chapter 2).

The patterns of learning in likely places described here might be seen as an introduction to a Japanese "social technology" – a body of cultural practice used to achieve social learning purposes. In apprenticeship and other forms of experiential learning, we can appreciate the rich variation of educational processes in Japan. The culturally supported pedagogical techniques of embedded tutoring include many strategies that nurture the observational skills of a motivated learner, as well as showing the rewards of persistent practice. Our cases depict Japan as a society eagerly engaged in lifelong commitments to learning – as well as an exporter and importer of a spirited social technology of learning in likely places.

Notes

1. Classic accounts, in addition to those presented here, are Hori (1994), Rohlen (1973), Kondo (1990), Peak (1986), and Philip (1989), as well as Herrigel (1953) described here. Japanese scholars, too, have written about apprenticeship in crafts, commerce, and the arts. See Irie (1988) for a survey of this work. (Japanese publications reviewed in an English article.)
2. The book became a key text for alternative education in the 1960s. It is, ironically, best known in the United States by an American appropriation of the title, *Zen and the Art of Motorcycle Maintenance* (Pirsig 1974). In Japan, Herrigel's account of education is widely appreciated. During a short visit in 1995, I heard enthusiastic reactions to his book from Japanese colleagues in (1) an academic conference on educational research at Kyushu University, (2) an evening drinking session at the archery practice hall of Onta, a small Kyushu pottery hamlet, and (3) a pottery workshop in Mashiko, a large pottery town near Tokyo.

3. Geertz (1983:157) calls such academic communities "intellectual villages" in his proposal for ethnographic studies of modern thought.
4. See the accounts of apprenticeship in Coy (1989) for examples from other parts of the world. Also see the account of a Peace Corps trainer in Oklahoma who used a Zen-like antididactic pedagogy, what Hori calls "teaching without teaching" (1994: 11), with volunteers preparing for service in Africa, without any connection to Japan or Zen (Tidwell 1990).
5. See Sigaut (1993:111–112) for a summary of the contrasting features of apprenticeship and school learning as "diametrically opposed processes" with characteristics derived from a review of ethnographic studies of apprenticeship in Europe.
6. The workshop on "Apprenticeship Education in Japan" was sponsored by the Asian Studies Program, the Japan Studies Council, and the National Resource Center for East Asian Studies of the University of Pittsburgh, on April 22–25, 1993, with funding from the Japan Iron and Steel Federation, Mitsubishi, NKK, and Sumitomo Endowments and with grants from the Toshiba International Foundation. L. Keith Brown, Jonathan Wolff, and Dianne Dakis of the Asian Studies Program staff, special assistant Frank Dressler, and colleagues in the Japan Studies Council gave indispensable assistance and gracious encouragement.
7. See Irie (1988:16–17) for discussion of implicit expectations for learning through *nusumi keiko* (surreptitious learning, stolen lessons) in the artisanal trades.
8. For example, the Chinese movie, *Farewell My Concubine,* graphically illustrated the squalor and inhumane treatment of young apprentices in a Chinese opera theater.
9. We also do not cover the communities of practice whose purposes appall us. Japanese military indoctrination of young men leading up to World War II was notoriously brutal. More recently the Aum sect depended on the learned commitment of its highly schooled converts for its terrifying projects.
10. Although these cases occur in nontraditional settings, we should note the equally creative adaptations associated with "traditional" settings. The dynamic learning arrangements that are described in this volume show individually creative adaptations of pedagogy and learning – from Zeami to the auto mechanics.

References

Anderson, Jennifer, 1991, *An Introduction to Japanese Tea Ritual,* Albany: State University of New York Press.

Becker, Howard S., 1982, *Art Worlds,* Berkeley: University of California Press.

Coy, Michael, ed., 1989, *Apprenticeship: From Theory to Method and Back Again,* Albany: State University of New York Press.

von Durckheim, Karlfried Graf, 1962, *Hara, The Vital Centre of Man,* London: G. Allen and Unwin.

Geertz, Clifford, 1983, "The Way We Think Now: Toward an Ethnography of Modern Thought," in *Local Knowledge: Further Essays in Interpretative Anthropology,* New York: Basic Books.

Goodenough, Ward, 1961, "Education and Identity," in Frederick C. Gruber, ed., *Anthropology and Education* (The Martin G. Brumbaugh Lectures in Education, Fifth Series), Philadelphia: University of Pennsylvania Press.

Goody, Esther N., 1982, *Parenthood and Social Reproduction: Fostering and Occupational Roles in West Africa,* Cambridge: Cambridge University Press.

Herrigel, Eugen, 1953, *Zen in the Art of Archery,* Boston: Routledge & Kegan Paul.

Hersh, Sarah, 1995, *Music Educator Shinichi Suzuki: His Teacher Development Program and Studio Teaching,* Ph.D. dissertation, University of Minnesota.

Hori, G. Victor Soogen, 1994, "Teaching and Learning in the Rinzai Zen Monastery," *The Journal of Japanese Studies,* 20: 5–35.

Irie, Hiroshi, 1988, "Apprenticeship Training in Tokugawa Japan," *Acta Asiatica,* 54: 1–23.

Kondo, Dorinne, 1990, *Crafting Selves: Power, Gender, and Discourses of Identity in a Japanese Workplace,* Chicago: University of Chicago Press.

Kuhn, Thomas, 1970, *The Structure of Scientific Revolutions,* Chicago: University of Chicago Press.

Lave, Jean, 1977, "Cognitive Consequences of Traditional Apprenticeship Training in West Africa," *Anthropology and Education Quarterly,* 8: 177–180.

1982, "A Comparative Approach to Educational Forms and Learning Processes," *Anthropology and Education Quarterly,* 13: 181–187.

Lave, Jean, and Etienne Wenger, 1991, *Situated Learning: Legitimate Peripheral Participation,* Cambridge: Cambridge University Press.

(Peak), Lois Taniuchi, 1986, "Cultural Continuity in an Educational Institution: A Case Study of the Suzuki Method of Music Instruction," in Merry I. White and Susan Pollack, eds., *The Cultural Transition: Human Experience and Social Transformation in the Third World and Japan,* Boston: Routledge & Kegan Paul, pp. 113–140.

Philip, Leila, 1989, *The Road through Miyama,* New York: Vintage Books.

Pirsig, Robert M., 1974, *Zen and the Art of Motorcycle Maintenance: An Inquiry into Values,* New York: Morrow.

Plath, David W., and Jaquetta Hill, 1987, "The Reefs of Rivalry: Expertness and Competition among Japanese Shellfish Divers," *Ethnology,* 26: 151–163.

Rohlen, Thomas P., 1973, " 'Spiritual Education' in a Japanese Bank," *American Anthropologist* (October 1973), 75: 1542–1562.

Sigaut, François, 1993, "Learning, Teaching, and Apprenticeship," *New Literary History,* 24: 105–114.

Singleton, John, 1989a, "Japanese Folkcraft Pottery Apprenticeship: Cultural Assumptions in Educational Practice," in Coy, ed., pp. 13–30.

Tidwell, Mike, 1990, *The Ponds of Kalambayi: An African Sojourn,* New York: Lyons and Burford.

Wolcott, Harry, 1991, "Propriospect and the Acquisition of Culture," *Anthropology and Education Quarterly,* 22: 251–273.

Part I

Actors, artists, calligraphers: Learning in the traditional arts

1 Transmitting tradition by the rules: An anthropological interpretation of the *iemoto* system

Robert J. Smith

> Above all, he was the mold-breaker within tradition. Yet he knew that ballet's tradition lay not in the art form as a whole, which could be changed radically through concepts; the tradition was in the dancers' training.[1]

The view that the household (*ie*) and the linked-household organization called *dōzoku* provide the model or template for the creation of other institutions of Japanese society is encountered at every turn. Almost every social scientist, Japanese and foreign alike, has argued that the structural principles of the household are to be found everywhere in Japanese social institutions. Schools, companies, factories, criminal groups, and virtually any other institution one can name are said to be family-like or familistic (e.g., Hayashi 1983, Hsu 1975, Ortolani 1969, and Rekishi Kōron 1978). Commentators of conservative persuasion argue that the whole of Japanese society is one big household, with the imperial family at its head. Whatever one's view of that claim, the connections between the imperial institution, the cult of ancestor veneration, and the strong emphasis on genealogical or historical depth among the *iemoto* must be acknowledged.

The reasons are not far to seek, as the following picture of the *ie* ideal shows. In it, I try to describe what a household was supposed to be; inevitably, many of the chief characteristics attributed to the *iemoto* as institution and person are brought to mind. First, the *ie* as an institution had social, economic, and sacred dimensions. It is the last of these that too often is overlooked. The sanctity of the Western family was predicated on the sacred bond of matrimony (linking husband and wife), but

We are grateful to Robert J. Smith and the Isabella Stewart Gardner Museum for permission to reprint this chapter from Isabella Stewart Gardner Museum, *Fenway Court 1992* (Special issue, John M. Rosenfield, ed., "Competition and Collaboration: Hereditary Schools in Japanese Culture"), Boston: Isabella Stewart Gardner Museum, © 1993, pp. 37–45.

that of the Japanese household was expressed in veneration of the ancestors (linking the head of the house and his successor). The congregation of worshippers in the ancestral cult were the members of the household. It is for good reason that David Plath has said that in Japan, the family of God is the family (Plath 1964).

Let me offer a brief outline of the design of the *ie*.[2] The household was a corporate unit, conceived to have originated far in the past and destined to persist into the future as its members die and are replaced by their successors in each generation. In theory, no household should ever die out, and in the interest of guaranteeing continuity, the head of the household exercised undivided authority. It was he who inherited the estate intact, and it was he who bore the responsibility to pass it on to the next generation. The authority of the head, which was transmitted to him by the ancestors, could be acquired only through succession. The household head exercised authority in the name of the ancestors, therefore, and chief among his responsibilities were the proper veneration of the ascendants of the house and the selection of his successor. He had the power to appoint as successor any person he deemed capable of filling the position. So important was continuity of the line that virtually any individual might be selected. Most often, to be sure, it was the firstborn son; alternatives included other sons, adopted husbands of daughters, younger siblings of the head, and even persons in no way related to any current member of the house. It was so like a corporation that a household actually could lapse for a time, to be revived upon the designation of an individual to become its head.

The head was in effect the custodian of the assets of the household (real property, other assets, business, trade, craft, or art, be it noted) handed down by the ancestors. It was his responsibility to nurture the estate and pass it on intact or enlarged to his successor. Like all offices that permit the exercise of authority over others, this one implied heavy responsibilities as well. Among them was the carrying out of ritual responsibilities toward the ancestral spirits, often in the context of a Buddhist temple or Shintō shrine, for the founding ancestor frequently was a deified human or a humanized deity.

The *ie* of *iemoto* means household, of course, leaving no doubt as to the origins of the core characteristics of what is called the *iemoto seido*. Its key features are commonly said to be: emphasis on the master–disciple relationship, hierarchical ordering of linked subgroups, unquestioned authority of the *iemoto* (whose authority is like that of a household head), emphasis on exclusivity, and an organizational style modeled after the household (*ie*).[3] For their part, those who study *iemoto seido,* closing the circle, treat it as providing the model for the social and psychological relationships within the institutions of Japanese society. They, too, argue that schools, companies, factories, and so on exhibit common features that reveal clearly the extent to which they are patterned after the *iemoto* system (e.g., Peak 1986).

Are these insights in any way surprising? Knowing what we do about Japanese society over the past two or three centuries, is it likely that its institutions would be organized on any other set of principles? Would we expect to find loosely structured groups, reaching decisions by majority vote, unconcerned with perpetuation of their descent lines, contemptuous of tradition, stressing individuality, disrespectful of seniority and experience? Of course not, and since it is undoubtedly the case that people who wish to construct new institutions look about for materials at hand rather than taking off in unprecedented directions, it is hardly surprising that the household proved to be the model on whose basis other undertakings were structured.

The term "fictive family" or "fictive kinship" occurs frequently in the literature on the *iemoto seido.* Before turning to the character of this particular fiction, let me reiterate that the family/household in Japan has never depended on genealogical, consanguineal descent for its continuity or the perpetuation of its enterprise. Fictive family relationships flourish throughout Japanese society, from the imperial household right down through the criminal gangs. The Meiji Civil Code of 1898, often said to require primogeniture, did nothing of the kind. Although it expressed a preference for succession by the eldest son, it left open the possibility that literally any individual might be designated successor to the head of the house and heir of all its assets. This notable flexibility in the rule of succession made it possible for households to avoid extinction, while the rule of impartible inheritance insured that assets were not dispersed at the death of the household head. Rules of succession and inheritance that did not demand genealogical relationship were ideally suited to the requirements of the *iemoto,* as it happens, for it could prove disastrous to pass the headship on to a child of indifferent talent or unsuitable personality. As the sociologist Nakano Takashi has demonstrated, any household's occupation takes precedence over the rule of descent; in fact, the descent rule is determined by the need for occupational continuity (Lebra 1993:109).

It is on the basis of a fictive family relationship that the authority of the *iemoto* rests. Here the social relationship is expressed in familial terms, and to some extent even behavior is modeled after family roles. The function of this kind of fictive family relationship is to confirm and reconfirm, over and over again, the legitimacy and authority of the *iemoto.* Assuming the existence of an ideology that specifies the character of the relationship between leader and follower (ruler and ruled), it becomes necessary to create a system for imparting that ideology that will facilitate the routinization of the desired behavior. Because virtually everyone becomes familiar with family roles and statuses in the process of growing up, fictive family relations are easily taught and readily established. The use of kin terms in *iemoto* groupings creates the proper semantic and psychological environment; employment of rituals, such as grave visits and wearing kimonos bearing identical crests or other insignia, serves to emphasize the family-like nature of the group. Once established, the leader needs no further logic to justify his paramount position, for his authority is both absolute and self-evidently legitimate.

The relationship in such a system is patrimonial; the position of *iemoto* is inherited, and the relationship between the leader of the group and his followers is based entirely on their willing consent. To operate effectively, and to survive, the *iemoto* system requires that its participants accept the fiction that familistic relationships are the prime basis for all human relationships. That day is passing in Japan,[4] but in an earlier time, the relationship between master and pupil (*shujū kankei*) was by no means limited to the teaching and learning of an art or skill, for the master was expected to function as a surrogate parent.

In the world of Tea, however, authenticity and commercialization have become especially closely associated: The *iemoto* system is based on the idea that a single lineage may claim to be the only true authority on the artistic technique and related philosophy of a focal ancestor or famous teacher. The integrity of the message is preserved by strict training. Unauthorized communication of information is usually controlled by a convention limiting instruction at certain levels to oral transmission alone. The unspoken implication that school leadership has access to secret documents pertinent to the tradition reinforces its exclusiveness. To aid prospective students in identifying its authentic representatives and to ensure consistency in the education of adherents, the lineages began to certify teachers and students at various levels of experience. Since instructors were financially recompensed according to the level of their expertise, fees related to these documents developed into a source of income for the families that originally issued them as well as for those below them in the hierarchy (Anderson 1991:60).

Having presented the normative picture of the *iemoto,* let me now turn to the issue of variability. Like many institutions that seem quite uniform in character when viewed from a distance, what is called *iemoto* or *iemoto seido* actually is a highly variable set of institutions and practices, some of which, tellingly enough, usually are referred to as *iemoto*-like. They have different historical origins; their current status in contemporary Japanese society is far from uniform; and their claims to legitimacy, genealogical continuity, historical depth, and purity of transmission are sometimes fanciful.

In this chapter, we discuss the role of the *iemoto* in the Japanese arts, but it is worth pointing out that "schools" (many of which safely can be assigned to the *iemoto* type) abound in an astonishing array of techniques, disciplines, and fields of endeavor. Broadly speaking, these schools are to be found in what today are called traditional performing, graphic, literary, and applied arts.

The performing arts include those of the stage *nō, kyōgen, buyō* (Japanese dance), perhaps *kabuki, ningyō jōruri, rakugo, manzai, nagauta,* and *kiyomoto*; the instrumental music of *biwa, koto, shamisen,* and *shakuhachi*; and (stretching more than a bit) even the court music and dance of *gagaku* and *bugaku.* The graphic arts are the familiar ones of calligraphy and painting, as well as woodblock printmaking. The literary arts appear to be limited primarily to poetry. The applied arts are especially numerous and include swordsmithing, horsemanship, swimming, the martial arts (archery, swordsmanship, dagger throwing, use of the *naginata, kendō, jōdō, aikidō*), *sumō* refereeing, native mathematics, the culinary technique of preparing living fish, fireworks manufacture, bell casting, ceramics, lacquer work, certain kinds of fortune-telling, and last but until recently the most widespread of all, the schools of etiquette like Ogasawara-*ryū.* To these lists must be added, of course, the great threesome that is difficult to classify in the terms just used – flowers, tea, and incense.

One thing they have in common is the claim to genealogical continuity, often extending back to the mythological age of the gods. Such claims are by no means limited to the *iemoto,* however, for scores if not hundreds of Japanese families (including many among the ex-nobility, for example) trace their ancestry back to one or another of the deities of the Age of the Gods, whose exploits are recounted in the eighth-century *Kojiki* and *Nihon shoki.* In her study of the remnants of the *kuge* class in contemporary Japan, Lebra has a great deal to say about their participation in the world with which we are concerned in this chapter. Her findings cast considerable light on a variant *iemoto*-like form that deserves our full attention.

About 40 percent of the *kuge* houses listed by the *Kasumi Kaikan* (The Ex-Peers' Club) were associated with certain arts, crafts, and areas of scholarship – poetry, calligraphy, the Chinese classics, Confucian studies, court music and dance, lute, flute, flower arrangement, incense, *kemari* kickball, *sumō,* court-costume dressing, sewing, culinary art, and many others. According to Lebra (1993:87), the art or skill of these houses was called *ieryū* (house style). Today they are often compared to *iemoto,* but the great difference is that they did not necessarily practice the art in question. During the Tokugawa period, it seems, the shogunate recognized in these artistic and courtly traditions a potential source of revenue for the impoverished nobility, and it assigned them exclusive rights to receive fees for certifying the nonnoble *iemoto* who actually practiced and taught the art.

Lebra quotes a remark made by one of the members of the nobility she interviewed: "My house is the *iemoto* of the Ikuta school of *koto* music. No, nobody [in my family] teaches or plays it. All my father does is affix the family seal to certificates." Another person, a woman, explained this kind of arrangement as something like *arubaito,* a side-job that provides extra income. Her house has long held the seal with which the higher rank of a certain *kiyomoto* school is authenticated: "Every *kiyomoto* practitioner who wants a *jō* rank must receive my family's seal" (ibid., p. 87).

Not surprisingly, many of the *ieryū* died out with the abolition of *kuge* status after the Meiji Restoration. Nonetheless, some noble houses then, and more commonly following the abolition of the modern peerage after World War II, revived their *ieryū* in order to earn a living from practicing and teaching them. They now do what their ancestors never did: hold classes, exhibit their work, and issue certificates to students they teach themselves. "In the seven-hundred-year history of this house," said one man, "I, the twenty-eighth-generation master, am the first to make a living from this art" (ibid., pp. 331–332). As a consequence of their changed circumstances, many *kuge* houses have adopted the term *iemoto* but boast that they do not build up *iemoto*-like networks for commercial gain.

The three best known probably are the Sanjōnishi in incense, the Sono in flower arranging, and the Reizei in poetry. Less well known, but in many ways my personal favorite, is the Shijō (known as *hōchō no ie,* the house of the slicing knife), whose art, called Shijō-ryū, is the culinary art of preparing living fish to be served as *sashimi.*[5] The present *iemoto* is a thirty-eight-year-old ex-rock-band drummer, who performed under the name of Jōji Shijō with a group called Izumi Yōji and Spanky. Although he did not anticipate a career as *iemoto,* he left the music world about ten years ago to assume the position, and only last year began selling licenses to chefs. The lowest grade costs ¥50,000, the highest ¥1,000,000 (about $400 to $8,000).

There are many reasons for the survival or revival of a school. Among them are prestige and enhanced identity, as is the case with those associated with the nobility and some others as well, in which the *iemoto* is regarded by his disciples as the embodiment of the art created by the founding ancestor and perpetuated by the line of more recent ones. By becoming attached to the *iemoto,* a disciple becomes associated with the long line of distinguished descent of the *iemoto* house and thereby enhances his or her own standing (Lebra 1993:5). The Shijō-ryū just mentioned is a good example, for the present head of the house is, after all, the *forty-first generation* head of a house established in A.D. 886. Another is economic, for the *iemoto* of some of the traditional arts and crafts make a very handsome living indeed, but money is by no means the only motivating force. It cannot be, for only a small percentage of all *iemoto* or heads of schools are full-time practitioners of their art, and only the very well-known among them derive much income from its pursuit. Nevertheless, money looms large in the criticism of the *iemoto,* among whose many alleged sins are those of authenticating inferior artifacts (tea bowls, paintings, and the like), multiplying levels of certification, and charging outrageous fees for advancement from one grade to the next.

Even a casual examination of the economics of the situation, however, does provide valuable clues as to how we may profitably distinguish among the performing arts of the world of traditional music and drama. The Japan Performing Artists' Organization annually provides figures on the average reported annual income of all performing artists (Table 1.1).

Seven of the top fifteen categories are traditional artists, but the differences among them as to the source of their income are instructive. What the figures show is that the earnings of those practicing the classic *iemoto* arts depend heavily on fees received for teaching rather than public performance. *Kabuki* actors top the list of fifteen; *nō* actors are third.[6] But *kabuki* actors report receiving 90 percent of their income from stage performances and less than 5 percent from teaching.[7] For their part, *nō* actors report receiving only about 25 percent of their income from the stage and almost 40 percent from teaching. *Buyō* performers (Japanese dance) get half of their income from teaching, and *koto* players one-third; neither reports deriving any substantial proportion of annual income from performances. The same is true for *rakugo* and *manzai,* who receive one-half and one-third, respectively, from performances and less than 5 percent

Table 1.1. *Annual income of performing artists*[a]

Occupation	Average income (¥10,000)[b]	Percent stage performance	Percent teaching
1. *Kabuki* actor	844	90.1	—
2. Broadcast "talent"	814	—	4.9
3. *Nō* actor	675	26.7	37.1
4. Popular musician	674	22.2	16.2
5. Solo musician	590	—	55.3
6. Orchestra member	512	71.1	18.0
7. *Rakugo* teller	502	49.3	—
8. *Manzai* duo	416	32.8	—
9. *Buyō* dancer	381	—	46.1
10. Jazz musician	363	42.9	—
11. *Nagauta* singer	362	33.9	38.9
12. New drama actor	336	37.8	—
13. Ballet dancer	317	—	—
14. Modern dancer	281	—	—
15. *Koto* player	279	—	31.4

[a] Adapted from *Japan Almanac 1993* (Tokyo, 1992), Jin-ichirō Ueda, ed., p. 238.
[b] ¥10,000 was about $80 in 1993.

from teaching. *Nagauta* singers, by contrast, receive one-third from performances and 40 percent from teaching. The details are less important than the tendency they highlight: There is a clear distinction between those performing arts that are transmitted directly and almost exclusively in the *ie* line to one's successor and a very few insiders, on the one hand, and those that are taught to the public as well.

So far I have said little about the internal organization of the *iemoto* grouping, which has been very well described by Yoshikami (1990). It is in these matters that the full implications of the household model are to be seen. Yoshikami identifies three core characteristics of the *iemoto* grouping, which I will paraphrase as authority, continuity, and exclusivity (p. 17). In taking the view that the *iemoto* is a charismatic individual, she follows a Weberian line of analysis earlier adopted by Kawashima Takeyoshi, the eminent sociologist of law, in his analysis of the phenomenon in the early postwar period.[8] The *iemoto,* recognized to possess superior talent and leadership ability, sets the standards of artistic style and functions as the head of the household, the fictive *ie.* As for continuity, the *iemoto*'s standards are imparted to the disciple through individual instruction in a prescribed course of study. In the process, it is thought important to foster group loyalty, solidarity feelings, and consensual sensitivity among the disciples. The exclusivity of the group is marked by rites of passage in which awards are presented; these may be titles, certificates, ranks, name changes, articles of clothing, or insignia of various kinds. The use of garments and insignia to signify level of achievement within the school's art differs not at all from similar practices in Buddhist temples and monasteries, schools, department stores, corporations, and many other organizations in contemporary Japan, where uniforms, pins, ties, and colors may be used to denote grouping and rank (Yoshikami 1990:66). Surely it is the case that ritual recognition of achievement promotes solidarity, but I would add that it is also a powerful stimulus to what we may call "constrained competition among group members."

The issue of external competition with practitioners of the same art is an important one, as the following remarks suggest:

> Group consciousness is created to overcome internal heterogeneity through socializing, working, and playing together and discussing group activities and goals. The style of the art assumes the distinctive characteristics of the *iemoto*'s, and a sense of exclusiveness or "us" and "them" is felt. Often other groups, even those of the same discipline, are viewed as enemies and are dealt with tacitly as competitors. Within the group, the hierarchy is determined by seniority, by the individual's length of time and rapport with the leader, and not by age or ability. A senior–junior relationship is established. A newcomer, no matter how old, is the lowest in the hierarchy. Group ties also involve individual relationships that extend into the private lives of people, even to the family. It is intrusive in one sense, but in another it provides a sense of caring and security. (ibid., p. 24)

As elsewhere throughout Japanese society, the penalties for violating the rules of exclusivity and secrecy are severe. Just as the rural community once had the power to ostracize a member household that had violated the basic norms of reciprocity and harmony, so too the *iemoto* grouping:

> If a student transgresses the implicit loyalty required of the group, he is reprimanded. In the worst cases, he is ostracized, expelled from the group, or not spoken too. To be psychologically orphaned is a fearful state in an emotionally bonded society. (ibid., p. 26)

In conclusion, let me review some of the criticism of *iemoto seido* in the postwar period. Much of it has been made by persons of substance. Kawashima Takeyoshi argued that Japanese society could never become democratic as long as familistic principles continued to dominate its institutions. Hayashiya Tetsusaburō denounced it as a feudal survival, like the imperial institution, and urged the destruction of both. He was not attacking the arts per se but rather was taking the not uncommon purist's view that the essence of true Japaneseness lay in those arts, in this case the Way of Tea (*sadō*) as it had been *before* it was distorted and transformed by the *iemoto* system into what it is today. Yanagi Sōetsu, whose passion for folk art made him a predictable enemy of *iemoto seido,* also denounced the baleful feudal influence on the Way of Tea of institutions like the great Buddhist establishment of the Honganji. In short, these critics hold that the *iemoto seido,* far from preserving the traditional arts, has instead distorted or destroyed them through its rigid formalism and stifling of spontaneity and creativity.[9]

Some of the criticism originates in other quarters. Perhaps the most famous case is that of the dancer Hanayagi Genshū, who in February 1980 attacked Hanayagi Jusuke, *iemoto* of the Hanayagi school of Japanese dance, backstage at the National Theater in Tokyo, slashing her in the neck with a knife. Asked why she had done it, the perpetrator said, "I did it to smash *iemoto seido.*" As usual, the story turned out to be somewhat more complicated. Genshū was born in Osaka to a couple of itinerant actors and throughout her childhood traveled about the country with them. Lacking formal schooling, she received dancing lessons instead and became a *natori* of Hanayagi-ryū under Daizō, a pupil of Jusuke. She had been expelled (*hamon*) some ten years before as a result of her insistence on giving what the press called "avant garde" performances, including dancing nude, while using her professional name. Needless to say, Hanayagi-ryū was not about to countenance the flaunting of its authority and the cheapening of its considerable reputation. After her expulsion, Genshū constantly criticized *iemoto seido,* denouncing it as "an institution of exploitation, related to the imperial institution."[10] As I suggested earlier, the connections between the imperial household, the cult of ancestor veneration, and the strong emphasis on genealogical or historical depth among the *iemoto* are obvious, perhaps especially so to the disaffected.

But set against all its critics is the widespread assumption that without *iemoto seido* many if not most of the Japanese arts of an earlier day would have died out altogether. There is no answer to its severest critics, whose position is that the death of the traditional arts would have been no loss to Japan or the world.

Notes

I thank my research assistant, Kuwakado Chō, for his invaluable help in locating published materials on *iemoto seido.* For an institution of such importance, there are surprisingly few general studies, although there are hundreds of accounts of one or another of the "schools" of tea, flowers, and the major traditional performing arts. Names of Japanese authors are given in the Japanese order, surname first.

1. This passage is taken from an article about Rudolf Nureyev that appeared in the *New York Times,* January 17, 1993.
2. I have freely adapted the description given by Yonemura (1976).
3. Anyone interested in pursuing research on the subject of *iemoto* must begin by consulting the work of Nishiyama (1962, 1971, 1980, 1982a, 1982b).
4. Among the many criticisms against the *iemoto seido,* lodged by Japanese and Western critics alike, are their authoritarianism and the tradition of hereditary leadership, although there is another position that they too often fail in orthodoxy. See Anderson (1991:89).
5. The following information is taken from a television interview broadcast in 1992. The program, one of a long, popular series, was *Iemoto seido: Soko ga shiritai.*
6. In second place, between actors of *kabuki* and *nō,* are so-called broadcast performers, primarily television personalities (*tarento* – i.e., "talent") and actors.
7. Of course, some *kabuki* actors who teach dance closely resemble *iemoto,* but they teach acting techniques almost exclusively to members of their house.
8. Kawashima (1957) is the classic sociological study of the household and *iemoto seido.*
9. For a particularly strident negative opinion, see Ishimori (1977).
10. This sensational story was reported in the February 22, 1980, editions of the *Asahi Shinbun* (Tokyo).

References

Anderson, Jennifer L., 1991, *An Introduction to Japanese Tea Ritual,* Albany: State University of New York Press.

Hayashi, Tadahiko, 1983, *Nihon no iemoto* [The Iemoto of Japan], Tokyo: Shūeisha.

Hsu, Francis L. K., 1975, *Iemoto: The Heart of Japan,* New York: John Wiley & Sons.

Ishimori, Eiko, 1977, *Sengo nihon no dentō o dame ni shita cha-kadō no iemoto* [The Iemoto of Tea and Flowers Who Have Ruined Postwar Japanese Traditions], Tokyo: Yamate shobō.

Kawashima, Takeyoshi, 1957, *Ideorogii to shite no kazoku seido* [The Family System as Ideology], Tokyo: Iwanami shoten.

Lebra, Takie Sugiyama, 1993, *Above the Clouds: Status Culture of the Modern Japanese Nobility,* Berkeley and Los Angeles: University of California Press.

Nishiyama, Matsunosuke, 1962, *Gendai no iemoto* [Iemoto Today], Tokyo: Kōbundō.

1971, *Iemoto monogatari* [Stories of Iemoto], Tokyo: Shūei shuppan.

1980, *Gei no sekai: sono hiden denju* [Secret Instruction in the World of the Arts], Tokyo: Kodansha.

1982a, *Iemoto no kenkyū* [Studies of Iemoto], Tokyo: Yoshikawa Kōbunkan.

1982b, *Iemoto sei no tenkai* [The Development of the Iemoto System], Tokyo: Yoshikawa Kōbunkan.

Ortolani, Benito, 1969, "Iemoto," *Japan Quarterly* 16, 3: 297–306.

(Peak), Lois Taniuchi, 1986, "Cultural continuity in an educational institution: a case study of the Suzuki Method of music instruction." In Merry I. White and Susan Pollak, editors, *The Cultural Transition: Human Experience and Social*

Transformation in the Third World and Japan (pp. 113–140). London: Routledge and Kegan Paul.

Plath, David W., 1964, "Where the Family of God Is the Family," *American Anthropologist 66,* 2, pp. 300–317.

Rekishi Kōron, 1978, *Tokushū: iemoto seido to nihon no shakai* [Special Issue: The iemoto system and Japanese society], 4 (April). See especially Moriya Takeshi, "Iemoto seido no seiritsu" [Formation of the Iemoto System], pp. 33–40; Tachikawa Hiroshi and Hirose Chisako, "Iemoto seido kenkyū shi: oboegaki" [Notes on the History of the Study of the Iemoto System], pp. 175–183; and Yoneyama Toshinao, "Iemoto no jinruigaku" [The Anthropology of Iemoto], pp. 130–140.

Yonemura, Shōji, 1976, "Dōzoku and ancestor worship in Japan." In William W. Newell, editor, *Ancestors* (pp. 177–203). The Hague: Mouton.

Yoshikami, Miyuki, 1990, The Iemoto System of the Arts: The Unacknowledged Philosophical and Institutional Basis of Japanese Education. Masters thesis, University of Maryland.

2 The search for mastery never ceases: Zeami's classic treatises on transmitting the traditions of the *nō* theatre

J. Thomas Rimer

Japan's modern century remains, in one sense, the icing on a very thick cake created from an amalgam of traditional cultural values. The fact that these traditions still retain their power in contemporary Japan, certainly in the case of the arts, can be easily observed in the fact that such traditional poetic forms as the 31-syllable *waka* and the 17-syllable *haiku* are still written and widely appreciated, and that such theatre forms as the *nō,* which continues to be performed in a thoroughly traditional manner, finds both amateur practitioners and relatively large, enthusiastic, educated audiences (often themselves amateur performers) throughout the country. As Gary DeCoker points out in Chapter 4, on the teaching and learning of Japanese calligraphy, such issues as "copying the model" and the importance of discipline and master–disciple relationship suggests that the kind of training process long associated with the *nō* can surely qualify as a kind of "situated learning," a method that can show a venerable and highly respected pedigree.

How does one function when one becomes involved in learning, possibly with the hope of mastering, such a classical means of aesthetic expression? The most important element in many of these traditional art forms might be described as experiential: Training by doing, rather than by explanation, remains the central core of the artist's or actor's experience. What is more, such training occupies not merely an early phase in a total career but continues throughout the artist's whole professional life. The search for mastery never ceases – indeed, must never cease.

In many ways, these Japanese attitudes and beliefs as to the nature of artistic creation and reproduction are understandable in Western terms, particularly in the realm of, say, opera or concert music, where the singer or musician's goal is to reproduce as accurately as possible a musical score. Nevertheless, the leeway is much greater in these Western forms. Many opera singers, for example, say that they never listen to recordings of great, older singers since they wish to re-create the music in terms of their own personality and self-understanding, without any "undue influences."

This Western attitude, it seems to me, even in examples that privilege "situated learning," therefore implicitly posits the ultimate centrality of the artist's individual personality. In the Japanese case, on the other hand, it is precisely this self-conscious personality that is to be set aside, or, to put it in a more appropriate perspective, to be harnessed and shaped for service toward a larger goal. Here is a passage from the notebooks of Matsuo Bashō (1644–1694), the greatest of the *haiku* poets and teachers, who, like Zeami, shares the traditional commitment to artistic creation (Yuasa 1966:33).

> Go to the pine if you want to learn about the pine, or the bamboo if you want to learn about the bamboo. And in doing so, you must leave your subjective preoccupation with yourself. Otherwise you impose yourself on the object and do not learn. Your poetry issues of its own accord when you and the object have become one – when you have plunged deep enough into the object to see something like a hidden glimmering there. However well phrased your poetry may be, if your feeling is not natural – if the object and yourself are separate – then your poetry is not true poetry but merely your subjective counterfeit.

Putting yourself in touch with a larger principle outside yourself, then losing yourself in it, is not a state of mind limited to the realm of Japanese aesthetics. The virtue of developing a natural alignment of the individual and his "untrained" nature toward a set of higher ideals is virtually a first principle of traditional East Asian morality and ethics. This experiential conception receives one of its most succinct expressions in this well-known passage from the Second Book of the *Analects* of Confucius (Waley 1938:88).

> The Master said, At fifteen I set my heart upon learning. At thirty, I had planted my feet firm upon the ground. At forty, I no longer suffered from perplexities. At fifty, I knew what were the biddings of Heaven. At sixty, I heard them with a docile ear. At seventy, I could follow the dictates of my own heart; for what I desired no longer overstepped the boundaries of right.

In this paradigm, understanding comes through the passage of time and the kind of virtuous application required to bend the ego, the untrammeled will, in such a way that the larger moral and ethical issues assume their right and natural, central place in the human scheme. Thus artistic striving is not only modeled on this pattern of naturally focused development but becomes the means by which to bring about the appropriate changes. As Bethe and Brazell (1990:168–169) remark, *nō* training is meant to develop not only the actor's body but his soul as well.

In this context, cultural acquisition requires the gradual development of an "understanding" by any apprentice that can be measured only in experiential terms. Apparently only a trajectory through self-subjugation can lead to the growth of an authentic internalized artistic "self" capable of moving an audience in the kind of aesthetic and theatrical terms appropriate to the challenge that the highly poetic *nō* theatre presents.

The *nō* theatre came into being in more or less the form in which it is still performed during the time of the great actor Kan'ami (1333–1384) and his son Zeami (1363–1443). Although changes have clearly come to the *nō* and its method of performance since this period, the performance tradition does remain unbroken. Would that we knew how Shakespeare, or Molière were first performed! It is precisely those demands made by the experiential actor training system employed by the *nō* that has kept this ancient Japanese performing art alive and supple. At the heart of this tradition lies the reciprocal relationship between teacher and student, master and disciple.[1]

For those not familiar with the *nō,* it is difficult to provide a brief yet effective description of such a synthetic form of theatre art. Suffice it to say that the *nō* combines singing, dancing, mime, acting, chanting, the use of masks, and exquisite costumes, all at the service of poetic, often profound, texts usually based on a range of subject matter to be found in legends, Buddhist and Shintō texts, and the poetic and literary masterpieces of the preceding periods, such as *The Tale of the Heike,* that chronicle the great civil wars of 1185, the early poetic *The Tales of Ise,* which describes the romantic and spiritual life of the courtier Ariwara no Narihira (A.D. 825–880), or the eleventh-century *The Tale of Genji,* doubtless the greatest of Japan's classical texts, which recounts the life and death of the fictitious Prince Genji and his complex entourage. Given the variety of skills needed for performance, the *nō* is essentially an actor's theatre (in the literal sense of the word, since women have never performed professionally). The actor must spend his lifetime mastering and remastering the skills needed at every level of performance.

Much of the "learning" that goes on between generations of *nō* performers is conveyed by means of imitation somewhat in the style of what used to be called "rote learning" when I was a child. The "text" is the master actor himself; his disciples, in copying, in imitating again and again the teacher's movements, gestures, and intonations as closely as possible, gradually internalize these skills and make them their own. Indeed, Zeami suggests, the master actor himself must use his teaching as one form of learning for himself (see Bethe and Brazell 1990:175). As

John Singleton has pointed out, Zeami, himself a great teacher, describes in his treatises the *learning* process, a subtle irony often missed.

Under these circumstances, one would not expect that there could be any written "textbook" for young performers. Remarkably enough, however, Zeami himself did compose a series of treatises for members of his company, possibly as a way of preserving the art at a time when his personal situation and the general political confusions of the time might have prevented him from passing these "secrets" on verbally to the next generation. My Japanese colleague Prof. Yamazaki Masakazu and I had the pleasure (and the hard work) of translating these treatises into English (Rimer and Yamazaki 1984). One of the things I learned in doing research on these now famous documents in the history of Japanese aesthetics was that they were kept secret until this century, when a copy was found by chance in a secondhand bookstore in Tokyo in 1908. These treatises were written for what we might term "professional adepts"; in that regard, it is remarkable that we as cultural and historical outsiders can grasp their meaning as clearly as (we think) we do. One reason for this possibility is practical: Zeami was a real man of the theatre, who measured success in terms of pleasing his audience. Therefore the advice he gives in these treatises, despite the profundity of his thought, is always aimed at the learning process, and through this focus, we too can enter into the dialogue between teacher and student that he has created.

It might be mentioned here that many famous modern *nō* actors have indicated in interviews that they have never read these treatises of Zeami. On the surface, this may seem surprising. Yet given the content of the treatises, some natural resistance is to be expected. Since these texts are written in difficult classical Japanese, actors without at least some special training in medieval grammar and poetic terminology might well find them difficult of access. *Nō* actors have also stressed the fact that they learn the texts of the plays they perform by memorizing the words, and often do not know the precise meaning of what they say. In the very roughest of terms, I suppose that it could be said that classical Japanese is at least as different from modern Japanese as perhaps Italian is from English. And to extend my parallel between the *nō* and Western opera, there are many American opera singers who do not know precisely, linguistically at least, what all the words sung by Tosca, Lucia, or Mimi might be. Indeed, the fact that an artist like Maria Callas studied with extreme care the *texts* and so the psychological, even philosophical, aspects of her operatic roles constitutes one of the chief reasons for her extraordinary mastery of her art.

Zeami's treatises serve many purposes. John Singleton has mentioned the importance of the sociocultural setting for learning, which can often involve a need to explicate the sources of the "tradition" and so to provide legitimacy. This issue was very much in Zeami's mind. In the fourth chapter of his first long treatise, "Style and the Flower" (*Fūshikaden*), he took great pains to trace the lineage of the *nō* back to the age of Japanese myth, as a way of justifying the lineage, and so the high importance, of his art; since, socially speaking, actors were regarded as little more than beggars at his time, there were doubtless a number of compelling explicit ideological reasons for Zeami's urge to include this material as a means for communal self-justification. (See Rimer and Yamazaki 1984:31–37.)

Because the tradition is venerable, then, it must be followed then passed along, by adepts who have experienced and mastered this training, to the next generation in turn. A number of issues impinge on this implicit concept of experiential learning, as set forth in the treatises. Although the treatises discuss a wide range of elements that go into any successful performance, the principle of *internalization* remains paramount. The performer, beginning with his training as a child, must continually work so that what he internalizes in terms of movement, chant, and so forth will eventually become fully natural; a great performer will no longer need to "think" about what he is doing.

This internalization, in turn, is aided by a deep rhythmical process, moving through three stages from slow to fast: *jo, ha, kyū.* For Zeami, this basic rhythmical development, so much stressed in the musical fabric of the *nō,* will inevitably, like some natural psychic heartbeat, help the actor move through the various stages required. At one point, Zeami cautions against placing these rhythmic developments, centered in the chant, in any subsidiary consideration (Rimer and Yamazaki 1984:46).

> If the actor bases his chant on his movements, he shows himself as a beginner. For an artist of experience, movement will grow from the chant. The audience hears the text and watches the movements. In any aspect of life it can be said that our intentions give rise to the various aspects of our behavior. It is through words that these intentions are expressed. In the case of the *nō* as well, therefore, the chant provides the substance of which the movements of the actors serve as a function. This is because functions grow out of substance and not the other way around. Thus, at the time of an actual performance, the actor stresses the importance of the chant. In this fashion, a performer will be able through experience to blend chant with gesture, and the dance with the chant, so as to become the kind of accomplished player who has within him every element of his art.

Without this relentless drive for internalization, the actor can never achieve the kind of distinctions in performance necessary to give an accurate presentation. Zeami's remarks on the role type of mad persons (which he felt were the most difficult to create) shows something of the high standards required (Rimer and Yamazaki 1984:13).

> This skill represents the most fascinating aspect of our art. In this category there are many types of roles, and an actor who has truly taken up this specialty can successfully play all types of roles. I must repeat again and again that an actor must fully commit himself to rehearse and practice continuously, as I have admonished.
>
> In general, there are various types of possessed beings; for example, those inhabited by the curse of a god, a Buddha, the spirit of a living person, or of a dead person. Therefore, if the actor studies the nature of the spirit who possesses the character, he should be able to manage the part well. On the other hand, the really difficult parts involve those characters whose thoughts have become confused because their minds have become crazed – a parent searching for a lost child, for example, a wife thrown over by her husband, or a husband who lives on after his wife. Even a relatively skillful actor may fail to make the distinction between them, and he will create his mad gestures in the same manner, so that no emotional response is engendered in those who watch him. In the case of characters of this sort, the actor must have as his intention the manifestation of the precise feelings that can indicate the character's emotional disturbance, and make them the core of his Flower.

In terms of apprenticeship modalities, Zeami's remarks on training are extremely revealing. Given the physical dexterity required of *nō* performers at all ages, training must begin early. The apprentice actor receives emotional support from older actors and, indeed, from appreciative audiences. A reciprocity of shared understanding between the actor and his public not only spurs on amibition and creativity but controls artistic standards. In that regard, the audiences must be as active during a performance as the actors. Indeed, the audience assists by its positive response in helping to "create" the tradition that the performers serve.

Zeami suggests that a child actor's training should begin by age seven (Rimer and Yamazaki 1984:4).

> When a boy practices at this age, he will naturally of his own accord show some elements of beauty in what he does. If, by chance, he should show some special skill in dancing, movement, chanting, or in the kind of powerful gestures required for demon roles, he should be left free to perform them in his own manner, according to his own desires. He should certainly not be instructed as to what he did well and what he did poorly. If rehearsals are too strict, and if the child is admonished too much, he will lose his enthusiasm. If the *nō* becomes unpleasant for him, his progress will cease.

At this age, of course, only experiential learning would surely be possible, since any abstract or theoretical "explanation" of the *nō* as an art form would be beyond a child's understanding.

And so the pattern is set. At each stage of the actor's growth, until he is over fifty, Zeami makes striking comments on the nature of the kinds of training and self-discipline to which the true artist must subject himself (see Rimer and Yamazaki 1984:4–9). At eleven or twelve, Zeami indicates, "an actor can begin to comprehend the *nō*," and various explanations can be made concerning performance. The basic skills – first the chant, then the requisite movements and dance positions – must be thoroughly absorbed.

During the difficult years of puberty, Zeami notes, when the actor's voice is changing and his physique is awkward, he must practice by himself and, most importantly of all, "vow to himself that, although he is now in a crucial period, he will truly stake his life on the *nō* and never abandon it."

At the age of twenty-four or twenty-five, voice and physical appearance alike will have settled in. The actor at this stage in his career may now appear a skilled performer to the uninitiated, yet the true artist knows he is still not fully mature. "He will ask every detail of those who have already achieved a real reputation for their performances, so that he may rehearse all the more diligently." Otherwise, "if an actor thinks he has attained a higher level of skill that he has reached, . . . he will lose even the level that he has achieved."

For Zeami, the peak of an actor's perfection can be reached at age thirty-four or thirty-five. "Therefore it is in this period that the actor must perfect his self-discipline. At this time in his career, he must recall all that he has learned; it is also the moment when he is able to plan for the means to accomplish what he wishes in the future." By the age of forty-four or forty-five, a decade later, the actor must seek new ways to show his skills, for "although his real art may not as yet be in decline, as his years advance, his physical presence and the beauty others find in him will be diminished." By this time, an actor of note will have his own disciples, who can take over certain flashy or physically demanding roles; yet "even if he has no young successor of a suitable caliber, an actor should not himself perform any highly complicated and strenuous roles. A master . . . must most of all know himself, and, therefore, work to give the younger actors proper training. . . . One who truly knows how to see and reflect upon himself – it is he who has really grasped the nature of our art."

At fifty (an age beyond the ordinary life span at Zeami's time), even though the master actor's skills must diminish and his art fade, "in the art of the *nō*, even if the foliage is slight and the tree grows old, the Flower of the artist still retains its bloom." Thus is the cycle completed.

Scattered through these texts are certain terms that need some explanation. Again, given the complexities of the form and its history, these words are difficult to reduce to any simple translation. Still, some context will be helpful in understanding the level of discipline required during the whole gamut of an actor's career.

The first is Role Playing (*monomane*). This term means literally "the imitation of things," but Zeami's meaning is unrelated to our Western concept, derived from Aristotle, of *mimesis*; for him, Role Playing might rather be defined as "essentialization," with the actor's looking for the key movement, gesture, or bodily carriage that will identify the deep human truth of the role being undertaken.

The second is a term already mentioned, the Flower (*hana*), that sign of true artistic accomplishment as understood by the audience. An actor has a different kind of "flowering" at different stages in his career; his continual determination to refine and expand his skills will work toward the development of the proper "flower" for each phase of his career.

The third, and most difficult, term to explain is Grace (*yūgen*). The word literally means something like "deep, dim, mysterious." Zeami used the same term to mean different things over the years in the course of composing his treatises. He generally used the word to represent the elegant grace suggested by the behavior and dress of court ladies; yet on some occasions, he seems to have adopted from the medieval Japanese poetics (with which he was quite familiar) significant overtones of transcendental mystery and depth. Whatever the niceties of these shifting definitions, however, it is clear from the treatises that Zeami wishes his actors, by "essentializing" their characters, to move away from the external attributes of the role they play toward a high level of poetic suggestiveness. The actor must learn to imitate, then manifest the interior spirit, not the external features, of the type of role being performed. This concept is very far from our understanding of realism in the contemporary American theater. Zeami requires his audiences to make the kind of effort necessary to look beyond the familiar surface of things, a talent possibly altogether atrophied in our television generation.

Zeami's ultimate challenge for actors lies in the schema set forth in his treatise "Notes of the Nine Levels" (*kyūi*) (Rimer and Yamazaki 1984: 120–125). Here, in highly complex and allusive language, he attempts to show the whole range of possibilities, from literally the sublime ("The Art of the Flower of Peerless Charm") to close to the ridiculous ("The Way of Crudeness and Leadenness") necessary for the mastery of *nō* performance. It is of the greatest interest that the performer should learn all nine possibilities, Zeami indicates, as he may sometimes need to call on even the crudest possibilities in the context of a particular performance.

For the *nō* actor then, his apprenticeship never ends. In Zeami's treatise "A Mirror Held to the Flower" (*Kakyō*), he indicates that "the ultimate keys of our art [involve] understanding the *nō* with one's very being" (Rimer and Yamazaki 1984:105). "If an actor really wishes to master his art," Zeami continues, "he must set aside all other pursuits and truly give his whole soul to our art." In order to "revere" the art of *nō* properly, however, "an actor must deeply believe what his teacher conveys to him and take those instructions to heart."

It is here, in this crucial partnership of student and teacher, adept and beginner, that the art of the *nō* can be reborn in each generation. In this subtle and evolving relationship, we are far from the kind of didactic learning usually associated with formal education.

A final consideration. Since the *nō* is an art form dedicated, as Zeami always insisted, to pleasing its audiences, it may be worthwhile to speculate a bit, in terms of this system of experiential learning, as to how, in the words of Robert Smith, "talent, abilities, and creativity can combine in the end to *differentiate* those who have undergone the same *un*-differentiated training." The question is certainly an appropriate one to ask. It is true that, even to a casual visitor to a *nō* performance (assuming some prior interest in the theatre), the crucial differences between a merely competent and a truly brilliant actor will at once be apparent, however difficult those differences may be to articulate successfully on the part of the spectator.

In one sense, the matter is one of intuition: It is difficult to explain objectively and convincingly, as our newspaper critics know all too well, why, say, prewar recordings by such concert pianists as Solomon or Schnabel, despite the far less refined recording art of the period, often remain more satisfying than many of those now made by their often flashier and sumptuously recorded juniors. "They serve the music better" is the most common explanation given, and in terms of *nō* actors as well, that phrase might serve to tell us something that is useful.

Zeami himself never addressed this question directly in his treatises, although, in his sequence on the "Nine Levels" mentioned previously, he does suggest that a truly mature artist can shift his performance into unexpected areas in order to create something fresh and new. If he himself could be asked this question directly, however, I suspect, on the basis of what he has written, that he might wish to remind us first of all that any performance of *nō* represents an ensemble effort; even a great performer cannot succeed if all those on stage – actors and musicians alike – do not work closely, intensely, and effortlessly together.

Second, Zeami would doubtless add that much of the success of a performance consists of the tacit yet profound relationship that must be established during that performance between actor and audience; for Zeami, creativity can only truly reveal itself in a context of intuitive understanding. At least a part of the burden is thus shifted away from the performer and onto the audience; and as audiences have changed over the years, so have the demands and expectations of performance. Perhaps then, at least in one sense, a measure of the actor's supreme skill lies in his ability to intuit the needs of each particular audience and to respond to those needs. Zeami mentions the need for this intuition on the part of actors, but he does not, perhaps cannot, address the means by which it can be achieved. Communication cannot take place in a void; and for those who give of themselves, there must be present as well those who can take what is offered with enthusiasm, gratitude, and understanding.

As in all great art forms, the mystery of the performing genius thus surely lies ultimately beyond any explanation. And, perhaps, that is how it should be.

Note

1. For a number of relevant details concerning the function of the family or *iemoto* system of passing on the art of *nō,* see Keene (1993).

References

Bethe, Monica, and Brazell, Karen, 1990, "The Practice of Noh Theatre" in *By Means of Performance: Intercultural Studies of Theatre and Ritual,* ed. Richard Schechner and Willa Appel, Cambridge: Cambridge University Press.

Isabella Stewart Gardner Museum, 1993, *Fenway Court 1992* (Special issue, John M. Rosenfield, ed., "Competition and Collaboration: Hereditary Schools in Japanese Culture"), Boston: Isabella Stewart Gardner Museum.

Keene, Donald, 1993, "The *iemoto* system (Nō and Kyōgen)," *Fenway Court 1992,* Boston: Isabella Stewart Gardner Museum, pp. 30–36.

Rimer, J. Thomas, and Yamazaki Masakazu, 1984, *On the Art of the* Nō *Drama: The Major Treatises of Zeami,* Princeton: Princeton University Press.

Waley, Arthur, translator, 1938, *The Analects of Confucius,* London: George Allen & Unwin, Ltd.

Yuasa Nobuyuki, translator, 1966, Matsuo Bashō, *The Narrow Road to the Deep North and Other Travel Sketches,* Harmondsworth: Penguin Books.

3 Education in the Kanō school in nineteenth-century Japan: Questions about the copybook method

Brenda G. Jordan

Introduction

From the sixteenth century to the late nineteenth century, the Kanō family of painters and their disciples played an important role in the development of Japanese painting. Founded in the fifteenth century, the Kanō school flourished due to the political astuteness of its leaders and its overall organization. Kanō families obtained the patronage of the shogunate and were the official painters for the ruling Tokugawa family from 1615 to 1867.

The Kanō family system followed the *iemoto* system (R. Smith, this volume; Kono 1992). They maintained their power and control in the artistic arena in several ways. They were versatile and skilled painters, producing works in different styles and subjects upon demand. Their versatility was one of the features that made them particularly suited to the varying needs of their military patrons. They had connections with important patrons, monopolized official government painting projects, kept the leadership within the family, and transmitted their artistic styles and techniques through teaching. Knowledge of Kanō styles and techniques was passed down from masters to pupils and disseminated widely, resulting in the school having a far-reaching and continual influence on Japanese painting throughout the Tokugawa period. Many artists were affected either directly or indirectly by the Kanō style.

There is some evidence to indicate that one basic instructional method of the Kanō school involved moving a student up a prescribed series of steps on an educational ladder. In those cases, the student went through a methodical system of study that provided concrete, step-by-step training in the techniques of the use of the brush. Central to what we might call a core curriculum was the use of *funponshugi* (literally "doctrine of *funpon*") or what we shall refer to here as the "copybook method."[1]

The process involves laying a piece of paper over a painting to be copied and tracing the critical portions with *gofun,* a pure white paint, using dotting (and similar techniques). The copier could then set the tracing aside and, looking at the original, complete the copy of the work with ink (Hosono 1988b:18). When a student had practiced a model many times, he would make a clean copy and take it to the master for his evaluation. After receiving the teacher's permission, the student was then allowed to proceed to the next item in the lesson. In this way, a *mohon* (copybook) made up of teacher-approved copies was created and later bound up into a volume(s) or put together as a handscroll for professional use. When a graduate returned to his native place, these volumes were loaned to his own students as teaching materials. The graduate thus acted as the representative of the Kanō family in his home vicinity, disseminating the Kanō style with his teaching (Hashimoto 1889).

There were clear reasons for the use of this method of teaching, and the teaching method virtually guaranteed certain results. At the same time, the method of *funponshugi* as it was used in the Kanō school came to be questioned, both from inside and outside the school. Furthermore, there has been the perception that the Kanō system, using the copybook method, became increasingly orthodox and dogmatic as time went on. It is still a matter of debate as to whether or not the school lost its artistic vitality after the passing of the important painter Kanō Tan'yū (1602–1674); the fact remains, however, that many well-known painters received training from Kanō teachers.

Two Kanō-trained painters in particular left us with enough information to begin to formulate a picture of how students may have been trained in the Kanō school, at least in the mid–nineteenth century. Kawanabe Kyōsai (1831–1889) was a painter and print designer who began his career using the name of Kanō Tōiku Noriyuki.[2] Hashimoto Gahō (1835–1908) is considered to be one of the pioneering figures, along with Kanō Hōgai (1828–1888), in the formulation of new directions in modern Japanese painting. Both men wrote about their experiences as young pupils. Kyōsai left a collection of stories, illustrations of his experiences, a painting manual-cum-autobiography, and much anecdotal and hearsay evidence passed down by the Kawanabe family, friends, and colleagues.[3] Gahō gave certain specific information concerning training in the Kanō school, but Kyōsai's story is perhaps the more intriguing because the man's life, personality, and *oeuvre* so often seem to fail to fit into the image of the sober, diligent, and upright Kanō master that he was to have become.

The following, therefore, takes somewhat the shape of a historical case study organized loosely around Kyōsai, with the writings by Gahō and other information included to complement what we know of Kyōsai and to flesh out the story of his Kanō training. Kyōsai's individual case should not be misconstrued as the standard for all Kanō students in all periods of Kanō activity, but it will become clear why Kyōsai's case is both an interesting and informative one from the standpoint of the nature of mid–nineteenth-century Kanō school education and the copybook method.

Kawanabe Kyōsai

Kyōsai is known for his lively painting style, weird and fantastic subject matter, and exploits as a drinker and teller of tall tales. He was a versatile artist, with a broad *oeuvre* that covered a range of sizes, formats, subjects, and stylistic traditions. Kyōsai was also notable for his creative twists on conventional subjects. Into ostensibly traditional pictures, he interjected images of the modern age, certain Western techniques such as foreshortening, and a considerable amount of playfulness. Significantly, he was extraordinarily skilled in brushwork and technical facility, and he possessed an expansive knowledge of traditional subject matter.

As a youth, Kyōsai was greatly affected by two artistic forces, the example of the woodblock print artist Utagawa Kuniyoshi (1797–1861) and the years of training in a high-ranking Kanō atelier (painting studio/workshop). In 1837, at the age of six by Western count, Kyōsai was entered into the studio of Kuniyoshi. Kuniyoshi was a major figure in the area of woodblock printmaking during the last decades of the Tokugawa shogunate. He had a profound influence on the young Kyōsai. Although Kyōsai is said to have already demonstrated an interest in *shasei* (meaning, in this case, sketching or painting directly from nature), it was Kuniyoshi whom Kyōsai later credited with impressing upon him the importance of *shasei*. Kuniyoshi is said to have advised: "in order to draw [warriors], look carefully at the way a person suddenly throws down another person, and the position that person takes while falling. Or else, focus on the appearance of a person who pins another down, and of the man resisting him. You must paint that spirit and force" (*Kyōsai Gadan* 1983: Plate No. II 66-03).

This passion for *shasei* remained with Kyōsai throughout his career. The stories of his adventures in this regard express an underlying theme (irrespective of the veracity of their details) that seems to contradict what some claimed was the essential nature of the Kanō curriculum to which he was exposed. How did Kyōsai become a versatile and individualistic painter when he had not only trained in but graduated from one of the academic Kanō ateliers? As will be seen, Kanō education was not intended to focus on creativity; particularly in the first years, the primary focus was *not* on fostering imagination, originality, or expressiveness. Yet, for Kyōsai, the apparently opposing Kanō training and his love of *shasei* were, in fact, contrapuntal elements in the creation of an individual style.

The case of Kyōsai, therefore, opens the door to issues concerning the relationship between training and the artistic process. These issues include how Japanese artists were trained in traditional settings prior to the late nineteenth century, what kinds of skills the masters sought to transmit to their pupils, what relative weight was given to the development of technical skills and craftsmanship, when creative imagination or originality would be allowed, the balance between individualism and tradition, and the role that training in hereditary family workshops played in the development of an individual career.

After the mid–nineteenth century, the influx of Western ideas brought changes not only in artistic styles and techniques but also in the view of what art was. This, in turn, affected ideas about individuality and creativity. Yet within Japanese art, there remained a delicate balance between skill and creativity, planned production and "happy accident." Traditional training in the arts continued to play an important role in the late nineteenth century in transmitting artistic skills and knowledge from one generation to the next. The particular type of training that aspiring practitioners of the arts received allowed for the development of superior technical ability among able students, which was highly valued and may not have been the impediment to the creative process that might at first be assumed. Kyōsai's case serves as one model of how at least some young mid–nineteenth-century Kanō artists appear to have received their training.

Entrance into the Kanō school

In 1840, Kyōsai entered the school of Maemura Tōwa Aitoku (?–1853), a Kanō-trained artist. In 1841, through Tōwa's introduction, Kyōsai entered the studio of Kanō Tōhaku Norinobu (1818–1851), head of the Surugadai Kanō family. The Surugadai Kanō were an *omote eshi* family, second only to the high-ranking *oku eshi* Kanō families; all of these families served as official painters to the shogunate, with the accompanying prestige and respect that their position demanded. At that time, admittance into one of the higher-ranking Kanō schools gave a student the chance of obtaining a prestigious position in the future, such as being an official painter for a *daimyō* (lord).

Kanō school education in the mid–nineteenth century combined a curriculum developed specifically for Kanō students with the multifaceted educational process common to training in other traditional arts in Japan. Hashimoto Gahō provided a model for what Kanō school education may have been like at this time in an 1889 article in the journal *Kokka* entitled "Kobikichō Edokoro" (the Kobikichō painting studio/workshop).[4] In this article, Gahō revealed the process of training *deshi* (pupils) in the *oku eshi* Kobikichō family. Gahō was attempting to reconstruct events of many years past, and his recollections should not be accepted as indisputable fact. Nevertheless, this basic model is useful when compared with what is known about education in other areas of Japanese art, such as research on folkcraft pottery apprenticeships (see Singleton 1989a). When taken together with the information available on Kyōsai's experiences, a picture of life as a *deshi* in the Kanō school at this time can be tentatively presented.

In order to receive training in a Kanō atelier, one had to gain entrance to a painting master's studio. As revealed in the "Kobikichō Edokoro," membership in the samurai class was the normal prerequisite for entrance to the school. In addition, new students entering the school from the outside, with no previous connection to the Kanō family, had to have an introduction from the *daimyō* of their *han* (feudal domain). Kyōsai's entrance was possible because his father was of samurai status, and Maemura Tōwa provided an introduction through his connections with the Surugadai branch.

Gahō wrote that Kobikichō pupils began their painting lessons around the age of seven or eight, but a formal entrance into the school took place, generally speaking, when they were fourteen or fifteen. The teacher was treated with a great deal of respect. He was referred to as *tonosama* (a term of address for a feudal lord) and had a relationship with his students not unlike that of *daimyō* to retainer. In the Kobikichō family, the master would not relegate teaching to anyone else, and even if there were superior senior students whose skills had surpassed his, they would still receive guidance from the teacher in the production of works.

The first step

A Kanō student seems to have moved through a series of steps in his education. Initially, there were housekeeping or menial tasks that the student was expected to perform. Kyōsai entered the school at age nine, with some previous training in painting, but for a long time he was employed much like a servant, working long hours and helping to provide the basic labor needed to keep the studio running. Very little time was left for painting. This period was a time of testing the student's interest, sincerity, motivation, and patience. It was also a time for learning the art of unobtrusive observation (Singleton 1989a:19).

Unobtrusive observation is an important factor in the training of artists and craftsmen in Japan, in which the student must discover the method of knowing for himself. In apprenticeship situations, the first thing learned is to anticipate accurately the needs of both the master and the household. In painting, in addition to menial tasks, students also assisted in technical aspects of painting. The Englishman Josiah Conder (1852–1920),[5] who was Kyōsai's pupil in later years, commented that much of his own instruction under Kyōsai "was gained by watching the master execute painting, in listening to his comments and explanations, and in assisting him with such purely technical details as generally fall to the share of the pupil" (Conder 1911:v). This may have included such things as bringing water and grinding ink. In Figure 3.1, from the *Kyōsai Gadan,* Kyōsai's autobiography and painting manual, Kyōsai is assisted in painting a dragon at Togakushi Shrine in Nagano by his pupil Sugimoto Tomekichi and others who rush back and forth carrying water, grinding ink, and bringing large bowls of ink to the painter as he works.

The instruction that Conder received may have been exceptional in that Kyōsai provided him with verbal comments. The key to learning by observation lies in the word "unobtrusive." The student was expected to go about his tasks while still observing the master at work. A pupil might be scolded for presuming to ask a question or standing idly by to watch (Singleton 1989a:26).

Kyōsai probably learned how to observe unobtrusively while going about his various assigned tasks. This early "pre-painting" period in Tōhaku's studio served the purpose of teaching the young Kyōsai both social and artistic aspects of the Surugadai Kanō family. This initial period seems to have lasted some two years before he was allowed to pick up a brush for systematic learning (Iijima 1984:29).

During the first few years in a studio, the beginning attempt at actual practice of a technique may have had to occur on the student's own initiative. Kyōsai may have originally tried his hand at painting at night when the day's work was done and no one else was around. Kyōsai's daughter

Figure 3.1. Kyōsai paints a dragon at Togakushi Shrine. (From the *Kyōsai Gadan.*)

Kyōsui (1868–1935) recalled that Kyōsai was left with little time to study, but he was eager to learn and would spend his nights staying up late to paint (Iijima 1984:29). During those early years, Kyōsai apparently worked so hard that he undermined his health (Conder 1911:4). Thus the stories handed down from Kyōsai indicate that the virtue of diligent persistence was probably being tested and developed in him during those first years in much the same manner that apprentices in other Japanese arts have experienced.

The setup of the studio

In the Kobikichō studio, a system of study that provided training in brush techniques followed the period of menial tasks. Before explaining this in more detail, however, it might be helpful to understand something about the setup of a Kanō studio and the divisions of students therein. Learning took place in the classrooms of the *edokoro,* which in the Kobikichō family consisted of the master's private room and adjoining rooms. The master generally stayed in his private room, teaching, critiquing, evaluating, or producing works, and it was rare for him to come out to the adjacent rooms. Furthermore, the master normally would not give lectures to the students about painting, although Gahō did note that practice work was evaluated by the teacher.

In one of the rooms adjacent to the master's room in the Kobikichō studio were the senior *deshi,* who were allowed to sit near a window. New students sat in an inferior position, back out of the light. There was another room for mid-level students, which was like a hallway between the master's room and the painting room for the senior students and new students. Each student would have a two-*tatami* (straw floor mat) area and a chest of drawers for their painting and drawing supplies. The chests acted as partitions between the students, and each student therefore had his own space. During the day, students used this area for their studies. At night, they would clean up their things and lay down their bedding in the same area.

Figure 3.2, from the *Kyōsai Gadan,* gives an idea of a variation of the Kobikichō arrangement in the Surugadai school, as drawn by Kyōsai. Older painters, in the upper left, work in a separate room from the seemingly larger room in the center, which opens onto a veranda. Here a variety of men of various ages are engaged in various activities. Trays are scattered throughout the room. In the upper center, folding screens lean on either side of the sliding-door partitions. Adjacent to these are rolled hanging scrolls, books, and cabinets filled with supplies. These and other items clutter the floors and walls of the crowded room.

There seems to have been a hierarchy of pupils in some cases. In the Kobikichō atelier, from one to three of the highest-ranking senior students would be designated as *deshi gashira* (head students). The head students were responsible for such things as the conduct of the rest of the *deshi* and managing the business of the school. Next were the *ehon kata,* a group of six or seven senior students responsible for the management of copies of famous old masterworks made with the *funpon* technique. They were allowed access to the storehouse to retrieve the copies at the requests of the master or students. They also had free access to the models themselves. Particularly valuable copybooks and old paintings were kept in a separate storage house. A student could receive special permission to copy these. The *ehon kata* also were in charge of the conservation, repair, and inspection of the copybooks. Under them were seven or eight *enogu kata,* who took turns cleaning the master's painting chest and making *gofun* and glue for the entire *edokoro.* These tasks presumably were not part of the menial tasks required of beginning students but were reserved for certain, selected students.

Figure 3.2. The school of Surugadai Kanō Tōhaku. (From the *Kyōsai Gadan.*)

The daily routine

According to Gahō's description, learning ran from around 7:00 A.M. to 10:00 P.M.; most of the time would be spent in *mosha* (copying), with the evening spent in *keikogaki* (drawing practice). In the middle of winter, there would be *kangeiko* (mid-winter practice), when the students would produce thirty to forty drawings from about 2:00 A.M. to daybreak.[6]

During *keikogaki,* when practicing from one's own copies of the copybook models, students used a *yakifude.* Similar to charcoal in the West, *yakifude* was produced by burning the tip of a sap-free stick of *hinoki* (Japanese cypress) or *maki* (Podocarpus chinesis). The tip was then used to make a rough outline or sketch of a composition. After the drawing was done, a feather brush would be used to clear the particles from the paper or silk surface.[7] This technique was used by professional painters as well as students.

Set rules for the *deshi* had been passed down for years, first orally and then written. Among these were not being able to leave the school without permission unless the student was on official business. If a student were by chance to stay overnight somewhere, he had to bring back a certificate showing where he had been and to notify one of the *deshi gashira*. Students also were not to engage in drinking bouts, arguments, or gossip. In addition to these and other rules pertaining to daily life, the acts of associating with *bunjin* (scholar-literati) painters, attending *shogakai* (painting and calligraphy gatherings), and painting in the popular *ukiyoe* style were strictly forbidden. Student life as presented by Gahō was a fairly strict and rigorous regime.

The core curriculum

In *funponshugi,* the element of rote practice, still a vital part of learning in Japan, was important for several reasons. In the *Gadō Yōketsu* (The Secret of the Way of Painting; 1680) by Kanō Yasunobu (1613–1685), founder of the Nakabashi Kanō, there is a distinction made between paintings produced with the native traits that one is born with – that is, innate talent (*shitsuga*) – and paintings produced as a result of systematic training (*gakuga*) (see Hosono 1978:151–152; 1988b:27–28; Kono 1992). Talent and individual differences were acknowledged, but these things were not praised. They could not be passed down through generations and were secondary, therefore, to methods of painting that could be taught. The technique and style of a particular workshop could be transmitted better from generation to generation through rote learning of established patterns, ensuring uniformity of production. Individuality and natural talent were subordinated to more important considerations.

For a nineteenth-century Kanō pupil, the first systematic lessons corresponded to similar stages in other Japanese arts, where the assigned practice was (and is) regular repetition of a particular skill. Training in the Kobikichō school began by painting objects with simple shapes, such as melons or eggplant. Gahō noted that if one were the child of a painter, he would normally start this process at around the age of seven or eight, although, as mentioned earlier, Gahō also wrote that students generally were around fourteen or fifteen when they formally entered the school. (Many students were related to someone in the Kanō school.) The next step in the Kobikichō studio was the *sankan mono,* three handscrolls of *tehon* (practice/model books), with a total of thirty-six leaves of paintings of *kachō* (bird-and-flower), *sansui* (landscape), and *jinbutsu* (figures). This model book had been prepared by Yōsen'in Korenobu (1753–1808) and was the fundamental teaching device.

Gahō wrote that many students were able to master this basic level and then proceeded to the beginning of the atelier education with the *Okashi gahon,* containing sixty leaves of landscape and figures, drawn by Kanō Tsunenobu (1636–1713). The copying of the *Okashi gahon* was completed in about one and a half years. In the next half year, students would copy Tsunenobu's *kachō* drawings in twelve leaves and then progress to a series of single-sheet compositions (*ichimai mono*) copied from famous artists. These models focused on figures and included works by Chinese painters, Japanese ink painters, and Kanō artists. The last step in the Kobikichō ladder was copying Tan'yū's *Kenjō shōji,* "paintings of Chinese sages for the sliding doors in the Throne Hall (Shishin-den) of the Kyoto Imperial Palace" (Kono 1992:23–24). Because students varied in talent and energy and differed in the time it took to master each step, some completed the entire course in ten years, and others were still not finished in twenty.

Kyōsai's course of study is said to have been along the same lines; students were first taught how to paint gemstones and then proceeded to flowering plants and feathers. When a student became more proficient, he copied the works of old masters. Kyōsai improved in technical skill rapidly and spent a great deal of time copying old masters. At the same time, he also came to feel that he should be working from life (Iijima 1984:29).

In the West, too, the copying of old masters was a time-honored method of learning painting through self-study. Traditional Japanese artists, however, went one step beyond copying of masterworks to achieve mastery by regularly repeating certain subjects. In later years, around 1881, Kyōsai began to produce paintings daily of Kanzeon Bosatsu (Sanskrit: Bodhisattva) and Sugawara Michizane (845–903), a Heian-period (794–1185) court noble and scholar admired by those who hoped to develop artistic or academic achievements. The reason for engaging in this practice was expressed in the *Kyōsai Gadan* as a desire to reach a higher level of achievement by daily practice of different techniques and compositions and by altering brushstrokes while using the same subject matter as the starting point. This practice can be explained in the context of many Japanese artists' lifelong study of certain forms that served as a standard repertoire. These paintings were not sold or exhibited (although Kyōsai did donate his finished sketches to temples and shrines); rather, they were the tools with which the painter continually challenged his abilities, working within an established framework yet striving to vary the new image in such a way that his technical mastery moved to a higher level. This mastery of execution, so often regarded in the West as mere technical finesse, was the springboard from which a work of art could be created.

Additional learning opportunities

Three years after beginning the *ichimai mono,* students in the Kobikichō atelier would begin to assist their master in coloring paintings. This included helping their master with commissions from the Tokugawa family, a type of internship not uncommon in traditional arts. For this work, the students would receive an exemption in their room and board.

Another form of learning involved a kind of game playing. During a monthly connoisseurship session in the Surugadai school, students would be asked to identify a painting without looking at the signature and seal of the painter. Every pupil would decide for himself what he thought, and then the group would vote. Those students who incorrectly identified the painting would have to pay a small sum of money to a collective pot. Twenty or more members usually attended these meetings, and the money collected in this way would be spent to cover the expenses for the day. Sometimes money would be left over even after expenses had been paid (due to the large number of wrong answers). However, Kyōsai is said to have made mistakes rarely (Iijima 1984:31).

Like the Surugadai school, the Kobikichō atelier also had competitive games in which two teams headed by *deshi gashira* would compete in painting skills. These games naturally had practical application. Later in his life, the master painter Kyōsai was often called upon to evaluate the authenticity and value of old artworks and to give opinions regarding, for example, which Japanese or Chinese painter may have been responsible for a particular unsigned work. In the Kobikichō school, the *deshi gashira* made appraisals for works of art at the requests of clients and shared one-fourth of the enormous fee that their master Kanō Shōsen'in Tadanobu (1823–1880) charged for this service.

Unorganized, informal ways of learning also existed. There was a role to be played by stealing the master's secrets, a way of learning a craft skill that is still employed today. In fact, it was often expected that the master would guard his "secrets" and the learner would "steal" them. Conder told a story of the young Kyōsai that illustrates this point. Kyōsai told Conder that he would steal into Tōhaku's storehouse at night to inspect old paintings by early Kanō masters that were considered too valuable to be loaned to the students for study. Kyōsai had earlier seen his master handling a painting in which the depth and softness of a monkey's fur had impressed him. Frustrated by his own attempts to obtain the same effect, Kyōsai found himself confronted one night with the very painting that he had admired. Taking a sharp knife, he carefully cut and peeled up from the mounting a part of the silk. Peering underneath, he found, as he had half anticipated, that the hair had first been painted on the underneath side of the semitransparent fabric. Darker hair had then been painted on the front side of the material to produce the desired depth of texture. Afterward, when using silk as his material, Kyōsai would follow this method of under-painting in the more elaborate works of monkeys, tigers, other furred animals, and even human hair (Conder 1911:4).

Whether or not the event actually happened as described, Kyōsai apparently related this story to Conder as fact, and Conder accepted it as such. Thus, whether Kyōsai was recalling an actual experience or driving a point home by embellishing a story, the fact remains that the passing of the "secret" to Conder, who was clearly a favorite of Kyōsai's, was the act of a master directly passing on his most precious knowledge to a deserving pupil. This was yet another way in which a student could receive carefully guarded information once he had proved himself.

Less or more rigidity

In the Kobikichō *edokoro,* the *ehon-kata* had access to stored works, and the average student would not have easily obtained such works. It may also be that the Surugadai branch was less rigid in the way they managed their school than the higher-ranking Kobikichō family seems to have been. Some indication of this comes from the story that the Surugadai master Kanō Tōhaku Chikanobu (1772–1821) allowed Maemura Tōwa to enter his school without the benefit of either an introduction or samurai status (Iijima 1984:28–29). The possibility of a less dogmatic attitude on the teacher's part is suggested by the underlying theme of a group of stories about Kyōsai, which are said to have occurred during these years. The following is perhaps the best-known example.

Unsatisfied with studying animal paintings, Kyōsai said that he also used his free time to study directly from life. According to the story, Kyōsai went boating on the Sumida River one day. The boatman in his company captured a large golden carp in his net, which Kyōsai excitedly carried back to the Surugadai studio, where the carp was placed in water in a large shallow vat. Kyōsai then sketched every part of the fish, down to the thirty-six rows of scales. When he finally put the brush down, he discovered that while he had been absorbed in his study, the other students had placed a cutting board beside him, along with a big plate, a large bowl, and other items. Kyōsai was shocked at their heartlessness. He protested that, in sketching the carp, something new had been created and that, in effect, the carp had acted as his teacher. He was grateful for this and planned to release the fish. The other students laughed uproariously at this and proceeded with their plan. However, just at the moment the knife was about to cut into the carp, the fish gave a great flip, and from its mouth a golden-colored breath came out. Everyone was totally astonished (*Kyōsai Gadan* 1983: Plate No. II 66-06). The result was that Kyōsai's fellow students agreed to help him release the carp in Benten Pond, and Kyōsai himself thereafter developed considerable skill in portraying carp in his painting.

In the illustration of the studio of Kanō Tōhaku from the *Kyōsai Gadan* (Figure 3.2), students dance about in surprise as their proposed dinner flips off the veranda and out of their reach (lower right). Clearly this story is colorfully embellished, and those embellishments serve a larger purpose, illustrating more than Kyōsai's passion for working from life (which seems to have been its original intention). The illustration also suggests that drawing directly from nature may not have been particularly frowned upon in the Surugadai studio or that some leeway was given for students who demonstrated talent and enthusiasm for their studies. This view is supported by Gahō, who wrote that students in the Kobikichō studio sometimes did experiment with *shasei*.

Nevertheless, Kyōsai claims to have done much more than occasionally experiment, as attested to by numerous related "incidents." He related a story in which he sketched a severed head that he had discovered in a river. He also told of becoming engrossed in sketching a huge fire in 1846 rather than helping his family protect their possessions. The carp story and one other in which Kyōsai ventures out to sketch the Niō images at a temple are thought to have occurred when Kyōsai was around fourteen or fifteen years of age (Iijima 1984:30). According to the "Kobikichō Edokoro," a student such as Kyōsai should not have gone off on his own on nonofficial business and would, in any case, have had to account for his whereabouts the next day. Thus there was a discrepancy between the stated case in the Kobikichō atelier and what Kyōsai claims to have done in the Surugadai studio.

Hashimoto Gahō described his painting education as consisting of long hours of study each day and numerous rules governing behavior. But in the Surugadai school, there seems to have been the time and freedom for other activities. According to the *Kyōsai Gadan,* the students slipped out of the studio during free time to partake of various amusements. These amusements included going to *jōruri* lessons, to battle-chronicle recitations, to *rakugo* storytelling, and to other entertainment halls in the evenings. Kyōsai himself secretly took lessons in *nō* and *kyōgen* and maintained an interest in these art forms throughout his life.

Kyōsai also said that he drank and visited the brothels, expensive entertainments for which he needed money. Thus he began to paint *takoe* (kite pictures) and *hagoita* (racquet boards) and branched out to produce such things as *ema* (votive plaques) and *shōji* (sliding doors) for hairdresser shops. Kyōsai later said that he studied hard in order to learn how to paint these works for popular consumption, but when he took the finished work to the store, the clerk would not even condescend to look at him. The young painter would simply be asked how many paintings he had done and then would be thrown some coins as payment. Painting for these store owners was thought to be a shameful thing to do if one were a Kanō student (Iijima 1984:31–32).

In isolation, the details of the stories told by Kyōsai and others have to be regarded with some suspicion. Yet they all share the theme that Kyōsai had an overwhelming interest in working directly from life. Kyōsai, in his eagerness to emphasize his passion for sketching from life, gave us some clues regarding the possible exceptions and variations in the education of Kanō students.

Funponshugi: Pro and con

As noted previously, Kyōsai proceeded rapidly through the course of study but still felt an urge to paint from life (Iijima 1984:29), a statement substantiated by numerous stories about his efforts in this vein. There is the suggestion that he may have felt some frustration with the copybook method, and one wonders if others might have also felt that way. In fact, the copybook method as it was used in the Kanō school had come under attack long before Kyōsai's time by Nakayama Kōyō (1717–1780) and others.[8] The emphasis on *funponshugi* created problems for at least some of the students as well.

Hashimoto Gahō commented in the "Kobikichō Edokoro" that the system of Kanō school education was that of copying from beginning to end. Although the students did sometimes experiment with *shasei* or creating new pictures, these efforts were on their own initiative. The master did not usually critique the practice work of students done in this regard. Copying and imitation were so important that some students were unable to go beyond the bounds of their predecessors. Gahō alluded to one extreme case where someone was reported to have actually given up painting and moved to another line of work when a fire destroyed the copies of old paintings upon which he was so dependent.

Kanō Hōgai and Hashimoto Gahō are said to have rebelled from the system by agreeing together to study the famous ink painter Sesshū (1420–1506) (Hosono 1988a:84). However, as Sesshū seemed to be too lofty a height to attack immediately, the two settled on another well-known ink painter, Sesson (1504–1589?), for study. This plan reportedly outraged their colleagues, who tried to have Hōgai and Gahō expelled on the grounds that they were breaking the rules of the Kobikichō school.[9] Hōgai, in fact, was said to have often been on the verge of being expelled from the school for his criticism of his master Shōsen'in and the copybook method of teaching (Hosono 1988a:84).

However, there were reasons for the use of copybooks. One of the purposes from the point of view of Kanō ateliers was to produce artists capable of a certain consistently high level of technical facility. This method of mastering brush techniques seems to have been appreciated afterward by artists, despite their resistance to its overwhelmingly one-sided approach. In the same "Kobikichō Edokoro" article in which Hashimoto Gahō criticized the dogmatic copying of model books, he also wrote that when it came to obtaining technical skill with the brush, the Kanō education gave rise to skill that would have otherwise been difficult to obtain. For an exceptionally talented artist, such intensive training was a springboard from which he could go on to develop his own style.

Most students were, no doubt, incapable of going beyond the parameters of their training and instead became skilled painters for whom it was enough to produce a high-quality product for their patrons. It must be remembered that this level of skill would have been greatly appreciated. In many traditional arts, both the artist who is superb at recreating his or her craft and the one who is a creative innovator are valued.[10] In the case of Kyōsai, Hōgai, and Gahō, an important feature of their Kanō training was that, in the end, they ruled over it rather than being controlled

Figure 3.3. First lesson in the Kanō school. (From the *Kyōsai Gadan.*)

by it. Christine Guth perhaps worded it best when she commented of Hōgai that "he, like other great Kanō masters before him, had so completely internalized the technical requirements of this profession that he was able to transcend them" (Guth 1990). The same can be said of Kyōsai as well.

In later years, the methods by which these painters learned influenced how they taught. Kyōsai himself produced his own variation of a Kanō copybook, the *Kyōsai Gadan* (1887). This manual contains some 165 illustrations. The initial illustrations in the painting manual are samples of Kanō brushwork (Figures 3.3 and 3.4), and various Kanō painters' examples are included, particularly Kanō Tan'yū. However, the *Kyōsai Gadan* freely draws on sources from nearly all schools of Japanese painting, from medieval times to the nineteenth century, not to mention Chinese and Western examples. To those making use of the manual, Kyōsai

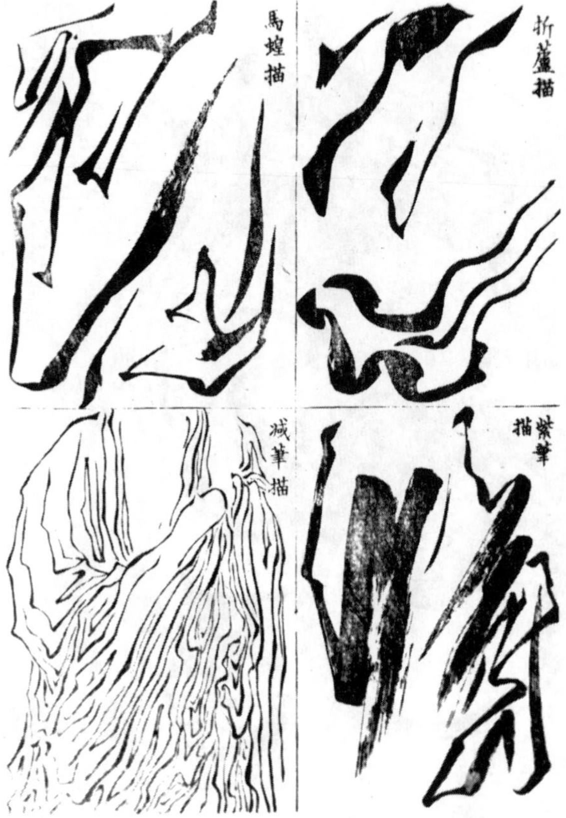

Figure 3.4. Styles of brushwork of the Kanō school. (From the *Kyōsai Gadan.*)

emphasized the importance of studying old and new masters. At the same time, he also revealed his equal devotion to sketching from life in the biography portion of the *Kyōsai Gadan.*

Master teachers' spirit of versatility

A stereotype of the Kanō school is that the school was artistically stagnant by the late eighteenth century. Later Kanō painting is probably most identified with Chinese subjects such as sages like Confucius or bird and flower themes, produced in a stylized, outdated manner, and based on copies of copies of paintings. In recent years, however, we have become more aware of late eighteenth- and nineteenth-century Kanō masters who were not nearly as fossilized as one might think. A number of late Tokugawa period Kanō artists attempted to retain the original spirit of versatility and artistic vigor that had helped to make the school strong (see Yasumura 1987, 1989, 1990). Pupils observing their masters work and helping them with commissions may have been exposed to an unexpected variety of subjects and painterly styles that were outside the realm of what might be expected of late Kanō work.

Kanō masters were collectors of copies of famous old masterworks for the purpose of study. These included copies of Chinese paintings from the Tang, Sung, Yuan, and Ming dynasties, as well as a range of Japanese paintings from *yamatoe* to scholar-literati works (Hosono 1988a: 83). They copied from classic Japanese handscrolls but also incorporated *shasei* into their painting. They painted native *yamatoe* styles and subjects, something that had always been part of their tradition. They even worked in subjects and styles that were normally thought to be outside the realm of reputable Kanō painters, such as the reportedly forbidden *ukiyoe* style (see Yasumura 1987, 1989, 1990).

Kanō artists also experimented with current styles other than *ukiyoe.* Some produced works in the decorative Rinpa style, and others combined techniques common to Chinese painting of the Ming and Qing dynasties as well as Western elements such as "illusionistic shading and naturalistic perspective" (Kawai 1984:185; see also Kawai 1983). Kanō masters, thus, spread their artistic nets beyond what is sometimes thought to be the traditional stereotypical production of the Kanō school. Clearly, not all high-ranking Kanō artists were immune to different influences and ideas, including those from abroad (both China and the West), and thus it is fair to speculate that their students may have been exposed to a greater variety of paintings than was previously assumed.

Graduation

Kyōsai's case also provides an example of how completion of training and graduation proceeded in mid–nineteenth-century Kanō ateliers. Kyōsai graduated in 1849 at the age of eighteen, completing the coursework in about eight years, counting from his entrance into Tōhaku's studio in 1841.[11] This was less than the ten or more years that most students required to reach an acceptable level of competence (Hashimoto 1889; Iijima 1984:32). In the "Kobikichō Edokoro," Gahō wrote that those who finished the Kanō curriculum usually had reached the age of thirty. Furthermore, graduation in itself was not permitted for every Kanō student.

At the time of graduation, one of the student's paintings accompanied by a resume would be presented to the central Kanō family in Nakabashi, and, after examining these two items, they would confer a diploma upon the student. The student also received a small sum of money as a graduation reward (Iijima 1984:32). The student would also be granted an art name that incorporated one or more *kanji* (Chinese characters) from his master's name. The student was then authorized to practice professionally on his own, or he could be appointed as official painter for a *daimyō* (Hashimoto 1889; Iijima 1984:32).

In the Kobikichō school, some seven or eight years after beginning the *ichimai mono,* a student would receive a *kanji* from one of the art names of his master's house. Two years later, he would be granted another *kanji* from his master's given name. Presumably a similar practice was followed in the Surugadai studio, for Kyōsai's art name upon graduation became Tōiku Noriyuki, a name that incorporates two *kanji* from Kanō Tōhaku Norinobu's name.

As was custom in those days, Kyōsai shaved his head, perhaps sometime after graduation. It seems to have been the normal practice for painters working for the shogunate at this time to shave their heads and become *sōgō* (a term generally used for a high rank of Buddhist priests but also applied to painters). The drawing of the Surugadai atelier (Figure 3.2) illustrates this custom of shaving one's head, and Kyōsai pictures himself as having a shaven head in Figure 3.1.

Conclusion

Kyōsai subsequently left the Kanō school and became an independent artist. In his day, he was extremely popular with Japanese and foreigners alike, and he was constantly busy up to the time of his death with commissions, teaching, and other art-related activities. The evidence presented about his early learning experiences provides some clues about the Kanō school during its final decades and the effect the school had on young artists of that period who studied with Kanō masters. In Kyōsai's case, the possibility of the Surugadai branch of the Kanō school being less dogmatic and conservative than might be ordinarily assumed becomes an important consideration. The best of the mature artist Kyōsai's work is technically superior yet versatile and creative. While credit must go to the natural abilities of the artist himself, the Kanō training he received must have contributed a great deal to Kyōsai's ability to wield a brush like a natural extension of his own arm. His reputation as a connoisseur and collector may have had its roots in the monthly connoisseurship classes, and his flexibility and open-mindedness in switching from one style, subject, or format to another might not have developed so thoroughly had his Kanō masters been as dogmatic as they are thought to have been. Finally, Kyōsai was not without opinions and passions concerning art. Some tolerance on the part of Tōhaku must be assumed, or the lively youngster would probably never have made it through the Kanō curriculum, graduated, and received the right to use a Kanō art name.

Kyōsai's experience thus provides a case study of what life as a Kanō student might have been like in Edo of the 1840s. The Kanō ateliers are said to have placed great emphasis on the copybook method. There may have been an underlying idea that while natural talent was not denied and one's individual differences were acknowledged, these things were secondary to transmitting the style of a particular workshop from generation to generation through rote learning of established patterns. Yet there seem to have been possibilities for learning in other ways, for "stealing the master's secrets," for seeing works outside the usual production of the Kanō school, for learning through unobtrusive observation and games of connoisseurship. Furthermore, there is evidence that high-ranking Kanō masters themselves were not bound to only a few styles, and there were those who painted styles and themes from the *ukiyoe* school as well as branching out to embrace Western methods. The conservatism of Kanō families and their teaching methods may have varied from one family to another, therefore, with some ateliers being less dogmatic than others.

Finally, it may also be that the intensive training in the Kanō school was not as stifling as might be thought, and that in the hands of certain individuals, the training would act as a foundation from which a talented artist could go on to develop his own style. The case of Kyōsai demonstrates how an apparently dogmatic teaching method gave him many of the very skills that he needed to pursue an independent career. The art of Kyōsai, Gahō, Hōgai, and others all owe a great deal to the forward-looking influences to which they were exposed during their formative years.

Notes

I would like to thank all those who have contributed to the completion of this paper – in particular, Stephen Addiss, Karen Gerhart, Hiroshi Nara, John Singleton, Tom Rimer, Christine Guth, and John Rosenfield. Any errors, however, are mine alone.

1. Although *funponshugi* and "copybook method" are used interchangeably here, a fruitful discussion might be held in regard to the proper translation of *funponshugi*.
2. For more on Kyōsai and the incidents mentioned in this chapter, see Jordan (1993).

3. Kyōsai was notorious for his tall tales, and the veracity of stories told herein can be questioned. However, the underlying themes of the stories are consistent, and there is a great deal of material about him that can be corroborated with other evidence. This issue of veracity of the information about Kyōsai is taken up in greater detail in Jordan (1993).
4. All of the following material in regard to the Kobikichō atelier is taken from this 1889 article. For recent discussions of this article in English, see Jordan (1993) and Kono (1992).
5. Conder arrived in Japan in 1877 and became one of the most influential figures in the early development of Western-style architecture in Japan. Conder was clearly not the average student and was treated differently as a result, which is why his comments about assisting Kyōsai are all the more interesting.
6. Gahō used Western time designations here. He was probably estimating the time in Western terms without taking into account the seasons that would have affected the traditional time designations. Thus the times listed should be taken as a general guide.
7. The term *yakifude* used here literally means "scorched brush." See Shimizu (1981: 45–46). The use of *yakifude* is evident in a number of Kyōsai's paintings and sketches.
8. Kōyō wrote the *Gadan Keiroku* in 1775, criticizing *funponshugi.* For more on criticisms of *funponshugi,* see Hosono (1988b:18–26).
9. From an article by Imai Sōhō in the *Shoga Kottō Zasshi* (May 1939). Quoted in Hosono (1988a:84).
10. In the Confucian Analects, Confucius stated that he was a transmitter and not a maker; he believed in and loved the ancients (Legge 1971:195).
11. Kyōsai's graduation painting, *Bishamonten no Zu* (Picture of Bishamonten; 1848), is the earliest known extant work by the artist.

References

Conder, Josiah, 1911, *Paintings and Studies by Kawanabe Kyōsai,* Tokyo: Maruzen Kabushiki Kaisha / Messrs. Kelly & Walsh, Ltd.

Guth, Christine, 1990, *The Myth of the Meiji Artist* (unpublished paper), The Artist as Professional, CAA Annual Conference (February).

Hashimoto Gahō, 1889, "Kobikichō Edokoro," *Kokka* 3 (December): 15–20.

Hosono Masanobu, 1978, "Edo Kanō to Hōgai," *Book of Books, Nihon no Bijutsu 52,* Tokyo: Shōgakukan.

1988a, "Kanō Hōgai – Pathfinder in Modernization of Japanese-style Painting," in Botsugo Hyakunen Kinen Tokubetsuten, *Kanō Hōgai, Sono Hito to Geijutsu* (exhibition catalogue), Tokyo: Yamatane Art Museum.

1988b, "Edo no Kanōha," *Nihon no Bijutsu 3* (262), Tokyo: Shibundō.

Iijima Kyoshin, 1984 [publication of original manuscript from the late 1890s], *Kawanabe Kyōsai Ō Den,* Tokyo: Perikansha.

Jordan, Brenda G., 1993, *Strange Fancies and Fresh Conceptions: Kyōsai in an Age of Conflict,* Ph.D. dissertation, Lawrence: University of Kansas.

Kawai Masatomo, 1983, *Kanō Kazunobu Hitsu Gohyaku Rakan Zu,* Tokyo: Minato-ku Kyōiku Iinkai.

1984, *Study of a Set of "500 Rakan" Paintings from the Edo Period,* Proceedings of the Nitobe-Ōhira Memorial Conference on Japanese Studies, May 23–25, 1984, Vancouver, British Columbia: The Institute of Asian Research, University of British Columbia, pp. 182–234.

Kōno Motoaki, 1993, "The Organization of the Kanō School of Painting," in Isabella Stewart Gardner Museum, *Fenway Court 1992* (Special issue, John M. Rosenfield, ed., "Competition and Collaboration: Hereditary Schools in Japanese Culture"), Boston: Isabella Stewart Gardner Museum, pp. 19–29.

Kyōsai Gadan, 1983 [1887], Saitama: Kawanabe Kyōsai Memorial Art Museum.

Legge, James, translator, 1971 [1893], Confucius, *Confucian Analects, The Great Learning and The Doctrine of the Mean,* New York: Dover Publications, Inc.

Shimizu Yoshiaki, 1981, "Workshop Management of the Early Kano Painters, ca. A.D. 1530–1600," *Archives of Asian Art 34*: 32–47.

Singleton, John, 1989a, "Japanese Folkcraft Pottery Apprenticeship: Cultural Assumptions in Educational Practice," in Michael Coy, ed., *Apprenticeship: From Theory to Method and Back Again,* State University of New York Press.

Yasumura Toshinobu, 1987, "Bakumatsu Edo Kanōha Ibun," *Nihon no Bijutsukan 3,* Tokyo 1 (August): 100–105.

1989, "Funpon to Mosha: Edo Kanoha no Baai," *Nihon no Bigaku* 13 (January): 25–39.

1990, *Edo Kanōha no Henbō* (exhibition catalogue), Tokyo: Itabashi-ku Art Museum.

4 Seven characteristics of a traditional Japanese approach to learning

Gary DeCoker

I have based this chapter on my own experience as a student of various traditional Japanese arts and on *Jubokushō*, a fourteenth-century treatise on the teaching of calligraphy.[1] I began my study of the arts as a student at the Oomoto School of Traditional Japanese Arts. Oomoto, a "new religion" founded in 1892, includes the arts in its religious training. In the early 1970s, Oomoto organized a series of traveling exhibitions in Europe and the United States. In response to requests from people they met overseas, Oomoto founded a summer seminar for foreigners, held at their headquarters west of Kyoto.[2]

I attended the first seminar in 1976 and continued studying at the headquarters for four years. During the summer seminar, I acted as translator and assistant for some of the teachers. For the rest of the year, I was a student of the arts in classes for the Japanese who were working at the headquarters. Most of the nearly 200 people at the headquarters also study the arts. The 20 acres of grounds include three *nō* stages, a martial arts hall, and numerous rooms for the tea ceremony.

My classes included *nō* drama, tea ceremony, martial arts, and calligraphy. My interest, however, extended beyond the arts themselves. I also became intrigued by the methods of teaching the arts such as the repetitive practice and emphasis on basic techniques. My curiosity led to my dissertation, a translation and analysis of two medieval treatises on the teaching of calligraphy (DeCoker 1987). In those treatises, I found a discussion of some of the methods that I had seen as a student of the arts. I also came to realize the difficulty of making generalizations about the arts. The more I learned, the more I had to narrow my study. I left for Japan planning to write on the historical development of the teaching of the arts of calligraphy, *nō*, and tea ceremony. I returned to the United States with a study of two calligraphic treatises separated by only 160 years.

Jubokushō, written in 1352 by Prince Son'en (1298–1356) for Emperor Go-Kōgon (1338–1374, r. 1352–1371) of the Northern Court, was a guide for the young emperor's study of calligraphy. It consists of twenty sections of varying length, some a few sentences, others nearly a thousand words. Go-Kōgon asked Son'en to write the treatise, probably realizing that as emperor he would need a certain level of mastery in the art. In addition to the approach to study, Son'en includes sections on the history of the art.

In this chapter, I describe seven characteristics of a "traditional Japanese approach to teaching," relating each characteristic to my own experience as a student and to *Jubokushō*. The approach to teaching the arts, of course, has changed over the centuries. And each art has unique methods. The seven characteristics, however, exist in a wide range of pursuits in Japan and will probably continue to play a part in the way the Japanese approach teaching and learning.[3]

The seven characteristics

1. *Copying the model* – Mastery of the model is of foremost importance. Unique interpretations are discouraged. Creativity is allowed only after years of study.
2. *Discipline* – Teachers often stress the need for severity in teaching. Enduring hardship, both physical and psychological, is thought to promote personal growth. Above all else, students are encouraged to endure.
3. *Master–disciple relations* – The roles of the teacher and the student are clearly defined. An image of the ideal practitioner of the art exists and is held up as a model.
4. *Secrets, stages, and the hierarchy of study* – Teachers impart the skills or techniques of the art in hierarchical stages marked by the granting of certificates, titles, and ranks. Progress in the study of the art takes place by increasing the repertoire of movements or patterns. In many of the arts, "advanced" skills are often no more complex than those taught to beginners.
5. *Established lineages* – Schools or franchises exist for most of the arts. They often gain legitimacy for their teachings by tracing their lineage to the founder of the art.
6. *Nonverbal communication* – Teachers rely on nonverbal communication by having students imitate a model provided and explained by the teacher. Oral communication often is in the form of metaphors or parables.

Figure 4.1. A calligraphy teacher guides his student's hand to help her feel the flow of the brush. (Courtesy of The Oomoto Foundation.)

7. *Art as a spiritual quest* – The study of the art is a gateway or a means to a higher spiritual plane. The ultimate goal is not mastery of the art, but mastery of the self.

Reflections on the seven characteristics

This section of the chapter includes a discussion of each of the seven characteristics, first, from my own experience as a student of the arts, and second, as represented in *Jubokushō*.

Copying the model

Mastery of the model is of foremost importance. Unique interpretations are discouraged. Creativity is allowed only after years of study.

At the beginning of each lesson at Oomoto, teachers usually presented us with a model – a five-minute demonstration in martial arts, *nō,* or tea ceremony, or the writing of a few characters in calligraphy. The students then copied the teacher's form. While watching the teacher's demonstration, I often focused on a specific point of difficulty for me such as the placement of the feet or the turn of the wrist. Sometimes I would repeat that part of the movement, moving my feet from one place to another or turning my hand this way and that. At these times, my teachers rarely offered assistance. In fact, they often showed displeasure.

I realized later that they saw the movement very differently than I did. For me, it was a combination of parts. For them, it was an integrated whole. The calligraphy teacher emphasized the movement of the brush from one stroke to the next: The flow of the brush was not to stop until the character was completed. *Nō,* martial arts, and tea were the same. The movement continued from beginning to end. The flow unbroken.

In martial arts, the teacher repeatedly told us that the source of the movement was the *koshi* or hips. If moved correctly, the hips would move the rest of the body in a coordinated way. The upper half of the body should be relaxed. The shoulders, arms, and hands curved slightly with no edges. The goal, according to the teacher, was to allow one's *ki* energy to flow from the hips, through the upper body, and into the sword.[4] The other teachers described similar postures, movement, and energy flow. When the parts of the movement were not joined together into one, an edge or break would result. Here the energy would dissipate. The beginner needed to remember only two things: Start with the correct, rounded posture, and move from the hips. With these things in mind, the student repeated the model, gradually working toward the teacher's form.

Son'en and the model. Son'en begins *Jubokushō* with a detailed description of the correct brush grip, including a diagram from an earlier manuscript. He then states:

The correct shape of the hand when holding the brush is rounded and attractive. Although a difficult position at first, this grip will be especially beneficial later. Such a grip is fundamental in order to use the brush with facility and to write characters well. (1)[5]

He later adds, "In the beginning of your studies you should practice by taking the correct posture, concentrating while you move the brush quietly" (4).

Son'en suggests that his student set aside at least two to four hours for daily practice (11). He advises the student to repeatedly copy a few lines of poetry until "the image of the model merges clearly in your mind and you are able to write an almost identical copy from memory, then proceed gradually further into your studies" (2). For the beginner, Son'en warns, mastery of those few lines may take longer than expected, perhaps as many as ten days. Concentration and continued practice, however, will lead to good results.

In *Jubokushō,* Son'en also stresses the need to choose appropriate models for practice. Throughout the treatise, he points to the "classic works" of *wayō* (Japanese-style) calligraphy, those by the Three Masters who distinguished *wayō* from *karayō* (Chinese-style) calligraphy.[6] He acknowledges that the classic pieces are seldom available for perusal. For that reason, calligraphers used *ōrai* or copybooks, collections of characters originally written by a famous calligrapher and subsequently copied and recopied.

Son'en also cautions his student against being misled by his own taste or by what the public desires (7, 14). The classic works must guide the student.

> In the end, everyone who studies a model should be in accord with it, and there should be no difference between his writing and the model. Those who practice incorrectly try to imitate the form of the characters. The form looks similar, but they cannot reproduce the vigor of the brush, and so their characters seem to be without life. This is futile. (4)

Discipline

> Teachers often stress the need for severity in teaching. Enduring hardship, both physical and psychological, is thought to promote personal growth. Above all else, students are encouraged to endure.

When I first met my teacher of tea ceremony, I introduced myself and bowed. He responded with a slight dip of the head and the statement that he is a strict (*kibishii*) teacher. Although my tea teacher said very little beyond his first perplexing greeting, I realized later that he had presented me with his credentials – his sternness.

We entered the disciplined world of practice through cleaning. Tea practice began and ended with a thorough cleaning of the utensils and rooms. Everything was swept and scrubbed, even though nothing was dirty. The students from the previous day had just performed the same tasks. We began *nō* practice on our knees, washing the stage floor. And to start martial arts, we first held a broom, not a sword.

In other ways, too, the teachers added an element of discipline to practice. In calligraphy, the teacher insisted that we grind the ink ourselves, even though he sometimes used ink from the grinding machine. During the coldest month of the year, the martial arts teacher held a week of predawn practices called *kangeiko,* or mid-winter practice. All of this, we were told, would help us focus. The ritual beginnings and the practice itself had the same goal – *seishin tōitsu,* or mental concentration.

Son'en and discipline. Son'en realized that repetitious copying of a small number of characters could lead to carelessness and an inability of the student to perceive his own progress. "At such times you will become inattentive and entertain idle thoughts. Pay no heed, and just continue to practice as usual" (10). Perhaps to overcome boredom, Son'en instructs his student to write a finished copy every five or ten days. These works were to be dated and used in further study.

A disciplined approach to study, however, is of foremost importance. "The words of T'ai-tsung are very appropriate: 'Set your standards high and you reach the middle; set your standards in the middle and you attain the lowest' " (14). Son'en ends the treatise with a last word on the importance of discipline. "Here let me repeat, the most difficult thing is to turn your attention to the correct path and devote yourself to your practice" (20).

Master–disciple relations

The roles of the teacher and the student are clearly defined. An image of the ideal practitioner of the art exists and is held up as a model.

During my years of study, a teacher would occasionally miss practice. When this happened, a senior student, the one who had been studying for the longest time, would take over. Practice continued the same way, except that no one used the term "*Sensei,*" the honorific for teacher, literally "born earlier." On a few occasions, the senior student, perhaps because of a lack of talent or diligence, was not the most knowledgeable. In that case, the other students would help the senior by filling in the gaps.

When a senior student taught, I was struck by how well everyone assumed the proper role, although in some cases no one was really sure how to proceed. In the ritual chant and bows at the beginning and end of practice, everyone treated the senior student like the teacher, showing respect to the position of teacher, if not the person occupying the role.

The martial arts teacher once explained to me that the teacher was merely the oldest student of the art. He illustrated his explanation with a metaphor. During the chant before and after practice, everyone faces the same direction, but the teacher leads from a position a few feet in front of the students. The chant focuses their attention toward the ideal world of the heavens where true perfection in the art exists. From the students' point of view, the teacher's level may appear unreachable. But, according to my teacher, all that separates the teacher from the students is a few years of study. In the infinite distance between the worldly practitioners and the perfection of the heavens, the teacher stands only slightly ahead of the student – about as far as he is ahead of the students during the ritual chanting. A far greater distance separates all of them from perfection.

Son'en and his student. Jubokushō does not offer much insight into the relationship between Son'en and his student, the young Emperor Go-Kōgon. One role of the teacher, according to Son'en, is the selection of appropriate models.

> A beginner's calligraphy will surely suffer if he says "Here is a work from the brush of one of the Three Masters," or the like, and without consulting his teacher, he studies a piece because the text is intriguing and the characters are interesting. (12)

The teacher also should critique the student's calligraphy every week or so (9). The unstable political condition of the period, however, may have prevented Son'en from meeting very often with Go-Kōgon.

Secrets, stages, and the hierarchy of study

Teachers impart the skills or techniques of the art in hierarchical stages marked by the granting of certificates, titles, and ranks. Progress in the study of the art takes place by increasing the repertoire of movements or patterns. In many of the arts, "advanced" skills are often no more complex than those taught to beginners.

The martial arts teacher often told us that if we could master one movement, we could do them all. That statement captured the simplicity and difficulty of the arts. Each art had a few basic forms. In calligraphy, the character 永 contained all of the calligraphic strokes. Martial arts consisted of eight basic movements of the sword. Tea and *nō* seemed more complex, but they, too, could be reduced to a few central principles.

The teachers introduced the basic forms in the first few lessons. Then, in subsequent lessons, they taught us variations of these forms. A definite hierarchy of forms existed. But the forms learned in the fourth and fifth years of study did not seem any more complex than those of the first few months. In tea, for instance, we learned the procedure for making tea for an honored guest. This way of preparing tea included a wooden saucer under the tea bowl as a symbol of respect for the guest. The procedure was not more difficult, merely a bit more elaborate: It took a few more hand movements to manipulate the tea bowl.

In the Japanese arts, in general, it would be possible to start at almost any point in the hierarchy because each lesson consisted primarily of the basic forms. The student, therefore, constantly returned to the basics, in a different context and with a higher level of skill.

The hierarchies also had clear markers, making it obvious where students were in their study. In tea, we could purchase certificates indicating our completion of a certain level. These were the equivalent of the "secret teachings" of former eras.[7] The publication of the tea procedures during the Meiji period (1868–1912) opened the secret world. And at that point, each school created a standard schedule of study followed by all of its teachers. Instead of transmitting secret teachings, the schools began issuing certificates. Our tea teacher occasionally labeled something a "former secret teaching," but they were not otherwise identifiable.

Son'en and secret teachings. Son'en mentions "secret teachings" in section sixteen of *Jubokushō,* where he explains how to store an ink stick. "Place it unwrapped in a lacquer container and always wipe it. This is the utmost secret" (16). Son'en probably transmitted other, perhaps more profound, secret teachings to Go-Kōgon in the form of "oral transmissions" (*kuden*) during their meetings. At the end of the last section, he states:

> As we proceed, I will explain such things as poem sheets, plaques, and so on. These are the essentials of the Way, but you have already received the oral transmissions and have a general understanding of the Way of calligraphy, so these matters will not present any difficulty to you. (20)

The possession of secrets, such as the method of writing characters for poem sheets and plaques, helped a family carve out a place in the social hierarchy.[8] Although the secrets appear trite from our twentieth-century viewpoint, they gave certain families an exclusive relationship with the Imperial Family and the military leaders.

Established lineages

Schools or franchises exist for most of the arts. They often gain legitimacy for their teachings by tracing their lineage to the founder of the art.

After about three years of studying calligraphy, I had to change teachers. It was my teacher's idea. He told me one day that he had nothing more to teach me. This statement revealed more about him than about my ability. Among his students, I was one of the few adults; most were elementary schoolchildren. He said that he thought of himself as more of a student than a teacher and recommended that I begin studying with his teacher.

So a week later, instead of walking a few minutes to the local temple classroom, I made a ninety-minute commute to my new teacher's house. When I arrived, I realized it would be my only trip there. The students in the room, most of them teachers themselves, were far beyond my beginning level. Later, my first teacher apologized for sending me to his teacher. He explained that he had no choice. Had he sent me to a local teacher out of his school's lineage, he would have risked insulting his teacher.

Tea and *nō* at Oomoto also had a lineage, the Urasenke and Hoshō schools.[9] Moving between schools in these arts was impossible because of differing procedures and, of course, student loyalty to the teacher and school. The tea world stressed lineage more than *nō*, especially on our trips to the Urasenke headquarters in Kyoto. Everything seemed to be connected to Sen no Rikyū. In contrast, my *nō* teacher once responded to my question about Zeami's approach to teaching with his own rhetorical question: How do we know that Zeami was right?[10]

Son'en and established lineages. Son'en ends *Jubokushō* with three sections on the heritage of *wayō* (Japanese-style) calligraphy. In section eighteen, "Japan's Superiority to China in the Art of Calligraphy," he connects his own tradition to the foremost era of Chinese calligraphy. He begins with Wang Hsi-chih (ca. 307–365), revered in both countries as the "father of Chinese calligraphy," but incorporates Wang's tradition into his own Japanese lineage and implies that Chinese have veered from it. According to Son'en, subsequent Chinese calligraphers could not match Wang's achievements. He takes further liberties by telling a story linking one of Japan's most famous calligraphers, Kūkai (774–835, posthumously known as Kōbō Daishi), with Wang Hsi-chih.

At the time of Kōbō Daishi's visit to China, part of Wang Hsi-chih's calligraphic writing on the palace wall was in a damaged condition, and it had remained in this state because there was no one to rewrite it. Responding to an imperial command, the Daishi rewrote it, thereby reviving the Way that had been extinct from the Chin until the T'ang era.

Son'en continues by tracing Japanese calligraphy generation by generation from Kūkai to the "Three Masters" and the beginning of *wayō* calligraphy. "These Three Masters – Michikaze, Sukemasa, and Yukinari – have been admired as exemplars of this Way throughout succeeding generations to the present day, and we use the styles of each as models. Thus, the Japanese style has not changed."

By establishing a connection between Kūkai and *wayō,* Son'en implies that the classic tradition of China remains only in Japan. To bolster his claim, he states that the *wayō,* unlike many Japanese art forms, avoided the influence of China's T'ang era (618–907). *Wayō,* it seems, is pure Japanese, except for its origin in the calligraphy of Wang Hsi-chih. Later, Son'en criticizes currently popular forms of Chinese calligraphy, including the Sung (960–1279) style brought to Japan by Zen monks. Here again Son'en attempts to manipulate tradition. Sung calligraphy was recognized as superior to contemporary *wayō.* In fact, Son'en himself absorbed Sung elements into his own *wayō* calligraphy, giving new life to the stagnating *wayō* of his day.

Son'en writes, "Sung-style writing forms lack mystery and divinity" because they use "many variant and unsuitable forms." Given the difficulty of sustaining the argument that *wayō* of the fourteenth century is superior, he reverts to his former criteria, that of hereditary connections.

In Japan we always follow the examples of the past and thus do not lose our national heritage. In China this is not so. They change the old style of the past and allow contemporary styles to circulate. As a result, writing forms change. (18)

In section nineteen, Son'en continues to take his student through the centuries, from the Three Masters of the eleventh century to the present head of the Sesonji school. He concludes the section with this statement:

In order that you understand how these things have come about over time, I will mention the following. Lord Yukinari's descendants all copied his works without changing the writing forms in the least. Although the external appearance of these forms may seem to have changed over the ages, in essence they are all the same and were not mixed with other styles. From the time of Lord Yukinari to Yukitada of today, the form has remained quite the same. It would seem to have been faithfully transmitted.

Nonverbal communication

Teachers rely on nonverbal communication by having students imitate a model provided and explained by the teacher. Oral communication often is in the form of metaphors or parables.

On the first day of his study, an American student asked the martial arts teacher about the purpose of the art. After listening to the teacher's brief reply, he asked another question. The teacher shot back, "You don't even know enough to ask a question. Practice a few years; then, if you feel the need, ask me." The tea teacher, on the other hand, encouraged our questions, especially about the details of tea practice. He had an explanation for every action, every object, every phrase in the tea room.

The difference in these two teachers' response to questions lies in the questions themselves. Most of my teachers were very willing to talk about the details of artistic practice. They carefully guided us, using models and explanations, step by step through the hierarchy of movements (*kata*). When our questions turned to the purpose of the art, however, the teachers said less, often relying on the maxims of the past. For example, the purpose of the tea was "to make tea and drink it"; the purpose of *nō* was "to communicate with the audience." The purpose of calligraphy – "to write beautiful characters" and of martial arts – "to defeat the opponent."

The tea teacher once responded to a question about the goal of practice by saying that you just have to keep pushing until you break through. Here, too, he drew on a tea concept – *shū, ha, ri* (or observance, break away, detachment) from Kawakami Fuhaku's (1718–1809) *Fuhaku Hikki* ("Fuhaku's Jottings"). The purpose of the art becomes visible when the student breaks away from the details of the art and achieves a more personal understanding. The teachers acknowledged that the higher levels of *ha* and *ri* existed, but they left those for the students to achieve. At this level, students had to "steal the art," as another maxim said. But when it came to the specifics of each new form, things much easier to explain, the teachers had more to say.

Son'en and nonverbal communication. Son'en clearly states his preference for the classic works as models for his student. He tells the student to "apply your brush according to the examples of the ancient masters; leave nothing to chance, and you will naturally gain proficiency" (4). Son'en is less clear, however, about the qualities that make these works superior.

His attempts to define exemplary calligraphy take place in section five, "The Brushwork of the Classic Calligraphers." He begins by acknowledging the difficulty of describing the classic works and adds that he will "try to write about them as far as words and brush will allow." His description of exemplary calligraphy relies on metaphors from nature. Calligraphy should achieve the life that exists in natural forms.

The brushwork of classic masters is filled with life and displays no weakness.... The talented calligrapher pays close attention to every point of the stroke and puts his soul into it – the striking start, the pulling through, the turning, and the concluding lift. The writing of the untalented is as useless as a broken tree....

In broader terms, the energy of a floating cloud, a waterfall, or a spring, the curving shape of a dragon or a serpent, and the bent form of an old pine – these in their own right are your models. The brushwork of the classics is simply this. In his *Yōhitsu no Zu*, Hsi-chih describes the narrowing downstroke as a withered wisteria ten thousand years old. You should understand such matters. After all, the calligraphy of the talented is a living thing and looks as if it has been given life. (5)

Son'en also discusses the final stage of freedom in the art. In section six, he states: "Superior work that has attained a level of expertise is free in every respect." Later, he continues, "Then having mastered the brush, follow your heart and you will be able to write in the style of unlimited freedom" (6). Son'en's suggestions for achieving this freedom, however, focus on the restrictive nature of practice. It is only after advising his student to concentrate, precisely follow the model, and take the correct posture that he alludes to a larger goal for his art:

After you have achieved proficiency, your writing will not depart from the rules of calligraphy even though you let the brush follow its own bent. Confucius said that by the age of seventy he could follow the desires of his heart and not transgress what was right. It is the same in this case, and it will be enough if you practice calligraphy in this way. (4)

Art as a spiritual quest

The study of the art is a gateway or a means to a higher spiritual plane. The ultimate goal is not mastery of the art, but mastery of the self.

The words of Onisaburo Deguchi, one of the founders of Oomoto, guided the study of the arts at the headquarters: "Art is the mother of religion." For those who worked or worshipped at the headquarters, pursuit of the arts became part of daily life. The monthly worship services included a performance, referred to as an offering, of one of the arts, held on the *nō* stage inside the worship hall. At the time of the performance, worshippers merely turned ninety degrees from the altar to the stage. After the service, and on other occasions three or four times a month, the tea room behind the worship hall filled with people enjoying a formal tea ceremony.

The arts, indeed, permeated Oomoto. How they translated into religious practice, however, was less clear. Some teachers talked about the religion but usually in a personal context – a meeting with one of the leaders or a recent event at the headquarters. Other teachers made detailed comparisons of Oomoto doctrine with the philosophy of their art. Still other teachers focused on artistic principles. Mastery of *jo, ha, kyū,* the basic rhythmical movement of many of the traditional arts, for instance, was said to put one in tune with the rhythm of the cosmos. The artwork of the leaders, too, entered our practice in the form of a tea bowl or hanging scroll. Regardless of the teacher's approach, each student operated on the principle that artistic practice equaled religious practice.

Son'en and religious practice. In two sections of *Jubokushō,* Son'en equates artistic practice with Buddhist practice.

> [For] the reality of this Way (i.e., calligraphy) had its origin in Buddhist enlightenment and from there entered the secular arts. In wind and stringed instruments, songs and lyrics, Chinese and Japanese poetry – in all of these Ways (i.e., the arts), there is right and wrong, and you should be discriminating.

Son'en continues by describing a Buddhist concept meaning that all things in the universe have the same basic essence. "There is no duality of principle in anything, and there is but one enlightenment. While there are myriad modes of being, in reality there is but one principle" (6). Later, he again connects Buddhism and art.

> In all things, the Ways requiring practice are ever without limit. When you study Buddhism, you explore the witness of Buddha and our virtuous predecessors; you try to attain to the knowledge and insight of Buddha, but it still remains unattainable. It is surely the same in the secular arts. (14)

In addition, Son'en's use of the character for *michi* (the Way) adds a spiritual tone to this treatise. He uses *michi* (sometimes in the Sino-Japanese pronunciation *dō*) twenty-two times, usually referring to calligraphy or the arts in general. Some of the times, however, *michi* refers to something broader. This expansive use of the Way is most apparent in the sentence, "The Greater Way is distant and difficult to follow, and false paths are near and easy to tread" (7). Here he uses the word "*daidō,*" which has a normative meaning as the proper course of action. In this context, he is pointing to the existence of a lengthy and carefully followed approach to the study of calligraphy, a study equivalent to Buddhist practice.

Oomoto and the arts

Although the arts were linked to Oomoto from its inception, it was Naohi Deguchi (1902–1990), the third spiritual leader, who brought them to the followers. Her grandmother Nao (1837–1918), the foundress, grew up in extreme poverty without the opportunity to pursue any of the arts. When she founded Oomoto in 1892, however, she shared her spiritual insight through the vehicle of calligraphy. Over a period of twenty-six years, Nao wrote over 100,000 pages of calligraphy in a crude *hiragana* phonetic alphabet.[11] These writings became the Oomoto scriptures, and the calligraphy itself became the object of religious veneration.

Naohi's father Onisaburo (1871–1948) married Nao's daughter and, by virtue of the strength of his interpretations of the scriptures, became the leader of the religion. During his most active years, the two decades before World War II, Oomoto grew from a rural religion of a few thousand members to a powerful organization of over three million. Government suppression, the war, and a suspicious U.S. occupation force resulted in a reduction of that number to a few hundred thousand, where it remains today.

Naohi's parents, Onisaburo and Sumiko (1883–1952), also used the arts as a vehicle to express their spiritual power. Their calligraphy, ink painting, and pottery became, to the followers, the embodiment of the divine. Even though neither of them have extensive formal training, their work attracted the acclaim of artists and art critics. Naohi, in contrast to her parents, had a more thorough initiation into the arts. As an adolescent, she studied many arts including swordsmanship, tea ceremony, and *nō* drama. Even through the war years, secluded in a mountain village with her children to avoid persecution, she continued to practice.

After the war, Naohi's family again gathered at the Kameoka headquarters. Her father passed his later years making tea bowls. And Naohi studied the arts, especially tea. As she neared fifty years of age, however, Naohi's responsibilities grew. Upon becoming the third spiritual leader in the matriarchal lineage of Oomoto, she began receiving more attention from the followers who looked to her for guidance after the death of her father in 1947.

Naohi gave the followers what she knew best, the arts. Over the next two decades, the rebuilding of the Kameoka headquarters included the construction of tea houses and gardens, *nō* stages, and martial arts halls. The Banshōden worship hall itself contains a *nō* stage and tea rooms. Worshippers attending the monthly religious ceremony also view a performing art and attend a tea ceremony. Even the religious service itself, reflecting Naohi's artistic interest, begins and ends with music from the two-stringed zither (*yakumo koto*), a Heian-period instrument.

To nurture the arts at Oomoto, of course, Naohi needed practitioners. Early in the 1950s, she recruited teachers from the various hereditary schools of the arts (*iemoto*) and began offering classes to everyone working and studying at Oomoto – from seminary students to the grounds crew. For the next two decades, Oomoto's artistic energy focused inward. Following Onisaburo's maxim, "Art is the mother of religion," the followers of Naohi practiced their arts as a spiritual discipline.

In the early 1970s, international visitors, drawn especially by the work of Onisaburo, began to show an interest in Oomoto and its arts. By this time, Oomoto had produced dozens of accomplished artists, many who had become teachers of one or more of the arts. Finally, at the invitation of Dr. Vadime Elisseeff, the French art historian, Oomoto took its arts to the outside world. They began by holding exhibits and performances in European museums. Then, reflecting the religious origin of its arts, Oomoto proceeded to the Cathedral of St. John the Divine in New York, Grace Cathedral in San Francisco, and Canterbury Cathedral in England. These activities increased foreign interest in Oomoto's arts and religion, resulting in the creation of the summer seminar and the organization of joint religious services held with various religions throughout the world.

The arts truly changed Oomoto and its followers. Country bumpkins and urban ruffians became teachers of the arts. And the small, rural religion gained an international following. The arts, first viewed as lifelong pursuits for Oomoto followers, became a means of sharing the religion with the world. Kyotaro Deguchi, Naohi's only son, writing in English for the seminar students, describes the goal of artistic practice:

> In the controlled creation of beauty that is art in action, we harmonize spirit, energy, and form. By attuning ourselves in this way with divine activity, we benefit ourselves and all around us. Art can be an active, creative meditation, a spiritual practice.... We wish only to offer the opportunity to learn the arts to all who feel moved for whatever reason to experience them in actual practice, and to find, if not always what they thought they were looking for, something of value to take home with them.[12]

Oomoto, in turn, took things from its foreign guests. The seminar's inquisitive students prompted the teachers to develop explanations for things that might otherwise have gone undiscussed. Teachers also tried to distill the teachings of their art, so the essence could be transmitted in a concentrated time period.

Over the years, the teachers continued to refine the seminar into a carefully choreographed experience. Gradually, however, interest began to wane. The seminar now attracts fewer students and less attention from Oomoto followers. The four-week course still occupies a place on the yearly calendar, but it receives little notice during the rest of the year.

The changes at Oomoto reflect a decline in Oomoto's energy as it enters its second hundred years. The decade of the 1980s produced many misfortunes. After the third spiritual leader, Naohi, died, a bitter split arose over her succession. Although now resolved, the dispute left Oomoto depleted in funds and followers. And, more importantly, the fourth spiritual leader occupies her position out of a sense of obligation. Naohi, who according to Oomoto scriptures was the last leader to be the embodiment of the divine, appointed her youngest daughter to succeed her. The daughter's appeal, however, was her neutrality rather than her spiritual power. Although her followers have united behind her, they do so only out of respect for her mother's wishes. And the spiritual leader, too, is unhappy, admitting that she longs for the quiet days when she served as director of the botanical gardens.

Without a strong leader, Oomoto and its arts languish, perhaps slowly to expire. In fact, the international efforts of the 1970s, fueled by the arts themselves, might have been Oomoto's last sparkle. On the other hand, the religion may have just changed the focus of its international efforts from the arts to ecumenicalism. Early in 1994, for instance, three of its leaders along with some followers went to Mecca and circumambulated the Kaaba. Upon returning, they began working on a joint statement with Muslim leaders, trying to express the Oomoto belief in a universal god in a way that would not diminish Allah. The place of the arts in Oomoto's future is uncertain. To survive, they must continue to bring people together – the followers to each other, and the world to Oomoto.

Notes

1. This chapter includes a discussion of four "traditional Japanese arts": *nō,* tea ceremony, martial arts, and calligraphy. For a translation and analysis of *Jubokushō* and a brief introduction to Japanese calligraphy, see DeCoker (1988) and DeCoker and Kerr (1994).
2. There is little scholarly writing about Oomoto. References to it can usually be found in discussions of the Japanese "new religions" (*shinkō shūkyō*), many of which were founded by women during the Meiji era (1868–1912). See Ooms (1993) for one recent work.
3. The author wishes to acknowledge the assistance of Alex Kerr in the development of the seven characteristics.
4. In Oriental philosophy, *ki* is said to be constantly flowing through the body. Control of one's *ki* is thought to bring various physical and psychological benefits.
5. The numbers in parentheses refer to sections in *Jubokushō.*
6. Ono Michikaze (894–966), Fujiwara Sukemasa (944–988), and Fujiwara Yukinari (972–1027).

7. "Secret teachings" in the arts existed from the late Nara and early Heian periods (eighth to ninth centuries). They were transmitted orally and in secret treatises, handed down from teacher to student through the generations. During the Meiji period, many of the secrets were published for a wider audience. See DeCoker (1988: 201–203) and DeCoker (1996).
8. Poem sheets are square sheets of decorated paper on which calligraphy is written; plaques are large wooden signs that hung above gates and temples in the capital.
9. There are five schools in *nō* theater and two major and several minor schools in tea ceremony.
10. Sen no Rikyū (1522–1591) and Zeami (1364?–1443) are considered founders of their respective arts.
11. The Japanese writing system consists of three elements: two phonetic alphabets (*hiragana* and *katakana*) and Chinese characters.
12. From a guidebook for summer seminar students published in 1981.

References

DeCoker, Gary, 1987, *Education and the Art of Calligraphy in Japan's Middle Ages: The* Jubokushō *and the* Saiyōshō, Ph.D. Dissertation, The University of Michigan.

1988, "Secret Teachings in Medieval Calligraphy: *Jubokushō* and the *Saiyōshō*," *Monumenta Nipponica,* 43: 197–228 and 43: 261–278.

1996, "'Traditional Approaches to Learning' in Japan: *Michi* and the Practice of Calligraphy in Japan's Middle Ages," in *The Distant Isle: Studies and Translations in Honor of Robert H. Brower,* pp. 105–124, edited by Thomas Hare, Robert Borgen, and Sharalyn Orbaugh, Ann Arbor: Center for Japanese Studies, The University of Michigan.

DeCoker, Gary, and Alex Kerr, 1994, "*Yakaku Teikinshō:* Secret Teachings of the Sesonji School of Calligraphy," *Monumenta Nipponica,* 49: 315–329.

Ooms, Emily Groszos, 1993, *Women and Millenarian Protest in Meiji Japan: Deguchi Nao and Omotokyo,* Ithaca, NY: East Asia Program, Cornell University.

5 Why was everyone laughing at me? Roles of passage for the *kyōgen* child

Jonah Salz

A four-year-old child dressed in a monkey suit and mask cavorts on the bare *nō* stage, scratching his behind and picking lice from his head, to the delight of the audience. But spectators looking directly in back of the frolicking boy would see in the not-quite-deadpan faces of the Monkey Trainer and stage assistant the proud but anxious demeanors of a father and grandfather participating in their heir's initiation into the *kyōgen* vocation. This mixture of comic abandon and rigid correctness that permeates the early career of the *kyōgen* professional is the subject of this chapter. After briefly mapping the path "from monkey to fox," it will chart in detail the early years of training, inventory the technical skills acquired, and suggest a pedagogic subtext to the two requisite plays of childhood, "Learning the Alphabet" and "The Monkey-Skin Quiver."

Introduction

Kyōgen is classical comedy, performed together with masked, lyric *nō* for the past 600 years. A full program of *nō-kyōgen* today might consist of two or three *nō* plays, typically ghost plays on themes of martial or romantic loss, in which the *kyōgen* actor appears during the interval as a village local. Sandwiched between these metaphysical operas are full *kyōgen* comedies, independent plays on more down-to-earth themes involving fatuous masters and lazy servants, cowardly husbands and shrewish wives, quack doctors, arrogant priests, and hapless bandits.[1] *Nō*'s spiritual monodramas combine with *kyōgen*'s situational comedies to portray the timeless depths and ironies of the human condition.

This chapter relies primarily on interviews, writings, and performance observation of the Sengorō Shigeyama family. They are the largest and most popular family within the Okura school, the older of the two "schools" (*ryūgi*) of *kyōgen* players, whose current *iemoto* (headmaster) is the twenty-fifth generation, dating back 600 years. When I mention "the Shigeyama family," I refer to an extended *ie* household of kin and non-kin.[2] The thirteen professional members of the Shigeyama family are based in Kyoto, performing throughout the Kansai (Kyoto, Nara, Osaka, Kobe) district and regularly in Tokyo.[3] What follows is a sketch of the typical childhood training of a *kyōgen* professional.

The way of *kyōgen*

The actor's career is considered a *shūgyō,* or "course of learning," implying the diligent, assiduous, quasi-religious quality of lifetime training: "a Way." Although *kyōgen*'s themes and more naturalistic acting methods are less obviously a spiritual discipline than its more refined cousin *nō,*[4] theorists and practitioners from Zeami on have long recognized the importance of *kyōgen* parodies, puns, and inversions as philosophically complementary to the *nō,* revealing "society upside-down" (Lafleur 1983:138). *Kyōgen*'s lifetime training, notes Motohide Izumi (1983:134–135), while seemingly cruel in its insistence that new forms be learned at each stage of one's life, develops not merely the techniques themselves but the disciple's spiritual qualities. And Manzō Nomura, another great actor raised before World War II, believes that "the old training method attempted to produce a tension in the disciple, like that toward an acolyte at the temple gate; rather than 'teaching,' it attempted 'to lead you to a realization'" (*satoraseru*) (Manzō Nomura 1982:347). Manzō's classic memoirs on the spiritual path of *kyōgen* is entitled *The Way of Kyōgen* (1955; reprinted in Manzō 1982).

The professional's training is said to be steady and progressive, where continuity becomes strength. It consists of an accumulation of details and remembering perfectly the *kata* (the deconstructed, named, patterned forms) as they are taught. Training is progressively difficult – complex patterns are taught as combinations of, or variations on, previously absorbed (and therefore second nature) *kata* patterns. Yasushi Maruishi, who speaks with the hard experience of one who began *kyōgen* as an adult, stresses that fundamental patterns (*kihon no kata*) need to be recalled automatically – they are as vital to the progress of a *kyōgen* actor as the foundation is to the construction of a building.

Kyōgen acting is a lifetime Way, of continuous and changing challenges for each stage. Such stages in the actor's career are marked by debuts in a progression of specially significant roles. The first-time performance is called an "opening" (*hiraki,* using the character for "revealing," "opening out," a homonym for the blossoming of a flower bud), not merely the "first-time performance" (*hatsuen*) or "first-time role" (*hatsuyaku*) of a play from the standard repertoire. Such crucial performances are sometimes referred to as a *musubi,* or "knotting" the separate strands of training knowledge into a solid, permanent bundle of mastered techniques; completion creates a *fushime,* the bamboo knob marking seasonal growth. These are extraordinary performances whose proper accomplishment requires special ablutions, intensive practice, a substantial supporting cast in a carefully weighted program, and an appropriately dignified performance venue.

Teachers and students alike treat lessons for *hiraki* pieces with special care and intensity, knowing that these contain the intangible family treasures, the jealously guarded tools of their trade. The family's continued survival depends upon their proper transmission. Although there are great variations in careers according to talent and circumstance, regardless of the route or pace taken, the path of the professional *kyōgen* actor narrows to the steep incline of the *hiraki* pieces. Once mounted, the actor resumes his journey on the next plateau, with a far wider perspective on the ground already covered, newly aware of the next steep mountain to come.

Table 5.1 depicts the *hiraki* roles and plays, the ideal ages at which they are performed, their "debut" features, and their special challenges. "The *kyōgen* career begins as a monkey and ends as a fox."[5] These animal roles frame the first decades of the professional actor's life, but in fact there are many more roles that must be challenged in between, and afterward, for full masterhood to be achieved.

The actor debuts as a frisky trick monkey in *Utsubozaru* at age three to six, teaching the child the importance of stage presence and imitation. *Iroha,* the debut play in the Okura school, demands that the child memorize dialogue in a plot *about* learning. The teenager (at age fourteen to fifteen) enters the world of *nō* actors and musicians with the ritual dance-play *Okina-Sambasō.* For this coming-of-age piece, he receives his first *kuden,* or secret, oral transmissions, undergoes "hundred-day practice," and eats by a "separate fire." He also wears a mask as an expression of self rather than disguise for the first time since his monkey debut; he is also accompanied in the *Sambasō* dance by full orchestra for the first time. At around the same age, he performs the *ai,* or interval *kyōgen katari* narrative "Nasu no Yoichi," within the *nō* play *Yashima.* The solo tour de force demands careful breath control, utilizing *ma,* subtle time and space intervals, in order to command attention for this tale of martial heroism. Once these two plays have been performed, with the proper

Table 5.1. *Major* Hiraki *roles of passage in the Okura school*

Age[a]	Role	Play	"First-time" aspects	Special challenges
3–5	Child	*Iroha*	lead role	partnering, mimicry
3–5	Monkey	*Utsubozaru*[b]	mask, dance	animal mimicry, rhythmic dance, 60-minute stage presence
14–15	Nasu no Yoichi	*Yashima* (*nō*)	solo narrative, active *aikyōgen* (interlude in *nō* play)	breathing, use of *ma*, storytelling, stage presence
14–15	Sambasō[c]	*Okina-Sambasō*	secret teachings, ritual ablutions, drum accompaniment, mask	rhythmic stamps, both "old" and "young" dances, dignity (*kurai*)
20–25	Fox-priest	*Tsurigitsune*	studying "first to last," "18 secret teachings"	animal mimicry, man/beast tension, physical "torture" of inverted *kata*
25–30	Master	*Hanago*	lengthy singing, self-accompaniment while dancing	difficult melodies, acting/dancing/singing simultaneously
25–30	Badger-nun[d]	*Tanuki no Haratsuzumi*	double masks, animal/nun mimicry	spiritual tension, dignity
60–80	Grandfather	*Makura Monogurui*	refined improvisation	dignity, sexiness
60–80	Old Nun	*Bikusada*	refined improvisation	dignity
60–80	Old Nun	*Iori no Ume*	refined improvisation	dignity, charm

[a] There is actually wide variation.
[b] *Utsubozaru* is the debut piece of the Izumi school.
[c] Sambaso may precede the Nasu no Yoichi *katari*.
[d] *Kanaoka* is performed instead in the Izumi school.

kurai (ranking, or dignity), the young man may regularly perform *ai* interval narration on *nō* stages.

Tsurigitsune ("Trapping the Fox"), performed around age twenty, is likened to a graduation thesis for a college student, marking the end of regular training and the creation of a full-fledged (*ichininmae*) actor. Depicting a Fox transformed into a Priest in the first act, and the Fox itself in the second, *Tsurigitsune* is a severe challenge due to the physical "torture" of inversing the normal stance, walk, and vocalization style, coupled with the psychological tension of portraying the half-beast/half-priest for the long first act. It also requires a great capacity to memorize the eighteen secret teachings (*narai*) contained in the secret transmissions (*hiden*). Among the lifetime *hiraki* roles, none is considered as important.

Tsurigitsune is the first of the three very important learning pieces. *Hanago,* featuring a long, lyrical tribute by a man for his mistress (while his wife secretly eavesdrops), is performed at age twenty-five to thirty and challenges the mature actor to demonstrate simultaneous abilities to sing, dance, and act, largely alone and simultaneously. *Tanuki no Haratsuzumi* ("The Badger's Bellydrum") is similar to *Tsurigitsune,* but here the actor copes with two masks, one worn on top of the other, with the added challenge of portraying a nun and pregnant female badger.[6] Finally, there are the "three old-person pieces,"[7] performed when the actor is in his sixties or seventies. *Makura Monogurui* ("Pillow Crazy"), *Bikusada* ("The Old Nun Sada"), and *Iori no Ume* ("The Plum Hut") contain no extraordinary techniques but are especially static and open-ended, relying on the actor's accumulated technical mastery and mature personality to express their refined grace and gentle humor.

Debut pieces emphasize specific aspects of the *kyōgen* art that must be acquired before proceeding to the next stage, keys that unlock doors to the next room of the fortress of the actor's art. Some plays emphasize rote memorization or unique vocal expression; others stress rhythmic song and dance; still others probe nuanced acting expression. A few test all three. Each challenges the actor with an opportunity to prove his acquired technique and to "shed his skin" (*dappi*) and be renewed as an actor, capable of going deeper in one's art (Koyama 1990:342). I argue in this chapter that the *kyōgen* actor's "promotion" (*sotsugyō*) plays are carefully chosen not only to stress certain physical and psychological techniques but also to provide a running metacommentary on the art itself.

The actor's "initiation" to *kyōgen* professionalism through these "roles of passage" are the occasional spotlights in a long career, a chance for rising stars to challenge themselves publicly, for famous masters to prove their continued mastery, and for perennial bit players to take center stage. The triangulation of expectations of teacher, student, and audience give these plays a dynamic tension and fascination, focusing on the vital junctures where an actor's career is made – both personal milestones and public proof of his achievement. And the basic tools for the journey along this lifetime path are provided at infancy.

Basic training

It is imperative that children born into professional *nō* and *kyōgen* families be taught the basic forms early; these become second nature. At the same time, children are imbued with a sense of respect for, even gratitude toward, the *kyōgen* profession. With *kyōgen* as in *nō,* many insiders believe that those outsiders who attain professional status without undergoing this childhood training will always "lack a certain something" (Bethe and Brazell 1990:174). Perfectionism is essential for the young professional; Izumi (1983:64) agrees with those who say that a year of severe training in childhood is equivalent to ten years of such hard training as an adult.

Even before the first lessons are given, mothers acquaint their children with the home practice rooms (*keikoba*) and Green Rooms of *nō* theatres, immersing them in the atmosphere of their future lifelong profession. Akira jokes that he began learning *kyōgen* even before he was born, inside his mother's womb as she attended practices and performances! Even when they are living in the house where lessons are given, on practice days, *kyōgen* mothers holding infants will press their heads down to force a bow when greeting an adult, teaching them to respect the *keikoba* (practice hall), the Green Room, senior students, and especially their teachers.[8] This "in-body learning," to use Zarrilli's phrase,[9] marks the beginning of the physical enculturation of proper roles that typifies the child's learning method throughout his *kyōgen* career. And like the forced bow, there is something automatic about their heir's assumption of the family mantle: For first sons at least, there is no choice.[10]

Traditionally, the child's first lessons came when he was six years, six months, and six days old.[11] Some say this only applied to amateur students; in fact, many professional households began much earlier. Sengorō was quickly "seized" by his grandfather, Sensaku II, who refused even to yield to Sengorō's own father.[12] "As soon as I'd learned it, he wanted to show me off, so we performed here and there" at temples and ladies' club meetings before formally debuting on a *nō* stage (Sengorō 1983:9). Soon brother Sennojō, three years younger, began practicing together with him, and the two became popular "Little Sprout Stars," child prodigies of Kyoto's *kyōgen* world. As a consequence of the demand for the popular brother combo, sometimes partnering with their grandfather, they had many opportunities to perform. Sengorō learned thirty to forty plays before graduating from elementary school (1983:11–12).

But Sengorō's days as his grandfather's spoiled pet were soon over. He proved a slow learner, and lessons grew more severe:

> The two things he most often warned me about were "Stop fussing about, with your eyes darting from side to side" and "Don't fiddle with your hands," followed by "Lower your buttocks [*koshi o ireru*]." Granddad would repeatedly warn me, "Stick out your chest," "Open your eyes wide," "Use a big voice." Meanwhile little brother Sennojō would perform flawlessly. (Sengorō 1983:16–17)

In fact, Sennojō debuted three years earlier than Sengorō; he was not only a quicker study but had the experience of training together and watching his older brother perform. *Kyōgen* training and touring can even precede toilet training: Sennojō relates how a delay in a building dedication ceremony led to a shameful disaster. His overanxious grandfather dressed them a full two hours before the performance. Poor Sennojō, unable to contain himself, left a wet trail "like wagon-wheel tracks" on the *tatami* mats. A servant dutifully mopped up behind him (Sennojō 1987: 6–8).

Sennojō was apparently afraid of being hit by his short-tempered grandfather, a not uncommon occurrence for those raised before World War II. Izumi (1983:137) considers it a "necessary evil" for teachers to scold, slap, or hit students with their fans. And although he resented such punishment at the time, Sensaku III admits that, "I never forgot or repeated the mistake I was hit for" (Shigeyama and Shigeyama 1982:25).

Since World War II, universal education has made the early preschool years even more important for *kyōgen* training, since *kyōgen* actors, like everyone else, must attend school. "You have to devote oneself to practice until the third year of elementary school, or wait until after entrance to university," Sengorō admonishes. If fundamentals of *kyōgen* are not forced into the child's body by eight years old or so, they never will be (Kobayashi 1972:136).

The child's mastery of the basic forms through exploration in *keiko* (practice) is likened to childhood games: He learns by playing, with energetic attention, maintaining the rules or seeing what happens when he breaks them (Izumi 1991:138). Similarly, new *kyōgen* skills are absorbed entirely within the framework of entire performance pieces. There are no warm-up exercises or regular scales to practice.[13] The plays themselves are the systematic curriculum; correct progression will inculcate the techniques needed for performance and further study. New forms are simply studied as variants or exceptions to the already learned patterns. Actors thus "learn to learn": Progressively difficult pieces are taught at an increasingly faster pace.

In the beginning of *kyōgen* study is the word. Dialogue and singing are learned in the same way: Kneeling in the painful *seiza* position, directly in front and far apart from the teacher, the child bows in gratitude to the master and for the *kyōgen* lesson. The master sits, enunciating clearly, sometimes beating time on his thigh or even "conducting" the student with his fan. The student intently observes the contractions of throat and formations of lips before repeating it back, as loudly, clearly, and exactly as possible. This method, known as *kuchiutsushi* (mouth reflection), continues with ever-longer phrases until the disciple memorizes the entire play. Belting the words out with the loud, clear, and above all sincere and obedient (*sunao*) expression, as though shouting to a friend on the playground, is key.

After mastering the entire play, the student recites it, interrupted by the teacher only when needing specific corrections. Mansaku suggests that the student "learns the full expressiveness of the words" rather than learning the words by heart. This training method shows the child that he cannot act while looking down at a script, nor depend on a prompter, nor cover up for verbal mistakes with physical improvisation. At the same time, it encourages good seating posture and proper breathing methods (Mansaku 1991:24).

After the entire vocal text has been mastered, *tachigeiko* (standing practice) begins. The child is first taught the basic stance (*kamae*), molded physically until he achieves the proper shape: feet slightly apart, knees bent, chest out, hands on thighs, elbows bent, arms curved, chin tucked in, eyes level, back "so straight that you can tie a bamboo pole to your spine," leaning slightly forward, in the "ready position." Mansaku recalls that when his back was curved, his father would yell, "Sloucher!" (literally, "Cat back!") and strike his spine with his fan (Mansaku 1991: 25–26). Gestures and movement blocking are likewise taught through strict imitation of the master. The teacher usually models the role to the side and slightly in front for the student to shadow, or he alternatively faces him to be mirrored. An older disciple may play a secondary role to the teacher at these times so that the child learns proper timing through practice with a partner. The disciple will also sing accompaniment to the dances, allowing the master and child to concentrate on dancing to the proper rhythms.[14]

Before the *kyōgen* child can move or dance, he must learn to walk. Actors refer to the walking style in *nō* and *kyōgen* as *hakobu,* not *aruku,* implying "moving oneself" rather than mere walking. The particular glide is called *suriashi*: The tabi-sock clad foot is slid firmly along the stage floor in small steps, feet straddling an invisible pole, maintaining a low, steady center of gravity to create a serene but powerful glide, emanating suppressed energy.

Komai ("short dances") are the lively dances, often appearing within plays, that are now performed independently. These are continuously practiced throughout childhood as a kind of parallel training to the basic forms molded in full *kyōgen* plays. For a very young child, the teacher may stand behind him, raising the child's hands in the proper patterns while kicking his feet forward. Singing *kouta* ("short songs") develops breathing techniques and the special undulating rhythms of *kyōgen* vocalization. Dancing *komai* produces the proper "moving *kamae*" form essential for nondance gestures and movements within plays (Mansaku 1991:24). The youngest generation is often introduced to the public through these short, simple dances at all-*kyōgen* performances, as their doting relatives figuratively and literally back them up as chorus.

After about a year of training in basic songs and dances, the child will increase the frequency and intensity of lessons, in a soon-to-be-familiar pattern, preceding a performance. Soon he will perform his *hatsubutai* (first stage appearance) in his *hatsuen* (first performance), in the *hatsuyaku* (first role) of the monkey in the *hiraki* piece *Utsubozaru* ("The Monkey-Skin Quiver").[15]

Monkey business

Utsubozaru is highly unusual in many ways: Instead of the "top banana and straightman" of most *kyōgen,* it depends on four almost equally balanced roles. *Kyōgen* are usually unaccompanied; in *Utsubo,* there is a full chorus. Most plays are fifteen to thirty minutes long; *Utsubo* lasts a full hour. Most plays have simple, comic plots; *Utsubo* shifts into a wide range of *kyōgen* performance techniques: highly melodramatic posings, narrative (*katari*), psychologically complex acting, and a variety of songs and dances. For actors and audiences alike, *Utsubozaru* is a very special spectacle.

The monkey business of *Utsubozaru* is serious fun. Although the silent *kokata* roles, with which the *nō* actor makes his first appearance on stage, are deemed successful if he sits still, selflessly, and "does not spoil the play" (Johnson 1977:194), the monkey is not merely a charming, stoic plot appendage. "If the monkey is not done correctly, the whole piece won't come together," warns Sengorō (1983): "The cues (*kikkake*) are especially difficult, and so severe training is crucial. But it's no good if it's *too* correct either, or the childlike innocence will be lost" (170). Training the child to achieve this proper balance of spontaneity and discipline requires a masterful teacher, especially when coping with the rather sudden shock to the youngster's sense of security when thrust from the intimacy of his home practice hall into the bustling backstage of the *nō* theatre. In an extreme case, a boy refused to budge from the dressing room. A "sudden illness" was announced, and the actors already on stage as Lord and Servant neatly segued into a different two-character play! But Kobayashi (1976:134) emphasizes that this was an older, amateur child, however, and so was not taught with the same ardor as a born professional.

Despite its length, difficulty, and the discomfort of its costume, *Utsubozaru* is a splendidly appropriate debut for the fledgling professional.

A Lord out hunting with his Servant happens across a performing Monkey and his Trainer. The Lord demands the Monkey's skin, whose supposed magical qualities will enable him to make an invincible quiver for his arrows. The Trainer refuses, threatening them with bow and arrow; the Lord stops the fleeing pair. Acquiescing in the cruel demand, the Trainer requests permission to kill the pet himself. The Trainer explains to the Monkey that although he holds him as dear as a son, he has no choice. He raises his stick to strike, but the Monkey, imagining it his cue, grabs it, and proceeds to perform the "rowing the boat" trick. The Trainer bursts into tears: "Such a dumb beast doesn't even know when he is about to be killed!" The Lord, moved to tears, drops his weapon and agrees to spare the Monkey's life.

Overjoyed, the Trainer dresses the Monkey in formal red costume and has him perform a series of cute dances and tricks for the Lord. So amusingly "humanlike" are the Monkey's antics – pointing to the moon with his fan, falling asleep on his arm – that the Lord chortles in appreciation. He is even drawn to imitate the Monkey, who playfully "attacks" him. The Lord gladly offers his fan, sword, and even his robe to the Trainer, and the play ends with the "*saru uta,*" a celebratory song and dance which blesses the Lord, the audience, and the boy-Monkey. He exits down the bridgeway, this time carried "piggy-back" by the Trainer.[16]

As it invites him in with song and dance, *Utsubozaru* subliminally teaches the child many things about the *kyōgen* world. Kobayashi (1976: 133) notes the significance of the child wearing a mask and rather realistic fur costume. Later, he will be able to imitate through his face and body; this first play's highly mimetic costume allows him to act the monkey by being his childlike, fidgety self. During the first half of the play, he rolls on his back, does somersaults, bites his paws, chatters "kyaakyaakyaa," and scratches himself. Koyama suggests that, while this harkens back to the natural *monomane* imitation essential to *kyōgen*'s origins (more properly *sarumane,* or monkey imitation, a common word for copycat), the true learning occurs in the second half of the play. Accompanied by a chorus, the boy expresses the Trainer's gratitude in a series of religious and folk dances: Hopping up and down, pulled by the rope if he should wander too far or off the beat, the child learns through "physical mastery" (*taitoku*) the quintessential rhythms of *kyōgen* (Koyama 1987:341). This transition from scampering beast to cultured trickster can also be seen as a public metaphor: The child's natural mimicry and playful energies have been tamed; he has become a *kyōgen* actor.[17]

Mansaku believes *Utsubo* fulfills two related pedagogic functions: The child is made to realize the importance of imitation – the child imitates a monkey, in turn imitating a human – and these two levels of imitation stress the basis for *kyōgen* as drama. But, importantly, the transformation is not complete: There is a bit of the child in the monkey, and a hint of the child in the human posings. Rather than create an entirely separate, stylized stage persona, the child learns that he should allow his own personality (*kosei*) to seep into his characterization – that this is, in fact, *kyōgen*'s "bottom line." And while the Lord and Trainer converse, the boy scampers freely between specific actions determined by the cues, learning to improvise (1991:22).

Kobayashi (1976) notes the child's realization, during his arduous first lessons in *Utsubo,* that *kyōgen* is not merely a game but his future profession, as the father or grandfather suddenly cuts off his affectionate indulgence, replaced by the severity of a teacher. "Ripped from his mother's knee," the child is suddenly confronted with the adult world. As Manzō's father explained to him, "In art, there are no fathers and sons, only masters and disciples" (quoted in Kobayashi 1976:133). And audiences are moved to tears by the knowledge that the infant is performing what he has been taught as best he can, ignorant of the overall meaning of his actions (Kobayashi 1976:133–134). Moreover, the pathos of the dumb animal, performing on cue exactly what he has been taught, even in the face of death, parallels the tiny *kyōgen* tot, performing his rote-learned monkey business and dances in the full glare of the public eye. In so doing, the monkey-child gains the sympathy, affection, and finally rich gifts from the Lord, who in real life is frequently, not coincidentally, also the head of the acting family or school. The most glorious *Utsubozaru* in Shigeyama family history occurred in the 1967 performance where four generations of once and future heads of family performed: grandfather Sengorō as the Lord to son Masayoshi's Servant, great-grandfather Sensaku III as Trainer to great-grandson Masakuni's Monkey. The final fertility dance could be read as the Shigeyama family's own dance of rejuvenation and evidence of their continued prosperity.

There is thus a consistent ironic subtext to this elaborate family affair. Just as the Monkey pleases the Lord and receives magnificent gifts, so too has this peewee professional, by pleasing the school Master, received the beneficence of the tradition: applause and affection, further training, a livelihood. This success is physically and materially evident. The naked Monkey becomes "clothed," first in his "human" costume, then figuratively in the rich Lord's garments, just as the immature boy will inherit the treasured traditions. He crawls onto the stage by himself but is carried off on his father-Trainer's back, no longer wild and independent but having become human, a member of a glorious family.[18] Meanwhile, the pleased Lord strips himself of weapons and finery and returns to a second childhood by imitating and frolicking with his grandson-Monkey; the tradition is renewed. To welcome the boy into the tradition, the entire extended family of *kyōgen* players joins him on stage as chorus in the final half, symbolically expressing supportive membership in the tradition.[19] The child is made aware, however subconsciously, of the fellow passengers on the lifetime journey down the path of *kyōgen.*

On another interpretive level, the Lord's appreciation is a stand-in for an audience comprised of diehard *kyōgen* fans and family friends. They attend with great anticipation, sighing "how cute!" over the little boy's playful scamperings, even interrupting important dialogue within the play with applause for the tot. The Trainer's farewell to the Monkey is often interpreted as a father's tender love for his son, bringing tears to some fans. Paralleling the on-stage Monkey's receiving of the Lord's beneficence, off-stage a variety of gifts commemorating the occasion are offered to the young professional by family, friends, and fellow professionals: mostly flowers, sweets, and toys, but also professional tools such as fans (with crests of various *nō* and musician schools), and costume.

Learning the ABCs

Utsubozaru requires the boy to be on stage in fur and masks for almost the entire hour-long play, requiring great concentration and patience. Perhaps because of this, the Shigeyama family begins the training with the simpler, mimicking play, *Iroha.*[20] Like *Utsubo, Iroha* concerns an "uncivilized" youth getting the upper hand on an older, wiser man, but here the actual learning process is displayed:

> A Father (or Elder Brother, depending on the age of the *ado* partner) instructs his recalcitrant son (or younger brother) in the Japanese alphabet using the traditional mnemonic device of a poem. When the child twists the mnemonic phrases into puns, it infuriates his mentor, who insists that the child follow his lead exactly. When the naughty pupil repeats even this order, an escalating series of scoldings and ear-pinchings ensue. Finally the elder throws down the child, whereupon the boy springs up and, following orders to imitate everything, throws down the tutor. He runs off shouting, "I did it!"

Iroha is another certain crowd pleaser. Audiences ooh and ahh over the cute little tyke's attempts to imitate the *kyōgen* form. Kobayashi (1976: 134) notes the charming nature of the child, whose tongue is not yet even moving smoothly, reciting the difficult tongue twisters in a clear, loud voice. Needless to say, audiences delight in the spectacle of the boy's father, grandfather, or even great-grandfather, illustrious older actors, being tossed roughly to the ground by the tiny, gleeful child. The cry, "I did it!" is not just the son's song of triumph over his parent but one of mastery of his first *kyōgen* itself.

There are practical and philosophical reasons that make it easy to imagine why *Iroha* was chosen for the Okura school's stage debut piece. At ten minutes long, *Iroha* is one of the shortest plays in the *kyōgen* repertoire. Much of the dialogue is an exact repetition of the previous line, the child merely mimicking the teacher. *Iroha* is also a play about teaching: The oral, mouth-to-mouth transmission method becomes the subject of the play itself. The reversal within the narrative – the student treating the teacher disrespectfully – resonates within the actual familial relationships of the players (grandson–grandfather; younger–older brother). The child debuts appropriately in the irreverent *kyōgen* tradition by breaking powerful taboos: publicly mocking, even physically attacking, his teacher. The disciple will eventually need to go beyond role imitation of his master to forge his own career.

An unintentional overturning of his grandfather as teacher gave Sennojō a premature start on his *kyōgen* career. In fact, Sennojō's first teacher was not his grandfather but his nanny, Umedon, who had picked up the play while overhearing Sengorō, three years older, studying it. Umedon was apparently jealous when Sengorō's stage debut caused such a commotion and so, while on their daily strolls in the Imperial Palace grounds, "taught" it to the infant Sennojō through the *kuchiutsushi* method, which she had overheard in the practice room. When she proudly reported to Sennojō's grandfather that he had learned *Iroha,* she was roundly scolded. But his grandfather was forced to begin teaching Sennojō years ahead of schedule (1987:6–8).

Despite the brouhaha, Sennojō cannot recall a thing from his debut at two years and seven months in 1926 in *Iroha*: "I was learning *kyōgen* before I even knew it" (1987:6). In fact, few actors can recall their stage debuts. Even during the event, the infant *kyōgen* actor striving to perform the right words and actions may completely miss the point of the play. When Dōji Shigeyama performed *Iroha,* he made a few mistakes the first night – with his nervous father (as stage assistant) and even grandfather, as Father, visibly moving their lips in anticipation of a slip. They apparently trained him hard the next day, as he was letter perfect the second night. Yet he came backstage afterward annoyed and perplexed: "I tried my best – why was everyone laughing at me?!" Caught up in the seriousness of the training, he had forgotten (or never realized) that *kyōgen* was funny! His mother Kinuko told me this with obvious pride that he had taken the art so seriously, and indeed Dōji's error of overearnestness is deemed far better than not taking *kyōgen* seriously enough.

One final anecdote may best illustrate the importance for the fledgling actor of being earnest, of learning the backstage proprieties, and of keeping promises. Dōji's stage debut was not *Iroha* but as Whirlpool in a dance version of Goethe/Dukas's "The Sorcerer's Apprentice," which I directed with the Noho Theatre Group in the summer of 1986. I had asked Akira (who was playing the Mickey Mouse/Apprentice lead) if I might "borrow" Dōji; he told me to ask Kinuko, who told me to ask Dōji (then three) himself. I showed him the Disney video, and Dōji was delighted of course; he agreed, and after carefully confirming his commitment, Kinuko made him seal the deal with a pinky "handshake." But the first day of rehearsal, Dōji was whisked in the air by an overenthusiastic American dancer playing the lead broom. Frightened, Dōji burst into tears and ran to his mother, refusing to budge. Before the next day's rehearsal, Kinuko called me to the side, and I found myself playing the straight man in the following melodrama:

Kinuko: Dōji, don't you have something to say to the Producer?

Dōji: (*bowing formally, mumbling through stifled tears*) I'm sorry, Mr. Jonah, for any inconvenience I am causing you . . .

Me: (*returning the bow formally*) That's okay, you don't have to—

Kinuko: (*sharply*) Louder, Dōji! Speak clearly!

Dōji: (*hands on floor, head lowered in abject humility*) I'm sorry, Mr. Jonah, for any inconvenience that I may cause, but please excuse me from appearing this time.
Me: (*sympathetic, but formal*) Certainly, you are excused.
Dōji: Thank you very much, and please consider me in the future.

Kinuko's erect posture and cold glare betrayed no hint of irony; Dōji had made a promise, and had to fulfill it, or learn the heavy consequences of withdrawal.[21]

Conclusion

The *kyōgen* child is quickly inculcated in the traditional forms of practice, performance, and backstage behavior. By the age of five or six, the child has left his mother's side to enter the male world of the professional player. He has learned to master the rules of a serious game that he will play throughout his life. He knows how to sit still for lessons, to vocalize, to sing and dance to a variety of rhythms. He has learned how to be on stage for up to an hour, to "change gears" within a play, to accommodate different partners, to adjust to various audiences. He has become familiar with how to dress and with Green Room conventions. And he has been introduced to his lifetime colleagues of *kyōgen* and *nō* actors and musicians using their special ritualized greetings.

Moreover, he has absorbed the implicit teachings belied by the explicit comic content of *Utsubozaru* and *Iroha*. Consciously or not, the child has learned four essential *kyōgen* methods that will serve him well throughout his career:

1. the importance of perfect mastery of the external forms,
2. the necessity of blending his own personality within those rigid forms,
3. the significance of "imitation" in practice and performance (child of monkey and monkey of human; child of teacher), and
4. the potential, should all of the above be mastered, to win over (or overpower) the traditional "authorities" (Lord, Teacher, Father, audience), earning by his artistry their laughter, accolades, gifts – and, eventually, a livelihood.

Notes

Writing about contemporary *kyōgen* actors is complicated by actors' names. Inherited at birth or changed during one's lifetime, acquisition of illustrious forbears' names often parallel actors' completion of particular roles of passage. Unless otherwise specified, the names referred to in this chapter are as follows: Sengorō (XII, now Sensaku IV), Sensaku (Sensaku III), and Manzō (Manzō VI). [Ed. note: References to works by actors in this chapter use their stage names rather than their family names, which are included in parentheses in the list of references.]

1. For more general information on *nō,* see Keene (1966); for *kyōgen,* see Sakanishi (1960) and Hata and Yoshikoshi (1982).
2. *Kyōgen* is often called a home-made art produced in a "cottage industry," whose *ie* (household) organization follows many of the same principles of other family-run businesses such as farms or small shops.
3. My relationship with the Shigeyama family is rather complex, built over sixteen years of regular contact as student, director, producer, tour manager, and researcher. I have studied ten *kyōgen* plays with Sennojō, have translated, arranged lecture-demonstrations and workshops, and produced tours of *kyōgen* in Kyoto and the United States, and have directed *kyōgen* actors in intercultural experiments in plays by Beckett, Yeats, and Shakespeare with the Noho Theatre Group.
4. The *nō* actor's more transparent Way is described in Bethe and Brazell (1990), Emmert (1987), and Johnson (1977, 1982, 1985).
5. First written by Manzō Nomura, this phrase has become a somewhat inaccurate cliché (Mansaku 1991:21).
6. *Tanuki* was originally taught only to the first sons of the family (*isshi sōden*), but now all professionals must learn it. Izumi school players, who until recently have not had *Tanuki* in their repertoires, instead perform *Kanaoka,* similar but simpler than the next true test, *Hanago.*
7. Probably a parody in content and typology of the "three old-person plays," including *Seki-dera Komachi, Higaki,* and *Obasute,* marking the peak of mature *nō* artistry (Komparu 1983:15).
8. Emmert (1987:130) stresses the importance and complexity of *aisatsu* (polite greetings) as ways of knowing how to behave toward senior and junior players from various schools within the *nō* world.
9. Much of what Zarrilli (1990) says of Indian martial, spiritual, and theatrical arts holds true for *kyōgen* training: "daily repetition of physical exercises and/or performance techniques encodes the techniques *in the body.* By daily practice all physical and mental obstacles in the way of correct practice are gradually eliminated. The goal of all such virtuosic systems is reaching a state of 'accomplishment' [Skt. *siddhi*] in which the doer and done are one. Through such actualized practice comes both control and transcendence of 'self' " (131). Where *kyōgen* training differs from this, and from *nō* practice, I would argue, is that the child is taught from infancy *not* to abandon the self in order to inhabit the form, integrating, rather than transcending, the self.
10. The "in-body learning" of "becoming a *kyōgen* actor" exaggerates childhood discipline (*shitsuke*) practice of society at large, well documented by Hendry (1986).
11. Since the child was considered one year old on the day he was born, and the lunar calendar was then used, a six-year-old might be the modern equivalent of a 4½-year-old.
12. There are a number of related reasons why grandfathers rather than fathers teach *kyōgen* children: (1) direct training can minimize transmission "static," which might occur with succeeding generations, insuring a more faithful line of transmission;

(2) semiretired or famous grandfathers are generally freer than their mid-career sons, whose teaching and performing duties might take them away from home more often during the child's available practice time; (3) the custom may date from before the Meiji era, when rival *nō* schools would not permit *kyōgen* actors to "contaminate" their stage if they had stepped on another school's. Thus, in Kyoto, two "teams" of *kyōgen* actors developed, centered on alternating generations within the family.

13. At a summer retreat for my amateur *kyōgen* group in 1989, such Western rational methods were imported to brush up on their *kyōgen.* Specific techniques were decontextualized in a so-called American-style workshop, led by actors who had offered 90-minute *kyōgen* workshops at colleges and theaters abroad. Successful, it was repeated in subsequent years.
14. The disciple thus brushes up on songs while learning to accompany various dancers' personal idiosyncrasies. In fact, assisting professional and amateur *keiko,* which begins in the teenage years, acts as a sort of parallel training process, allowing the young master to observe how to teach and, by scrutinizing novices studying plays and dances he has long since mastered, to recreate the beginner's mind, which is so important to keeping these fixed texts fresh.
15. This play is preceded by *Iroha* in the Okura school, as detailed later. While *Utsubozaru* has long been given special status in *kyōgen, Iroha* appears to be of more recent establishment as a stage debut piece: Sensaku debuted as Tarō Kaja in *Busu* in 1901 (Sensaku 1984:21).
16. See translations in McKinnon (1968) and Kenny (1989).
17. Ohnuki-Tierney views the play as depicting the monkey as artist but also, on a ritual level, as cultivator: Monkey performances were originally held at horse stables, where their magical properties were said to pacify wild horses. She sees the "Monkey as culture-bearer" as domesticating the uncivilized Lord's murderous impulses (1987:174).
18. The child also receives his first performance honorarium – becoming a true professional.
19. This sense of symbolic family embrace is further enhanced backstage. Professional stage debuts are usually on the same program with other rarely performed and auspicious *nō* and *kyōgen* plays, often featuring invited *nō* actors of rival schools, creating a "this is your (future) life" collection of musicians, *nō* and *kyōgen* actors, and patrons (all often listed in excruciating detail in autobiographies).
20. In the Izumi school, where *Utsubozaru* is the debut piece, *Iroha*'s precocious student is the child's first lead role.
21. There was a happy ending to the story: Dōji, relieved of his obligation, stayed to watch the rehearsal and, with the gentle coaxing of some of the female brooms, eventually decided to participate after all. His official stage biography lists his stage debut as Noho's *Sorcerer's Apprentice,* followed by his *kyōgen* debut in *Iroha.*

References

Bethe, Monica, and Brazell, Karen, 1990, "The Practice of Noh Theatre," in *By Means of Performance: Intercultural Studies of Theatre and Ritual,* Richard Schechner and Willa Appel, eds., Cambridge: Cambridge University Press, pp. 167–193.

Emmert, Richard, 1987, "Training of the Nō Performer," *Theatre Research International,* Vol. 12, No. 2: 123–133.

Hata Hisashi and Yoshikoshi Tatsuo, 1982, *Kyogen,* Don Kenny, transl., Osaka: Hoikusha Color Books, no. 39.

Hendry, Joy, 1986, *Becoming Japanese: The World of the Pre-school Child,* Manchester: Manchester University Press.

Izawa, Toshiharu, 1993, *Kamigata Oiribukuro: Meijin no Kokoro to Gei* [Kamigata Souvenir: Spirit and Art of the Masters], Vol. II, Osaka: Tōhō Publishing.

Izumi, Motohide, 1983, *Kyōgen o Miru* [Watching Kyogen], Tokyo: Kodansha.

1985, *Kyōgen de Gozaru* [This Is Kyogen], Tokyo: Kodansha.

1991, *Kyōgen e no Shōkai* [An Invitation to Kyogen], Tokyo: Kodansha Culture Books.

Johnson, Irmgard, 1977, "The Child Player and His Training for the Nō Profession," *The Denver Quarterly,* Vol. 12, No. 2 (Summer): 190–196.

1982, "The Adolescent and His Training for the Noh Profession," *Asian Thought & Society,* Vol. VII, No. 21 (Nov.): 303–314.

1985, "The Life of the Adult Noh Player in Japan Today," *Comparative Drama* 18, no. 4, pp. 289–310.

Keene, Donald, 1966, *No: The Classical Theatre of Japan,* Tokyo: Kodansha.

Kenny, Don, transl., 1989, *The Kyōgen Book: An Anthology of Japanese Classical Comedies,* Tokyo: The Japan Times.

Kitagawa, Tadahiko, 1964, *Kyōgen Hyakuban* [One Hundred Kyōgen Plays], Kyoto: Tankōshinsha.

Kobayashi, Seki, 1976, *Kyōgen o Tanoshimu* [Enjoying Kyōgen], Tokyo: Heibonsha Color Shinsho, No. 33.

Komparu, Kunio, 1983, *The Noh Theater: Principles and Perspectives,* Tokyo: Weatherhill.

Koyama, Hiroshi, ed., 1987, *Kyōgen no Sekai* [The World of Kyōgen], No. V, Iwanami Koza Nō-Kyōgen, Tokyo: Iwanami Shoten.

Koyama, Hiroshi, ed., 1990, *Kyōgen Kanshō Annai* [Guide to Kyōgen Appreciation], Vol. VII, Iwanami Koza Noh-Kyōgen, Tokyo: Iwanami Shoten.

Lafleur, William, 1983, *The Karma of Words: Buddhism and Literary Arts in Medieval Japan,* Berkeley: University of California.

McKinnon, Richard, 1968, *Selected Plays of Kyōgen,* Seattle: Uniprint.

Mansaku (Nomura Mansaku), 1984, *Tarō Kaja o Ikiru* [Living Tarō Kaja], Tokyo: Hakusuisha; Hakusuisha U-books.

Manzō (Nomura Manzō VI), 1982, *Manzō Nomura Chosaku Shū* [Collected Writings of Manzō Nomura], Hisashi Furukawa and Seki Kobayashi, ed., Tokyo: Satsuki Shobo.

Ohnuki-Tierney, Emiko, 1987, *The Monkey as Mirror: Symbolic Transformations in Japanese History and Ritual,* Princeton: Princeton University Press.

Sakanishi, Shio, 1960, *The Ink-Smeared Lady and Other Japanese Folk-Plays,* Rutland, VT: Charles Tuttle.

Salz, Jonah, 1997, *Roles of Passage: Coming of Age as a Japanese Kyōgen Actor,* Ph.D. dissertation, New York University.

Sengorō (Shigeyama Sengorō XII), 1983, *Sengorō Kyōgen Banashi* [Sengorō's Kyogen Tales], Tokyo: Kodansha.

Sennojō (Shigeyama Sennojō), 1987, *Kyōgen Yakusha: Hinekure Handaiki* [Kyōgen Actor: Chronicle of a Perverse Half-Life], Tokyo: Iwanami Shinsho no. 396.

Sennojō (Shigeyama Sennojō) and Sensaku (Shigeyama Sensaku III), 1982, "Geidō: Kyōgen Tokushū" [The Path of Art: Special Kyōgen Issue], *Geinō Sō Series,* No. 8, Ishikawa Prefectural Nō Cultural Hall, pp. 8–25.

Sensaku (Shigeyama Sensaku III), 1984, *Kyōgen Hachijugonen* [85 Years of Kyōgen], Tokyo: Kodansha.

Zarrilli, Phillip, 1990, "What does it mean to 'become the character': Power, presence and transcendence in Asian in-body disciplines of practice," in Richard Schechner and Willa Appel, eds., *By Means of Performance: Intercultural Studies of Theatre and Ritual,* Cambridge: Cambridge University Press, pp. 131–148.

Part II

Potters, weavers, mechanics, doctors, and violinists: Learning in artisanal apprenticeship

6 Learning to be an apprentice

Bill Haase

Stumbling into apprenticeship

I fell into a pottery apprenticeship with my *sensei* (teacher) when I was visiting Japan in the early 1980s. I had come to Japan planning to stay only a few months and then pursue apprenticeship training in Britain. Instead I was introduced to Sensei and given the opportunity to become his *uchi deshi* (live-in apprentice). The ancient pottery community, which I will call Kamamura here, became my home for more than a year. What follows is a reflective description of what I found there.

I met Jane, an established American potter, at her exhibition in a Japanese department store. I told her of my interest in a pottery career. She responded by asking if I would like to study in Kamamura. I was taken aback, stuttered awhile, and then said yes. She introduced me to my teacher, in whose household she had studied several decades earlier. I had no idea what I was getting myself into.

Jane had been a student of Sensei's father. When Sensei as a young man was ready to leave his natal family for training in an outside workshop, it was decided that he should go to Europe to study. Jane arranged his apprenticeship with a potter there and kept in close contact with him after he returned to his father's workshop. She thought it would be good for him to have an American apprentice.

Jane introduced me to Sensei and suggested that I try this apprenticeship for three months. Then I could decide with Sensei whether to continue. With this in mind, I heard Sensei tell me he took students for "just one year." I assumed he meant not more than one year. I agreed without hesitation, and we set up a starting date.

This was the first of a string of misunderstandings. I later found out his "just one year" had meant not less than one year. But I began my stint in Kamamura thinking I was there for a three-month trial period, hoping that I would be invited to stay on after that. When people asked me how long I would be there, I could only respond that I'd be there three months and would have to see after that.

This, of course, got back to Sensei, but he didn't say anything. I guess he just assumed I would be leaving soon enough and it wasn't worth his time to confront me about going back on our agreement. It was several months before I became aware of this misunderstanding. By that time, it was almost too late to regain credibility as a serious student.

The importance of an apprentice's initial commitment cannot be underestimated. In consultation with my *senpai* (senior apprentice in the workshop) and her friend, I was encouraged to clear up this misunderstanding by telling Sensei how long I planned to stay. The friend made the point, "You must tell Sensei how long you will stay so that he will know how to teach you."

Learning to be an apprentice

You don't just become an apprentice. You have to learn how to be an apprentice. I had finished my college education in art with a concentration in ceramics just before coming to Japan, so I thought I knew a bit about pottery. I had also spent half a year in 1978 as an apprentice in a pottery studio in Pennsylvania, so I thought I knew more or less what apprenticeship was about.

The first thing I learned was that I didn't know anything and couldn't do anything. During my first month there, I was the proverbial bull in a china shop. Almost every day I broke something. I lived in fear of my own actions from one day to the next.

On one of the first days, I was getting water at the outside faucet, and I busted the flimsy spigot clean off. Sensei's wife chuckled and called the plumber right away. Another day, as I was sieving some glaze, I pushed the screen through the wooden frame. Later, as fresh pots were drying outside, I picked one up to turn it, for even drying, only to find that Sensei had just applied a fresh coat of slip (liquid clay for coating pots) to the outside of the pot, and I'd ruined the design.

My worst mistake happened when we were hurriedly mixing glazes, and a bag of some raw material had to be removed from the area. The bottom had gotten wet from sitting on the floor and was about to rip. When I picked up the bag and swung it over another bucket of slip, the contents were rapidly disgorged from the bottom of the bag. Not only had I made a huge mess, but I had thoroughly contaminated a whole bucket of slip.

These actions initially elicited only a grin from Sensei but soon were being met with piercing glares and scornful comments. Our already tenuous relationship was getting worse.

When I arrived at the workshop in April, there was one other apprentice there. Keiko-san, my *senpai* (senior), had entered the workshop six months ahead of me and was familiar with the workshop routines. She was the person most helpful to me in figuring out what was going on or what was expected of me. When I finished a chore, I went to her to see what to do next. It was already becoming very difficult to talk with Sensei, so I just followed Keiko-san's lead and advice. She seemed to have a good relationship with Sensei, so I took her advice as credible. Keiko-san started work at 8 A.M. and finished about 5 P.M., so I did the same. Keiko-san also said she took one day a week off, so I figured I could, too. I didn't know that more was expected of me.

There were two crucial differences between her situation and mine, which I did not initially understand. (1) She was a woman, so she wasn't being given the "professional" training thought necessary to become a potter. It was assumed that she would be in the workshop only about a year and then move on to bridal training and marriage. (2) She was a day apprentice, and I was *uchi deshi.*

As *uchi deshi,* I was a twenty-four-hour-a-day apprentice. This meant surrendering almost total control of my life. After working all day in the shop, I was summoned by the "bing-bong" of the intercom for dinner and then again for my bath, when everyone else was through.

Meal times varied considerably, so I often didn't know when I would get dinner, but the food was excellent and plentiful, with rice from their own rice paddies and vegetables from Sensei's mother's vegetable patch.

Learning what was appropriate during meals was difficult. The number of family members present varied according to each individual's schedule. Initially, I tried to speak to Sensei in English. Early on, he was quite civil and sometimes friendly, but soon we fell into an all-but-silent relationship. Japanese craftsmen have often been characterized as *mukuchi* (taciturn; literally "having no mouth"). Sensei was known as a man who avoided verbal communication. He didn't speak much with the rest of the family either, unless he was feeling particularly jovial.

With the rest of the family, I would try to communicate in my poor Japanese. It seemed odd to just eat in silence with eyes glued to the TV, so I would make it a point to say at least something during the meal. We would often talk about the food or what was on the television. Almost invariably the focus of attention was the television above the dining table, which blared out soap operas, game shows, or the news.

I slowly came to realize that it distressed Sensei and his family whenever I left the family compound to go into the village or rice paddies on my own. In my first months, after Keiko-san had gone home, I liked to go sketch in the fields, take a stroll in town, or pick up some things at the store. Sensei scoffed at my "going shopping" as I passed him one day on my way out.

I didn't understand how strongly the family felt about this until some time later. They were distressed for several reasons: (1) I was not in the workshop practicing at the wheel in my spare time, as any serious student would; (2) whenever I went off on my own, they were responsible for whatever trouble I would get into; and (3) they were afraid of what sorts of information I might spread or receive about the family. As far as Sensei's family was concerned, it was better if I had no relationships with people outside of the workshop.

I was given a room adjacent to the workshop, up behind the main house. This was the room designated for foreign apprentices. It even had a Western-style bed. To leave the compound, I had to pass right by the house, so they were able to monitor my coming and going. It was quite comfortable, although I would have done anything to have my own bath or shower. I did my own laundry in the workshop washing machine, which barely worked.

Sensei's best pots, which had been selected for exhibition, were stored in the room next to mine, so I was able to inspect these pots often and carefully. In fact, I often secretly borrowed one at a time to sketch. Sensei later told me that to learn pottery you have to be surrounded by good pots. This fit the description.

The first couple of months I was at the workshop, I gave the family ¥30,000 each month for food and other expenses. Jane had suggested that I do this, and I thought it was a good idea. I certainly didn't want to be a burden. After this initial period though, my money was firmly refused. As an apprentice, it was my labor and loyalty that was expected. Payment was seen as a way of shirking my responsibility.

Shortly after I arrived as an apprentice, the family got two puppies. I can't help but suspect they were there to keep an eye on me. They were kept at my front door. The dogs were yelpers, and they let the rest of the family know when I was coming and going. I was also expected to take care of the dogs when no one else wanted to.

The standard routine

After the first few months, I became accustomed to the standard routine in the workshop. I learned my role within that routine primarily by watching and being taught by my *senpai,* Keiko-san, who showed me how to do many of the required chores. I also took over some of her duties, which freed her to spend more time doing wheel practice.

A typical day would start with cleaning up the shop (I usually swept the night before), straightening the tea cups and things for tea, burning the garbage, and making sure everything was in order. Then I would clean and straighten Sensei's wheel (if I hadn't done it the night before), which meant dumping the overflowing ashtrays, wiping down the wheel deck, changing the throwing water, cleaning out the slip container, arranging the tools so he could find everything, and washing or replacing his hand towel. If he would be throwing that day, I had to prepare and leave clay for him. I usually cleaned up Sensei's father's wheel, too.

Often I would take the dogs for a walk in the rice paddies or behind the workshop to the mountain, if no one else had done it. This was my favorite job, and I relished these moments away from the workshop.

If the weather was good, it was my job to take all the finished pots outside to dry. These pots would have to be turned occasionally through the day, in a direction opposite to the path of the sun, as Sensei's father explained to me. If the weather became threatening or raindrops began falling, it was a mad dash to get all the pots back inside again.

My work days were spent doing chores like making clay, making slabs, wedging clay for Sensei or his father, and helping Okabe-san, a local woman who helped in the shop on a regular basis, with the jiggered production (mechanical mass production of molded forms).

Making clay was done by Keiko-san and myself. We passed filter-pressed slabs of clay from the village clay cooperative through a pug mill two or three times until the clay was the proper hardness. It takes quite a bit of practice to get just the right consistency of clay. It was the apprentices' duty to make sure there was always an adequate clay supply on hand.

Occasionally, Keiko-san and I would clean out all the trimmings from under the wheels and throw these into the clay pit in the far corner. It was my job to climb down into the pit, after the clay had been moistened, and dig it up with an adz-like tool. This reclaimed clay was first passed through an ancient pug mill (usually with great difficulty) and then through the regular pug mill several times. This clay was most often used for the jiggered ware.

Learning to wedge clay for Sensei was something I could not do well for quite a while. When I started wedging clay for him, Sensei had snarled that there was too much air in the clay that I had prepared for him. I asked to look at his copy of Bernard Leach's *A Potters Book* in which I had seen a description of correct wedging. Sensei refused to lend me the book, saying only that I should watch him or his father when they wedged. Since I was wedging all of Sensei's clay, I hardly ever got a chance to see him wedge, but I did watch Sensei's father. I wedged all of Sensei's clay and some of Sensei's father's clay until a new apprentice, Sugiyama-san, arrived. Then Sugiyama-san inherited this job.

They say "it takes three years to learn to wedge clay." To wedge clay correctly is very difficult to master. It is a skill that many Japanese potters consider critical to an apprentice's training but is considered trivial in American ceramics classes.

Making slabs for press-molded or slab-built pieces was another of my jobs. I would wedge up the clay and bang the clay into rectangular shapes of correct size before cutting them into slabs of appropriate thickness. After cutting them, they had to be smoothed again with a wooden rib and moisture to create a perfectly flat surface. It was very good wedging practice, because all the air left in the clay showed up when I cut the slabs and smoothed them.

Once every few weeks, when enough pottery had been produced and Sensei decided it was time for a bisque firing, Keiko-san and I would carry out all the green pots to the oil-fired bisque kiln. It was usually Sensei's wife who would stack the kiln, and Sensei might stop by just to check on things once or twice. Once the kiln was loaded, Keiko-san and I would build the door and mud it shut. Sensei started the oil burner first thing in the morning and turned it up a bit at a time throughout the day. The firing was usually finished by later afternoon, so we would unload the next day.

After all my other chores were done, I was allowed to practice my throwing. But I had to keep an eye open for other things that I should attend to, even while I practiced.

Keiko-san, as my *senpai,* was allowed to continue her practice on the wheel unless a special job required her help. She was also given certain orders to fill (like a series of small plates requested by some *mingei,* folk art, shop), or sometimes she helped trim some of the jiggered ware.

Ten o'clock and three o'clock were designated times for *ippuku* (tea break). Everyone in the shop stopped work for tea and sweets. We all gathered around the tea drinking spot: In summer, it was by the door where the cool breeze blew in and you could see that side of town below; in winter, it was huddled around the kerosene stove. Everyone sat on low stools except Sensei, who had a normal-sized chair in which he usually sat cross-legged. Sensei's father, wife, and mother had medium short stools, and the apprentices had the shortest stools, only inches off the ground. Local news and gossip would be traded over cups of cold tea in summer and hot tea in the cooler months. Everyone was served tea in their designated teacup.

It was during these *ippuku* that I heard interesting tidbits of family history from various people – stories from Sensei about his time in Europe, or from Sensei's father about Yanagi, Leach, and Hamada, the famous founders of the Japanese folkcraft movement, coming here on visits. The conversation was usually in Japanese, and I had to ask Keiko-san to translate what she could remember later.

Departures from the standard routine

The normal routine was suspended as glaze firings approached. These were usually just before a scheduled exhibition, of which Sensei had three or four each year. "Firing" usually meant two or three back-to-back (or simultaneous) firings. First, the seven-chamber climbing kiln was fired, although usually only four or five chambers were used. Several days later, the single-chamber salt kiln would be loaded and fired. Occasionally, a third firing would be done in the newer three-chamber climbing kiln to refire the underfired pots. I will describe only the routine involved with the large climbing kiln here.

Exposure to these wood-firing kilns exploded my previous conception of what a kiln was. These kilns were alive, breathing fire and spewing smoke, gobbling up dried pine wood, bundles at a time, and cackling with glee. As much as I was enamored by this kind of firing, I dreaded the period leading up to a kiln firing because there was no normal routine to fall into. I often had to ask someone what I should do next, and I couldn't go back to my wheel to practice in free time, because the wheel deck had become a glazing platform.

Mixing the glazes was the first job. We apprentices would roll up our sleeves and dive into the large glaze buckets to scrape the hardened glaze sludge up from the bottom. This often took hours for a single bucket, and the glaze was extremely cold during fall, winter, and early spring. Sensei would occasionally take out an electric drill with a glaze mixing attachment for his own use, but this was not available to us.

On the first day I began work upon entering the workshop in April, glazing was in progress. I had been given a board of sake cups to glaze, and Sensei's wife showed me how to glaze first the inside with clear glaze, then the outside with black glaze. To get the glaze to go up inside the foot ring, she set the pot in the glaze with the foot barely submerged, then quickly pushed it down and pulled it back up again. Presto! I followed her example exactly up to that last part, but for the life of me I couldn't get the glaze to go up inside the foot ring. By the time I had finished glazing this board of *guinomi* (large sake cup), I'd splashed so much black glaze around that I'd speckled the clear inside glaze on most of these cups, and Sensei told me to wash them all and start again. That was the last time I was allowed to help glaze for quite some time.

Wiping the bisque ware with a damp cloth was my main job while others glazed pots. Sensei's wife, Okabe-san, and Keiko-san glazed the production ware while Sensei and his father glazed their own pots.

After Sensei's wife and Okabe-san had finished glazing, we filled saggars (clay containers to protect ware during firing) with glazed pots and handed the saggars inside the kiln to Sensei's wife, who was the designated kiln loader. Certain glazes had to be put in certain places in the kiln, so experienced guidance was necessary even here. After a column of saggars was set in place, Sensei would come out and stack his pots on shelves atop the saggars. He had to remember what glazes were on what pots, so that he could "read" the temperature during kiln firing from the way the glazes looked. No pyrometers or cones were used to measure temperatures in this kiln.

After a chamber was loaded, it was usually my job to stack the rounded, crumbling door bricks into place. I then mixed up a clay-mud slurry in the scrap clay pit and smeared this over the door bricks to seal the door completely. It was endlessly frustrating trying to stack these ancient bricks into a secure door. I had to be both careful and quick, or else Sensei would sneer, "It'll be evening before you're done." Sensei was always in a hurry to start preheating the kiln, so I often found myself rushing to put up the last doors as smoke from the oil burner came pouring out at me. Fear of asphyxiation was a strong incentive to get faster at door building.

Preheating the kiln with the oil burner brought the kiln up to red heat in the first chamber by morning. This oil preheating saved a lot in wood fuel costs, which were very high. It also allowed the fireman to start fresh in the morning after a good night's sleep, with the glazes in the first chamber close to melting already.

After I had been there for six months, it became my job to tend the oil burner at night. The most explicit instructions I ever received from Sensei were about adjusting this oil burner. He explained that I must turn the oil up a little at a time through the evening and then adjust the air to create a clean flame – not too much smoke, not too much air. "You have to look and adjust. Every time different." The calibrations on the adjustment handles were not to be trusted.

Sensei always had an experienced helper come to fire the big kiln with him. My only designated job during firing was to fix the cracks in the door and to seal the stoke holes after a chamber had been finished. I also moved the wood that was stored atop the kiln's upper chambers off the kiln at the appropriate time, before it started to smolder. This wood-storage method was a way of ensuring perfectly dried wood.

I learned to steer clear of Sensei during firings. The more tired he became, the more abusive he was, sometimes becoming quite sarcastic with me. The large kiln usually finished firing about 9 P.M., but even if it was quite late, Sensei's wife always prepared a great feast afterward. These postfiring feasts were a time when Sensei was more vocal and loose. It was on such an occasion that he said to me, "You can't do anything! If you want to do *yakimono* (this word for pottery can also mean grilled food), you'd better do *takoyaki* (a grilled snack food)."

Unloading the kiln, done two days after the firing, was a wild time with hot pots flying everywhere. I never understood why they didn't wait a little longer for the pots to cool down, or unload a little slower. Once the doors were taken down, Sensei's wife would hand out the still-hot pots and saggars. It was a scramble to place the pots in places where they wouldn't roll away and to stack production ware in flat wooden fish boxes, then haul everything down to the workshop. Invariably, a few small pieces were broken because of the hurry. Everybody except Sensei helped shuttle pieces into the workshop where they were lined up on the floor. The rejects were taken off behind the kiln to be smashed. At first, Keiko-san was responsible for this, and she was given orders to smash the pots into very small pieces. She was sent back on one occasion because the shards were not small enough.

Sensei came up to see the results of the kiln sometime during the day of unloading. He never showed any elation or dismay at the results. He might take a particular pot and inspect it or try to clean up a minor imperfection, but more often than not he would go off to do other things.

Cleaning the pots began as Okabe-san, Keiko-san, and I sat on low stools, ground the foot ring of each pot smooth with a piece of carborundum stone, wiped the pot clean, and placed Sensei's pots on the wheel deck. These pots were then filled with water and wiped dry to check for leaks. After making sure they were not leaking, they were carefully priced by Sensei and his wife.

Numbers and prices were assigned to each of Sensei's pots, and a list of the numbered pots and corresponding price was compiled for the gallery. In Japan, most expensive pots are sold with a special paulownia wood box – measurements were taken, and boxes were ordered to these specifications. Once the boxes were finished, Sensei would do *hakogaki* (writing a description of the piece on its box lid and signing it).

The standard production pieces not destined for exhibition were also cleaned and taken to the showroom or storage area. Some pots were packed up and sent off to shops that had ordered them. Occasionally, small pots being sent to a *mingei* (folk art) shop would be wrapped in rice straw to underscore the *mingei* image of the work. It was fun to sit there with Sensei's mother and Okabe-san learning to wrap pots in this way.

Kiln repair and kiln building was another deviation from the normal routine. In the last few months I was in Kamamura, Sugiyama-san joined the workshop as a second *uchi deshi.* With the manpower of two *uchi deshi* available, Sensei decided to rebuild the large kiln, which appeared to be in danger of having its arch collapse.

This design of the Kamamura-style kiln is a more rudimentary technology than the climbing kilns found in most other Japanese pottery villages. Except for the use of manufactured refractory bricks, this kiln was being rebuilt in the style of the Edo-period Kamamura kilns.

Sugiyama-san and I worked as a team, demolishing and removing certain segments of the kiln, according to Sensei's instructions. As the work progressed, an apprentice status inversion took place. Sensei was giving us instructions in Japanese, and I had to look to Sugiyama-san to clue me in. It soon became Sensei and Sugiyama-san working at laying up bricks, as I looked on and helped as an assistant. By this time, I'd pretty well gotten used to being the odd man out.

The kiln building went on for two months. After rebuilding the large kiln, we rebuilt the bisque kiln, rebuilt part of the salt kiln, and finished by building a new single-chamber kiln for natural ash glazed pottery. It was hard work, but the chance to see how these kilns were put together from the ground up was an important part of my education there. There was no explanation attached, but it was all there to see.

As well as being a rare educational opportunity, the hard work of kiln building could be seen as a way of paying the family back, with physical labor, for the training I had received.

Sensei and I: Learning to be a failure

During the first few days I was in the workshop, I was surprised at how friendly and open Sensei was. He seemed to laugh easily, and he spoke about his time in Europe. My Japanese was very limited and his English was very good, so we spoke in English. As I quickly fell from his good graces, less and less English was spoken; in fact, we hardly spoke at all.

After awhile, his commands came in Japanese, or first Japanese, then English if I hadn't understood. For instance, when I wasn't paying attention and he'd run out of clay to throw with, he'd yell "*Tsuchi!*" Once when he'd just gotten up on his wheel to throw, he couldn't find his throwing chamois (a strip of leather to smooth the lip of pots), and he started yelling in Japanese at me because I had cleaned the wheel. The chamois was right there in front of him and he just hadn't seen it, but I was learning that Japanese was the language of choice for chastisement, although I was scolded and ridiculed in both languages.

Sensei also began talking about me to others while I was present, using Japanese. I might catch a few words or the gist of the conversation, but I was helpless to defend myself. During these exchanges, he ridiculed my jogging in shorts, or talked about when he'd seen me going to the store for a beer, or how a twenty-four-year-old could look like a high school boy.

As these kinds of exchanges continued, and I found it harder and harder to speak directly to Sensei, I was learning, painfully, to be a failure. I found it difficult to do anything right in his eyes, and I often had no idea of what he expected of me.

My first main fault in Sensei's eyes was that I showed a lack of commitment to studying pottery. He saw my daily jogging as a diversion from serious study, and he thought I might be in Kamamura for reasons other than studying pottery. He told me at one point that "there is nothing else for you here." He also told me that "even one year is not enough to really learn about making pottery." At least on this second point, we agreed.

My second main fault was that I couldn't "see." He made this clear for the first time at an end-of-the-year party when nearly everyone from the workshop was present. He said simply, "You have to learn to 'see'." I asked Keiko-san later what he meant, and she replied that neither she nor any of the others present had understood either. Sensei referred to this again when he told me my *sakazuki* (small sake cups) were not acceptable, after I'd been in the shop for more than ten months. He said, "Your *sakazuki* are weak because you can't see."

Learning to throw

Sensei did not require me to spend an extended period of time doing only workshop chores before he assigned me to a wheel and allowed me to start wheel practice. I knew an American apprentice in Bizen who had survived a year of sweeping floors and cleaning rocks out of clay before getting to use the wheel. I was assigned the electric wheel by the door the first day I arrived, when Sensei walked me through the workshop and told me whose wheel was whose. He also told me that I should try to make some small shape and make them all the same, although he didn't say what shape.

After five months of my practicing the *guinomi,* which Keiko-san had suggested I make, Sensei said abruptly, "What are you trying to make, anyway?" Then he gave me my first real assignment, which was a tiny *sakazuki* (small sake cup) about 1.75 inches tall, of which only half was thrown and the lower half was trimmed into a tall foot. He gave me a fired example of the shape and said only, "Make them with as little trimming as possible." I never received a model of what the *sakazuki* looked like in the freshly thrown state, although Sensei's wife asked him if I shouldn't have an example to work from. Sensei had always produced freshly thrown models for Keiko-san to work from in practicing her assignments. It was never demonstrated to me how to throw these tiny cups correctly. I was on my own, like a Zen student with a *koan.*

I accepted this challenge and thought I'd be able to make a decent *sakazuki* in a few weeks of practice. This shape was simple in appearance but very difficult to duplicate. I would take my *sakazuki* to Sensei every few weeks to see if they were all right, trying to catch him during his least negative moods. At first, the shapes were all different, then the lip was too thin, then the trimming wasn't right. There was always something wrong with them.

A strange transformation gradually overtook me during the six months I was trying to throw these tiny pots. As I was straining to distinguish almost imperceptible differences in shape and thickness in these forms, in order to produce them perfectly, I began feeling myself shrink to the size of these tiny sake cups. I was feeling very small!

Finally, after six months of *sakazuki* practice, Sensei told me to try making teacups, since these *sakazuki* were too difficult for me. He did condescend to fire the hundred or so that I had saved, and they were sold in the workshop's showroom.

I started all over again with the teacup shape and its designated measuring stick. Although these cups were only about 2.5 inches tall, after throwing *sakazuki* for so long, I felt like I was throwing huge pots! Again I played cat and mouse with my teacher, trying to catch the shape and feel that he was looking for in this form.

I learned a lot from just watching Sensei and his father throw. In fact, this was the primary mode of instruction. My wheel was right next to Sensei's father, so I could watch him from time to time through the day as I practiced. I was always amazed at how quickly and vigorously he worked, kicking his wheel like a madman and making the whole wheel deck shake, while I was straining at my wheel to get my tiny sake cups just right. On one of the first days I was in the shop, Sensei's father came over to show me how to squeeze the spinning clay just below the cup being formed, to separate it from the mass of clay below. With this move, you could cut the pot off and remove it without stopping rotation of the wheel. This was probably the only time I was explicitly "taught" anything about throwing.

Sensei's wheel was on the far side of the workshop. He would allow me to stand to the side of his wheel deck after everyone else had finished work (he usually started and finished work an hour or two later than the others) and watch him throw. He never addressed or acknowledged me, but he didn't seem to mind my looking at all. From this vantage point, I could see exactly how he moved on the clay, and I tried to memorize the sequence.

Two things were especially interesting to me. One was the way he wiped his hands clean of slip and tossed it back in the pot or wiped it into the waste clay container. This move was like a hand dance. The other thing was the way he would roll and nod his head as the clay revolved. Sensei's father also did this, and at some point I found myself doing it, too.

An unusual opportunity to hear Sensei's father speak about his philosophy of teaching came when an American friend visited the workshop in the company of his host family. Mark was an art school graduate and had brought some examples of pottery he'd made in art school. Sensei's father looked carefully at the unskillfully thrown pots and was very diplomatic at first, but later he began telling Mark through the translation of his host family that the most important thing in learning to be a ceramic artist is developing a strong foundation of skills (*kisozukuri*). He went on to say that to try to express yourself without first establishing a *kiso* (foundation) is no good. After Mark and his host family had left, Sensei's father admitted to me that the pots had been "very, very bad."

I am sure Sensei agreed with his father about the importance of *kisozukuri,* but he stressed the importance of learning to "see" as the most important step in my becoming a good potter. What I believe he meant was that to be able to replicate specific shapes and also just to throw "good" shapes, a highly developed visual acuity is necessary. Sensei demonstrated this visual acuity in his highly successful expeditions to the mountain to collect edible wild plants that were difficult for the rest of us to locate.

Leaving the workshop

After extended and torturous deliberation, I decided to leave the workshop upon completing thirteen months of work there. I told Sensei almost two months ahead of time that I would be leaving after June of my second year, when the heavy work of kiln rebuilding was completed. My decision to leave was partly due to the fact that most of my jobs had been taken over by Sugiyama-san, and I felt that my usefulness in the workshop had ended. I wasn't yet able to help out with production for filling the kiln, but I didn't have the hackwork to make me feel useful either. I felt even more alienated when I saw Sugiyama-san getting on so well with Sensei, and then the apprentice status inversion took place, which further convinced me that leaving was the best thing to do.

I had seen other apprentices in Kamamura in situations I considered to be much more tolerable, living in their own apartments, working with teachers who treated them well. My dissatisfaction was enhanced by this contrast.

I also found my goals coming into focus through this period. I wanted to learn the kickwheel after being inspired by Sensei's father's example. I had a great desire to learn about wood firing but wanted a teacher with whom I could communicate, one who would talk to me. I believed I also needed a better command of the Japanese language to accomplish these goals.

When I confronted Sensei with my decision to leave the workshop, he responded with a truly shocked look and said, "But you have a chance to study with us now!" as if I were throwing away the opportunity of a lifetime. He said he didn't mind if I left but didn't think it was a good idea. I was probably the ultimate failure in his book, but I was elated to be getting out of there. I do have to thank Sensei for this: If I wasn't a "serious student" of Japanese pottery before I arrived, I surely was by the time I left.

7 Craft and art education in Mashiko pottery workshops

John Singleton

The pottery town of Mashiko is a famous setting for the Japanese folkcraft (*mingei*) pottery art world, conveniently accessible to Tokyo, and attractive to tourists and aspiring potters. During six months of fieldwork in 1987, I observed pottery craft learning and pedagogy there. Mashiko potters, students, and other residents introduced me to the practices of pottery production and the social networks of potters. They included me in the social relations of learning and teaching.[1]

In 1987, there were about 350 workshops,[2] mainly mom-and-pop home enterprises, located in a town of 20,000 people. About half of the population, and kilns, are in the urban strip of Mashiko, which begins at the railroad station. There is one main business and tourist street that leads from the station to the workshop of Mashiko's most famous recent resident, Hamada Shoji. Hamada was one of the first "living national treasures" of Japanese folkcraft, so named in 1954.

Hamada made Mashiko famous. Not a native son, he moved to Mashiko in 1924 because of his attraction to the simple functional pottery production there. It exemplified for him the *mingei* ideals articulated by Yanagi Sōetsu[3] and his small circle of intellectual colleagues. In the 1920s, the group included Hamada and his close friend, the English potter Bernard Leach. Yanagi and his friends invented the Japanese word *mingei* to stand for their conceptions of folkcraft and art; established a museum in Tokyo, the *Mingeikan*; and tirelessly promoted the *mingei* movement. They achieved public recognition for, and retention of, functional folkcraft pottery styles and technology, which they associated with premodern peasant production. The *mingei* movement created an art world that has had a major influence on several generations of artist–craftsmen and their patrons in Japan, Europe, the United States, Australia, and elsewhere.[4]

The major economic supports of the town of Mashiko in addition to pottery production, and tourism associated with the local reputation for folkcraft pottery, are agriculture and small manufacturing industries, including a camera assembly plant.

The people of Mashiko, potters and others, have made profitable postwar careers out of their association with the folkcraft movement. The Chamber of Commerce and the development section of the town office emphasize in their promotions the symbolism of *mingei* pottery. The town is also, however, the home of famous artist potters working in very different idioms, modern sculptors, and workshops and factories that make simple molded flowerpots or generic tableware. (See Shimotsuke Shimbun [1984] for descriptions of the outstanding potters of Mashiko.)

Two well-promoted pottery craft festivals a year bring thousands of tourists and buyers to Mashiko to buy at reasonable prices from younger potters, factories, and other producers not connected to the high-class gallery and art circuits. Competent potters are thus able to survive economically – while nationally recognized folkcraft and fine artists can make a very good living. Certain galleries in San Francisco and Germany sell Mashiko ware exclusively.

The social construction of *mingei* images in Mashiko is fairly recent. Though strongly associated with Japanese and international public images of unchanging tradition, pottery making started here only a little more than a century ago.

Pottery learners

Over the last half century, Mashiko has attracted many aspiring potters at various stages in their careers. It was a place to learn from the recognized masters, especially Hamada, and from the native artisans. After the economic recovery from World War II, it was one of the few folkcraft pottery centers that allowed outsiders to establish new workshops and kilns.

Would-be artists, craftsmen, and *mingei* specialists come to Mashiko workshops from all over Japan and the world. In 1987, there were three groups of student potters: (1) native sons and daughters of the local community who had grown up with pottery as a convenient career model; (2) graduates of fine arts schools, usually two- or four-year universities, who needed practical experience for entry to a pottery art career; and (3) people searching for alternative and independent lifestyles, dropouts from the corporate middle class, not associated with conventional educational, industrial, corporate, or marital expectations.

International students, too, are a small group in this community – there are generally ten to fifteen foreigners in residence. Their origins and aspirations parallel those of the Japanese novices, including some whose parents are potters. They, too, come to work with and learn from the Mashiko potters.

Folk model of pottery apprenticeship

In several communities, widely regarded as traditional centers of folkcraft pottery, there is a model of highly formal but implicit expectations for pottery apprenticeship.[5] Sometimes the model is presented as an historical artifact, undermined by current demands for extended schooling before setting out on a craft career.

One is told that apprentices were expected to accept an extended state of dependence on their masters, during which they would be subject to demands for long repetitive practice of standard wheel-thrown forms. They were obliged to demonstrate their persistence in pursuit of the craft skills and to endure patiently the tacit testing of their motivation and spirit.

The folk model of pottery learning seems to have five stages, centered on the symbolically important skills of throwing pots on the wheel. In that model, stage one begins with a long period of unobtrusive observation while the aspiring potter is assigned menial jobs in the workshop – a kind of waiting period that tests the learner's character and ability to persist in a desire to learn, without allowing direct participation in pottery production. It is a time for learning how to learn, to develop the strategies of unobtrusive observation.

Stage two begins when a learner takes the first tentative trials at the wheel – often a self-initiated activity in the evening or on holidays when nobody else is in the shop. At stage three, a learner is explicitly assigned to a wheel in the shop and directed to practice the forming of specific shapes on the wheel when other chores have been finished. The forms come from the standard production of the workshop. Learners are told to make 10,000 copies of the first form before they go on to a second form. These practice pieces are not fired; they are returned each day for recycling in the shop's clay pit. One is never released from the tasks begun in the first stage, but a successful apprentice becomes efficient in anticipating the needs of the master, gaining time for practice at the wheel.

Only at stage four does the learner get assigned to actual production work, in which the pots will be glazed and fired for sale as work from the shop. Stage five, after one is acknowledged to have developed the necessary craft skill, is a period of productive labor in the shop to repay the master for the training received. In elite shops, it may lead to a formal show of the learner's original work in an appropriate gallery, sponsored by the master.

The model is important for understanding the course that an apprentice experiences, but it does not suggest the many variations of learning ideology and experience in Japanese folkcraft pottery villages today. We might think of it as the folk curriculum of apprenticeship. It presumes a naive learner, but apprentice applicants have often studied in another shop, in art schools, or in special craft training centers. Neither does it account for the dropouts, runaways, or pushouts that occur along the way. Personality clashes might well be expected, and apprentices are as quick to judge the sincerity of their teachers as the masters are to judge them. Since labor is exchanged for teaching, the labor may be judged exploitative by the learner – and the teacher may be concerned by the laziness or ineptitude of the learner.

Few people enter one shop as raw novices, stay for the three to ten years expected of apprentices, and emerge from the same shop as fully recognized professionals. Many aspiring potters move from one shop and community to another – in and out of apprenticeships, jobs, and schools – in the process of their pottery education. Along the way, they experience a wide variation in the nature of masters, the ways in which workshops are organized, and the expectations held for their work and education.

Four brothers from one Mashiko pottery family are described here in order to illustrate widely different constructions of pottery art and/or craft. They also differ in the ways in which they organize their work and their relations with aspiring potters who come to study with them. Even their conception of learners – as apprentices, students, or laborers – is at issue. In their workshops, pedagogical arrangements are as distinctive as their separate styles of pottery. They constituted, in themselves, a unique typology of teaching styles and motivations, associated with their individual ideologies or philosophies of pottery work.

A family of potters

As third generation potters, the four brothers were born and raised in Mashiko. They grew up in an established family workshop and are recognized in the folkcraft art world for their work. They have been directly influenced by personal contact with the *mingei* folkcraft "promoters," especially Hamada, and their work is marketed in the *mingei* art world with which he was associated.

The workshop with which I was related most directly during my stay in Mashiko was that of the oldest brother, then sixty-six years old. He had inherited the family workshop originally established by his grandfather. His wife, until her death, had worked with him in pottery production. His twenty-five-year-old son, the fourth potter generation in the family, lived and worked with him. The workshop head and his three younger brothers were well known in Mashiko, and each had established separate recognizable pottery styles and separate forms for a pottery career. The four brothers could be roughly described, in order of seniority, as artist, businessman, craftsman, and salaried teacher. All of them were locally known as teachers.

The artist potter

The elder brother was an artist (*sakka*) and philosopher, a learned but unschooled teacher of advanced students of pottery. His workshop was a kind of "graduate school" of folk pottery, where graduates of pottery training centers, art schools, or other workshops might come to perfect their skills and philosophies. He made pots in occasional spurts, usually timed to meet the obligations of gallery exhibitions, but he did not produce much and was seemingly unconcerned about household finances. He was looked after by friends and students. One young patron made specific efforts to arrange periodic shows of his work.

His workshop was artlessly but artfully arranged in the epitome of a *mingei* ideal. Kick wheels were lined up in a wood platform in front of the rough *shōji* windows. The workshop floor was dirt, and the furniture was improvised. Sliding doors worked only with some difficulty and were usually left open. There was no sign on the road directing one to the workshop, and a two-rut dirt driveway led up from the rice fields and through a bamboo thicket to the house and shop. The immediate neighbors were a single lady potter and a dairy farm. But the workshop was only a short walk from the tourist plaza of the main pottery marketplace in the center of town.

A personally sculpted and smoke-blackened wood teakettle hanger, in the form of a woman who held the bamboo tea dipper in her arms, was one of the few deliberately decorative items there. A random assortment of teapots and teacups were kept on the workbench platform near the fireplace for purposes of hospitality, together with scrap paper to be used for kindling the fire and a shifting collection of sweets and snacks left by visitors – to be passed out to the next round of visitors and students.

The workshop had an aura of ancient peasant use, a *mingei* style cultivated by Hamada. Urban visitors were impressed by the setting and honored to be invited to sit at the fireplace.[6] The only electrified appliances were the bare light bulbs, a large pug mill (clay mixer) of uncertain vintage, and the radios and heaters occasionally brought in by students to use next to their assigned wheels. Chickens, housed in hutches just outside the shop door, would occasionally walk into the shop and pick up food crumbs from the floor. Water for tea was drawn by a bucket on a rope from an open well a few steps away.[7] Wood-fired kilns were adjacent to the shop, and firewood was stacked under the eaves – when the household had enough money to purchase it.

In this workshop, I was able to drink tea with the potter, his son, his students, alumni of this workshop, and his visitors. As the students liked to point out, "tea drinking" was an important activity and not just a break from work. It seemed to be the potter's favorite activity. Indeed, the students had to develop strategies to be able to slip away from the tea drinking to work on their wheels. There was no payment to students in this workshop, and they were not expected to make pots for sale by the master. Foreign students were drawn to this shop when their Japanese language competency was adequate for the "tea drinking" conversations.

"Drinking tea" was an explicit pedagogical technique of the artist potter – conversation with his students and other visitors. Summer or winter, an iron kettle of water hung over the firepit. The first student chore of the morning was to start a fire and fill the kettle. Tea was regularly served to anyone in the shop – a major (but never stated) duty of the students, regular visitors, resident ethnographer, and, as a last resort, the potter himself.

It was conversation around the teapot on important topics of the day that constituted "teaching." The potter and his students did not, however, talk about pottery making. "Anybody can make a pot," said the potter. "We have many more important things to talk about." Topics ranged from current political issues, philosophy of life and esthetics, to a review of plans for upcoming shows of the potter or his workshop "alumni."

The potter was the center of any conversation, and he used various rhetorical strategies to maintain a professorial authority over his firepit-centered "classroom." An outsider quickly learned to avoid side conversations.

He and his students worked exclusively on kick wheels, and they fired their work in wood-burning kilns – using the traditional technologies honored by the *mingei* movement. But the potter saw these as advanced techniques for self-expression; he encouraged novices to learn to throw first on an electric wheel. One could, he felt, better experience the spontaneity of pottery forms on the kick wheel at a later stage in their learning. There was no formal assignment of chores in this workshop, though new students were expected to pick up on the chores done by their seniors – and occasionally chastised in private by the seniors if they were not doing their share. Unlike the potter described by Haase (Chapter 6, this volume), the artist Master did not express displeasure with his students. It was left to the students to convey the unstated expectations.

The shop was a regular gathering place for a circle of local potters, alumni of the shop, people working in other shops, and international students. Folding chairs were sometimes brought in for special literary or political events, and the shop became a lecture hall. At other times, a busload of schoolchildren might show up at the door for an introduction to pottery work.

The businessman potter

The second brother was a wealthy local businessman and entrepreneur, as well as a potter. Among other enterprises, he owned a local shopping center for tourists, where he sold his brothers' pots exclusively, as well as retailing and wholesaling the works of many local potters. He maintained a private pottery collection of high-class pots from the famous folkcraft centers of Japan in his shopping center.

At home, separate from the shopping center, he had his own pottery workshop and regularly hired young people to work there in producing a variety of pottery wares. He used modern technology, gas and electric kilns, and mass-production techniques. Occasionally, he had a chance to produce his own handmade pots; he was recognized as a potter in his own right.

For the novices in this workshop, he was more of an employer than a teacher. Young newcomers to Mashiko, who needed a way to support themselves, would work for the businessman for a while and then would move on to the artist or craftsman brothers' shops. The majority of Mashiko pottery workshops offered a similar kind of low-wage employment for novices, but with more direct contact with the working potters. A few students managed to continue their employment in such shops or factories while spending spare time "hanging out" at the artist brother's workshop.

The craftsman potter

The third brother was a craftsman, a man who had gone into pottery production immediately after the completion of his compulsory schooling (equivalent to American junior high school). He deliberately used the language of labor and described himself as a *setoyasan* (plate maker or merchant) without artistic pretensions.

His cramped workshop, close to the family workshop in which he had been raised, was shared with five to eight students who were attracted to him, his pots, and his enthusiasm for pottery making.

Highly productive and hard-working, he used only the traditional folk technology of kick wheels and wood-fired climbing kilns. His wife, graduate of a college-level art school, had her own separate workshop, which she used in those brief periods when she was free of home and child-rearing chores.

In talking about his work with his students, he would emphasize that he was just a potter who made functional household wares (*setoyasan*). He insisted that prices of his work should be kept at a level low enough for it to be used in everyday life. With his emphasis on an ideal of functional ware, he did not seek display of his work in art shows, though his older businessman brother sometimes would enter his pieces in such shows. His work and style was distinctive, recognized for its folkcraft quality. The influence of his designs could be seen in the work of his former students, though they were careful not to copy his pottery in their independent work.

Unlike common Mashiko workshop practice, the third brother did not pay his students – and he refused to use their practice pieces in his workshop production. The only work for the students, beyond the voluntary chores of cleaning the workshop and serving tea to visitors, was assistance in loading and firing the wood-fired kiln. He emphasized that the students' time with him was for learning to throw pots.

Over the years, he had established a graduated curriculum sequence of functional pot forms for their intensive practice – though he adjusted the sequence for each student's needs. Students were both novices and those with some experience in pottery. They often moved back and forth to the elder brother's workshop as well as participating in a common social network with students and alumni of the two workshops.

He believed that by restricting the students to practice forms at the wheel, they would build up a creative anticipation and appreciation for making their own pots once they established their independence from him. They were more likely to explode with creativity then – if they had been denied freedom to experiment during their practice in his shop.

Salaried teacher of urban hobbyists

The fourth brother, a widower, had always lived in the main family compound. He and his two school-age sons were members of the elder brother's household. He commuted to work as a teacher of pottery hobby classes at a newspaper-sponsored cultural center in Tokyo. He was also a jazz musician and seemed to enjoy his music practice more than pottery production. Though he often came to drink tea in the workshop, I never saw him working on a wheel there. On rare occasions, a student from one of his Tokyo classes would visit the family workshop. Then he would receive from his student the same forms of student respect accorded his older brothers in their workshops.

Teaching and commoditized labor

Mashiko potters obviously find many reasons to be engaged with aspiring potters. In a narrowly economic view, students can contribute substantially to workshop production – in doing the workshop chores and assisting in tasks that require many hands. Firing in a wood-burning kiln is almost impossible without some outside help – though a few mom-and-pop potters manage to do it with just two people. Fortunately, some aspiring potters are motivated by considerations of quality and participation in the processes of production as its own reward. Most potters who depend economically upon student labor also feel a responsibility to pay for it, though they sometimes cannot afford to pay the legal minimum wage.

In this respect, the first and third brothers are unusual. They do not regularly pay for the labor of their students – and, indeed, they do not use it for their basic household production. The student labor is essentially not given a cash value or commoditized – only that labor is used that is freely offered by the students, treated as a kind of free-will offering in return for the learning opportunities allowed. This keeps the student–teacher relationship separate from those based on commoditized labor.

The teachers do assume a kind of paternalistic responsibility for their students. One alumnus of the artist's shop was said to have been paid because he was so poor and needed money to survive. The exchange of labor is a kind of gift that requires an exchange of teaching responsibility and the provision of a context for learning. So much gift giving in Japan is itself commoditized – as in the hired services of department store gift advisers and managers – that it is important to recognize the uncommoditized and unverbalized exchanges of some teacher–learner relations (cf. Madono, Hill and Plath, Chapters 8 and 12, this volume, respectively).

Potters do not enter lightly into teaching relationships, given the implications and responsibilities of an acknowedged teacher's role. Some never take in students.[8] Even those long established in a teaching role may deliberately avoid the language of superordinate teacher status. Students of the craftsman brother, for instance, very quickly learned not to defer in the language they used to refer to him. In private, they would readily acknowledge their indebtedness to him as teacher (*Sensei*): "Some of us think we ought to be paying him tuition," said one. But to his face and in reference to him elsewhere, he was always referred to by his locally familiar nickname.

Conclusion

This chapter suggests, then, that the simple folk model of apprenticeship described here is only the beginning of a description of apprenticeship experience and relationships in Japanese pottery workshops. The steps and rules of the model given here do not describe the actual sequences of learning or predict the ways in which students will be treated in a shop.

The simple economic exchange of labor for the opportunity to learn holds in most of the workshops I observed (such as the businessman brother's shop) but only in one of the four brothers' shops. A few teachers deliberately reject the commoditization of student labor in their shops – and gain in return a more powerful sense of collaboration with and loyalty from their voluntary associates. The satisfactions of teaching seem to outweigh, for them, the economic rewards of cheap student labor.

For students, there is, indeed, a variety of patterns of participation in pottery production and opportunities to learn the skills, perspective, and "secrets" of the masters. In this, each student reinvents something of the traditional craft and finds his or her own place in one of the pottery art worlds. Despite distinctive origins, the learners blend together in the Mashiko pottery art community of practice and become potters together, no longer distinguished by their different paths to potter status.

Notes

I am an amateur woodworker and novice blacksmith, not a potter. My son, Willi Singleton, introduced me to the idea of apprenticeship when he entered a Japanese family workshop and later introduced me to the Mashiko pottery workshops and worked with me as a research assistant during my time there. My wife Anne, also a potter, accompanied me for a part of this research and participated with me in the potter networks of Mashiko. The potters and students of Mashiko were gracious hosts and consultants for the fieldwork reported here.

Other colleagues who have been helpful to me in fieldwork and analysis include the authors in this volume (especially my longtime co-conspirators Jacquetta Hill and David Plath) and L. Keith Brown, Michael Coy, Kazuhiro Ebuchi, Margaret Eisenhart, Esther Goody, Jean Lave, Mark Lincicome, John Roberts, and Satoru Takeuchi. I am grateful for their advice and encouragement.

The research on which this paper is based was made possible by a Senior Fellowship award of the Japan Foundation. I also received support from the Japan Studies Group and the Japan Iron and Steel Federation endowment of the University of Pittsburgh.

1. Some 25 years earlier, I lived in a similar community not far from Mashiko while studying a middle school in relation to its community (Singleton 1967). In Mashiko, I studied a different educational institution, apprenticeship, and its relationship with its community, a craft community of practice.
2. In 1995, there were said to be over 500 workshops in Mashiko. The pottery community of practice continues to expand, even though the *mingei* boom of the 1960s and '70s has dwindled.
3. Yanagi Sōetsu is best known outside of Japan for his writings translated in *The Unknown Craftsman* (1972).
4. It should be noted that the *mingei* ideology is influential but contestable. It is a common topic for argument among potters (see Moeran 1984:9–27). It is also a successful marketing strategy.
5. See Singleton 1989a for the source of this model. The present chapter is an elaboration of the wide range of variation in ideology and experience among potters and learners in more cosmopolitan networks.
6. The shop was used as a "natural" stage setting by some Japanese film and TV producers who brought in a tractor trailer full of equipment and set up their cameras, reflectors, and sound systems in the muddy yard of the workshop for a week or more.
7. Running water was discreetly available outside of the family living quarters.
8. Among the many independent potters who spent significant time with the artist or craftsman potter brothers, I know of only one who took on a teaching role in her own workshop. The brothers take obvious pleasure in their role as teachers, but they derive minuscule economic rewards from their teaching practice. I find it ironic that the masters have conveyed their pottery skills effectively, but they have not conveyed their desire to teach.

References

Moeran, Brian, 1984, *Lost Innocence: Folk Craft Potters of Onta, Japan,* Berkeley: University of California Press.

Shimotsuke Shimbun, 1984, *Tōgenkyō Mashiko: Mashiko no Tōkō, Hito to Sakuhin* [Earthly Paradise of Pottery Mashiko: The Potters of Mashiko, People and Works], Utsunomiya, Japan: Shimotsuke Shimbunsha.

Singleton, John, 1967, *Nichū: A Japanese School,* New York: Holt, Rinehart and Winston.

1989a, "Japanese Folkcraft Pottery Apprenticeship: Cultural Assumptions in Educational Practice," in Michael Coy (ed.), *Apprenticeship: From Theory to Method and Back Again,* State University of New York Press, pp. 13–30.

Yanagi, Sōetsu, 1972, (Adapted by Bernard Leach), *The Unknown Craftsman: A Japanese Insight into Beauty,* Kodansha International, Ltd.

8 Craft and regulatory learning in a neighborhood garage

Kathryn Ellen Madono

I decided to look for apprenticeship in a neighborhood garage because I believe that any significant cultural form should be evident in the most mundane settings. The social status of an auto mechanic is problematic in both the United States and Japan. We call such a mechanic a "grease monkey"; the Japanese equivalent is "cockroach" (*aburamushi,* literally, grease beetle). Yet it was clear in the garage that apprenticeship was central in the education of auto mechanics.

Two Yamura brothers employed fifteen workers in the garage I chose to study. Their skilled journeymen offered highly crafted complex repair services while less skilled apprentices did more routine, bureaucratically regulated, state vehicle inspections.

I spent four months observing daily life in the garage and interviewing workers. Interviewing involved being interviewed – they wanted to know about me. I presented myself as a local Japanese–American homemaker turned educational anthropologist. Using my foreign, feminine identity, I could ask naive questions.

Learning relationships in the garage

The brothers preferred to hire journeymen mechanics, but they also advertised for *minarai* (apprentice; literally, novices who learn by observation of skilled workers). Thus apprentices are those who will learn through observation. Rough labor can be learned by trial and error, but the fine points of auto mechanics are acquired when novices work in intimate and loyal cooperation with more skilled seniors.

Two Yamura family houses and separate sheds for painting, inspection, electrical work, and testing surrounded the yard. The yard was always full of vehicles in some stage of repair or inspection. To move vehicles in this crowded space, mechanics cooperated in pairs. One stood outside a vehicle guiding, while the other drove. They avoided asking for help from workers with whom they did not share obligations. I recorded "who helped whom" to identify viable alliances. These alliances reflected the reciprocal relationships of garage apprenticeships.

Hierarchies of learners, or alliances, spanned at least three cohorts in the Yamuras' relatively successful apprenticeship system. Where experts and learners become deeply involved in cooperative tasks, they form teams (*han*). In different activities, one person can move from expert to learner. These work relationships are based on reciprocal obligations, within which they exchange loyalty, legitimacy, and caring.

Learning cannot be separated from everyday practice. Exchanges in work relationships validate a wider Japanese gift economy. Communities of customers and service industries, as well as the families of workers, practice similar exchanges.

Apt learners focus on the ritual patterns of daily life (*kata*). Both regulatory bureaucracy and the reciprocal exchanges of craft alliances focus on the details of practice. In contrast to the implicit ritual of *kata,* auto inspection regulations are explicitly defined in contracts, textbooks, and guidelines. Various state bureaucracies regulate state-mandated services, such as auto inspection. These regulations are founded on abstract rules. Auto inspection was a major source of income for the Yamuras. It has been the entry-level job for all apprentices. Unlike gift exchanges of craft, bureaucratic regulation assigns monetary value to skilled services. Through regulation, the inexact craft of auto mechanics can be commodified. That is to say, it can be sold at a market price without a personal relationship between buyer and seller.

Even in the family garage, two foundations for the practice of auto mechanics could be distinguished: regulatory knowledge (an instrument of commodification) and craft skills (as a gift for reciprocal exchange). Auto mechanic apprenticeships are vitalized by the interdependence of these contrasting sets of interests.

Craft transmission through journeymen

In 1962, with the help of his sister, the president of the garage transformed a roadside portion of his father's suburban farm property into a gas station. He wanted to attract orders for repair work, so he hired journeymen who would teach him their mechanical skills. In those days, he was a novice in auto mechanics. Those journeymen are now gone and have been replaced by two of their apprentices. At the time of my research, those two former *minarai* had become the garage's most

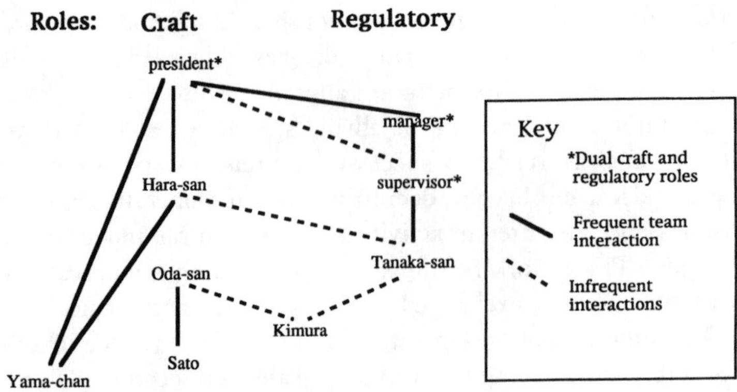

Figure 8.1. Team interaction.

experienced mechanics. One of them was the garage supervisor. He had learned bureaucratic as well as mechanical skills. The other, Hara-san, was limited to mechanics. Figure 8.1 shows their rank, just below the Yamura brothers, who are the president and the manager. "The way we [the mechanics] do things" was seen as a smooth transmission of skills between generations of journeymen and *minarai.*

Closer observation of learning, however, suggested that stress and tension are important aspects of the transmission process. *Minarai* actively acquired their skills. In the process of doing their assigned tasks, teams not only confirmed tradition but also had to invent it.

Teams

Journeymen belonged to multiple teams (*han*). The number of learner–mentor relationships were fewer than the appointed teams on the official organization chart. Many appointed teams did not function. Figure 8.1 shows some of the active learner–mentor relationships that are described in this chapter. Part of the reason why some such teams did not function lies in the intricate social manipulations that multiple team membership requires of learners. That is, many workers had not developed the social skills necessary to alternate between leading and following. Such role switching is a difficult social skill.

Several journeymen switched hierarchical roles throughout the day as they joined in teamwork. The president was among the few who switched roles easily. By manipulating hierarchical language to transform social context (Bachnik 1992), for instance, the president switched from his customary boss register to a subordinate learner register. Technical skill and social flexibility, rather than formal roles and the norms of seniority, qualified mentors. The explicit educational system of the garage was based on formal appointment of teams as well as cultural norms that supported the conventions of the seniority system (*senpai–kōhai,* senior–junior). Skilled learners had to manage contradictions between these culturally understandable appearances and actual practice (cf. Bachnik 1992:226).

The president wanted to learn hydraulic repair from a journeyman whom he had recently hired. Sensitive to the incongruity between boss and learner roles, he manipulated both the physical and the linguistic symbols of hierarchy. In the yard one day, the president had been standing high on a large truck. Mumbling that he lacked the skill to unscrew a bolt, he invited the new journeyman to climb the truck engine so that he could show him how to do the job. He physically exchanged places with this chosen mentor who had been looking up at him from ground level. The rusted bolt that he was trying to remove had little to do with the skill he wanted to learn. By symbolically adjusting their relationship, however, he was reinforcing his temporary subordination.

Linguistic manipulations of terms of address illustrate the president's social skills. He slipped easily from a superior's language to the coaxing voice of an intimate boyhood friend or an adult stooping to speak to a child (Suzuki 1974). A switch from more formal terms of address was appropriate because the two were close in age and they were peers on community service committees. The president chose to call his mentor by a nickname, Yama-*chan.* The suffix, -*chan,* added respect to intimacy. By mixing the language of respect and intimacy, he drew attention away from his position as boss to his temporary subordinate position as *minarai.* He subtly closed a normative social distance. The journeyman did not follow the president in making this switch. Instead, he maintained a standard, respectful distance from his employer.

In working contexts, other much younger employees also addressed the new journeyman as "Yama-chan." Instead of calling him Yamanaka-san (a family name with a standard honorific suffix), they addressed him with a familiarity that asserted their position as peers. In many ways, they were not his peers. Yama-chan had only two years more seniority than the newest *minarai.* Younger and less experienced employees were his seniors. They were emphasizing their seniority at the garage and the journeyman's outsider status. They were not taking the position of a learner with him. Thus, depending on one's status, the same nickname had different implications.

Hara-san (see Figure 8.1), who also wanted to learn from Yama-chan, adopted a less forthright tactic than the president. He simply avoided any direct address. Many workers had not mastered role switching. They were unhappy with the stress that switching roles caused. Hara-san said that if he had to give orders to subordinates or if he were addressed with nonstandard intimacy, he would quit. In other areas, too, Hara-san was unable to switch roles. He performed technical tasks in the inspection garage, but he refused to lead. Hara-san and Tanaka-san felt that they should maintain a consistent social image and should be called by only a formal standard form of address. They did not feel that the image of self, expressed in terms of address, should shift with context.

While team membership was designated from above, team participation was an individual choice. Much of the hydraulic repair team's work was on garbage trucks. The youngest inspection-shed workers refused to join in. The work was too dirty, they said. In contrast to the older "grease beetle" image of auto mechanics, they were dandies. They sported crimped hair styles and wore white cotton gloves. The hydraulic drives that open the back hatches of garbage trucks often broke when they were filled with rotting garbage. Young mechanics refused to tolerate the stench or to expose themselves to garbage "germs." Although they were asked to join the hydraulic repair team, they chose to limit their work to routine inspections and only simpler repairs. They preferred quick, clean, and easy jobs on sporty consumer vehicles. Unlike older family men, they would not sacrifice personal image for livelihood or ambition.

Delicate manipulations of linguistic symbols were particularly important because workers genuinely believed in personal equality. They held to this popular belief in the face of obvious inequality.

Paternalistic practices

Teamwork was based on a Japanese cultural model of paternalistic management (*oyabun-kobun*). Seniors of work gangs derive status from loyal followers (Bennett and Ishino 1963). They lead alliances. The paternalistic bosses are called *oyabun*. *Oyabun* imagery is derived from child–parent relationships. *Oyabun* are figurative parents (*oya*). They are responsible for their followers as children (*ko*) (Nakano 1964:77). This is also reflected in the boss organization of Japanese gangs.

In these kinship metaphors, the suffix *bun* means a role that is similar to a bureaucratic office (Nakano 1964:147–154). This organization is characteristic of entrepreneurial families (*shōka dōzoku*). It joins what Westerners dichotomize as either family or bureaucracy.

Shop apprenticeships (*detchibōkō*) at the turn of the century used similar paternalistic forms. In traditional shop apprenticeships, apprentices were treated like family members. They were, however, expected to pay back their mentors with free service for a year following their apprenticeships (cf. Singleton 1989a). Contemporary garage apprentices are paid and contractually employed. They are never expected to pay for their education. Nevertheless, daily garage practices followed the shop apprenticeship tradition of learning relationships based on reciprocity.

The traditional name for this system, *oya-kobun,* was uniformly rejected by garage workers. They preferred to say that their social organization was based on senior–junior relations (*senpai–kōhai*) – that is, seniority. Simple seniority was complicated by the higher priority given to actual kinship ties. Workers also showed respect for skill, age, belief in personal equality, and, in a few situations, differences in certification. To the contemporary Japanese sensibility, traditional images of shop apprenticeships and boss gang organization are antidemocratic and feudal.

Oda-san was, nevertheless, widely recognized as *oyabun.* It was whispered to me that Oda-san's father, a construction worker, had been an *oyabun,* too. Pride in his job experience, valuing in-group identity, and his control of teamwork all supported Oda-san's paternalism. His avowed role model, the president, also emphasized explicitly the seniority system and the ethos of paternalism.

Workers used the rhetoric of paternalism to critique their employee benefits. Although the garage did not operate as a contemporary Japanese family, many workers espoused a paternalistic management model when discussing the duties of an employer. Workers implied that the president should take care of their personal needs, as well as their workplace life (cf. Smith 1988). Their stories about the president emphasized his duty to care for his employee "family." He visited them when they were sick and acted as a marriage go-between. They resented his lack of financial support during emergencies.

In turn, the president complained about the heavy obligations that his workers placed on him. He argued that paternalism consisted of symbolic gestures rather than substance. Anyway, he played the role, he added. The company trip and the company banquet were his gifts. By continuing such "big man" rhetoric, he implicitly acknowledged the legitimacy of worker demands for paternalistic responsibility.

A teamwork model

How does paternalism affect the transmission of working knowledge? Teamwork is an idealized and observable model of cooperative learning. Oda-san and Sato's teamwork comes close to the idealized model. As mentor and learner, they shared both work and leisure activities. They were known as the twins. They hung onto one another in the manner of Japanese schoolboys. They chose to work in a relatively small garage rather than a large dealership (where most of their vocational school classmates were employed) because they hoped for greater working independence. In club and classroom organization, their *alma mater* vocational school had emphasized the ethos and rituals of paternalism.

More typical workers were not trained in vocational school, they lacked financial resources, and their parents were less involved in artisanal occupations. Apprentices generally attempted to control their learning situations through resistance. They were less involved in alliances. Their cases illustrate some of the limits to the completely cooperative teamwork model of Oda-san and Sato. Nevertheless, learners participated in teams despite their discomfort.

Oda-san had a reputation for efficiency. He bragged that he was the fastest inspection worker because, to save time repairing them, he avoided mistakes. The rhythm of teamwork supported his explanation. It was also the most convincing explanation for his reputation as the most efficient inspection garage mechanic.

Oda-san grinned in agreement when I described his teamwork routines as his *kata*. If I had not used this elegant word, Oda-san would probably not have used it. The related, more pedestrian, term that Oda-san had volunteered earlier when he described his work was *dandori* (stages of work). Others talked about *tejun* (order of hand movement). All of these terms objectified a personal embodiment of working practice.

Kata is a technical term that refers to the embodiment of form and practice in the Japanese arts (Ikuda 1987). It is a distillation of fundamental skills and concepts that are also integral to the everyday practice of an art. These practice forms introduce novices to an art. Because they are aesthetically valid, they continue to inspire mature practitioners. In contrast to *kata*, novice learners of Western music practice scales and arpeggios. But mechanically simplified forms lack the artistic substance of a musical performance. *Kata* embodies the essence of an artistic style. It is associated with a founder and a lineage of followers. Legitimated by such lineages, *iemoto* schools and individual teachers identify with their distinctive *kata* (Nishiyama 1982; R. Smith, Chapter 1, this volume).

Oda-san's *dandori* expressed the rhythm of teamwork. His team members worked as if their actions were choreographed. Many stages of their dance were repeated as they used a tool on one side of a vehicle and then on the other. Then they replaced the tool in their storage carts. They selected the next tool and repeated the pattern on the other side. Finally, they returned the tool to its original storage position. Each procedure had its ritualized pattern. While Oda-san worked on the two front wheels, his *kobun* carried out the same *dandori* in back. Because Oda-san finished the two front wheels before Sato's four, he had time to fill out an inspection form and to watch Sato working. This timing organized the work process. It resulted in quality control and a guide to cooperation.

Waiting and observing were leisurely activities. There were no workbenches in the shop. Instead, mechanics squatted or kneeled on the ground where others could easily see their work. They were accustomed to working under an observing gaze. On the truck inspection team, breaks in movement were as much a part of the work rhythm as rests in a musical phrase. Careful observation of the work process was not a conscious effort.

The unintended result of attentive waiting may have been learning, cooperation, or supervision, but participants understood waiting as timing. During this quiet interaction, conversations were unusual. If there was consultation, it occurred after a team had completed its *dandori.* Until then, a teammate observer must continue to participate in the work process. He can smoke or fill in inspection forms, but one eye is always on the continuing movements of his partner.

While seniors worked, juniors never left the work site, even for a smoke. Their attention focused on the work rhythm. Juniors were often in the observer role. Instead of emphasizing the specialized role of each participant as I have observed in individualistic work patterns in an American machine shop (Madono, in progress), teammates followed a rhythm set by the *oyabun.* Staying together within each *dandori* maintained the rhythm of teamwork.

Struggles

In contrast to an abstract rule, its conceptual counterpart, a *kata* can be the source of quiet tension between learner and mentor. This tension was evident in the behavior of some juniors who resisted Oda-san's leadership. They avoided sharing regular teamwork and leisure. Nonetheless, they too said that Oda-san showed them how to do their work. With no vocational schooling, they had learned auto mechanics on the job. This section describes learning among these resistant young *minarai.*

Minarai reach journeymen status when in one context they are team leaders, even when in another context they are subordinate team *minarai.* Few switched roles with ease. Tanaka-san and Oda-san, for instance, had refused to join the hydraulic repair team. Many learners, however, struggled to attain skills that were withheld or that "belonged" to unattractive mentors. In these relationships, a *kata* was not passively accepted; rather, it was actively sought – or rejected.

Kimura had entered the garage through his father's friendship with the president. Most garage employees had been personally introduced. During his first year of high school, he had been expelled for his participation in a motorcycle gang. Shamed, Kimura's father begged the president to hire his delinquent son. Seven years later when he talked to me, still contemptuous of bureaucratic regimentation and fiercely loyal to his gang, Kimura emphasized his debt to his father and the president. He included these parent figures in his world of *oyabun–kobun* relationships.

In separate interviews, the president's sister and mother explained that delinquent boys make good workers (cf. Wagatsuma and De Vos 1984: 37–39). Gang leaders are also called *oyabun.* Apart from the technical value of auto mechanics to a motorcycle gang, the similarity between gang and garage organization is a factor in integrating delinquents. Relative to Kimura's gang membership, his job status was low (see Figure 8.1); he had only seven years of seniority, and the year before, his first and only *kobun* had quit. In direct address, the honorific suffix *-san* would not be added to his name until he had a regular *kobun.* Nevertheless, because paternalism was so important to him, Kimura was becoming a loyal worker in spite of himself. On the day after a drunken night with his gang, Kimura spoke to me through a hangover. He made the foregoing confessions while he was hiding behind a vehicle, pretending to work on a wheel.

One of his silent protests concerned commonplace disruptions by seniors. While seniors were observing, often out of boredom rather than with didactic intent, they would grab tools from their juniors. These seniors could freely force a junior into the observer role and continue their subordinate's work. Equally abruptly, they might return the tools to their junior's hands. These privileges of seniority irritated Kimura. On better days, he became engrossed in his job and resented any interruptions.

In one instance, the president had usurped Kimura's work. Over the intercom, the president was called to the telephone. He dropped Kimura's hand tool and left. I asked Kimura how he felt. He sneered, "Yeah, at first when he did that, it upset me. I was serious then. Now, I don't care. If he wants to wreck his own work, it's his responsibility."

Until the previous year, Kimura had refused requests for collective overtime work. This resistance conflicted with his need to belong. During the busy holiday season, he began shifting his loyalty; he was working seven days a week and fifteen hours per day.

Many years ago, to test *minarai* before they were permanently obligated to them, employers hired them for two probationary years. Under those conditions, hiring "bad boys" was a safe decision. The president explained that currently employers have less opportunity to try and test *minarai*; there is only a three-month probationary period. A lack of prospective *minarai* among a generation that has received more child-centered education is a problem for him. Entering *minarai,* today, often quit before they can be profitable for their employer.

Hara-san belonged to the middle cohort of workers. He recalled his early years of apprenticeship with pride. Soon after he graduated from junior high school, his teacher visited the garage to warn the management that their job applicant had been a "bad boy" at school. Fortunately, the president ignored the teacher's warning. Resentful of Hara-san's teacher, the president's mother recalled that the boy once begged a customer to allow him to rebuild his automobile engine, after working hours. Hara-san had to struggle for access to learning opportunities. "Today," she boasted, "he's our treasure."

These frustrations made Hara-san feel that the skills that he was learning were all the more valuable. Because he was functionally illiterate, he could not study for certification exams. He even lacked a driver's license. Luckily, he had improvised other approaches to learning. During the probationary employment period, he had been allowed to perform only menial labor, such as washing cars or tools. While he endured these long stints of hard labor, he observed his seniors at work. Deprived of the opportunity to participate in more valued work, his desire to learn grew.

Difficulties continued after this testing period. In contrast to the limited technical difficulties that contemporary inspection routines require of *minarai,* then novice Hara-san was thrown directly into complex repair. In 1972, when parts were scarce, a mechanic's job focused on repair.

Unlike younger vehicle inspectors, he did not spend fourteen years doing routine inspections. As a novice, he was doing the work of the most experienced contemporary journeymen.

Without lectures or textbooks, Hara-san had many questions. "You have to badger them for good answers. Ask them until they are tired of you." Implying that his inspection juniors were more passive, he commented, "people who don't ask questions don't learn anything." Nondidactic seniors, however, avoided explicit questions. Some seniors might have viewed his aggressive learning tactics as antisocial. Yet Hara-san's habit of persistent questioning about immediate experiences was an effective learning technique.

Nondidactic mentors

Oda-san helped me to understand his nondidactic method of "showing how." His instructions to novice *minarai* contrasted sharply with his explanations to me. To an outsider, he lectured on his work in the didactic manner of "head learners." He was eager to illustrate the patterns of his routines and to convince me of their rational value. Instead of similarly instructing juniors, he told them only enough for them to begin working.

When the manager entered the inspection shed with orders to fill, he would first consult with Oda-san about the progress of each inspection job. Oda-san was responsible for predicting *minarai* work efficiency. Actually, because of his seniority, Hara-san had been formally assigned to lead the inspection garage, but he refused. Instead, Oda-san informally replaced Hara-san as the supervisor of the inspection garage. Because Tanaka-san and Hara-san did not work closely enough with inspection juniors, Oda-san had been asked informally to help make job assignments.

To predict the amount of time required to finish a job, Oda-san anticipated mistakes. Because novices make more mistakes, he explained that prediction is more difficult. For example, novices frequently forget that the two sides of engines are designed as mirror images. Rather than warning them, Oda-san waited until novices committed such common mistakes. Then without a word, he took over the job, leaving the novice to observe his work process.

By showing, rather than by talking, he avoided novice resentment. Workers remembered seniors who had been forced to quit because they had used excessive commands to "instruct" juniors. Oda-san said that he had learned to stay out of personal conflicts. He watched from the sidelines. His personally elaborated work routines were one means to avoid conflict. Shared belief in personal *kata* helps to organize kinesthetically and socially complex activity. Such "body learning" (Harper 1987: 117–121; Plath, Epilogue, this volume) is not necessarily individualized.

The paternalistic ethos of the seniority system contributed to the legitimacy of Oda-san's *kata*. Direct enforcement would have undermined his sense of informal leadership. Without paternalistic loyalties, he could not have transmitted the *kata*. Novices imitated the movements of nondidactic seniors. Their work processes became similarly patterned. When work activities were highly predictable, embodying a senior's *kata* avoided conflict resulting from direct supervision. Seniors who were critical of a junior's work refrained from verbal criticism; instead, they usurped their work. Although juniors resented this practice, seniors interpreted their interference as "getting the job done."

Because of such conflicts, even apparently harmonious *oya-kobun* relationships may have been transient. Journeymen were less powerful than they appeared in their face-to-face behavior. Juniors repeated innuendoes explaining why a senior had quit. Drawing from such stories and complaints, there were three journeymen behaviors that juniors resented: refusal to share skills, oral criticism, and giving explicit orders (see Table 8.1, in the conclusion to this chapter). Learners were not explicitly so privileged, yet they exerted a formative degree of control over their mentors.

Regulatory craft

Among inspectors, Tanaka-san was best prepared for a career in regulation. Although he had avoided teamwork with his juniors, he was the supervisor's loyal *kobun*. The supervisor had a reputation for both craft and regulatory skills. Tanaka-san's interests were more narrow. He was concentrating on mastering regulatory rather than mechanical knowledge.

The supervisor was tired of working at the garage. Because he was obligated to the president, however, he could not quit without a successor to his responsibilities. Before trying a second career, he was passing on the lore of regulatory customer service to Tanaka-san.

In preparation for further certification, Tanaka-san attended night school lectures on the regulations governing testing of finished inspections. He showed me his two-inch-thick reference book for vehicle testers.

The examination was more difficult than those he had already passed. Whereas examinations intimidated less-schooled mechanics, schooling sharpened Tanaka-san's testing acuity. Yet the knowledge that he learned through schooling and examinations was not the substance of his regulatory craft. Regulatory specialists also learned their craft in practice. Even regulatory craft cannot be learned in the abstract.

In contrast to Oda-san's embodied mechanical craft choreography, regulators had to learn both the regulations and an oral lore. This lore is embedded in practice. It is inside knowledge that is partially observed in practice. Examinations required Tanaka-san to know the law in theory. Lore is situated in reciprocal-exchange relationships, not only in teamwork but also in a wider reciprocity network. Such lore included Tanaka-san's introduction to the significant names and faces of garage customers and outside supporters. Like mechanics, regulatory specialists learned their lore while working in teams. The supervisor recited the lore of regulation evasion, for instance, when he and Tanaka-san delivered vehicles to a customer and as they encountered appropriate applications of that lore. While the supervisor introduced him to customers, Tanaka-san associated faces with embedded oral histories. Their names were entwined in complex networks of obligations, reputations, rate negotiations, and past conflicts. Tanaka-san was a *minarai* in the oral lore of customer service.

Much like the idiosyncratic nature of repair, this lore could not be standardized; although it could have been recorded and filed, it was not. Those who had interacted with customers privately possessed that valuable knowledge. If learner–mentor relationships were viable, mentors passed on their personal knowledge.

Reciprocity in craft learning

Craft learning is nurtured through reciprocity. Reciprocity relations depend on continual exchange. To control their situations, loyal learners became increasingly involved in exchange relationships. By giving and receiving, they set the stage for increased interdependence. Because *kobun* learners were in a subordinate position, they were necessarily dependent on their *oyabun* mentors.

Such paternalistic dependency relationships are not bureaucratically mandated. Within the relations of dependency, resistant learners still became aggressive agents of their personal learning agendas. Kimura resented the interference of his seniors; Hara-san badgered them with questions; and Tanaka-san concentrated on mastering regulatory skills. Otherwise, through teamwork, reciprocal obligations increased interactions between mentors and novices. Informal reciprocity could also ease role-switching stress.

Mutual dependence in craft education contrasts in other ways with the autonomy of a student studying for a regulatory exam. Many aspects of auto inspection are normally learned independently or through individualistic classroom study. Among inspection workers, lectures, manuals, and free telephone advice from parts suppliers were common resources for independent learning. In addition to learner agency and free access to knowledge, however, teamwork provided a cooperative structure for learning. Further comparison of the two inspection seniors will help us to understand the importance of reciprocity in structuring craft learning relationships.

No one recognized Tanaka-san as "one who shows you how to work." He had no interest in attracting loyal *kobun,* and he did not act as an *oyabun.* He was, instead, a didactic teacher. This academically apt senior would teach the principles necessary to do a task. Then he left juniors to discover their own working procedures. Juniors felt that his explanations were complete and useful. He promoted their independence. Eschewing paternalism, he avoided strings of obligation. He was indifferent to sharing *oya-kobun* reciprocity with them. Juniors enjoyed freedom when they worked with him. Their preference for free didactic instruction dampens optimism that craft learning is either pleasant or efficient.

These tensions were also evident in comments made by Oda-san. He recognized that he educated future competitors by showing his work to his juniors. From the learner's perspective, sources of conflict and stress in cooperative learning were also evident. In reference to Sato's complete deference to Oda-san, an older artisan empathized, "he bows his head, but under his breath he's cursing."

To learn a craft, reciprocal relationships offer an advantage over didactic instruction. The educational limitations of Tanaka-san's didactic teaching style were illustrated by a comparison with Oda-san's tool cart.

Because novices generally lacked funds to buy their personal tools, they borrowed hand tools from their seniors. When Tanaka-san's tools began to disappear, he suspected theft. Instead of using a personal *dandori* that would organize his tool cart, he left them tangled in a pile. Because he did not incorporate his tool cart organization into his work process, he had difficulty accounting for missing tools. After he noticed that a few tools were missing, he moved his cart into a vehicle testing shed with his supervisor. There, juniors did not dare to help themselves or, he suspected, take them home.

In contrast to Tanaka-san, Oda-san's preoccupation with his possessions never waned. His *dandori* included tool replacement in a prescribed position on his tool cart. His cart was equipped with special drawers, boxes, hooks, and shelves where he meticulously arranged each tool. Since missing tools were obvious, borrowers had to return them. Furthermore, he doggedly demanded their return. Such tool borrowing added to cycles of exchange.

Oda-san and the president claimed that they gave more than they received (Sudō 1984:216; also cf. Strathern 1971:168–169). Their reputations for generosity depended on their ability to convince their *kobun* that they gave more. To indirectly portray generosity in work relationships, Oda-san continually elaborated on the details of his *kata*. The "unbalanced reciprocity" (Lebra 1969) created by a mentor who must always give cannot continue without returns from learners. Prompt return gifts were a social imperative. Thus *kobun* fulfilled Oda-san's demands for minor personal services during their shared leisure. Their efforts then led to further giving by the mentor.

The reputation as the "one who gives more," or in this case "the one who shows more," is not only created by boastfully declaring a *kobun*'s debt. The reputation of a generous leader is created by *kobun*. Eager learners placed mentors in the center of activities that allowed mentors to perform a "big man" role. In the earlier example of this chapter, the president placed his journeyman-mentor, Yama-chan, in the social center when he framed him as an intimate friend and coaxed him to take a higher position.

In more typical situations, even when subordinates had superior skills, rather than monopolizing more highly valued repair work, juniors assumed the inferior position and handed tools to seniors. Juniors took the most valued roles only when their tasks were bureaucratically designated as their individual responsibility and seniors joined them to "help."

Loyal *kobun* minimized their role as givers and emphasized their role as receivers. They offered deference to maintain their self-constructed subordination. If *kobun* refused to work intimately with an *oyabun*, the *oyabun* would lose reputation. This was the predicament of Tanaka-san and Hara-san. They were appointed to be leaders, but eschewing paternalistic reciprocity, they failed to lead.

Had regulatory knowledge dominated learning, it could have influenced the transmission of craft negatively. Craft could have become boring to mechanics who devalued "body learning," intuitive experience, a personalized exchange community, and *kata*. The mechanic's efforts could then be seen as commodified labor.

For Tanaka-san, who had a reputation for ability in what craftsmen called "head learning" (*atama de oboeru*), indeed, mechanics had become boring. After fourteen years of routine vehicle inspections, Tanaka-san felt that he had learned all that he theoretically needed to know about auto mechanics. He said that compared to scientific knowledge his craft work was inferior. Furthermore, the technology of automobiles would soon be outmoded. His work no longer interested him. Only when his tinkering succeeded did auto mechanics become a kinesthetic pleasure. But those moments were rare. He spent his free time recuperating from physical labor. Work tired him so much that he did not enjoy exchanging his mechanical skills with friends or "souping up" his car.

Because of this lack of interest in teamwork and shared leisure, he had little to share with younger co-workers. His generosity expressed in giving free knowledge did not lead to the paternalistic relationships in cycles of giving and receiving. Juniors did not even interpret his free help as generosity. To them, Tanaka-san was just a nice guy.

Total dominance of Tanaka-san's regulatory perspective could have undermined craft learning. Withdrawal of Tanaka-san's cart represented only a minor breakdown in junior–senior reciprocity. Nonetheless, it is symptomatic of the potential separation of craft and regulatory learning practices. Craft and regulation are interdependent in the garage.

Conclusions

This chapter draws attention to the transmission of skills through personal relationships. Table 8.1 contrasts the attributes of craft and regulatory learners. In the context of the garage, I have chosen "body learning" as the central metaphor for craft learning. The "head–body" distinction is also preserved in personal alliances.

When asked about their apprenticeships, workers typically described regulatory learning experiences. Therefore, I took pains to gather evidence for the characteristics of craft learning (the right column of Table 8.1) through participant observation. With the exception of the category "Mentor behavior violations," observed body learning was confined to specific garage practices that were rarely explicitly stated. In contrast, I have not observed head learning attributes. Because head learning

Table 8.1. *Regulatory and craft learning compared*

	Bureaucratic regulation	Artisanal craft
Central metaphor	"Head learning" (*atama de oboeru*)	"Body learning" (*karada de oboeru*)
Forms of knowledge	Text & curriculum, standardized vocabulary Public knowledge Vocabulary of abstract principle	*Kata* Private knowledge Experience
Transmission	Didactic lecture Individualized study	Model the first step; participation in production Team interaction
Learning strategies	Memorization; answer explicit questions Passive	Observation, experimental Aggressive
Sources of legitimacy	Certification Judicial or scientific authority	Superior performance *Oya-kobun* loyalty
Mentor behavior violations	Favoritism, bribery	Direct supervision, skill hoarding, verbal criticism

is institutionally legitimized, informants agreed on broader, commonly shared social experiences and observations.

The hierarchy expressed in *oya-kobun* alliances undermines democratic and bureaucratic sentiment. At the same time, *kata* shifts the focus of this contradiction between equality and hierarchy from difficult interpersonal relationships to ritually shared activity. If there is personal conflict, team members could relate through leisure reciprocity. An overwhelming concern with reputation joins learning and leadership.

Bureaucratic policy not only regulated the enterprise, it also mandated services, such as vehicle inspection, and thereby supported economically all of the services that the garage offered. Embodied, on-the-job craft is far more difficult to regulate. Other than in the reputation of an *oyabun* or in the loyalty of a *kobun, kata* lacks an outside source of legitimacy. Only participants recognized it. This problem is evident in the number of appointed teams where cooperation was not observed. Although team membership is appointed, learners ultimately choose whether they will participate.

The artisan's ritual view of work organizes more than technical efficacy. Oda-san's *kata* marked his work as distinct. He possessed his *kata* and expected *kobun* to mimic it. When Sato followed Oda-san's *kata,* he momentarily reified his work process.

Such affirmations were only one moment in a myriad of exchanges. "Body learning" refers to the embodiment of cultural knowledge. A personal and a group sense of *kata* are momentarily objectified in ritual practice. In this sense, craft is embodied. But this objectification is the subject of daily negotiations. Craft expertise is contested in minor but pervasive ways.

The regulatory knowledge that workers learn through preparing for examinations is unrelated to this life world. Unlike the academic and legal systems that support head learning (i.e., regulatory bureaucracy), *oya-kobun* paternalism requires what regulatory bureaucracy might label as "bribery" or "favoritism." Nevertheless, the two systems are not easily separated (Befu 1990). The apparent dichotomy of "head" and "body" learning fails to encompass the practical interdependence of the two ways of learning. Only in the practical application of regulatory knowledge do craft and regulation become mutually dependent knowledge forms.

References

Bachnik, Jane, 1992, "Kejime: Defining a shifting self," in Nancy R. Rosenberger, ed., *Japanese Sense of Self,* Cambridge: Cambridge University Press.

Befu, Harumi, 1990, "Conflict and Non-Weberian Bureaucracy in Japan," in S. N. Eisenstadt and Eyal Ben-Ari, eds., *Japanese Models of Conflict Resolution,* London: Kegan Paul International.

Bennett, J. W., and I. Ishino, 1963, *Paternalism in the Japanese Economy,* Westport, CT: Greenwood Press.

Harper, Douglas, 1987, *Working Knowledge,* Chicago: University of Chicago Press.

Ikuda, Kumiko, 1987, *Waza Kara Shiru* [Learning the "Knack"], Tokyo: Tokyo Daigaku Shuppan.

Lebra, Takie S., 1969, "Reciprocity and the Asymmetric Principle," *Psychologia,* 12: 129–138.

Madono, Ellen, (in progress), *"Learned it by Myself:" Solitude, Community and Craft in a Machine Shop,* Ph.D. dissertation, School of Education, University of Pittsburgh.

Nakano, Takashi,1964, *Shōka Dōzoku no Kenkyū* [Research on the merchant *dōzoku*], Tokyo: Miraisha.

Nishiyama, Matsunotsuke, 1982, *Iemoto no Tenkai* [Social Change in the *iemoto* System], Tokyo: Yoshikawa Kōbunkan.

Singleton, John, 1989a, "Japanese Folkcraft Pottery Apprenticeship: Cultural Assumptions in Educational Practice," in Michael Coy, ed., *Apprenticeship: From Theory to Method and Back Again,* Albany: State University of New York Press, pp. 13–30.

Smith, Thomas, 1988, "The Right to Benevolence: Dignity and Japanese Workers, 1750–1920," in *Native Sources of Japanese Industrialization, 1875–1920,* Berkeley: University of California Press.

Strathern, Andrew, 1971, *Big Men and Ceremonial Exchange in Mount Hagen,* Cambridge: Cambridge University Press.

Sudō, Kenichi, 1984, "Jyōhō to Chiiki no Zōyo – Kōkanron – Daikushūdan no Zōtō no Bunseki" [Information and local gifts – exchange theory – analysis of the gift exchange (in the apprenticeships of) carpenter guilds], in Kurita Yasuyuki and Itō Mikiharu, eds., *Nihonjin no Zōtō,* Tokyo: Mineruva Shōbō.

Suzuki, Takaō, 1974, "Language and Behavior in Japan: The Conceptualization of Personal Relations," in Takie S. Lebra and William P. Lebra, eds., *Japanese Culture and Behavior,* Honolulu: University of Hawaii Press.

Wagatsuma, Hirōshi, and George A. De Vos, 1984, *Heritage of Endurance,* Berkeley: University of California Press.

9 Developing character in music teachers: A Suzuki approach

Sarah Hersh and Lois Peak

Talent Education, or the Suzuki Method as it is commonly known, is a Japanese method of music instruction that has attracted the attention of musicians and parents throughout the world. The method is particularly famous for the high levels of performance achieved by large numbers of young children. Suzuki students as young as five or ten years old perform spirited renditions of concert works that were previously considered the province of occasional prodigies. The approach has had a revolutionary effect on techniques of music instruction for young children.

Although Talent Education is best known publicly for its effectiveness in teaching children to play musical instruments, Suzuki himself sees character development as the primary goal of his teaching activities. More than the ability to play the violin or piano, Suzuki espouses nurturing the *kokoro,* or heart, as the primary purpose of Talent Education. He believes that development of the *kokoro* is accomplished through cultivation of every human's natural *sainō,* or ability.

Suzuki opens *Nurtured by Love,* his classic statement of the Talent Education philosophy, with the question:

> What is man's ultimate direction in life? It is to look for love, truth, virtue, and beauty. That goes for you, for me, for everyone. (Suzuki 1969:8)

Throughout Suzuki's sixty years of teaching children and young people according to his Talent Education method, he has always put education in love, truth, and beauty first. His efforts and those of his students have brought about a worldwide movement that attempts to replicate Suzuki's vision of happiness for the world's children.

> I feel respect and friendly feelings for everyone. In particular I cannot help but feel respect and warm friendship for small children. And my heart brims over with a desire to help make all the children born upon this earth fine human beings, happy people, people of superior ability. My whole life and energies are devoted to this end. (Suzuki 1969:119)

Figure 9.1. As a teacher, Shinichi Suzuki is 100 percent engaged and 100 percent engaging. In this photo, taken in 1976, Suzuki is a guest teacher at a summer institute held in Wisconsin. (Photo: Arthur Montzka)

In this chapter, we examine the means by which Suzuki strives to develop character and ability in his students. Some of Suzuki's methods of character development are traditionally Japanese, while other of his methods reveal strong foreign influences. His goals are the highest ideals of Western humanism, with overtones of Buddhist philosophy. The interpersonal means are primarily Japanese, yet instruction for foreigners is typically conducted in English. The medium is Western violin repertoire and instruction in fine points of musical technique.

To understand better Suzuki's approach to character development, it is necessary to understand how Suzuki perceives his own character to have been shaped through his life experiences, and how this in turn has shaped the teaching method he conceived.

Development of Suzuki's own character

Shinichi Suzuki was born in 1898, the third son of an important samurai family in the Nagoya region. Ten years before Suzuki's birth, his father had converted the family's *samisen* factory into a violin factory, becoming one of the earliest Japanese manufacturers of this newly introduced instrument. Over the next decade, the factory evolved into the largest producer of violins in the world. Much of Suzuki's childhood was spent in the violin factory, playing with the instruments as toys.

Suzuki's father was a member of Japan's National Assembly, an early and avid student of Western culture, and one of the pioneer Japanese visitors to the West. In addition to a life filled with music and violins, Suzuki inherited from his father excellent social connections and a strong interest in things foreign.

As an adolescent, Suzuki prepared for an increasing role in the business by studying at a commercial college. There he held various leadership positions and came to recognize the importance of fine character and high principles. At about this time, Suzuki became enthralled by the beauty of a gramophone recording of Schubert's "Ave Maria." He brought home a violin from the factory and tried to imitate the recording. Day after day of self-taught attempts finally produced a rudimentary ability to play the violin.

Even as an adolescent, Suzuki was an intensely philosophical, artistic, and spiritually oriented young man. He read and reread Tolstoy's *Diary*, carrying it wherever he went. Suzuki determined to live a moral and virtuous life according to the highest principles of humanitarian ideals. He also studied Zen Buddhism seriously, developing a deep understanding of spiritual philosophy and meditative practice. Through studies with the renowned Zen master Fuzan Asano, he developed signs of accomplishment that are evident even seventy years later, including the need for very little sleep and virtually imperturbable equanimity and compassion.

When Suzuki was twenty-one years old, he was invited to live as a family member in the Tokyo mansion of the Marquis Tokugawa so that he could study the violin and Western musical theory with the best teachers in Japan. It was undoubtedly within this environment that Suzuki developed his flawless and gracious dignity and ease among society's elite. Beginning in October 1920, Suzuki accompanied the Marquis on a world tour but left the Marquis' party in Berlin. There he searched for an artist to whom he could devote himself as a student. One evening, during a performance of the Mozart Clarinet Quintet in A Major, K. 581, by the Klingler Quartet, he had an artistic and spiritual experience that had a profound effect on his life.

> That evening I seemed to be gradually drawn into Mozart's spirit, and finally I was not conscious of anything else, not even of my own being, I became so immersed. . . . An indescribable, sublime ecstatic joy had taken hold of my soul. . . . Through sound, for the first time in my life, I had been able to feel the highest pulsating beauty of the human spirit, and my blood burned within me. It was a moment of sublime eternity when I, a human being, had gone beyond the limits of this physical body. . . . Mozart, the man, had shown me immortal light. . . .
>
> When I listen to Mozart, he seems to envelop me in his great love. . . . It was Mozart who taught me to know perfect love, truth, goodness, and beauty. And I now deeply feel as if I were under the direct orders of Mozart, and he left me a legacy; in his place I am to further the happiness of all children. (Suzuki, quoted in Hermann 1981:21–22)

Although Klingler did not accept private students, he agreed to accept Suzuki. As Klinger's only protégé, Suzuki became an active participant in the musical and social life of prewar Berlin. From Klingler, he learned to appreciate the fine points of musicianship and violin technique. Through his musical circle of friends, Suzuki came to know and be influenced by many people of fine character and artistry, including Albert Einstein.

In 1928, Suzuki returned with a German bride to his family's home in Nagoya. There he began to concertize and to teach young children. By the eve of World War II, his young students had won national acclaim. The war years brought great hardship and a temporary halt to musical activities.

In 1945, Suzuki formalized his philosophy and approach to teaching under the new name of Sainō Kyōiku, or "Talent Education." From a modest new beginning with five students and one violin, the movement grew rapidly, and by 1951 Suzuki had a following of students and training teachers too large for his house. During the 1950s, the method continued to grow throughout Japan.

In 1964, Suzuki and ten young students made a tour of the United States. American music educators and parents responded to the children's performances with amazement and enthusiasm, and the reputation of the Talent Education method began to spread around the world. Today, 300,000 children in forty-one countries are taking "Suzuki" lessons. Suzuki has been awarded nine honorary doctorate degrees and was nominated for the 1994 Nobel Peace Prize. Into his ninety-sixth year, Suzuki-*sensei* (the Japanese honorific term for "teacher") still worked each day with future teachers and was the widely revered head of a large international organization, respected by and positively influencing all who come in contact with him. Now retired from teaching, he still graciously welcomes and advises former students.

Goals for character development in the Suzuki method

Suzuki has two primary goals for character development, *kokoro* (heart) and *sainō* (ability). Suzuki usually describes a fine *kokoro* as the result of the full development of the *sainō*. Yet the relationship is not unidirectional. *Kokoro* and *sainō* are explicit goals in the sense that they are ubiquitous in Suzuki's writing, admonitions to students, and the example of his own daily life. However, he does not precisely define what he means by these terms. Each student must forge the meaning through countless stories, personal observations, and gradually approximated guesses.

Kokoro seems to include love, integrity, humility, honesty, service, respect, purity of mind, and optimism in the face of suffering.

> That we are born and that we finally die is the work of Mother Nature. It is not the responsibility of each one of us. Each human being has only the responsibility for living. That is my view of life. And I pray that my life may be lived in the midst of love and joy. . . . Love can only be had by loving. Our life is worth living only if we love one another and comfort one another. (Suzuki 1969:93–94)

Suzuki has authored many poetic aphorisms, which he has written as fine calligraphy, to be distributed to students and families studying the Suzuki method. His own favorite, which he calls his "motto," is *Oto ni inochi ari, sugata naku ikite.* This reflects what Suzuki believes to be the central relationship between character and its expression in an individual's life or musical activity. Although the many nuances of the phrase elude a single translation, it could be rendered variously as "tone has a living soul without form" or "sound breathes life – without form it lives" (Selden's translation 1980:49). In practice, Suzuki uses this phrase to remind students that the quality of their *kokoro* or soul is revealed by every sound of their instrument or action in their life. Therefore, through the process of striving to perfect their tone or activity, they perfect their soul.

> The very way one greets people and expresses oneself is art. If a musician wants to become a fine artist, he must first become a finer person. If he does this, his worth will appear. It will appear in everything he does, even in what he writes. Art is not in some far-off place. A work of art is the expression of a man's whole personality, sensibility, and ability. (Suzuki 1969:94)

Even when speaking informally in his studio – for example, to Australian teachers visiting in 1974 – Suzuki is eloquent on the relationship between art and character:

> I was determined to know what art is. And, at least, I came to understand that art is not at a distance from life – something very high or very far away. No, art is studying how to

bring my own feeling to a higher level. And my heart, having a nice heart. And how correct each of my everyday actions is. I studied how to improve myself. And, now, this is at the heart of the Talent Education movement for children. (in Hersh 1995:58)

Suzuki's motto is a statement of his own philosophy, yet it is similar in some respect to thoughts expressed by European musicians of Suzuki's age. English violist Lionel Tertis, born just two years before Suzuki, echoes Suzuki's belief that a musician who wants to become a fine artist must first become a finer person. In his advice to musicians, he writes:

Do not forget that your playing will reflect yourself. Therefore, to make your power of expression worth listening to, it is necessary to mould your mind and action through life to all that is of the utmost sincerity. (Tertis 1938:22)

In Matsumoto, a scroll hangs prominently at the entrance to the Talent Education Institute. On the scroll Suzuki has written in his own fine calligraphy, "Tone has a soul which exists without form." Suzuki repeats the aphorism frequently to his students, and a replica of the scroll is presented as a diploma to graduates of the teacher development program.

Another of Suzuki's favorite aphorisms that adorns the wall of the institute is *Ai fukakereba, fusu koto ōshi* (Where love is deep, much can be accomplished). To Suzuki, the phrase means that the development of *kokoro* through the practice of loving kindness and compassion for others will certainly bring about happiness and accomplishments that are of great benefit for oneself and others. This aphorism has had international appeal, and its first phrase, "where love is deep," has been used as the title of a collection of Suzuki's articles.

The second of Suzuki's explicit goals for character development in the Talent Education method is *sainō*, or ability. Some have translated this as "talent," whence comes the official name for the method, Sainō Kyōiku, or "Talent Education." In fact, *sainō* includes the meanings of both "ability" and "talent," and Sainō Kyōiku is better translated as "Ability Development." Although English speakers prefer to divide behavior into that which is inherited (talent) and that which is developed (ability), Japanese usage is less specific about such origins. Instead, most Japanese believe that a wide variety of qualities such as intelligence, personality, and personal habits are determined primarily by experience and education rather than heredity (Stevenson and Stigler 1992:91–99).

Suzuki's entire life's work has been focused on demonstrating that *sainō* can be developed. By *sainō* he means self-discipline, perseverance, effective habits, and high mastery of particular skills. Not only can *sainō* be learned; through the learning process, character is developed. An individual has the responsibility to develop his own *sainō*, and the responsibility of parents is to develop their own *sainō* and that of their children.

> Shortcomings or weak points in children are usually blamed on "character" or "nature" and are left at that. But through training, the contrary – points of excellence – can be brought out in a ten-year program. If he or she really goes about it in earnest, anyone can cultivate ability [*sainō*] in ten years, I believe. Even in one year, shortcomings can be changed into good points if only we set our aims high enough. . . .
>
> There is no limit to our shortcomings. Until we die, we should spare no time or effort in changing our weaknesses to merits. To do so can be pleasant and interesting. We can become like the horse that starts last and yet outruns the field, reaching the wire first; it is the same fun. (Suzuki 1969:51)

Teaching children to play the violin well is Suzuki's chosen method of fostering *sainō*. The gradual maturity and improved personal habits that come from serious study of the violin develop the character. Suzuki believes that development of a fine ability to play the violin (*sainō*) both brings about and reflects a fine character (*kokoro*).

The processes of character development in the teacher development program

Explicit curriculum

The teacher development program is located at the Talent Education Institute in Matsumoto, Japan, the headquarters of Sainō Kyōiku Kenkyūkai (Talent Education Research Group) and the International Suzuki Association. At any given time, approximately forty young people roughly between the ages of eighteen and twenty-five participate in the program for *kenkyūsei* (apprentice teachers). Most *kenkyūsei* are violinists, and the preponderance are women. A small number of pianists, flautists, and cellists participate in the program. They take lessons and instrumental classes with leading Talent Education teachers and join the violinists for recitals and classroom work. Suzuki personally directs the *kenkyūsei* program and devotes most of his teaching time to his work with apprentice violin teachers. Since the 1970s, the very great opportunity of studying with Suzuki has been limited to training teachers and a handful of extremely outstanding students.

There are two routes of entrance to the *kenkyūsei* program. Young Japanese violinists usually enter immediately after high school, recommended by the teacher from whom they have studied since childhood.

Foreigners usually apply by corresponding with Suzuki and are of a wide variety of ages, although most who remain for at least a year are between the ages of eighteen and twenty-five. Suzuki accepts all students who ask to enter the program, and this sometimes temporarily swells the program to as many as sixty students. The minimum level of violin performance required of a potential *kenkyūsei* is completion of the ten volumes of violin repertoire published by Suzuki, which culminates in the Mozart Concerto No. 4, in D Major. However, few *kenkyūsei* would be considered outstanding performers, and many are easily outplayed by the best among the method's ten-year-old students.

The weekly schedule of the *kenkyūsei* program consists of one or two formal activities each day. Those led by Suzuki include a recital at which each *kenkyūsei* performs a solo, an individual lesson that is observed by the other *kenkyūsei,* and a group lesson for all *kenkyūsei.* Suzuki's remarks at these lessons focus on remediating problems in study skills, bowing technique, tone production, and musicianship among the *kenkyūsei* themselves. Other teachers lead a music literature class, a master class on artistic expression, a reading group to discuss Suzuki's many books, and a calligraphy class. Ikebana (flower-arranging art) is also sometimes offered.

Suzuki constantly holds up to *kenkyūsei* his models of musical excellence, particularly cellist Pablo Casals and violinist Fritz Kreisler. He speaks of them as great human beings with wonderful hearts, as well as musicians of the first order. Students are constantly reminded to listen to recordings of these artists, to study their tone, and to try to emulate them. Suzuki delights in repeating, "I am your coach; Kreisler is your real teacher."

Note a few of the ways in which Suzuki referred to artists at lessons. After two months of study, Suzuki-*sensei* and Hersh exchanged these comments at the end of a lesson:

Suzuki: You catch something these days. You are changing. Congratulations.
Hersh: Congratulations to you!
Suzuki: Please ask Kreisler more questions. I cannot help you; he can, OK? Please listen to Kreisler. I like Kreisler's tone. If you do, study with Kreisler, not Suzuki. I am his assistant. You've improved a lot! (Hersh 1995:92)

Three months later, *Sensei* had this to say about Hersh's progress:

Suzuki: OK. Very good! [Your playing was like] Kreisler's playing at, perhaps, age *four*! (Hersh 1995:134)

Suzuki: Now, please play [the theme from Corelli's *La Folia*] again, as music from the heart. [*Student plays.*] Very good. So *that* is a musical performance. It must be at least this high [a level] to be a musical performance. [You must] make the level higher and higher to reach Kreisler. (Hersh 1995:144)

Five months later, Suzuki encouraged Hersh to study the playing of Ginette Neveu, a French violinist (1919–1949). Suzuki gave Hersh the following advice regarding the Sibelius Violin Concerto:

Suzuki: Please change your teacher to Neveu. When you hear her, you'll acknowledge that she plays with fine tempo and musicality. She changes tone color and tone character. For although tone is tone, and all human beings are similar, humanity speaks in several voices: small children, adults, older persons. It is not only the volume but the inside character that is different. Therefore, case by case, you must vary your tone.

This piece [Sibelius Concerto, first movement] is a nocturne. But your tone is not "nocturne." Your tone is "afternoon" tone! You can study with Neveu. I cannot teach you this; I cannot play this piece. It is too difficult for me. I acknowledge that Neveu is a better teacher for you. OK? (Hersh 1995:93)

Suzuki acknowledges that he cannot execute with agility the pyrotechnics of complex concerti. However, he has demonstrated many times that he can analyze the demands of even the most difficult passages and help others build abilities (*sainō*) equal to these challenges. In matters of expressiveness and interpretation, Suzuki is uncannily insightful (*kokoro*). Suzuki uses his violin to show the precise nuances of tone arising from these insights. His recordings display an artistic use of sound; his playing is truly "from the heart." He reminds those who study with him that

[a] performance without spirit results in music without heart and tone without soul. Not only in music, but also in the formation of personality, it is necessary for all humanity to have spirit. Forming people who have spirit is one valuable goal of education. (Suzuki 1976:28)

We turn now to the *kenkyūsei* experience of the apprentice teacher program. Japanese students view themselves as separated into cohorts based on time of entrance. However, graduation is not necessarily in cohort order. In fact, there is no fixed length to the *kenkyūsei* program. Japanese students wait anywhere between one and a half and five years until the day that Suzuki asks them to begin to prepare for their graduation recital.

By graduation, all training teachers have greatly improved technique and exhibit Suzuki's approved positioning of the instrument and playing tone. The variation in level of performance is wide, however. Some *kenkyūsei* who remain for years perform much more complicated pieces than those who have been judged ready to graduate. Suzuki's own standards for determining when a student is ready to graduate are a mystery to *kenkyūsei,* who never know when Suzuki-*sensei* will broach the subject of their graduation. Suzuki himself is enigmatic about the criteria he uses, although these undoubtedly involve his judgment of individuals' tone and *kokoro.* When asked, he will jokingly say only that a *kenkyūsei* is ready to graduate when he or she intuitively brings Suzuki an ashtray before he has even moved his hand toward his cigarettes. (However, merely plying Suzuki with ashtrays is not effective in producing an invitation to graduate.)

Just as foreigners usually take a different route than the Japanese in entering the program, they also take a different route in leaving it. All foreign visitors who remain for even a few weeks are incorporated informally into the *kenkyūsei* program. Those who remain for only a few weeks or months leave without graduating. Those who remain for at least a year usually ask Suzuki to allow them to graduate when their allotted time of stay runs out. He often acquiesces. Other foreign *kenkyūsei* follow Suzuki's procedure and remain until Suzuki himself suggests that they are ready to graduate.

To graduate, each student performs a formal solo recital that includes set pieces from the core repertoire and one or two pieces beyond this repertoire. The concert hall wall is hung with an example of the student's calligraphy, and family and friends are invited. The graduate takes a teaching pledge, and Suzuki presents him or her with a scroll on which he has written, "Tone has a soul which exists without form."

The English version of the new teachers' pledge is:

> We realize the unlimited possibilities of early education. We also realize that every child can be educated. Our purpose is to develop this ability, and present this fact to the world.
>
> We are delighted to be teachers of the Suzuki Method and fully comprehend the responsibilities we have as teachers. We will continue to study teaching in the future with much reflection, and through this continuing study, we will be better able to concentrate energies toward better teaching.
>
> We solemnly affirm that we will keep this promise as Suzuki Method teachers, and always do our utmost for our common purpose of educating the children of the world. (Hersh 1995:124)

After graduation, Japanese students usually return to their city of origin, where they establish a circle of students. As their own first teacher usually has a waiting list of students, they quickly have a full-time practice. Some are invited to come to teach by Suzuki associations in other cities or, occasionally, in other countries. Many *kenkyūsei* cease teaching when their own children are born. Some of the outstanding teachers have chosen not to marry. Having been imbued with the Suzuki Method's high expectations (even for Japan) concerning the mother's role in providing a suitable environment for her child, many hesitate to attempt to combine teaching and child rearing.

Foreign students usually leave Matsumoto and return for at least a time to their homes. Most teach the Suzuki method, setting up their circle of students largely on their own. Some go to work as violin teachers for a local Suzuki association. In contrast to the Japanese students who were enrolled in the *kenkyūsei* program in lieu of higher education, most foreign *kenkyūsei* complete a degree in music education or a related field if they have not already done so.

Japanese graduates who continue to teach may participate in Suzuki's weekly teachers' meeting and violin class whenever their schedules permit. Teachers also attend an annual teachers' workshop and return to Matsumoto each year for two brief summer-school sessions. On these occasions, students of all ages from all over Japan spend three and a half days attending concerts and team-taught lessons. Association newsletters and regional events also keep teachers in touch with the Talent Education Institute. Foreign teachers have the opportunity to see Suzuki when he travels on teaching tours to various countries. Many foreign ex-*kenkyūsei* become leaders in Talent Education activities in their own countries.

Implicit curriculum

In addition to the methods explicitly espoused in the preceding section are implicit methods by which Suzuki shapes a trainee's character. The most obvious to even a casual observer is the tone and atmosphere of the lesson studio. Suzuki observes an elegant form of upper middle-class speech and etiquette. Suzuki demonstrates very dignified and circumspect behavior. This naturally triggers extremely polite behavior in the students, who also use their most polite behavior and language in the lesson room.

Such is Suzuki's natural kindness and excellence of character that this genteel atmosphere seems to bestow dignity upon those of all ages and cultures who come in contact with him. Suzuki miraculously manages to remain infallibly polite according to all international standards of etiquette simultaneously. He is at once thoughtful, spontaneous, dignified, inspiring, and humorous, despite language, cultural, or age barriers.

Another important means of implicit character development is the acquisition of self-discipline and learning habits that trainees absorb through the process of violin instruction. Three central aspects of this development of the *sainō* are repetition (*kurikaeshi*), self-reflection (*hansei*), and perseverance (*ganbaru*). Repetition is the cornerstone of Suzuki's method of developing ability and is the leitmotif of Talent Education. Everything is repeated – the more often, the better. Repetition continues until something becomes second nature, unconsciously and effortlessly correct. Suzuki frequently prescribes 100 repetitions to perfect a difficult passage, and 10,000 to develop a new skill.

> Ease comes with training. We simply have to train and educate our ability [*saino*], that is to say, do the thing over and over again until it feels natural, simple, and easy. That is the secret. (Suzuki 1969:51)

Self-reflection is the companion of repetition, because students should reflect upon and try to improve what they do each time. Suzuki constantly exhorts his students to listen carefully to their own tone or performance. Suzuki has students begin each lesson and practice session with a slow arpeggio in whole notes, while the student scrutinizes his or her own tone quality and playing position. After reflection and correction, the arpeggio is played again, and then a process begins in which a few notes are repeatedly played and scrutinized for at least a third of the practice session. This inculcates the habits of concentration and self-reflection.

In consonance with Japanese folk psychologies of learning, Suzuki also considers perseverance to be central to the development of ability. Among the stories he recounts of exemplary students that he has taught are many vignettes of dogged perseverance in the face of very difficult tasks: a child with infantile paralysis who required countless repetitions of each tiny movement to become able to produce a sound on the instrument and who later became a competent player; a blind child who practiced until he could unerringly touch his outstretched finger with his bow tip, a task difficult even for sighted people; and the like. Suzuki seems to hold close to his heart not those students who merely learn quickly, but those who exert great perseverance and sustained effort in the face of difficulty.

Suzuki describes the salutary effect of this combination of repetition, self-reflection, and diligence in his own experience:

Expend effort on improving yourself. . . . For instance, I recently wrote, "Tone has a living soul without form" on 1,500 *shikishi* [squares or oblongs of cardboard covered with silk]. . . . I presented one to each little graduate at the annual March concert.

Many people say this is a terrible task. I have to get up very early every morning to be able to do it besides my other work, but far from finding it terrible, I enjoy it, and want to write especially nice. . . . Not a calligrapher, I nevertheless try to improve my writing with every *shikishi,* and self-confidence is added with each one. I work with vigor, and it becomes, although only in my way, splendid calligraphy. Yet one sheet is not like another. I cannot tell how much satisfaction I get out of this work and how wonderful the repetition feels. (Suzuki 1969:53)

Afternoon tea with Suzuki is an institution and a visible aspect of the implicit curriculum. Midway through the afternoon, Suzuki emerges from his office with a box of delicacies. This is the signal for the *kenkyūsei* in the vicinity to stop their activities, prepare tea, and sit down for conversation with Suzuki-*sensei.* Suzuki acts as the host, speaking usually in Japanese with asides in his rough and ready English. He reminisces about his experiences, describes Talent Education activities at other locations, plays recordings, or tells humorous anecdotes. Occasionally, important guests visit the institute, and Suzuki invariably introduces the *kenkyūsei* over tea. He believes that such opportunities to meet important role models are good training for young people. Tea time at the institute is a combination of Japanese customs and elements of the German salon society that Suzuki enjoyed in the 1920s.

Tea time is a *kenkyūsei*'s best opportunity to develop an informal relationship with Suzuki. Japanese *kenkyūsei* rarely speak with Suzuki in private, and then almost never about personal issues. Foreigners are bolder and often speak to Suzuki without being spoken to; they may even request a private interview with him. At one level, Suzuki's speaking relationship to his *kenkyūsei* is warm, yet so even-handed as to be almost impersonal. However, his relationship to them through his intervention in their musical performance is at an intensely personal, soul-searching level.

After a few opportunities to observe a new *kenkyūsei*'s personality and performance, Suzuki seems to be able to identify that aspect of personal character most in need of remediation. He focuses on the manifestation of this character trait in violin performance and begins to confront it directly, using various techniques. Suzuki never explicitly explains to the *kenkyūsei* what personality trait he is working on. Instead, he prefers to model again and again more appropriate examples, mimic one's own incorrect approach, point out other students' strengths, and prescribe extraordinary numbers of repetitions of technical exercises that require direct confrontation with one's weakness. Suzuki's instruction is always smiling, never hurried, but relentless, and it forces the future teachers to confront themselves in a way that they may never before have had to do.

For example, one *kenkyūsei* among a new cohort of students was a classic *burikko* (one who coyly feigns helplessness in order to dodge responsibility) who manifested the excessively cute, shallow, and helpless behavior that is considered attractive by some Japanese high school girls. Along with all the *kenkyūsei* in her cohort, she spent the first several months of private lessons with Suzuki playing a whole-note arpeggio, which was a vehicle for him to remediate their tone and technique. At each lesson, Suzuki smilingly worked with her on this arpeggio, trying to realign her playing position, so that left foot, elbow, and nose were in line. In her typical giggling style, she listened to his repeated homework assignments of "foot, elbow, nose" but did not seriously undertake the hard work and discomfort of completely reworking her position. Gradually Suzuki assigned the other *kenkyūsei* in her cohort to study various repertoire works, and she alone was still left studying only the arpeggio. She continued for months on the arpeggio, largely ignoring his smiling reminders of "foot, elbow, nose." She began to feel discouraged and in the *kenkyūsei* room would sometimes half-humorously play for sympathy, saying with a coy pout that Suzuki-*sensei* had "forgotten her."

When almost a year had passed and she was still on the arpeggio, her constantly giggly behavior became tinged with depression. One of her private lessons began with the arpeggio as usual, and Suzuki asked her without comment to repeat it again. Then again. Then again. Feigning ignorance, he suddenly asked her, "What was your name again?" This confirmed her worst fears, and she replied with her eyes downcast, without the usual giggles. "When was it that you arrived?" She answered, "A year ago, Sensei," in a small voice. "Oh, oh, that's right." He let this sink in with her standing there in silence for a couple of long minutes. Then he asked her, "What homework did I give you at your first lesson?" Barely audibly she answered, "foot, elbow, nose." "And what homework did I give you last week?" She hung her head, unable to reply. Suzuki asked, "Is it so very difficult?" She nodded affirmatively. "Did you try?" Again, she nodded, "yes."

Long seconds passed as Suzuki watched her. Then he asked, "What did you think about last night after you closed your eyes, just before you went to sleep?" With eyes full of tears, she mouthed, "I don't know." "What did you think about this morning after you woke up, just before you opened your eyes?" After another moment or two of silence, he said quietly to her, "My dear, if you didn't think 'foot, elbow, nose,' you don't really know the meaning of the word 'try'." At that point, her tears overflowed, and she bowed and left the room. When she returned the next day, she was sobered and began to work on her position in earnest. Her behavior over the next months matured, and she began to work hard at the violin.

This approach of simultaneously confronting students with their own potential and shortcomings occasions great personal growth among the *kenkyūsei.* Suzuki is always patient, ever smiling, and unquestionably puts concern for his students' character closest to his heart. Despite the pain that accompanies growth, most testify that Suzuki is the most psychologically influential and most genuinely kind teacher they have ever had.

Although, in teaching children, Suzuki promotes *kokoro* and *sainō* by orchestrating a good environment, in teaching adults, he holds them responsible for their own self-improvement:

> Talent follows on the heels of efforts. You are hasty if you reflect on yourself as you are now and grieve over your present weakness, concluding that you have no talent. My belief is this: if efforts are made, talent develops before you know it, and this is the true nature of talent. (Suzuki 1990:59)

Senpai–kōhai (senior–junior) relationships also play a role in the implicit curriculum of the Talent Education Institute, although they are less formal than in many other educational settings. Less experienced *kenkyūsei* rely on those who have been at the institute longer, as well as on those who play more proficiently, for advice. Advice is solicited on a wide range of personal and music-related issues. Living conditions for the *kenkyūsei* contribute to their reliance on each other. Separated from their families, each lives in a rented room, usually substandard, somewhere in the institute's vicinity. Thus the implicit curriculum includes loneliness, learning to budget and keep house for oneself, and adjusting to life in a usually drafty and cold room. For foreigners, a serious language barrier is added to the mix.

To escape their rooms and to enjoy each other's company, *kenkyūsei* usually spend most of the day gathered in the *kenkyūsei* room, chatting, drinking tea, practicing (often three or four people at once), or waiting for class to start. Most spend no more than two hours per day in serious individual practice, although some practice more seriously for certain periods, such as the weeks or months before graduation. Serious practice requires exempting oneself on a consistent basis from the much more comfortable society of the *kenkyūsei* room.

Through *senpai–kōhai* relationships, trainees forge bonds of camaraderie and respect and come to share attitudes, beliefs, and skills. One noteworthy skill that training teachers learn from their peers is how to facilitate all manner of activities. New foreign students are mystified at the ways that *senpai* (experienced trainees) intuit the needs of persons and situations. A classic example is the deployment of *kenkyūsei* at children's concerts. An ashtray appears next to Suzuki's chair. The piano is moved by five or six people. *Kenkyūsei* sweep across the stage from both sides, moving chairs and stands as they go. An ample number of *kenkyūsei* tune all of the children's small violins in a matter of minutes. Does some *senpai* assign trainees to these various duties? No. In fact, people do different tasks as each situation seems to warrant.

Foreign trainees inevitably ask whether they have missed an orientation meeting. "No." Sitting as spectators through a few events, they feel left out. They later ask, "Why didn't someone point out a likely task? If we had been asked, we would have been glad to work." At subsequent concerts, they may preselect a task; they may plan, for example, to move music stands. But often, in the time it takes to get on stage, someone else has done "their" task, and they feel superfluous. Finally, they learn to be quick, observant, and flexible. They have become an intuitive member of the *kenkyūsei* team.

Kenkyūsei come to use this keen observation and intuition at school each day. During their years in Matsumoto, many develop special skills that allow them to contribute to the community in unique ways. Seeing a need, they take on tasks that use their abilities. A trainee skilled in calligraphy may design logos and illustrate programs. Foreign trainees become guides for overseas visitors and help with foreign language correspondence. By using these special skills, *kenkyūsei* move closer to the center of the Talent Education community and express respect for their mentor.

The explicit and implicit curricula surround each *kenkyūsei* with influences that shape the development of *sainō* and *kokoro.* Many of these influences are so embedded in the structure of *kenkyūsei* activities that they operate without much additional direct teaching from Suzuki. An example is the weekly cycle of concert preparation, performance, and evaluation that is the product of scheduling *kenkyūsei* recitals every Monday afternoon. Each person must prepare and perform one piece each week. After the concert, *kenkyūsei* engage in self-evaluation and may also receive a few comments on these performances at their lessons with Suzuki.

Several opportunities for development are embedded in this recital process. First, the trainee gradually learns to come to terms with the discipline of performing every week. *Sainō* is cultivated through learning an expanded repertoire of music, always being ready to perform, measuring one's progress every week, and observing the skills of one's *senpai* and *kōhai*. Each *kenkyūsei* gains the self-knowledge that is a part of *kokoro* by experiencing and acknowledging his or her own current level of performance each week. To become comfortable with musical performance, a person must learn to use and celebrate his or her current level of *sainō* and *kokoro*. The attitude to cultivate is articulated by Suzuki at weekly lessons. "Your playing is very good, except for its bad points." For many trainees, this aphorism seems as inexplicable as a Zen koan until they have experienced the recital process for months or years.

The "missing" curriculum

Western visitors to Matsumoto are often puzzled that the teacher development program lacks explicit discussions of pedagogy, an organized requirement for observing the lessons of small children, or a formal teaching internship. While *kenkyūsei* observe countless lessons of Suzuki teaching young adults, teaching two-year-olds is a very different experience. Each day in the 1970s, approximately five teachers gave lessons to small children in various classrooms at the institute, yet only some foreign *kenkyūsei* showed interest in observing them. Suzuki himself neither encouraged nor discouraged observation of other teachers' lessons, nor called upon the other teachers to interact with or guide the *kenkyūsei*.

While Suzuki is extensive and lavish in his explanations of how *kenkyūsei* may improve their personal tone production and bowing technique, he does not regularly discuss how to present these to small children. Nor does he dwell on such practical topics as methods of starting beginners, how to work with parents, or specific instructions for teaching each piece in the repertoire. Instead, he has authored an instructional philosophy upon which to base such work and, as the head of a large organization, highlights a few such teaching points each year at teachers' conferences and in pamphlet form.

Although Suzuki expends great efforts to improve each *kenkyūsei*'s personal playing technique, learning how to work with children is something that training teachers have to "steal" if they are to acquire it at all. Suzuki perhaps assumes that *kenkyūsei* have had sufficient personal experience in the method that they do not need explicit guidelines for teaching each repertoire selection. Perhaps he assumes that equipping each student with well-developed *kokoro* and *sainō* is sufficient, and that they can work out teaching methods for themselves, believing that "where love is deep, much can be accomplished."

Instead of explications, Suzuki provides future teachers with a direct experience of tuition with a master teacher. His work with each student utilizes tonalization exercises that have been honed into their simplest, most effective form. He models each step that each student needs to take and provides a focused, supportive environment for development. He communicates his respect for his students in each interaction and shares humor and expertise in equal measure with them. He also shares with them the joy he finds in being a teacher. It seems that Suzuki expects future teachers to apply these elements of their direct experience creatively to their work with students of whatever ages.

Conclusions

Shinichi Suzuki's teacher development program is a unique blend of Western and Japanese cultural elements. The program is Western in its medium of instruction and formalization of daily classes. It is Japanese in its use of violin performance as a means to focus on developing character. Suzuki's strong effect and direct psychological intervention to improve the character of his students is reminiscent of Zen master–disciple relationships.

Those who have met or studied with Dr. Suzuki for even a short time are inspired by his own example of fine character and his dream for the happiness of humankind. Those who have had the opportunity to study with him personally find that he forever changes their lives in increasingly positive directions. Each new *kenkyūsei* arrives at the institute expecting to become an apprentice violin teacher and leaves having discovered that he or she has been an apprentice human being.

Note

Sarah Hersh and Lois Peak were trained by Dr. Suzuki as teachers during the early 1970s at the Talent Education Institute in Matsumoto, Japan. Hersh, an alumna of Oberlin Conservatory, studied at the institute from 1973 to 1976 and graduated as a certified teacher. She has made a career in Talent Education, teaching violin and Suzuki pedagogy in London and Minneapolis. She is authorized by the Suzuki Association of the Americas to develop teachers and in that capacity gives workshops on the Suzuki Method around the country. She has completed her doctoral dissertation on Shinichi Suzuki's teacher development program and teaches string pedagogy at the Crane School of Music, State University of New York College at Potsdam.

Peak studied at the Talent Education Institute in 1972 and part of 1973 and applied Suzuki's approach for one year while a violin teacher in Seattle. She subsequently spent three years studying and teaching the Suzuki method as adapted for a preschool curriculum. In 1983, Peak spent another year at the Talent Education Institute studying cultural and pedagogical aspects of the methodology Suzuki has developed. This chapter is based on Hersh and Peak's personal experiences and observations and draws on some of Hersh's dissertation research. Lois Peak is an employee of the U.S. Department of Education; however, this chapter was written to promote exchange of views among researchers. No official support by the U.S. Department of Education is intended or should be inferred.

References

Hermann, Evelyn, 1981, *Shinichi Suzuki: The Man and His Philosophy,* Athens, OH: Ability Development Associates.

Hersh, Sarah, 1995, *Music Educator Shinichi Suzuki: His Teacher Development Program and Studio Teaching,* Ph.D. dissertation, University of Minnesota.

Selden, Kyoko, 1980, "Words of Shinichi Suzuki," *Talent Education Journal* 7 (Fall–Winter): p. 49.

Stevenson, Harold, and James Stigler, 1992, *The Learning Gap,* New York: Summit Books.

Suzuki, Shinichi, 1969, *Nurtured by Love,* translated by Waltraud Suzuki, New York: Exposition Press. (Originally published 1966)

1976, *Talent Education Teachers' Convention* (convention booklet), Matsumoto, Japan: Talent Education Institute.

1990, *Man and Talent: Search into the Unknown,* translated by Kyoko Selden, Ann Arbor, MI: Shar Products Company. (Originally published 1957)

Tertis, Lionel, 1938, *Beauty of Tone in String Playing,* New York: Oxford University Press.

10 Becoming a master physician

Susan O. Long

Where and how does one learn to be a professional in contemporary Japan? Some might assume that a modern, technical field such as medicine is best learned in classrooms, laboratories, and libraries. Yet both in the United States and in Japan, the "likely places" for learning to be a physician extend beyond these to the hospital and the research laboratory precisely because professional education involves more than memorizing formulas and listening to lectures. Becoming a professional means learning to take on a role in a complex social system. For physicians, that role requires the ability to apply classroom knowledge to imperfect real-life situations in diagnosis, treatment, and research. It demands that one be able to interact in expected ways with colleagues, clients, and sources of funding. The understandings that form the basis of a successful career as a physician are not often explicitly taught but are grasped in the course of a young physician's postgraduate education. Through practice and observation, they become part of the physician's definition of him or her self as a professional.

In the United States, postgraduate medical education begins with a residency. This is a formal program in which a young physician rotates through various departments or "services" for a fixed period of time. Through practice, observation, explicit teaching, and independent study, the physician learns not only how to apply the knowledge gained in medical school but also how to present "cases" to a senior physician in the appropriate style, when and how to consult specialists in other fields, and how to talk with patients' families. At the end of the residency, it is expected that the young physician will continue training in a chosen subspecialty or go directly into private practice (increasingly group, rather than solo, practice).

Japanese postgraduate medical education must accomplish similar goals regarding clinical expertise. However, differences in the structure of the medical system and cultural values have created a somewhat different system of postgraduate medical training. Rather than a formalized system of rotations, most young physicians in Japan establish a relationship with a single mentor in a highly specialized department of a university hospital upon graduation from medical school. The organization of work, leisure, and education within the department suggests similarities to apprenticeship training, as well as to the more bureaucratized training received by young American physicians.

Goody discusses the historical emergence of apprenticeship to provide nonfamilial training as the market introduced greater specialization and division of labor. It was no longer possible for any son to learn an occupation from his own father because skills were more varied and not universally known (Goody 1989). Yet in industrialized societies, further processes of rationalization and bureaucratization have resulted in age-segregated educational institutions in which "experts" teach their knowledge in a disembodied manner to their charges. Learning in such institutions is generally abstract rather than applied, passive rather than participatory. The nature of the transition from this kind of learning environment to the work setting is unproblematical if we assume that work institutions are rational and bureaucratic. In such a world of "modernity," there is no place for apprenticeship. Postgraduate medical education is a paradox: It involves "modern," professional work that occurs largely in bureaucratic settings, and yet its training is characterized by apprenticeship-type learning even in the last half of the twentieth century. Medicine in Japan is based on scientific theory and knowledge. It requires logical thought processes, careful observation, and controlled experimentation. In Japan, the medical labor market is highly specialized and competitive. Why, then, does this style of learning continue to characterize postgraduate medical education in contemporary Japan?

This chapter begins with a discussion of the nature of doctor training after medical school, indicating ways in which the apprenticeship model operates in the university hospital setting, where this training primarily occurs. During and for a number of years after the Allied Occupation of Japan, there was an attempt to divorce this training from the "undemocratic" structure of the university hospital departments. Modern medical education, it was believed, would be furthered by creating a rotating internship that liberated the learner from the constraints of a particular department and its autocratic professor. The young doctor would complete his or her internship more well-rounded and, I suppose, more objective, rational, and scientific. This reform, like others of the Occupation (see, for an example in the field of education, Duke 1989), ultimately did not work because it ignored the underlying structural and cultural components of the old system. Interns complained that they could not support themselves; they were not eligible for licensure until the year was completed and so could not moonlight. They claimed that by rotating from one department to another, no one took responsibility for their education, and the year as an intern only postponed the inevitable entrance into a single department for postgraduate work required by professional standards for them to practice medicine successfully (Bowers 1965). So by the mid-1960s, the rotating internship had been discarded, and young doctors directly entered a single department of a university hospital for their postgraduate training. They were allowed to take the licensure examination immediately after medical school but could not practice unsupervised until they completed two years of postgraduate clinical training.

But this model also was contested by student protesters in the late 1960s. They viewed the system as one in which young doctors' careers were at the mercy of an arbitrary professor who controlled their educations, their economic plights, and their employment opportunities. In a system in which young doctors worked as unpaid researchers to earn their doctorates (*igaku hakase*) while the professor's name went on the publications, the young doctors believed that their labor was exploited. The student revolt of the late 1960s began at Tokyo University Medical School where students were joined in their protest by young doctors. They were successful in shutting down the university for a time and in canceling the 1969 entrance exam. They demanded a greater role for themselves in decisions about their clinical rotations and research projects. Political mobilization did result in some modifications of the system. Nonetheless, postgraduate medical education continues to share a number of features with classical apprenticeship, an educational system considered by the protesters to be out of touch with a modern, democratic society.

I then turn to the question of why this is so. After all, medicine is highly specialized, its scientific basis is conducive to classroom teaching, and it enjoys relatively high social status as a "modern" professional career. Medical school is based on classroom education. Why then is postgraduate education so apprentice-like, particularly when it trains young doctors for a variety of medical careers – clinical employment, private practice, or research – rather than strictly for the "master" position of university professor? Both external and internal factors contribute to the continuity of a training system based on "legitimate peripheral participation" (Lave and Wenger 1991) and "feudal power relationships."

The concluding section raises questions about the relationship of this system of training to the larger sociocultural context. How do we define "community of practice"? Is there anything about this form of training that is specifically Japanese? Might this medical example provide support for the premise that an apprenticeship-like context of embedded tutoring is basic to learning life skills as opposed to abstract knowledge? What is the relationship between situated learning and social power?

Postgraduate medical education as apprenticeship

To become a practicing physician in Japan, it is necessary to complete a six-year university curriculum consisting of two years of general education courses, two years of basic science courses, and two years of exposure to the clinical sciences. Upon completion of this course of study, students take the national licensing examination but may not practice until they also complete a two-year residency program. Although residency does not mean an end to formal education, the new doctor may experience discontinuity in the content and style of education as he or she leaves medical school and gains membership in a university hospital department. Pregraduate university education was situated in classrooms and in educational laboratories and offered exposure to all of the disciplines that make up medical science in Japan. Postgraduate education is located in the university hospital and other clinical settings, and in particular, in one specialty department in that hospital in which the student has chosen to pursue a career. The focus of pregraduate medical education is acquiring facts; the new resident must focus on learning the lifelong skills that will enable the professional to expand and apply that knowledge to real-life situations.

Postgraduate medical education begins but does not end with residency. A university hospital department includes a variety of paid and unpaid positions. In addition to residents who do clinical rotations both at the university hospital and at affiliated public and semipublic facilities, there are young staff doctors, those doing a fellowship, graduate and/or research students doing research in the department, and finally, the three levels of permanent staff. At the national universities, the salaries of the permanent staff are paid by the Ministry of Education; other salaries come from the hospital and departmental budgets. Of the permanent positions, that of the single full professor is at the pinnacle of the departmental hierarchy. Each department also has an assistant full professor and several lecturers.

All clinical departments I observed espouse an ideology of threefold professional responsibility: research, teaching, and clinical work. Although each medical member of the department is expected to do all three, the actual distribution of responsibilities varies with rank. The residents and young staff doctors have primary duties for in-patient care. Although they must also spend time on research to further their careers, research is the key focus of the permanent staff (professor, assistant professor, and lecturers). Their professional identities frequently are bound up in academic specialty associations and/or in hospital politics, both of which measure reputations by personal and departmental research output. Technically, only the permanent staff are educators; that is, they lecture to medical students. But all medical members of the department are engaged in teaching in some form. Even the first-year residents educate the other doctors as they present the cases of individual patients or as they summarize recent literature in their field at journal club meetings.

Residency is a formal educational program in the sense that it is required for full licensure. But the learning that occurs in the university hospital department is better seen as what Lave and Wenger (1991) call "legitimate peripheral participation," or what Clark (Chapter 14, this volume) calls "embedded tutoring." Residents generally come into the department with book knowledge but no clinical skills. They become "master physicians" over a long period of years in which they gradually take on increasing responsibility under the "guided participation" of their seniors. The professor has ultimate responsibility for the clinical and research work in the department and is the source of legitimacy for the young doctors' treatment of patients despite their lack of skill. But a good deal of the guidance of the young doctors is done by those in greater physical and social proximity, the young staff doctors and fellows.

The learning of postgraduate medicine is more like apprenticeship than the classroom learning of medical school in four key ways. First, the recent graduate enters a specialty department to learn specific occupational skills. He or she goes through somewhat ambiguous but readily recognized phases of training under the guidance of those more experienced. The earlier stages involve more of the mundane work of patient care such as drawing blood, charting, and ordering medicines. Gradually, as clinical skills develop, residents and young staff doctors need less close supervision and are assigned patients with more complex problems. Serious involvement with research, which legitimates the department in the eyes of the professor and his peers, is intensified at later stages.

Like an apprenticeship, there is a clear beginning to postgraduate medical education. As in Japanese schools, many departments have ceremonies or parties to mark the entrance of a new group of residents into the department. But (unlike residencies and fellowships in the United States) there is no clearly marked ending, no ritual recognition of the end of the required two years of training. Because residents and other young doctors are commonly rotated out of the department to assignments at other hospitals for periods of months to years, there is in most cases no clear boundary between those who remain in and those who leave the department. The later in the doctor's career and the longer the time away, the more the doctor worries about a university-based career, but as long as she or he is responsive to the demands of the professor (or his designate) and participates in departmental events when possible, the doctor remains part of the department. Mastery is implicitly acknowledged when a doctor obtains a position as a permanent staff doctor at that or another university hospital. A kind of partial mastery may be recognized when a doctor leaves the department for a clinical position at a public hospital or in private practice. As described by Singleton (1989a) for pottery apprentices, even young doctors who expect to leave the university will spend a year or two after official training ends "paying back" the professor for his guidance. Departure depends on other opportunities and on interpersonal relationships and not on the acquisition of specific skills (cf. Singleton 1992).

The nature of interpersonal relationships in the department is also more reminiscent of master–apprentice relations than of "rational," institutionalized educational settings. A young doctor generally has a direct, personal relationship with one of the permanent staff, and the lecturers and assistant professor have direct relationships with the professor, so that structurally the department displays the hierarchical characteristics depicted by Nakane (1970), or the *oyabun–kobun* relationship described by Ishino (1953). When I asked young physicians why they had chosen their specialty, some indicated practical reasons such as a woman's need to combine work and family careers, or the expectation of taking over a parent's practice in a particular specialty. But many responded that they joined a department because they had developed a relationship with a particular senior physician. One senior in the medical school explained, "There's only one of my teachers I can talk to about my ideals and future plans." An older physician related how he became a pathologist:

When I was a medical student, I had a pathology exam and couldn't do any of the problems. I turned in a completely blank page. The professor said, "I can't grade a blank paper!" so assigned me a library report on a particular topic. I became interested in it, and when I turned in the report, the professor was surprised it was good. He was pleased, and said, "Come and study pathology with me." So I did.

Upon entering a department, the young doctor exchanges potential autonomy for guidance. The department's full professor is expected to have a paternalistic interest in all of the young doctors in the department. In exchange for his[1] concern, their activities in research and clinical rotations form the basis of the professor's reputation and social power. The guidance of the young doctors, however, is frequently indirect, delegated by the professor to mid-level managers or taken on informally by friendly *senpai* (cf. Singleton 1989a). Young doctors often have responsibilities for assigning and assisting with in-patient or out-patient activities. Most importantly for the social structure of the department, each physician is assigned to a research group headed by a lecturer or assistant professor. The mild competition among these groups has the potential to erupt into conflicting loyalties. A young doctor may be torn between allegiance to the department as a whole and fealty to the research team leader, for example, when one of the lecturers is promoted to the single assistant professor position in the department. The permanent departure of a group leader from the department may mean career changes for the young doctors affiliated with him as well, as they follow their research group leader to a new hospital or otherwise find it too difficult to readjust interpersonal relations in the department to allow the young doctor to stay.

As in apprenticeship, the "master" (i.e., professor) controls the labor of the young physician. Moonlighting jobs needed for the doctors' livelihood, out-of-university clinical rotations, and postresidency positions at other hospitals all come to the young doctors through the department. The professor generally delegates a senior "apprentice" to distribute these jobs, but maintaining good relations with the professor, one's research group leader, and this senior "apprentice" (chosen for administrative and political skills, unlike other positions in the department by which people are rewarded for research productivity) will help to guarantee good placements and opportunities. It is thought by the young physicians that the proverbial "nail that sticks up" in the department does not get hammered down so much as sent to an undesirable rural hospital hours away from the university. In such a setting, it is difficult to maintain important ties or to continue to do research, both of which are crucial to the young doctor if he or she intends to continue in a university track. One physician in his 40s who was recently "called back" to his department after many years at a public hospital several hours away described his surprise and pleasure at his new appointment:

> I enjoyed my work at the public hospital. I had been there so long I thought I would never be called back to the university! I was really surprised when the professor telephoned me. But although I was a little sad to leave my practice, I returned to the university department.

One additional similarity of postgraduate medical education to apprenticeship is the extent to which the young doctors' lives revolve around the department. In a classical apprenticeship, the young worker lives with the master's family and/or other apprentices, takes meals with them, and in general has only limited opportunities for a social or personal life outside the shop. The importance to learning of physical separation from the outside world is recognized not only by the master potter but also by the couple who run weaving workshops for urban women (see Chapters 6 and 11, this volume, respectively). As in these situations, postgraduate medical education creates an atmosphere at once intense and "natural." Although young physicians do have homes to which they return (frequently they are still living with their parents at least during the first few years of postgraduate training), many do so only to sleep, and at that, not every night. Some of the newer medical school hospitals provide dormitory rooms at subsidized rates for the young physicians, and outside hospitals, particularly those away from major urban centers, may provide housing for the young doctors sent to them for clinical rotations. The nature of caring for in-patients, moreover, may necessitate remaining at the hospital all night either for taking turns on-call, or in emergency situations with one's own patients. Moonlighting jobs needed for economic survival often require the young doctor to remain at an outside hospital several nights a week.

As in apprenticeships, training is not limited to the schedule of a work day or to the specifics of the job. The *ikyoku* (literally "medical office") generally contains two or more areas. One or more will contain desks, bookshelves, and so on for medical study. But the "office" will also contain a lounge in which a great deal of education of the young doctors goes on. Reminiscent of the *ippuku* described by the pottery apprentice (Chapter 6), when everyone gathered around the tea kettle, and of the *koya,* where the divers gather after the day's catch is tallied (Chapter 12), physicians gather around the coffeepot to discuss patients, research results, or new drugs, and to plan for the departmental trip, the welcoming ceremony for the new residents, and the departmental baseball team. Young doctors play mah jong or gather at the *ikyoku* in the evenings, gathering gossip about the next round of clinical assignments or the latest in sports cars from the pharmaceutical company representative.

There is little explicit teaching in the *ikyoku.* Rather it is a place that provides access to information that helps the learners to "grasp the secrets" of the professional world in which they are as yet "peripheral" participants. Young doctors frequently leave the *ikyoku* in the late afternoon or early evening, but only to go to their moonlighting jobs; otherwise, they can generally be found in the ward, the lab, or the lounge until 9 or 10 at night. For many, three meals a day are eaten in the hospital cafeteria, unless a group of young doctors goes out for an evening of dinner and drinking on the town. It is this type of education that cannot be replicated in the outlying hospitals where the young doctors are sent. The careers of young women doctors testify to the significance of this informal education and development of interpersonal skills. Though ideally free to participate fully in this, many married women feel unable to stay beyond their clinical and research obligations, in order to fulfill home and family responsibilities. Women are more likely to leave the department to take permanent jobs in public hospitals or in private practice.

Factors supporting an apprenticeship-like style of postgraduate medical education

This brings us to a point at which postgraduate medical education differs significantly from classical apprenticeship. What is occurring is actually training for three different jobs simultaneously. The absolute control of the professor for determining when his "apprentice" has become a "master" characterizes only that situation in which the young doctor is pursuing a university/research career. Although a good recommendation of the professor is often helpful and sometimes necessary to obtain a clinical job in a nonuniversity hospital, if the labor market is favorable and governmental licensure requirements are met, the declaration of mastery by the professor may not be needed. Certainly for private practice, licensure is the key. The *igaku hakase* (doctor of medicine degree based on completion of a research project and dissertation) may help the young private practitioner to recruit patients, but the degree is probably more important to intraprofessional relations than to recruiting patients. But the system of guided learning for young doctors is maintained because most of them, at least initially, wish to pursue a university career for as long as possible. This relates to motivations to enter medicine, which in turn are linked to broader cultural ideals influencing occupational status rankings and the symbolism of health and illness.

External factors

Three external factors support the continuation of "embedded tutoring" in postgraduate medical education: (1) funding, (2) the "closed" nature of Japanese hospitals, and (3) the maldistribution of doctors.

Departmental funds are obtained in two ways. First, there is regular funding from the university hospital budget. This pays the minimal salaries of the young doctors (although some young researchers are there without pay, as are graduate students) but does not provide enough for self-support. This situation necessitates living at home or in university dormitories and encourages the young doctors to moonlight at the jobs recommended by their seniors. Other funding is "soft money," which comes from grants from the Ministry of Education or the Ministry of Health and Welfare and from pharmaceutical companies. These grants support the research activities of the department and provide "extras" in terms of supplies, books and journals, conference attendance, and so on. Productivity in terms of published results helps to assure continued support. Without research money, the reputation of the department cannot be maintained, nor can the department afford to employ all of its support personnel. This structure of funding results in the dependency of the young doctors on the department for side jobs and of the senior members of the department on the labor of the young doctors for research rather than clinical work.

A second external factor has to do with the way hospitals are staffed. Japanese doctors call our American system, in which community doctors admit and follow patients in hospitals where they have "admitting privileges," an "open" system. Most Japanese hospitals, on the other hand, are "closed." They hire their own doctors, who are paid on salary and see patients only (as out-patients or in-patients) in that hospital. Community doctors whose patients need to be admitted must therefore refer them to a hospital doctor and may not have any input into their care once hospitalized (unless they have a particularly close relationship with one or more of the doctors in that hospital department). It is therefore crucial that private practitioners have a network of known doctors to whom to refer their patients for hospital care, and that hospital doctors have a network of private practitioners who will refer patients to them. The local medical association has only limited effect on developing this network because its most active members are generally private practitioners. Thus it is medical school alumni associations and, to a lesser extent, specialty associations that create and maintain such ties. These are based on the intensive, all-encompassing years of *ikyoku* affiliation with its baseball games and out-of-hospital rotations, its research teams and its drinking parties.

The maldistribution of doctors in Japan creates similar need for interpersonal networks. The university hospital department typically serves as employment broker, providing jobs for its members (after all, even for those remaining "in" the department, rotations outside of it are necessary, in part to maintain the size of the department staff and in part to develop clinical skills) and physician-employees for public and semipublic hospitals. In 1994, the overall Japanese ratio was 184 physicians for 100,000 people; however, in the rural Akita prefecture, the ratio was only 164, while in Tokyo it was 253 (Japan Statistical Yearbook 1997). The system of postmedical education may not be the cause of this imbalance; urbanization and centralization are trends that have characterized twentieth-century Japan in general. But the perception of young doctors – that the level of technology and the interpersonal networks needed to advance their careers are not available in rural areas – contributes to the sense that being sent to such a location is a kind of banishment from the department. This contributes to the difficulty that rural hospitals have in recruiting physicians despite their willingness to pay higher salaries than those offered in urban areas. By making rotations to such places part of the required training for young doctors, both as a test of departmental loyalty and a means of obtaining clinical experience, the brokering role of the professor is maintained and thus his political power reinforced.

Internal factors

In addition to these external factors that help to maintain an apprenticeship-like postgraduate medical education, the nature of the work itself encourages learning through apprenticeship. To some extent, this might be said for all jobs. Applying knowledge requires experience that can never be obtained only through the more passive modes of reading or listening. Recognizing this, many Japanese companies provide formalized on-the-job training programs for workers. (For examples of company-sponsored training, see Rohlen 1974 and Kondo 1990.) But I would argue that medical work in particular demands an experiential learning style; even in the United States, which has more formalized residency and fellowship programs, situated learning with gradual assumption of more and more complex responsibilities characterizes postgraduate medical education.

First, laboratory experimentation, not unlike pottery making, involves some degree of creativity, but it relies primarily on strong discipline and repetitious, mundane activity, which is hands-on work and cannot be learned in textbooks. Residents begin by doing this mundane work – feeding laboratory animals, measuring chemicals – while their levels of enthusiasm and care are observed by their seniors. They are gradually given more important responsibilities for the group's work, including co-authorship of papers reporting their results. They may even be assigned primary responsibility for a particular phase of the research. But they are given little leeway in defining their own projects or in determining methodology. In other words, the more creative aspects of laboratory research are considered the domain of the "master" physicians who head the research teams. Yet the young physicians are interested in promoting the publishing success of their seniors because as the department's reputation improves, so do their own prospects through their affiliation with a successful department.

In clinical work as well, book learning only goes so far. Graduating medical students are very knowledgeable about human anatomy and physiology in general. They are familiar with laboratory tests and normal values for the results. Typical presentations of diseases, including relatively rare ones, have been memorized. Yet they do not have the skills to take a medical history, to determine appropriate treatments, to recognize unusual presentations of symptoms, to telephone the referring community physician, or to tell family members that their husband or mother is dying. Much of the day-to-day work of clinical medicine, as in the laboratory, is routine. Yet it is only through repetition that the young doctors will come to "remember with their bodies," to develop the mental habits and the internal "calluses" (Plath, Epilogue, this volume) that will allow them to be consistently effective clinicians in all kinds of situations. (I have heard the physically and emotionally stressful on-call system of American residents justified in a similar way. Learning to work on little or no sleep is good training for emergency situations that require excellent rapid judgment.)

Medical talk and medical procedures are good examples of learning through repetitive practice. As described in the earlier chapters on traditional arts training, routines are observed and imitated until the form (*kata*) becomes "natural." The presentation of cases to the professor is done in a particular way, different from the style in which patients might be discussed with a physician only a year or two one's senior in the *ikyoku*. As Lave and Wenger (1991:109) point out for Alcoholics Anonymous participants, the point is not learning *from* talk, but learning *to* talk, in this case, as a professional. This learning *to* talk is not taught but becomes part of a young doctor's personal style through observation and practice.

Similarly, medical procedures cannot be learned by reading descriptions of how the procedure is done but rather only through practice. If the young doctor in charge of the endoscopy clinic has had plenty of experience inserting the tubes, he or she is happy to let the residents take turns doing so. Their physical movements and linguistic utterances have a rituallike rhythm and style that the physicians learn relatively early in their years in the gastroenterology department. But the interpretation of the findings is less likely to be routine, and it remains the responsibility of the senior apprentice and the senior members of the department. Responsibility for diagnosis and treatment must be taken on gradually as young doctors develop the experientially based skills and understandings needed for the job.

While medical students recognize that they are studying science, they only vaguely foresee that to be good clinicians they will need other kinds of skills as well. As they are increasingly exposed to clinical practice, primarily after graduation, they come to acknowledge that medicine is also an art. In a sense, they "learn to see" in new ways. As does the artist or the potter surrounded by good art (Chapters 3 and 6, this volume, respectively), an inexperienced doctor learns good medicine through coming to understand the diagnosis and treatment decisions of his experienced seniors, an understanding that comes through observing the seniors and through trying their techniques until they become his or her own. Medical science is for the doctor a "transparent technology," which is both visible and invisible (Lave and Wenger 1991:101–103). For the new resident with the endoscope, the task is to make the scope invisible, for the technique to become so much a part of him (cf. Chapters 2, 4, 12, and 18, this volume, by Rimer, DeCoker, Hill and Plath, and McClure, respectively) that he can do it effortlessly in order to concentrate on what he sees through the tubes. Yet the art of medicine lies not only in making the correct diagnosis, but in being able to see beyond the tube, to make the endoscope visible again as part of a whole picture of the patient and his or her disease course.

That art is not only a matter of such applied skills as adjusting medication doses based on intuitive knowledge of individual patients. It is also social, requiring an understanding of the broader system in which the physician and patient participate. Japanese education is more likely than that in the United States to insist on group responsibility for learning; still, the young resident may for the first time be part of a team responsible for the health or even life of another who is not part of that work group. Along with clinical medicine, residents learn routines and patterns of communication that have been developed around patient care: how to present a patient to the professor during grand rounds, and how to go back later to interpret the professor's medicalized comments to the patient or family in lay terms; responsibilities while on call; how to obtain information from nurses while maintaining occupational status distinctions; and so on. (See Graves 1989 on medical residents' acquisition of impression management skills.)

In addition, both career advancement and clinical skills depend on interpersonal skills in dealings with patients and with superiors and subordinates in the medical hierarchy. A young doctor knows that he or she must maintain good relations with the professor but learns *how* this is done by watching those just ahead of him or her. A doctor several years out of school must also learn how to guide the newer residents to the right decisions about treatment without creating bad feelings, which would threaten the cohesion that is supposed to exist in the department, and which ultimately forms the core of the networks that physicians need whether they remain in the university or leave for other types of practice. This kind of interpersonal skill is never, to my knowledge, taught didactically but rather is observed and gradually incorporated into the young doctor's behavioral repertoire. Because these skills are considered necessary to the practice of medicine and because there is no other way in which they are taught, this embedded education that accompanies the more acknowledged work of the department continues to reinforce the need for an all-encompassing situated learning environment.

"Community of practice" and professional identity

Postgraduate medical education is an example of apprenticeship-like training that occurs within a formalized educational system in a bureaucratic, postindustrial society. We have discussed both structural factors in the occupational world of medicine and matters of content that contribute to the maintenance of an apprenticeship-like system of training physicians after medical school.

There are also factors in their situated learning environment that weaken the applicability of the apprenticeship model. First is the issue of how boundaries of the "community of practice" are defined. For Lave and Wenger (1991:98), "community of practice" is an ambiguous concept. They view it as neither "some primordial culture-sharing entity" nor as a "co-presence, a well-defined group [with] socially visible boundaries." In the case of physicians, the state license to practice medicine clearly defines who is and who is not within the "community of practice." Since graduating medical students may sit for the examination before their postgraduate training begins, the "community" itself does not control its boundaries. Rather, the identity issues of postgraduate medical education relate more clearly to status within a diverse occupational group.

In a classical apprenticeship, the master certifies the skills of his apprentices. With licensure coming from outside the university hospital department, the physician's status is to some extent a given; like the people going to the public bath described by Clark (Chapter 14, this volume), young physicians are judged in part by how well their behavior accords with their externally conferred status. On the other hand, status *within* the medical world is achieved competitively, more reminiscent of the divers described by Hill and Plath (Chapter 12, this volume). There are a number of ways to dive for their catch (from a boat or from shore, with or without weights), but the single measure of their success is their market tally. Competition for status among physicians may be more subtle but can sometimes be severe. Ranking depends on such factors as having an advanced degree (*igaku hakase*), academic affiliation, the overall reputation of the university, and one's position in the university hospital hierarchy.

Although there are times when a physician will identify him- or herself as a physician, self-identity seems more often based on actual or anticipated place within that world. Depending also on the social context, physicians' self-definitions vary greatly. One physician saw her residency as required time and saw her postresidency work in the hospital radiology department as work that was an interesting and useful job for her until the time that she would take over her father's private family practice. Another, in a urology department, identified himself as a "legitimate peripheral participant" in the world of international research. As he did his clinical work, he also anticipated the time when he would go abroad for several years as a researcher. He had little understanding of or interest in the problems to be faced by his peers going into private practice.

The notion of a "community of practice" in which people participate "in an activity system about which participants share understandings concerning what they are doing and what that means in their lives and for their communities" (Lave and Wenger 1991:98) is challenged by the diversity of motives and career paths of people in an occupational category, not only among physicians, but also among the mechanics (Madono, Chapter 8), potters (Singleton, Chapter 7), and weavers (Creighton, Chapter 11) described in this book. The shifting boundaries of *uchi* (inner) and *soto* (outer) (cf. Rosenberger 1992, Bachnik and Quinn 1994) may be a more useful way to investigate professional identities in a postindustrial society than to assume (intuitive) community of shared understandings.

Conclusion

What then does postgraduate medical education tell us about Japanese society and styles of learning found within it? This chapter demonstrates that situated learning in Japan is not a feudal holdover, as the student radicals of the 1960s would have had us believe, but rather a style of learning that develops in response to external and internal circumstances, which explains why the student protesters had only limited success in altering this educational system. Without creating open hospitals on a large scale, without developing different sources for funding medical education and patient care, without providing similar opportunities for professional development for rural as well as urban physicians, their reforms would only have temporary effects. They succeeded in loosening the professor's control over the young doctors only because the supply of doctors had grown significantly, and their role as employment brokers became less important to outside hospitals searching for physicians. This situation is "Japanese" only in that it is a response to specific historical and social structures.

If situated learning in Japan is unique in some way, it is perhaps because Japanese culture explicitly recognizes that learning is a social process dependent on both individual drive and interpersonal skills. It downplays the importance of power differentials by stressing common goals and the hope of upward mobility. But the emphasis on spiritual quest or self-development (cf. DeCoker's Chapter 4 and Hersh and Peak's Chapter 9, this volume) that American popular culture has sometimes romanticized are only part of the picture. What the example of postgraduate medical education can point out is that there is a great deal of variation in possible responses to such a setting. My informants never forgot that they had the option of leaving the department, and some did by their own choice. They not only participated in guided learning but simultaneously evaluated the nature of that experience and the quality of the guiding. Though few chose to leave, rejecting the occupational status hierarchy, the potential of the learners to challenge the status quo seemed in my research to be always just below the surface. In this sense then, guided participation also means active learning in a context of obviously uneven power relationships, balancing personal goals with situational constraints. And perhaps it is that balancing activity that underlies the value of apprenticeship as not only occupational learning but also as learning for life. The understanding that young physicians achieve lies not only in advancing their clinical and research skills but also in the relationship between the visibility and invisibility (cf. Lave and Wenger 1991) of a set of social relationships.

Despite the "rationalization" and bureaucratization of workplaces in industrialized societies, most human work, regardless of how esoteric or technical, remains essentially social activity. Books may be written and crash courses developed on how to work as a team, how to be assertive, how to manage your time, and so on, but these cannot ever take the place of experience because they are meaningless unless practiced in a particular social context. Classroom education can teach one to become a better student or a teacher, but it rarely provides the kind of guided experience necessary for applying that knowledge outside the classroom. Postgraduate medical education in Japan suggests that apprenticeship changes in response to the postindustrial situation but that some form of situated learning must continue to form the basis of professional education and professional identity.

Notes

Data for this chapter come from participant observation and intensive interviews in Japanese hospitals and clinics in 1977–1978. Follow-up interviews and observations were conducted in 1987 and 1996. Comparative comments on American medical education are derived in part from the author's experience as a spouse of a medical student, resident, and practicing physician, and from participant observation in a large, private, American tertiary-care hospital, January–July 1993. Financial support for this research was provided by a Fulbright–Hays Doctoral Dissertation Fellowship, a National Science Foundation grant, and a John Carroll University Grauel Faculty Fellowship. The author would like to thank the authors of the other chapters in this volume, and especially editor John

Singleton, for stimulating discussions about learning, for guidance, and for helpful criticism on an earlier version of this chapter.

1. I purposely use masculine pronouns in discussing full professors since those who hold these positions are nearly always men.

References

Bachnik, Jane, and Charles J. Quinn, eds., 1994, *Situated Meaning: Inside and Outside in Japanese Self, Society, and Language,* Princeton: Princeton University Press.

Becker, Howard S., 1982, *Art Worlds,* Berkeley: University of California Press.

Bowers, John Z., 1965, *Medical Education in Japan,* New York: Harper & Row.

Duke, Benjamin C., 1989, "Variations on Democratic Education: Divergent Patterns in Japan and the United States," in James J. Shields, Jr., ed., *Japanese Schooling: Patterns of Socialization, Equality, and Political Control,* University Park: Pennsylvania State University Press, pp. 260–269.

Goody, Esther, 1989, "Learning, Apprenticeship, and the Division of Labour," in Michael Coy, ed., *Apprenticeship: From Theory to Method and Back Again,* Albany: State University of New York Press, pp. 233–257.

Graves, Bennie, 1989, "Informal Aspects of Apprenticeship in Selected American Occupations," in Michael W. Coy, ed., *Apprenticeship: From Theory to Method and Back Again,* Albany: State University of New York Press, pp. 51–64.

Ishino, Iwao, 1953, "The *Oyabun-Kobun*: A Japanese Ritual Kinship Institution," *American Anthropologist,* 55: 695–707.

Kondo, Dorinne, 1990, *Crafting Selves: Power, Gender, and Discourses of Identity in a Japanese Workplace,* Chicago: University of Chicago Press.

Lave, Jean, and Etienne Wenger, 1991, *Situated Learning: Legitimate Peripheral Participation,* Cambridge: Cambridge University Press.

Nakane, Chie, 1970, *Japanese Society,* Berkeley: University of California Press.

Rohlen, Thomas P., 1974, *For Harmony and Strength: Japanese White Collar Organization in Anthropological Perspective,* Berkeley: University of California Press.

Rosenberger, Nancy R., ed., 1992, *Japanese Sense of Self,* Cambridge: Cambridge University Press.

Singleton, John, 1989a, "Japanese Folkcraft Pottery Apprenticeship: Cultural Assumptions in Educational Practice," in Michael Coy, ed., *Apprenticeship: From Theory to Method and Back Again,* Albany: State University of New York Press, pp. 8–15.

1992, "Deconstructing Apprenticeship Models in Folkcraft Pottery: Traditional Arts and Alternative Careers in Mashiko Workshops," in Paul Greenough, ed., *Redefining the Artisan: Traditional Technicians in Changing Societies,* Center for International and Comparative Studies, University of Iowa, pp. 101–118.

11 Weaving the future from the heart of tradition: Learning in leisure activities

Millie Creighton

Extensive studies of Japanese early childhood education show that learning occurs within a participation framework (cf. Lewis 1984, 1989; Tobin, Wu, and Davidson 1989; Peak 1989, 1991; Hendry 1986; Ben-Ari 1987; White 1987). Japanese day-cares, preschools, and elementary schools all emphasize socialization into structured routines and cooperative group identities, such that it is these routines and interactive group processes that control and direct children's activities with very little direct teacher intervention. According to Rohlen (1989:25),

> It is important to note that the teacher is the first agent of a society that agrees very broadly on the importance of fixed patterns of daily order. The routines and group processes learned at three and four will certainly be confirmed and reinforced in other structured situations throughout life.

Studies of work in Japan have looked at ways that group processes and socialization for group identities central to early childhood education are reinforced in later life learning situations (e.g., Rohlen 1974; Cole 1979; Clark 1979; Dore 1973; Abegglen and Stalk 1985; McMillan 1985). This chapter discusses socialization and situated learning not in a work-related context but in another arena of modern Japanese life that is often equally structured – leisure. To do so, it presents and analyzes one-week residential silk-weaving seminars for vacationing women held in the Japanese Alps of Nagano prefecture. I originally participated in one of these seminars in 1986 out of a personal interest in weaving. I returned as a participant in repeated sessions during the summer of 1992 in order to conduct fieldwork on the processes of socialization, learning, and identity formation in the workshops. These live-in weaving workshops reiterate themes of learning found in childhood school education and discussed in work contexts of adult life, such as the interplay of individuality with socialization into a collective identity, expectations for both teacher–pupil and *senpai–kōhai* (senior–junior) relationships, emphases on structured routines, shared cooperative learning, group evaluation, group responsibility, and "consensus decision making." The ideology surrounding the workshops emphasize silk weaving as a traditional Japanese craft, and therefore, although a leisure activity, the workshop experience mimics learning in an apprenticeship situation. As the reconstruction of a traditional craft and apprenticeship-like experience, this educational-leisure activity involves the reinvention of tradition and reaffirmation of rural values that are part of the modern construction of Japanese identity (Robertson 1987, 1988, 1991). While participants learn about silk weaving, they are also learning modern constructions of Japanese identity.

The likely place

The workshops are organized and taught by a Japanese couple who have devoted themselves to the perpetuation of Nagano weaving traditions. Their attempts to construct the educational experience in accordance with prevailing concepts of "traditionalistic" Japanese learning is apparent in the asserted workshop philosophy, encapsulated in the theme slogan, "*Dentō no naka de genzai o* . . . ." Like many such Japanese slogans, part of the statement is assumed to be understood and therefore omitted, making literal translation difficult. Since *genzai* refers to the present, the slogan could suggest, "[Let's make] the present based on a foundation of tradition," or "[Weaving] the present from the heart of tradition." However, several Japanese speakers felt that the phrase implied actions in the present that would shape the future. This idea is also found in the Japanese word for tradition, *dentō,* used in the slogan. Consisting of two characters meaning transmit and heritage, *dentō* suggests things that have been transmitted in a line, or passed down through the generations, and implies that these will in turn be passed on into the future. With these considerations, the workshop slogan conveys the imperative of "Weaving the future from the heart of tradition."

Appeals to tradition make the workshop location particularly relevant. Situated in a remote mountainous area, the weaving seminars appear to be a rural, "traditional" phenomenon but are the product of a highly urbanized, industrialized, and consumer-oriented modern Japan. Part of their attraction is a prevalent modern nostalgia for rural peripheries and area folk traditions, which represent a "lost Japan." The women who participate in the seminars are mostly urban dwellers who form part of the exodus to these representative examples of lost Japan during their vacation periods. Traveling to remote rural areas suggests a return to Japan's preindustrial rural past and also a reunion with the pristine

Japanese *kokoro* (heart/mind), a *kokoro* that is nonurban and definitely non-Western. As discussed by Ivy (1988:22),

> the traveler's "self" equals an original Japanese self which equals the authentic *kokoro,* which in turn equals the rural, remote, non-American, and non-rational. Travel is the operator which connects the terms of the equation, by allowing the displacement of discovery to occur. Travel permits a temporary recuperation of a lost self.

This area of Nagano prefecture was the heart of Japan's silk-weaving industry during Japan's early industrial development in the Meiji period (1868–1912). In the past, sericulture (silk production) and silk weaving were common household chores for rural area wives, and young rural women from poor families were often forced into exploitive employment in the area's silk factories (Tsurumi 1990). Ironically, amidst Japan's modern affluence predominately urban, upper-middle-class women now travel to the area to learn *tetsumugi* (Japanese hand spinning and weaving) as a leisure pursuit to rediscover Japan's roots and reclaim a connection with an idealized Japanese identity.

As new participants approach the workshop site, their journey takes them precisely into the heart of the nonurban reality they have been romanticizing – but almost painfully so. The travel bus "station" nearest the workshop consists of a bus-stop sign, bench, and telephone plopped down in an otherwise totally isolated mountainous area. The experience of being alone, unattached, and uninvolved is heightened by difficulties in getting a taxi to the still distant workshop location. The two small taxi firms that service the entire area have difficulty on the days when the more than twenty workshop participants arrive, so many must wait alone at the bus-stop bench for over an hour, with nothing to do but gaze at the natural setting.

After finally arriving at the actual workshop site, newcomers again discover that they are not fully integrated into activities. Repeating participants are already actively involved in their pursuits, and the male instructor, referred to here as Mr. Sensei,[1] is fully occupied with them. Mrs. Sensei greets arriving newcomers briskly but is too involved with final preparations for the rest of the week to interact with anyone at length. Interaction between newcomers, all strangers at this point, is constrained. After taking several solitary walks around the natural environment, there is little left to do. By the initial evening dinner session, at which the soon to be all-encompassing structure of the workshop is explained, structure is less imposed than something for which participants long. Similarly, the initial experience of being unattached and not integrated into group activities makes participants welcome their socialization into well-defined group identities, a process which forms a very large part of the workshop learning experience.

Learning in relationships

The structure of learning throughout the week-long sessions prompts the construction of overlapping and situationally shifting group identities, along with individualistically motivated action and self-development. Although seasonal allusions change depending on the month, the patterning of the workshop activities and the daily routines never vary. Participants who repeat their involvement will not encounter a new structure in a succeeding session, but their own locus of placement will shift. Learners can be divided roughly into two types, newcomers and those who have attended the workshops before. This forms the basis of *senpai–kōhai,* or senior–junior relationships. Those with previous workshop experience are *senpai*; newcomers by definition are everyone's *kōhai.* Newcomers are divided into two small groups, or *han,* and nearly all of their learning experiences are shared with other *han* members. Among returning participants, there is an understanding of who is senior or junior depending on how often they have been involved. There is usually one woman (or at most two women) with extensive experience at the workshop who returns as assistant to the teachers; such assistants are referred to as *daisenpai* ("big seniors"). As in other contexts of Japanese life, there is the expectation that *senpai* assist in the education process in informal ways, by transmitting their own sometimes recently learned knowledge to *kōhai,* so that at every level people are transferring an understanding of what they have just succeeded in learning to those who have not yet mastered this level.

As commonly presented, people become *senpai* by length of membership in a particular frame of reference. However, this is linked to an implied assumption in Japan that one gains skill and knowledge over time, and hence length of involvement should mean that one has gained greater competency. Even if not true in particular cases, maintaining this idea as myth is important. Because I returned to the workshops in 1992 in part to research socialization processes, I repeated the newcomers' course of instruction more than once. I was never referred to as a *senpai,* or treated or conceptualized as a *senpai,* until I finally participated in a session on the same terms as other advanced students. In other words, *senpai–kōhai* relationships were not strictly equated with length of time one was involved. I did become a *senpai* and was referred to as a *senpai* by the instructors and other participants, but only when I took on a *senpai*'s work and role.

Commensality and the creation of community

Workshops begin on Sunday. Repeating participants (*senpai*) arrive in the early morning and begin to set up looms for the specific projects they have chosen to make for the session. Newcomers (*kōhai*) are told that they may arrive any time on Sunday as long as they are present by 6:30 P.M. for the initial group gathering to take place at dinner. All meals for the workshop from Monday's breakfast through Saturday's breakfast are included in the course fees and provided by the instructors. After registering, participants are informed, both by telephone and in writing, that they must bring their own *obentō* (box meal) because dinner will not be provided on Sunday evening and food cannot be purchased anywhere in the locale.

Like an opening ceremony, Sunday dinner serves as a marker punctuating the official beginning of the seminar. The meeting has an important informative purpose: The schedule for the week is explained, and participants are assigned to dorm rooms and their small work groups. The meeting is also highly significant in that something happens to transform the collection of diverse individual strangers into a group of interconnected and mutually involved session participants. This occurs over the sharing of food.

Commensality, whereby people eat together, is a common process through which bonds among people are created or reinforced. According to Ohnuki-Tierney (1993:98), "Commensality binds people together who interact face to face in almost all societies to establish a sense of community, or *we*" [author's emphasis]. The workshop instructors created a situation in which not they themselves but the session participants would initiate the sharing of food and hence the seeds of community sentiment.

Although instructed to do so, I did not bring a meal for Sunday evening the first time I attended a session. It seemed too much of a bother to carry an *obentō* along with my other luggage all the way from Tokyo during several hours of bus travel. Despite the instructors' warnings, my experiences living and traveling in Japan led me to believe that one could get a packaged meal at a travel stop or convenience store almost anywhere, no matter how "remote." I was wrong. My error, however, cannot be attributed to my being a foreigner; six of the Japanese women also arrived without a meal due to the same mistaken assumption.

As we sat down to the dinner meeting, a participant mentioned to the instructors that some women did not have anything to eat. This prompted a commentary from Mr. Sensei about the (limited) availability of shops in the area. He explained where smokers could buy tobacco and where the liquor store and only tavern were in case people were interested in drinking during the week. There were two small shops – distant, but within a 30-minute walk – that sold food, but it was Sunday evening, and all the shops mentioned in this discussion were already closed.

Even though we all had been well informed that Sunday dinner would not be provided, I thought the instructors would find something to eat for the several women who were without food – at least the ever available rice. However, as the teachers began to eat their own meals, it gradually dawned on everyone that no food would be forthcoming from them. Clearly, no one would starve before breakfast, but most of the women had traveled several hours to reach the workshop, heightening a sense of hunger. *Enryo* (restraint) and a bit of embarrassment prevented those without food from asking the teachers or their peers for anything to eat.

Eventually, a few of the women with food began to offer some to those without. One woman then stated that it would not work out well for two women to share a meal since neither would get enough to eat. Before long, all the participants, who until that time had only smiled politely or nodded silently at each other, were actively talking together about the food situation, moving between each other's tables, and dividing any food brought among all those present.

After my first workshop session, I interpreted this incident as the instructors' attempt to establish limits firmly, to the extent that participants would be allowed to *amae,* or depend on them. Education researchers assert that socialization for *shūdan seikatsu* (group life) in preschools and elementary schools involves inculcating the understanding that one must be responsible and cannot expect teachers to indulge the desires for *amae* (dependency) that are indulged within the family setting (Peak 1989:94–114, 1991:11–38; Tobin et al. 1989:70–72; Hendry 1986:66). Peak (1989:115) stresses that "Over-reliance on the teacher is one issue that Japanese teachers consider important enough to force children to the point of tears, if necessary." Therefore teachers try to make this point to newly forming groups.

> A common technique in these cases is to wait for an opportune chance early in the transition period to plant the seed of understanding that at preschool, one must try to do as much as possible for oneself. (Peak 1989:112).

The workshop instructors likewise used the initial dinner meeting to assert limits to their indulgence and hospitality and also to make the point that this was *shūdan seikatsu,* not family life. This was particularly important in the workshop setting, where dorm and work rooms were an extension of the instructors' household. Their refusal to provide food firmly established their relationship to participants as teachers, not as household hosts interacting with guests.

However, the instructors' performance had another purpose. After participating in only a few workshop sessions, I could accurately predict that out of the twenty-two to twenty-four participants each week, six to eight women would neglect to bring a meal for the initial gathering. If this was something I "knew" after only a few weeks, certainly the teachers who had run the workshops for years knew it as well. At every session, I witnessed the same process through which a sense of community began to develop among the newly gathered strangers as they began to communicate with each other and share their own food in order to resolve the meal problem, independently of the teachers. Sano (1989: 127) points out that "Japanese teachers seem to play their role more from offstage; American teachers seem to perform their role at center stage." It has been noted repeatedly that Japanese teachers do not step in to resolve conflicts or sanction negative behavior but instead prompt peer groups to discipline each other and maintain social control from within (Peak 1989:107–112; Sano 1989; Lewis 1984:78–82, 1989:145–155). The workshop's initial dinner meeting reiterates these same group processes in an adult educational experience, while also revealing the other side of the coin, in which the group becomes the locus not only of disciplinary sanctions but of support, nurturance, and sustenance for group members.

Workshop groups

The structure of the weaving workshops is focused around various group frameworks that create shifting boundaries of self-identification and collective identities. These shifting frameworks are consistent with the Japanese ideals of dependency and interactive group behavior; they are also consistent with pragmatic concerns for education in the workshop setting. The division of participants into small groups, combined with the fact that these Japanese women have been developing skills for cooperative group behavior from childhood,[2] allows for the efficient operation of the workshops and effective teaching in a situation where there are only two teachers with one assistant for a group of about twenty-four students learning at different levels.

The following constitute different *uchi* (inside) group boundaries. A strong sense of togetherness develops among all the participants of any session, creating a collective group identity. Of these twenty-two to twenty-four women, approximately six will be returnees. The returnees create a group of *senpai-tachi,* while all newcomers form an "entering cohort" group. Newcomers are divided into two groups, or *han,* called A-*han* and B-*han,* which become the dominant focus of group identity for all first-time participants. Since there are only two instructors, Mrs. Sensei conducts a lesson for A-*han* while Mr. Sensei conducts a different lesson for B-*han.* By rotating teachers and lessons throughout the week, all newcomers receive the same full course of instruction. The instructors' conscious purpose for dividing newcomers into *han* stems from this pragmatic concern rather than from a desire to maintain a Japanese proclivity for small groups. However, they are able to draw on participants' experiences with and expectations for small-group organization. Since members of a *han* spend nearly all of their time involved in the same activities at the same time, bonds among them become intense.

Dormitory and *tōban* (monitor) assignments break across returnee/newcomer and A-*han*/B-*han* dividing lines. The workshops incorporate a system of rotating monitors, called *tōban,* a practice also regularly found in school situations (Lewis 1989:144; Peak 1991:88). The four women assigned to each *tōban* group also share a dormitory room, which they together clean. Since *senpai* are familiar with the work routines, each *tōban* group is comprised of at least one *senpai* and a mix of A-*han* and B-*han* members. In a process of daily rotation, *tōban* groups are responsible for maintaining nonweaving maintenance tasks essential to the group-living situation, such as preparing meals, or the evening bath, and cleaning the common rooms. As in Japanese school education, where children must wash floors and clean erasers, learning in the workshops means involvement in the work necessary to maintain the educational process. Consistent with these Japanese attitudes toward education, Kondo (1990:92) shows how people at an ethics retreat were also required to assume many of the cleaning tasks.

The overlapping workshop groups reflect an orientation toward a relationally constructed self in which selfhood is situational and embedded in networks of relationships. Bachnik (1992) shows how even among close family and friends of a household, the boundaries delimiting *uchi,* or the "inside" group, constantly change as people enter and leave the situation.

The *uchi* group for weaving participants similarly fluctuates throughout the workshop; at any moment, it might be the cohort, a specific *han,* or a *tōban* group. For newcomers, the strongest locus of identity becomes the *han,* but the periodic affirmation of other *uchi* frameworks prevents identification with one's *han* from precluding a strong sense of collective identity among all members of a particular session.

Daily routines

The workshop day begins at 5:00 to 5:30 A.M. Kondo (1990: 84) discusses how on a spiritual retreat for company employees everyone must awaken at 5:00 A.M., which she relates to a cultural belief that waking early is the mark of an ethical person and sleeping in nearly equated with immorality in Japan. The weaving workshops are supposed to be a leisure pursuit and a vacation. Therefore, there is no stated assertion that the day begins at 5:00 A.M. Participants are officially told not to exert themselves excessively, that they may leave the activities at any time to take a nap (which no one ever does, and which group involvement seems to preclude), and that they do not have to wake up early. No buzzers or alarm clocks force people to get up early – just the sun, a focal symbol of Japanese identity (Ohnuki-Tierney 1990:208). Japanese society has resisted conventions such as daylight saving time, preferring to allow early summer sunrises. Windows in dorm rooms have only *shōji* (rice-paper sliding shutters), which block outside views but allow the sun to shine in, making it a struggle not to awake at 5:00 A.M. Everyone is supposed to be quiet at this time, supposedly out of consideration for those (nonexistent) women who might still be sleeping. The day's *tōban* (meal monitors) go to the common rooms to prepare breakfast, while other women silently clean their rooms or take walks outdoors until about 6:00 A.M., at which time it was understood that everyone really *should* be awake, and there was no need to worry about keeping quiet any longer. Women would then do "radio exercises" together or work independently on the looms until breakfast at 7:00 A.M. After breakfast, advanced students work independently, while the A-*han* and B-*han* receive an organized lesson. There is a mid-morning green tea and fruit break. The fruit is always the local specialty of the season, emphasizing connections with the natural environment of the place. The mid-morning break is followed by more group lessons for beginners, then lunch from 12:30 to 1:30, followed again by beginners' group lessons. At 3:00 P.M. every day, all workshop members together participate in "radio exercises," a program broadcast at the same time twice daily throughout Japan. Since Japan has only one time zone, radio exercises synchronize the activities of many people throughout the country and help to create a symbol of collective national identity in the process. Exercises are followed by the mid-afternoon green tea and fruit break, again followed by group lessons for beginners. Dinner begins at 7:00 P.M. After dinner, everyone is engaged in more individualistic pursuits, such as weaving on one's own sections of cloth, spinning thread, or socializing in the common rooms until people retire, usually between 11:00 P.M. and midnight.

Once established, the daily rhythm regulated behavior. There were only two slight changes in this daily pattern; one resulted in breakfast starting half an hour later, and the other did not affect the time schedule at all. These were the week's two "special events," designed to heighten a sense of involvement in the natural environment of the place. One of the special events was a group morning hike through the mountains before breakfast. The other special event was "eating out." From the initial meeting, participants were promised that Wednesday, the midway point of the seminar, would be marked as a special occasion on which we would all "eat out" for breakfast. The phrase used, "*soto de taberu,*" carries the literal meaning of "eat out" and, like the English phrase, suggests the idea of going out to a restaurant to dine. This double meaning was intentionally used as a source of workshop humor. New participants clearly thought we would break our solitary isolation in the mountains and "homey" lifestyle with a mid-week restaurant outing. As one participant stated,

> For the first two days I was really excited about going somewhere else to eat. I kept thinking that maybe there was a nice French restaurant, or quaint *kissaten* [coffee/tea shop] for travelers out here somewhere. But after a couple of days, I couldn't imagine something like that anywhere around here, so I thought maybe the teachers had a bus coming to take us all out to dine.

As Wednesday approached, there was more and more discussion about the mystery outing until finally, on Tuesday evening, the teachers answered students' questions about where we would "eat out" directly by stating that "We will eat out – out" as they pointed outside. On the long-awaited special day, all the women helped Wednesday's *tōban* carry the breakfast dishes from the common room in which we normally ate to the outside of the same building.

Educational socialization practices in school settings emphasize establishing routines that govern activities (Sano 1989:128). As Rohlen (1989: 21) states, "The crucial tools applied by the teachers in their management of surprisingly large numbers of students involve, first of all, the thorough teaching of selected basic routines that punctuate the day." The daily seminar schedule reflects this educational emphasis on routines and on "habituating the body." The workshops involved a great deal of learning with and through the body in terms of habituating the body into weaving or spinning, activities that involve coordination of hands, legs, and full-body movements. The well-defined and nearly unvarying daily schedule also reflects the Japanese ideal of training the body for a regulated life. Students were habituating their bodies to anticipate the same activities at the same time every day, while training those bodies to thoughtlessly perform the craft processes.

Instruction for beginners

First-time participants spent little time actually weaving. For the first several days, participants learned such things as how to raise silk worms, how to boil the cocoons correctly, how to remove dead worms from cocoons, how to make silk watting, how to spin thread, and how to dye threads with natural grasses that the participants themselves collected in the surrounding mountains.

Most of these practices are not going to be engaged in often, even by the active weaver. People who specialize in raising silk worms sell these to the initial processing centers, where thread is spun and dyed. When I asked about the rationale for teaching all of these aspects of the craft, the instructors expressed strong beliefs that if one is to understand weaving, one must know all aspects of the process. Learning the craft also meant learning about, and preparing oneself for, engagement in that craft. This involves preparing the *kokoro* (heart/mind), as in calligraphy, where for many teachers grinding the ink is at least as essential to the learning process as perfecting the style of one's written characters.

Apprenticeship and apprenticeship-like situations, according to Goody (1989), offer not only a way to learn a craft or skill, but a way to learn about learning. Expecting to learn weaving, I was initially surprised at the emphasis on learning these other background processes. The course of instruction for beginners reflected a belief that one cannot truly respect one's weaving endeavors (and hence fully learn) without an experiential understanding of the materials used, the entire nature of the process, and how aspects of it are "woven" together. As a participant, I can attest that one embraces a sense of awe and wonder at the nature of hand-woven goods, at the very existence of textiles, when through personal experience one participates in every stage of the process from raising silk worms, to separating the cocoons, to spinning and dyeing before one can actually weave.

Each *han* (group) of newcomers collectively chose the lengthwise threads for their looms, set their looms up together, and tied each of more than 3,000 lengthwise threads that would comprise their cloth to an analogous set of 3,000 threads ending the previous piece. Each member of the *han* then wove a section of each group cloth, according to her own tastes. Setting up the looms is difficult for any one person new to this type of weaving. However, group members relied on each other, thereby enabling the group to set up the looms without repeated coaching and without errors in tying the threads. Yanagi (1989:134–136) believed that because craft allows individuals to rely on each other and on a tradition, nearly everyone has the capacity to create works of great beauty, and this does not necessitate individual creative genius. Japanese attitudes toward education also tend to deemphasize individual brilliance or inborn abilities, emphasizing instead effort, character, and the advancement of learning for all in cooperative groups (*han*) (e.g., Tobin et al. 1989:23–25).

Collective responsibility and consensus realizations

Two aspects of Japanese group processes that have been widely discussed are collective responsibility and consensus decision making. Kondo (1990:80) describes a situation in which other members of a group had to cover for one irresponsible woman so that the whole group did not suffer for her shortcomings. As a result "the stress on group responsibility acted as a highly efficient self-policing mechanism." During the weaving workshops, an entire *han,* rather than any individual member of it, took the blame – accompanied by scornful reprimands from the teachers – if errors were made setting up the looms. In this situation, collective responsibility had less to do with the group suffering for one person's irresponsibility than with everyone trying their best so that others would not suffer because of their mistakes.

Tying the 6,000 silk threads was a tedious process that had to take place between or after other lessons. *Han* members rotated this duty, while at least one member of the *han* acted as "spotter" (someone who watched to make sure the threads were tied in their precise proper order), thus making spotters equally as responsible for errors as those tying the threads. On a few occasions, a *han* would make a mistake, which was typically discovered at the very end. If, for example, the last of the 3,000 threads of one set was left without a partner to be attached to, it meant that somewhere along the line someone had erred. There was no way of knowing which individual or individuals caused the error because it was impossible to determine who had been tying and spotting at the time it occurred. In such a situation, locating responsibility collectively among the group was the only possibility.

The process of setting up the looms also contained a lesson in consensus decision making. The consensus model of group processes in Japan is frequently attributed to a cultural emphasis on harmony. What emerged more strongly in the workshops was an emphasis on "rationality," which made "consensus realization" seem a more appropriate name for the process. When the looms were almost set up, each *han* was told that it had to decide on the best place to insert the *aibō,* sticks which separate the up and down threads while weaving. The instructors told each *han* to discuss this until the group reached a unanimous decision.

In my *han,* there was a flurry of discussion about this problem. When Mrs. Sensei came back to ask how we were doing, one or two women shouted out suggestions about where the *aibō* should go. This resulted in severe reprimands from Mrs. Sensei, who said, "Is that the group's sentiment, or are you just expressing your own opinion? Don't think for yourself now, you must express the group's understanding." When I first heard the *sensei* criticize us in this manner, I felt like I was experiencing a total reversal of my own educational background, in which teachers would criticize students for mimicking the opinions of others and prompt us to instead "think for yourself."

The reason that "consensus decision making" seems a misnomer is that there was at the background of our discussions some idea that there was a right way of doing things, external to any of us, and hence our individual ideas or opinions did not matter. We were not involved in a process of mutually or collectively "deciding" nor one of swaying each other's opinions to our own. The purpose of the extensive consultation required to reach a group consensus was to allow the "natural" and "more appropriate" solution to surface in all its rationality. Furthermore, through this process, every participant came to an understanding of why this was the more rational way. Campbell (1984:311) contends that the consensus model involves an "implicit theory," that by necessitating exchanges of information and opinions, consensus decisions produce more harmonious outcomes, and also the best solutions. According to Campbell (1984:310),

Japanese prefer the consensual model for two reasons: By avoiding open conflict it preserves the social fabric of the group; and it is likely to produce substantively better outcomes – decisions which are certainly more implementable and probably more rational.

Interwoven identities

The socialization and learning experiences within the workshops create strong concepts of group identity. As in the larger society, these frameworks of group identity are multiple and overlapping, with one framework emerging as the strongest locus of identity. Through shared living experiences, all participants in a given session develop a strong sense of group identity. However, group identity is strongest within smaller groups, especially the members of A-*han* and B-*han,* who do nearly everything together throughout the week, and who collectively make decisions about their looms and weaving materials.

In many ways, Japanese culture tends to deemphasize individualism, but the emphasis on group activity, and merging self with a group identity, does not negate individuality. Scholars such as Moeran (1984) and Hendry (1992) have shown that Japanese culture posits differential judgments about "individualism" and "individuality." An analogy for the relationship between personal and collective identity is manifested materially in the woven products of seminar participants. All new participants weave four placemat-sized pieces of cloth on four different looms. The lengthwise threads (*tatte ito,* warp) for the looms are either chosen by the group or already set in place by the instructors before the workshop begins. Each woman individually chooses her own crosswise threads (*yoko ito,* woof) for her segments. Thus each segment of cloth is both a collective product and yet an object affirming the individuality of each woman within the constraints of the group. Despite the fact that each cloth has exactly the same "framework" or lengthwise threads running through it, there is incredible variation among the segments individually woven by each woman.

If one considers only the workshop involvement of first-time participants, the workshops appear oriented toward only group activities and collective involvement. Like new recruits in companies, these women are socialized into strong cohort and small-group identities. However, once ushered into the ranks of advanced students, participants spend a great deal of time working independently on their own individually chosen projects.

At the end of the week, just before the big "*sayonara* party," all participants gather to watch the advanced students cut their own material from the looms, followed by A-*han* and B-*han* members cutting their cloths into segments so each woman can take her own pieces home. This is a highly ritualized and well-photographed event. It creates a marked emotional climax, which brings many women near tears. After an intensive experiential process of coming to understand everything that goes into making cloth, the women have great difficulty actually cutting it.

The woven silk cloth also becomes the material metaphor of personal relationships. For one week, everyone is intensely joined together. Although addresses are exchanged, participants generally realize that once back to their normal lives, their ties to fellow participants will recede. Separating – indeed, cutting – the cloth also stands for the separating of selves that women realize is an implicit part of the final festive "*sayonara* party." There is great sadness that the cloth is disturbed in any way, and separating the bonds that have developed between participants is also recognized with great sadness.

Conclusions

The leisure-pursuit weaving workshops presented here reflect many common themes of modern Japanese life. Their popularity reflects the idealization of a receding Japanese heritage and a nostalgia for a craft lifestyle associated with the rural preindustrial past. Because silk, like rice (Ohnuki-Tierney 1993), is constructed as a symbol of Japaneseness, the popular resurgence of silk-weaving traditions mirrors the modern desire for symbols of Japanese identity. As part of the burgeoning leisure consumer industry, they reflect Japan's increasing affluence, which has allowed more Japanese to engage in travel and leisure pursuits. Reflecting attitudes toward learning, such activities are recast as educational, with suggestions that they are not just for fun but for self-development.

To enhance an understanding of educational processes in the Japanese context, this article has made comparisons between early school education and the transmission of knowledge in weaving workshops. The context of learning in this nonschool setting supports Rohlen's (1989:25) assertion that the routines and group processes found in childhood education in Japanese schools are indeed confirmed and reinforced in other structured situations throughout Japanese life. Although this has been argued before, most notably in studies of work organization, this research shows that parallel processes are also apparent in leisure pursuits and in activities where people expect a relatively short time involvement rather than a lifetime commitment.

Theories of situated learning suggest that education involves more than the acquisition of propositional knowledge; it involves the social engagements essential for learning to take place (Lave and Wenger 1991). According to Hanks (1991:15), "Learning is a process that takes place in a participation framework, not in an individual mind." As such, learning also involves processes of socialization into the appropriate participation framework and processes of identity construction. As in Japanese early childhood education, the socialization and learning experiences within the workshops create strong concepts of group identity. As in the larger society, these frameworks of group identity are multiple, shifting, and overlapping, with one framework emerging as the strongest locus of identity. Within a short time period, unconnected strangers are socialized into interconnected identities to provide a participatory framework within which learning can occur, which is consistent with patterns permeating other contexts of Japanese life and experience. While creating strong interconnected identities, this participatory framework also allows for the expression of individuality and, particularly at the level of advanced beginners, engagement in independently motivated self-development.

Socialization is not just a cultural initiation process for children but something that reoccurs in different social contexts throughout the life cycle as an integral part of learning. This study suggests that socialization, education, and identity construction need to be considered as interrelated processes. If learning occurs within a participation framework involving relationships with others, then socialization into those relationships and the learning framework is an important part of the learning process. This study also suggests that perhaps all education involves the creation of identity, whether the intentional inculcation of a national or collective identity that others wish to transfer, or the emergence of a new sense of self from within that accompanies personal development. Education is tied to identity construction because it can prompt people toward a new sense of situated selfhood defining a collective identity, or it can prompt shifts in the boundaries of a person's individual sense of self. Extensive studies of work organization by other Japan specialists show that learning a new work role involves the construction of a new sense of self, frequently one in which selfhood is interconnected with one's work organization and career identity. Women learning at the workshops are participating in a leisure pursuit where education involves an expanding sense of selfhood. This is education for "self-development," where self-development implies the continual re-creation and redefining of identity. For women participating in the workshops, the socialization and learning experiences contribute to the emerging development not of a career identity but of a changing personal self.

Notes

1. Teachers and certain other professionals are commonly referred to as *sensei* in Japan. Since the couple who ran the workshops were also teachers, workshop students referred to them as *onna sensei* (female teacher) and *otoko sensei* (male teacher) to differentiate them. I use the terms Mr. Sensei and Mrs. Sensei as an attempt to capture this aspect of workshop interactions.
2. Lewis (1984:71) refers to experimental studies showing that children who learned to perform cooperative tasks in groups of constant rather than changing membership were later found to be more skilled at cooperative group tasks when grouped with other sets of children. This supports the idea that socialization into stable small-group membership, emphasized in Japanese early childhood education, builds the skills for cooperative group action in subsequent settings.

References

Abegglen, James C., and George Stalk, Jr., 1985, *Kaisha, The Japanese Corporation,* New York: Basic Books.

Bachnik, Jane, 1992, "*Kejime*: Defining a Shifting Self in Multiple Organizational Modes," in *Japanese Sense of Self,* N. Rosenberg, ed., 152–172, Cambridge: Cambridge University Press.

Ben-Ari, Eyal, 1987, Disputing About Day-Care: Care-Taking Roles in a Japanese Day Nursery, *International Journal of Sociology of the Family 17*(2): 197–215.

Campbell, John Creighton, 1984, "Policy Conflict and its Resolution within the Governmental System," in *Conflict in Japan,* Ellis S. Krauss, Thomas P. Rohlen, Patricia G. Steinhoff, eds., 294–334, Honolulu: University of Hawaii Press.

Clark, Rodney, 1979, *The Japanese Company,* New Haven: Yale University Press.

Cole, Robert E., 1979, *Work, Mobility, and Participation,* Berkeley: University of California Press.

Dore, Ronald, 1973, *British Factory–Japanese Factory: The Origins of National Diversity in Industrial Relations,* Berkeley: University of California Press.

Goody, Esther N., 1989, "Learning, Apprenticeship and the Division of Labor," in *Apprenticeship: From Theory to Method and Back Again,* Michael W. Coy, ed., 233–256, Albany: State University of New York Press.

Hanks, William F., 1991, Foreword, in *Situated Learning: Legitimate Peripheral Participation,* Jean Lave and Etienne Wenger, 13–24, Cambridge: Cambridge University Press.

Hendry, Joy, 1986, *Becoming Japanese: The World of the Pre-School Child,* Manchester: Manchester University Press.

1992, "Individualism and Individuality: Entry into a Social World," in *Ideology and Practice in Modern Japan,* Roger Goodman and Kirsten Refsing, eds., 55–71, London: Routledge.

Ivy, Marilyn, 1988, Tradition and Difference in the Japanese Mass Media, *Public Culture 1*(1): 21–29.

Kondo, Dorinne K., 1990, *Crafting Selves: Power, Gender, and Discourses of Identity in a Japanese Workplace,* Chicago: University of Chicago Press.

Lave, Jean, and Etienne Wenger, 1991, *Situated Learning: Legitimate Peripheral Participation,* Cambridge: Cambridge University Press.

Lewis, Catherine C., 1984, Cooperation and Control in Japanese Nursery Schools, *Comparative Education Review 28*(1): 69–84.

1989, From Indulgence to Internalization: Social Control in the Early School Years, *Journal of Japanese Studies 15*(1): 139–157.

McMillan, Charles, 1985, *The Japanese Industrial System,* New York: de Gruyter.

Moeran, Brian, 1984, Individual, Group, and *Seishin*: Japan's Internal Cultural Debate, *Man 19*: 252–266.

Ohnuki-Tierney, Emiko, 1990, The Ambivalent Self of the Contemporary Japanese, *Cultural Anthropology 5*(2): 197–216.

1993, *Rice as Self: Japanese Identities through Time,* Princeton: Princeton University Press.

Peak, Lois, 1989, Learning to Become Part of the Group: The Japanese Child's Transition to Preschool Life, *Journal of Japanese Studies 15*(1): 93–123.

1991, *Learning to Go to School in Japan: The Transition from Home to Preschool Life,* Berkeley: University of California Press.

Robertson, Jennifer, 1987, A Dialectic of Native and Newcomer: The Kodaira Citizen's Festival in Suburban Tokyo, *Anthropological Quarterly 60*(3): 124–136.

1988, The Culture and Politics of Nostalgia: *Furusato* Japan, *International Journal of Politics, Culture and Society 1*(4): 494–518.

1991, *Native and Newcomer: Making and Remaking a Japanese City,* Berkeley: University of California Press.

Rohlen, Thomas P., 1974, *For Harmony and Strength: Japanese White-Collar Organization in Anthropological Perspective,* Berkeley: University of California Press.

1989, Order in Japanese Society: Attachment, Authority, and Routine, *Journal of Japanese Studies 15*(1): 5–40.

Sano Toshiyuki, 1989, Methods of Social Control and Socialization in Japanese Day-Care Centers, *Journal of Japanese Studies 15*(1): 125–138.

Tobin, Joseph, David Wu, and Dana Davidson, 1989, *Preschool in Three Cultures: Japan, China and the United States,* New Haven: Yale University Press.

Tsurumi, E. Patricia, 1990, *Factory Girls: Women in the Thread Mills of Meiji Japan,* Princeton: Princeton University Press.

White, Merry, 1987, *The Japanese Educational Challenge: A Commitment to Children,* New York: The Free Press.

Yanagi Soetsu, 1989, *The Unknown Craftsman: A Japanese Insight into Beauty,* Tokyo: Kodansha.

Part III

Work and community socialization: Diversity in learning arrangements

12 Moneyed knowledge: How women become commercial shellfish divers

Jacquetta F. Hill and David W. Plath

> The attainment of proficiency, the pushing of your skill with attention to the most delicate shades of excellence, is a matter of vital concern. Efficiency of a practically flawless kind may be reached naturally in the struggle for bread. But there is something beyond – a higher point, a subtle and unmistakable touch of love and pride beyond mere skill; almost an inspiration which gives to all work that finish which is almost art – which is art.[1]

Each year from March to September, some 500 women who live along the coast of the Shima Peninsula go hunting underwater for one of the world's most pricey edibles, fresh abalone. An expert diver earns a high income, but her greatest prizes are self-satisfaction and the respect she gains from having mastered a risky, esoteric craft. It took us several seasons to decipher some of the mystery of that mastery. We continue to dive after its deeper structures.

In the opening quotation, Joseph Conrad is talking about the art of operating a merchant sailing ship. For a shellfish diver, the vessel is her own submersible body. Because the tasks are performed in total immersion, novices have very few opportunities to learn by casually observing veterans in action. And because the amount of a diver's catch depends upon how well she can judge where the abalone are hiding in the reefs, she is, like most hunters, not eager to have a potential competitor tagging along with her and stealing her moneyed knowledge.

A few days after we arrived in Shima for the first time, we asked (as good academics will) about training programs and apprenticeships for divers. There are none – was the answer, with the addendum that years ago, when several novices turned up at the beginning of the season, a veteran diver usually was asked to supervise them in the water long enough to be sure that they could be trusted not to drown themselves.

We were left pondering those clichéd notions about how traditional crafts are passed on either by apprenticeship or by direct transmission from parent to child. Japan's mass media routinely employ such notions, adding that traditional crafts are an endangered species in that so few young people are willing to stay home and learn them. And this in turn puts Japan's cultural identity at risk because shellfish diving as a female specialty is said to exist only in Japan. Japanese folklore scholars have been studying the divers for half a century but have said rather little about how the craft is learned. For them, the issue of choice is geographical rather than generational transmission, their goal being to trace the spread of diving techniques as they diffused across the archipelago in earlier centuries from a putative First Beach in Kyushu.

One afternoon during our second visit to Shima, several of the women came to our house to talk with us about their craft. With tea and questions, we tried to steer them to the topic of skill acquisition, but the affable muteness of the group suggested that we were not even getting close to what they thought important. An older diver eventually said to Plath in a tone of friendly correction, "*Sensei*, learning this work is not like what you do in school."

Mentally discarding that line of questioning, we suggested that it might help if each woman would tell individually how she came to be a diver. First to respond, of course, was the senior-most among them, then in her fifty-sixth season of diving. Her account of her early years was much like those we would hear later from the other women in her age bracket.

Born by the ocean, she was playing on the beaches and in the surf by the time she was a toddler. With help from older playmates, she acquired the basics of swimming and breath-hold diving. During primary school vacations, and again after she was graduated, she practiced hunting for shellfish on shallower reefs near shore. Eventually she was invited to join a group of working divers who went out by boat to exploit reefs farther at sea. It was her informal certification: She could begin diving commercially.

We asked who else was in that boat group at that time (divers recall their work histories in terms of the groups they dived with). Though half a century had passed, she quickly named the other women, one of them being her mother.

The investigators raised eyebrows to one another. "So your mother taught you how to find abalone?"

"My mother!" she said loudly, "*She* drove me away! I tried to follow her to the bottom to watch, but she shoved me back. When we were on the surface again, she practically screamed at me to move OFF and find my danged abalone BY MYSELF."

So we had to discard that second cliché about how artisans learn. But surely, we thought, even if the divers are not trained by anybody, they nevertheless must acquire their skills in some normal or typical sequence. However, we eventually had to abandon even this third piece of common sense, though it is backed by a "native model" widely used to indicate supposed stages of diving prowess.

Folklore scholars as well as media reporters have been propagating the model for decades, and maritime museums build displays around it. We were aware of it well before we first went to Shima. Stripped to essentials, it posits the following:

1. Diving is a female specialty. The word for "diver," *ama,* combines the graphs for "women" and "sea."
2. Women are more suited to the craft than are men. This is because women have greater lung capacity (can submerge for longer intervals) and/or thicker deposits of subcutaneous fat (lose body heat more slowly so can work longer without rest when the water is chilly).
3. As a diver's skills improve, she will shift to a different mode of practice. It will demand more of her physically, but she will make larger catches. Three such modes are recognized, with labels that differ from region to region; we use the terms current in Shima. (a) A diver begins her career as an *oyogido,* or "swimmer," as in the story already mentioned, who moves around under her own power exploiting reefs near the shoreline. (b) In time, she will join a group pf *okedo* or "bucketers." Each of these groups hires a boatman for the season; he ferries them to deeper waters, where abalone tend to be larger and more numerous. Once she drops from the boat into the water, however, an *okedo* operates independently, using a wooden tub (or nowadays a kapok-filled life ring) to rest on between dives and to serve as a container for her accumulating catch. (c) When she reaches peak prowess, a diver becomes a *funado,* or "boater." She and a male partner – typically her husband – operate as a two-person team. She dives directly from their boat, dropping swiftly to the sea bottom by holding a 15-kilogram weight. When she is almost out of breath, she tugs on a lifeline attached to her waist; at the signal, her partner hoists her quickly to the boat. While she is resting, he retrieves the weight so she can use it on her next descent. Since she expends very little energy going down and up, a *funado* maximizes her working time on the bottom.

This "native model" has the virtue of parsimony. And it sketches a clear gradient of increasing complexity, risk, and productivity from one stage to the next, culminating in the exquisite teamwork of a lifeline-using pair. Like most idealized schemes, however, it states a perfect career but does not even begin to suggest the diversity of practice that one hears about by asking only a few questions. For example:

1. Across the Japanese islands, almost as many men as women dive commercially for shellfish, though the men rarely have been studied and never appear in tourist posters. In many locales, the craft is gender-typed but not rigidly segregated. In Shima, diving is regarded as women's work, but in recent years men also have begun to take it up.
2. In an earlier era, men (and slender women) may have been at a disadvantage as divers. But the wetsuit reduces individual differences in cold tolerance, diminishing if not erasing the value of having layers of body fat. Furthermore, in our experience, it is not evident that the diver who is able to submerge the longest will capture the largest amount of shellfish. An *ama* with smaller lung capacity may be able to compensate by making dives more frequently but to lesser depth than those made by her barrel-chested colleagues.
3. Every *ama* starts out as a "swimmer" in near-shore waters, and some continue to work as *oyogido* until the day they retire. Many divers will deploy their maturing skills by shifting to another mode of practice. But the decision to do so is conditioned by so many different factors that we have not been able to compress the data into a tidy ladder of stages. If a suitable partner is available, for example, a "swimmer" may become a lifeline diver without ever working as a member of a boat group. In general, such shifts to another mode of practice are made at the beginning of a new diving season. But even during the season, a diver may switch to another mode temporarily if her own health fluctuates, or that of her boatman or partner, or if space becomes available on an *okedo* boat, and so on. On average, the lifeline divers bring in the larger and more lucrative catches, but the list of top moneymakers includes some women from each of the three supposed "stages" of career progress.

Lave and Wenger (1991) argue that common-sense ideas about apprenticeship as a mode of learning are not much help when one wants to understand how craft skills get developed to levels of high prowess. They suggest that the unit of analysis be a "community of practice": a cluster of persons engaging in an array of activities that link up to form a productive enterprise. For shellfish divers, one must add another dimension. Given the *localized* nature of *ama* work, the community of practice must be placed, for purposes of analysis, within an ecology of practice.

A diver who has incorporated a set of physical skills could move away and deploy them elsewhere. But her skills individually and the community's standards of practice collectively are formed through ongoing engagements with particular, localized niches in the environment. Already in our first reports on the divers (Plath and Hill 1987, 1988a, 1988b), we found that we could most effectively communicate the pattern of *ama* learning if we described it in "ecological" terms. A diver's skills have to be built into her body, but her moneyed knowledge is mentally recorded on the specific reefs and tidewater territory that her community of practice controls.

Put another way, the craft of shellfish diving involves not only learning many skills – that's true of most crafts – but studying at different sites. Of course, a diver can only learn certain essential skills underwater. But she is likely to acquire important items of knowledge, motives of competitiveness, senses of collegial duty, and so on while on land. From a pedagogical perspective, the coastal environment consists of an array of "learning resource centers" (in the jargon of campus bureaucrats), and in her ordinary daily round of activities, an *ama* will be engaged in several of these. En route to expertise, she must discipline herself to seize each new "learning experience" when it appears at one of these sites, much as she must train herself to pounce upon a live abalone when she detects it in the camouflage of reef vegetation. *Ama* learning, like *ama* productivity, is a catch-as-you-can business.

To illustrate this point, we sketch four key sites of learning and practice as we have observed them in Shima. Each site occupies a different niche in the physical environment that the community inhabits; each also occupies a different niche in the moral and cognitive ecologies of local human action. [For additional information on these sites, we refer you to our earlier reports (Plath and Hill 1987, 1988a, 1988b) and to a more recent video documentary made in Shima, and its companion study guide (Media Production Group 1993).]

Ichiba: The cooperative and its sales dock

By the sixteenth century, Japan's near-shore waters had been divided into small territories, each held as an exclusive economic zone, a marine commons, under the control of a nearby village. Control was transferred to local marine producers' cooperative associations when the state ordered these to be formed late in the nineteenth century. The point to remember is that a novice diver enters a community of practice that holds a heritage of information about its territorial waters and the fluctuations of marine species within them. It also holds a heritage of experience in adjusting the productivity of human shellfish takers to the reproductive powers of shellfish species. Measures to prevent overfishing were being taken generations ago, long before contemporary angst about "The Environment." The difference today is that the co-ops also artificially propagate abalone and attempt to micromanage many particulars of diving practice through size limits, bag limits, fixed diving periods, regulations on the equipment that one may use, and so on.

Already in the 1870s, for example, air hoses and hand pumps were imported from England and used in shellfish diving in Shima and elsewhere. It quickly became obvious that an air-equipped diver could remain submerged for long periods and soon would destroy the resource base. Air apparatus have been banned from *ama* diving ever since.

In order to dive commercially, one must reside locally and join the cooperative. One also must market all abalone and *sazae* ("top shells") through the co-op, which resells them immediately to local seafood merchants. But a diver is allowed to sell other species – found only in small numbers – privately.

During the season, which runs from March to September, an *ama* confronts her moment of truth as an artisan at the end of each day's work. Amid an audience of her peers and seafood dealers, she must offer her catch for weighing and public judging at the co-op's sales dock. Every diver is an independent producer. She does not share her catch with other *ama,* though once or twice a season the whole day's catch will be pooled and the money saved to pay for an annual postseason vacation trip that divers and their boatmen take as a group. From a diver's earnings, the co-op withholds 5 percent as its handling fee. In addition, a boatman who transports a group of *okedo* receives 10 percent of each woman's catch, and a lifeline diver shares fifty/fifty with her boat-handling partner.

Competition for the day's, and season's, biggest catch is heated and is reinforced by the public drama on the sales dock. The manager sings out names and weights, ostensibly so the recording clerk will hear him above the din. But this broadcasts the news of a big catch to all in earshot: divers, dealers, and sometimes other local people who stop by to savor the drama. News of an exceptional catch will be relayed to others in the community and rebound from them to the diver the next time they meet her (e.g., in the supermarket).

Divers' rankings and batting averages are a matter of general knowledge in the community. And people will say of someone who is exceptionally skilled, "She was born to be an *ama*." It is generally expected that a diver's curve of performance (and income) will move upward with experience for many years, turning down again only after she enters her sixties. But even divers in their seventies, obviously no longer able to claim top ranking, continue to compete against their age peers.

Dairyō ("big catch") is a central idiom in the *ama* world, as it is for hunters and fishers generally. Along with "safety at sea," the phrase is printed on boat pennants and on amulets that divers tie to their diving masks. Osaka merchants are supposed to greet one another in the street not by saying good morning but by asking "*Mokkarimakka*?" ("You making any money?"). The most frequent *ama* greeting in Shima, along with ritual complaints about the weather, is "*Dairyō kai*?" ("Y'all get a big catch?").

In Japanese popular imagery, stereotypic students cramming for university entrance examinations drive themselves with a vision of ultimate success: One day they will "capture the world" (*tenka o toru,* or, more literally, capture everything under the heavens). In *ama* imagery, the women dream that one day they will capture everything under the sea. Divers tell us that the secret of success is to be driven by lust for competition. The *ichiba* and its daily ranking spurs that lust not only among master divers but among novices on the periphery hoping that in time they too will break into the big money.

Koya: Houses of caring and cognition

In *ama* practice, one sees an exquisite brocade of rivalry and mutual caring. If the sales dock is the niche that nurtures competitiveness, the *koya* are nurseries for cooperativeness. Each group of five to fifteen or so divers has its own hut, or *koya,* just behind the beach. Here the women eat, change clothes, and rest before and after working. Most of these tasks could easily be taken care of at home – the women live only a few steps or at most a few minutes' walk away – so the *koya* are more than just a matter of convenience. In fact, *ama* often say that one of the appeals of being a diver is the opportunity to spend six months a year in the companionship of the *koya*: away from men, and perhaps even more important in rural Japanese society, away from the eyes of one's mother-in-law.

Except during naptime, the huts are alive with talk, teasing, and even impromptu singing. There is a blunt "backstage" quality to much of the interaction, like that in locker rooms and taverns where people gather after engaging in rugged sports or risky occupations everywhere. *Koya*-mates should be sensitive to one another's feelings, but the official norms of feminine modesty are left at the door.

Out in the water, you are in competition with *koya*-mates as with all other divers. But if you should be injured or meet danger in the water, your best hope for rescue will be from others in your *koya.* They are likely to be nearby – this is a matter of practice not prescription – and monitoring your rhythm of work in their peripheral vision.

In addition to lessons in caring, social interaction in the hut provides vital access to an ongoing flow of information about the reef environment, to moneyed knowledge in the narrow sense of where the abalone are likely to be found. Verbal replays of the day's dives will generate precious information about the peculiarities of each reef. A novice needs to spend as much time-on-talk in the *koya* as time-on-task in the water.

One time early in our research, we asked some of the women to sketch on paper the major shoals and deeps and their relation to the shoreline. After sketching and naming a few sites, their interest flagged. This was a bore. It was how you are forced to demonstrate knowledge in school but had little to do with the knowledge you need to have as a diver. As soon as we set the paper aside, however, they spontaneously ignited in animated discussions about particular reefs and about their experiences there. This was information with a purpose: stored and indexed for its value in predicting the probability of finding abalone again at a particular site.

Ama say that the physical skills of diving can be mastered in a season or two; and one probably will need another two or three seasons in order to perfect one's technique for extracting abalone – which cling tightly to the rocks and must be levered off using a steel bar. They must be pried off without cracking the shell or tearing the soft tissues: Only live, whole abalone bring in today's high prices. The procedure requires the skill and strength of a surgeon and the swiftness of an athlete.

Ama also say that it takes at least a decade to absorb the full corpus of moneyed knowledge about the reef environment and its inhabitants. One woman commented to us that she had tried counting sheep when she could not easily go to sleep at night, but the whole business was tedious. Instead, she names and counts reefs.

Hama: Collaborations made tangible

With prosperity, many cooperatives have built seawalls and docks to shelter their boats; the divers simply step aboard and put to sea. But in a few Shima locales, the boats still are launched across the beach, the *hama,* and into the surf, in a crescendo display of collaboration. This is how everybody had to do it in the old days – a drama of collectively breaking ties with the security taken for granted on land.

At the appointed hour, elderly boatmen who had been slouching in the sand suddenly seem decades younger as they pull on hip boots and hurry into position. Divers from different *koya* array themselves around the first boat to be launched. A low-key signal from the boatman triggers a minute or two of activity that is a perfect pantomime of Japanese "Togetherness." The two-ton vessel rumbles across greased logs and dips toward the surf, propelled by muscle-straining *ama.* Other divers drop skid-logs just ahead of the bow as the vessel enters that zone of uncertainty where it must prove that it can float. When all boats have been launched, the divers array themselves along the surf line. As their boat approaches, each group wades out to board it, splashing water on it for good luck.

Little may be said in the minutes during launching. Little need be said, other than heave-ho's to coordinate muscle thrusts. The body movements – at times a stunning, if impromptu, choreography – soon become second-nature, embodied knowledge. But the performance is a powerful daily reminder that safety at sea is everybody's mutual responsibility.

Iso: The obscured workplace

Immediately after the boat launch and its spectacle of high togetherness, the divers must shift into the competitive mode. Among the slide photographs we have taken of *ama* at work, there is one that consistently elicits little gasps of excitement from them. It captures that moment in the morning when all divers are on board and the last boat is turning seaward. For an athlete – and *ama* are athletes as well as artisans – it is that period when time stands still until the big game begins. Sometimes as they are wading out to their boats, the divers cannot control the rush of eagerness. Grandmothers act like schoolgirls pinching and shoving one another on their way to the volleyball court.

As soon as the divers are in the water, spaces begin to open in what had been the seamless togetherness of the beach. More often than not, many divers will cluster together, operating over the same set of reefs during a dive period. The *iso,* the tidal zone, is not only the place where you practice and polish your own diving and hunting skills; as a "learning resource center," it also offers opportunities for glimpsing, partially obscured by distance and by cloudy waters, how your rivals practice their skills.

After a few seasons, you know the work habits of colleagues almost as intimately as your own. You learn to identify each diver, even in poor visibility underwater, by her peculiarities – how she knots her headcloth or crooks her left arm. When a group of *ama* looks at slides we have taken of them underwater, they often erupt in spontaneous games of guessing from limited cues who is in the photo. Often the best information about the movements of the abalone comes from the movements of your rivals.

But distance must be maintained. If a colleague's movements suggest that she has come upon a large cache of abalone, you might trigger a fight if you rush over. Conversely, a diver who has just made a "find" may take evasive action (e.g., leaving the surface headed in one direction but making a U-turn once submerged).

To put it another way, greed and envy are occupational hazards that can bite you like moray eels or trap you like a discarded fishnet. A diver must learn to control them in the water just as she must learn to hold in her breath. In the *koya* after hours, one sometimes hears stories about an *ama* (she always is from some other community) who disappeared underwater and never was found. Her abalone knife, however, was retrieved from the spot where another diver had been collecting a huge cache of abalone. And *ama* lore includes the story of a mysterious "double" who appears suddenly while you are underwater. You don't recognize her, but you recognize her signals that point the way to a great cache of abalone deeper on the reef. Follow her, and you will never come back.

Discussion: Grasping fluid knowledge

The *ama* case poses an empirical challenge to the usual modes that are employed to explain how prowess and proficiency are acquired. There are no classrooms to observe, no master–apprentice dyads to interview, and apparently, a diver in training can't even expect much help from her mother. What then?

We all know that the way we study in school has little to do with how we study and learn the essentials of conduct in the everyday real world. And yet the specialized, even peculiar, scenario of the classroom so dominates the scholarly mind that it is almost automatically applied to settings outside the classroom, even when no teaching occurs in the setting. Events and processes end up being described in terms relevant to *more* schooling. Research techniques smell of chalk dust.

We slipped back into schoolish habits when we asked some divers to sketch a map of the *iso*. To them, it was like another classroom test, a regurgitating of information divorced from its contexts of use. A diver's knowledge of the reefs is largely carnal knowledge: In a quite literal sense, she "in-forms" her body by transporting it around the reefs. To this, she adds cognitive information she has collected by listening to talk in the *koya*. She can deploy this knowledge orally or kinesically; translating it into the two-dimensional symbols of a paper map is a bother. The women's reactions to the task showed us what *ama* expert knowledge is not; but this did not provide clues to what that knowledge is.

Notions of apprenticeship begin to move one away mentally from narrow fascination with the teacher as authority figure. Esther Goody (1989: 234), for example, seems to empower the learner in her formula for apprenticeship as a system that has "someone who doesn't know, learning from someone who does." Similarly, Cole (1985:156) says that what matters is not that a master gives instruction but that he arranges for the learner to come in contact with what needs to be learned. This is perhaps the minimal response to a "zone of proximal development" (Vygotsky 1978), referring to what a learner cannot do toward completion of a task without the assistance of someone who can carry out the task. Greenfield (1984) plays out the implications of this zone in apprenticeship, offering a metaphor of the master as one who provides scaffolding for an apprentice to stand on while learning to complete a task; the master, in this case of weaving, participates with the novice in completing a garment, doing those parts that the novice is unable to do. Both jointly get on with the primary object of finishing the job, while providing a situation for learning to occur through participation. Here one has the peculiar artisan form of instruction, where a successful "production" is as important to master artisans as is the novice's desire to know.

Sometimes a Shima boatman will invite an amateur *ama* to ride with him and the diving group that he taxis out to the reefs in order to test her skills in deeper waters. This is perhaps a form of putting the learner in proximity to practice, but boatmen do not claim to be master divers, only that they command enough diving skill that they are confident of being able to dive down and rescue an *ama* in distress. Skilled and novice *ama* engage in joint activity – which Greenfield regards as essential if scaffolding is to occur – in tasks such as launching boats or cleaning the *koya*. In contrast, master abalone divers compete directly with novices as well as peers. Operations in the *iso* might be tagged as a form of parallel activity, but it would be an exaggeration to call them joint.

The essential first step to take, analytically, is the one suggested by Lave and Wenger (1991): to uncouple learning from teaching. "Mastery," in their words, "resides not in the master but in the organization of a community of practice of which the masters are part" (1991:95). Instead of inspecting social relationships or asking what the master knows, we direct our attention to the novice as he or she searches for knowledge inside the "intricate structure of a community's learning resources" (1991:94). Learning is proactive, participatory. Novices are obliged to be responsible for organizing how they learn, for anticipating what they need to learn next, and for seizing it when it surfaces in the routine flow of work. To learn is to practice, and vice versa.

The notion of a *community* of practice, however, is a bit more troubling. The concept of community has been unpacked and repacked so many times in social science discourse over recent decades that using it could draw us into old debates that were abandoned, unresolved, in the backwaters of ambiguity. But if we can avoid these detours, the idea of a community *of practice* helps us break away from teacher–learner dyads by directing us to look instead for networks of distributed knowledge (Hutchins 1993). Different forms of learning may occur at diverse nodes in the social network – or to use the ecological idiom we employed earlier, at different niches in the social environment.

How the physical and mental dimensions of artisan practice interweave in a particular setting is illuminated in the Kellers' account of "thinking and acting in iron," the process going on while Charles Keller as blacksmith created a utensil called a skimmer (Keller and Keller 1993). They show how "the internal mental order, both the image of the object and other relevant knowledge, is continually transformed by external actions and their material constituents and results" (1993:127).

One literally "in-forms" the body. In diving, the body itself becomes an inner landscape, a model of the outer landscape, and at the same time a means for acquiring further mastery of that landscape. The body is not a passive repository of knowledge; it is our human requisite for the production of knowledge.

In smithing as in diving, one's knowledge can never be detailed or precise enough to anticipate all the possible outcomes of an act. *Ama* contrast the fluid, ever-changing conditions in their workplace with the tedium they would encounter in many of the other jobs open to a woman in Shima – seeding pearl oysters, for instance, or cutting up fish for canning and drying. The *iso,* they tell us, is never the same for two days in a row.

In an environment of endless change, one needs a flexible fund of knowledge that can be reworked, redirected, at any moment. *Ama* prowess includes some well-rehearsed actions, such as the technique for levering an abalone away from its host rock. These perhaps could be considered *kata*: essential forms to be practiced until one is close to perfection. But *ama* prowess is too labile to be forced into a toolbag of *kata*. *Ama* are more like airline pilots than like weavers or potters. If an artisan creates a product such as a cloth or vase, the product itself will carry evidence of how it was produced. The size of one's shellfish catch is an index of diving mastery, but the catch itself offers no clues as to how it was obtained. One can learn by imitating the practices of a high-ranking diver, but it is risky to imitate too closely. Shellfish hunting forces one to dance daily with fickle seas.

To paraphrase Rand Spiro (Spiro et al. 1987), information that will be deployed in many different ways needs to be learned in different ways. The very open-ended-though-not-random way that a diver educates herself is appropriate to the fluid conditions in which she will pursue the practices of her craft. Spiro and his colleagues speak of "ill-structured knowledge domains" as being like a landscape: No two sites are alike. And to master the territory, one has to criss-cross it, approaching all sites from an array of angles until one has constructed an internal "map" of apt flexibility. The artisan mastery of this kaleidoscope of day-to-day conditions of work is shaped through long years of experience: Top catches wait for years of experience. How that mastery of shifting complexity is forged, and how incremental, flexible expertise grows, is still poorly understood. Even less is known with certainty about how to teach so that the growth of cognitive flexibility is not shunted into oversimplified, inflexible constructions. How to organize teaching so as to shorten the tenure of years of self-directed learning required for mastery of complexity is the prize discovery awaiting a winner in the new age of oversupply of information.

The *ama* stand far out on the end of the continuum of difference among the array of apprenticeship arrangements in Japan. As in the others, mastery is accomplished by practicing productive work. Unlike others, learners are not held at a periphery of productive work until expertise is built through practice. What an *ama* should know and how she should come to know it is left up to her. No master diver manages her trajectory of development. The environment is not arranged for learning, nor does a co-participating master complement the amateur diver's partial skills or knowledge of the rocky shoals. While beach, *koya,* co-op market, and rocky shoals are learning resources, visited in the daily routine of diving, it is the amateur diver's own responsibility to appropriate and organize her own expertness. It all seems an anachronism beside the examples of well-ordered apprenticeship. This teacherless way, nevertheless, seems well suited to producing the cognitive flexibility for daily adaptation to changeable and fickle seas, coupled to embodied skills for capturing abalone, applied daily to produce the big catch and the money prize.

Notes

Our fieldwork on the Shima peninsula has been aided by financial support from several sources. For the summers of 1981 and 1982, we had travel moneys from our university's Office of International Programs and Studies and from the Center for East Asian and Pacific Studies. For the autumn of 1984, Plath held a research fellowship from the Japan Society for the Promotion of Science, and for the spring of 1985, one from the Japan–United States Educational Commission. During 1984–1985, he received research funds from the U.S. Joint Committee on Japanese Studies (co-sponsored by the American Council of Learned Societies and the Social Science Research Council). For the 1986–1987 and 1987–1988 academic years, our university's Research Board provided salary for a graduate research assistant for the project. From 1984 to 1990, the investigation became a joint venture carried on in collaboration with a team of faculty and graduate students from Konan University in Kobe, led by Professor Morita Saburo.

1. From J. Conrad, 1906 (1988), *Mirror of the Sea,* Marlboro, VT: The Marlboro Press, p. 20.

References

Cole, M. (1985) "The zone of proximal development: Where culture and cognition create each other." In J. V. Wertsch (Ed.), *Culture, communication, and cognition: Vygotskian perspectives.* Cambridge: Cambridge University Press, pp. 146–162.

Goody, E. (1989) "Learning, apprenticeship and the division of labor." In M. Coy (Ed.), *Apprenticeship.* Albany, NY: State University of New York Press.

Greenfield, P. (1984) "A theory of the teacher in the learning activities of everyday life." In B. Rogoff and J. Lave (Eds.), *Everyday cognition.* Cambridge, MA: Harvard University Press.

Hutchins, E. (1993) "Learning to navigate." In S. Chaiklin and J. Lave (Eds.), *Understanding practice: Perspectives on activity and context.* Cambridge: Cambridge University Press, pp. 35–63.

Keller, C., and Keller, J. D. (1993) "Thinking and acting in iron." In S. Chaiklin and J. Lave (Eds.), *Understanding practice: Perspectives on activity and context.* Cambridge: Cambridge University Press, pp. 125–143.

Lave, J., and Wenger, E. (1991) *Situated learning: Legitimate peripheral participation.* Cambridge: Cambridge University Press.

Media Production Group (1993) *Fit surroundings.* Color, 30-minute video documentary, VHS cassette and study guide. Dist: Asian Educational Media Service, Center for East Asian and Pacific Studies, University of Illinois, Urbana, IL.

Plath, D., and Hill, J. (1987) "The reefs of rivalry: Expertness and competition among Japanese shellfish divers." *Ethnology 24*(3): 151–163.

(1988a) " 'Fit surroundings' – Japanese shellfish divers and the artisan option." *Social Behaviour 3*: 149–159.

(1988b) "Athletes of the deep: The *ama* as artisans and as emblems." *Japan Society Newsletter* (Nov.), pp. 2–5.

Spiro, R., et al. (1987) "Knowledge acquisition for application: Cognitive flexibility and transfer in complex content domains." In B. Britton and S. Glynn (Eds.), *Executive control processes.* Hillsdale, NJ: Lawrence Erlbaum Associates.

Vygotsky, L. S. (1978) *Mind in society: The development of higher psychological processes.* Cambridge: Harvard University Press.

13 The self-taught bureaucrat: Takahashi Korekiyo and economic policy during the Great Depression

Richard J. Smethurst

Takahashi Korekiyo became finance minister for the fifth time in December 1931 at the age of seventy-seven – during the depths of the world depression. Prices were falling sharply, unemployment was high and rising, farmers suffered from the collapse of agricultural commodity prices (especially for raw silk and thus cocoons), the growth of industrialized productivity stagnated and many factories were under- or unutilized, and investment in plant and equipment virtually disappeared. To counter these problems, within six months of coming to office, Takahashi engineered Japan's recovery by introducing a series of reflationary, countercyclical fiscal and monetary policies that dramatically reversed his predecessor's conservative, deflationary policies. In monetary policy, Takahashi took Japan off the gold standard, ended the convertibility of paper money for gold, let the yen exchange rate float, lowered interest rates, and introduced legislation to raise the limit on the Bank of Japan's issuance of bank notes by over eight times. (Primary Takahashi biographies: Gotō 1977; Ōshima 1969; Imamura 1958.) Within a year, the yen had fallen 60 percent in value vis-à-vis the dollar, from ¥100 per $50 to $20, before stabilizing at ¥100 per $30 in 1933. Japanese exports boomed even while the rest of the world's trade contracted. The value of Japanese exports in constant yen increased by almost 2.5 times between 1931 and 1937. (Statistical references: Bank of Japan 1966, 1986; Ohkawa and Shinohara 1979.)

In the summer of 1932, Takahashi also introduced a countercyclical fiscal policy. Takahashi increased government spending and made up the difference not by raising taxes but by deficit financing – and deficit financing through selling low-interest, government bonds directly to the Bank of Japan, not on the open market. The government's spending increased the amount of money in circulation and thus effective demand. This together with expanding exports stimulated production and reemployment – people had more money to spend, and Japan began to recover from the Depression. By 1935–1936, Japan was back to full utilization of capacity and nearly to full employment. The number of nonagricultural gainful workers grew by almost 2 million workers from 1931 to 1936, an increase of 12.5 percent. Workers in the agricultural sector, the safety net for the unemployed during the Depression, declined in number by over half a million from 1932 to 1936. Because there was excess unemployment and thus un- and underused factories in the early 1930s, Takahashi's deficit financing was reflationary rather than inflationary – in fact, consumer prices did not return to their pre-Depression 1928 level until 1938.

By 1935, Takahashi recognized that the economy was nearing full recovery, and he introduced a plan to bring government spending gradually back into balance with revenues. It was here that the only (and unintended) weakness in Takahashi's fiscal exercise emerged. When he began his reflationary fiscal policies in June 1932, he had no choice but to increase military spending – he became finance minister, after all, during the euphoria surrounding the popular takeover of Manchuria in 1931–1932. The military, increasingly happy with their growing budgets, resisted his efforts, to the extent that on February 26, 1936, ultranationalist young army officers brutally murdered (shot seven times and then slashed with a sword) the eighty-one-year-old Takahashi while his wife looked on. His successor, Baba Eiichi, immediately doubled the military budget; he expanded it by 117 percent in the 1937 budget compared to Takahashi's 113 percent increase over five years from 1931 until 1936 – not only speeding the road to war but also to rapid inflation. In 1936, the consumer price index reached 87 percent of 1929; consumer prices grew by an annual average of only 1.9 percent during the Takahashi years from 1932 until 1936. Between 1936 and 1940, the four years immediately after Takahashi's assassination, the consumer price index (CPI) increased by over 15 percent per year, and during World War II, from 1941 until 1945, the inflation rate grew at an average annual rate of 57.8 percent. Takahashi's comparatively moderate increase in military spending and its concomitant modest rise in inflation were a far cry from what came later.

It is widely accepted by leading Western historians of the Depression that Takahashi was unusual in the world at the time. He introduced what we came later to call "Keynesian" monetary and fiscal policies before John Maynard Keynes published *The General Theory of Employment, Interest, and Money* in 1936, thus doing something that few of the world's finance ministers were willing to do and that few economists approved of in 1931–1932. Charles Kindleberger (1986:163), the author of the standard economic history of the Depression, describes Takahashi's record as "one of the most brilliant and highly successful combinations of fiscal, monetary, and foreign exchange rate policies the world has ever seen." He goes on to emphasize the Swedish, Finnish, and Japanese success stories in recovering from the Depression by the mid-1930s. Robert Skidelsky, Keynes's biographer, echoes Kindleberger's sentiment when he writes: "In the early 1930s what would now be called Keynesian methods of fighting the Depression were tried out in Japan and Sweden." Skidelsky adds that while the Swedish finance minister drew much inspiration from Keynes, "it is unlikely that Takahashi" did (1994:488). My question is, is Skidelsky correct – is it necessarily "unlikely" that Takahashi drew on Keynes?

The purpose of this essay is to explore briefly the education of Takahashi Korekiyo in an attempt to see how he became the finance minister whom Gotō Shin'ichi, one of his biographers, calls "Japan's Keynes." Did Takahashi read Keynes and other Western economists purveying Keynesian ideas? Was he influenced by Japanese Keynesians like Ishibashi Tanzan? Did he reach these ideas independently of Western influences? Or some combination of all three? But let me say here that what makes Takahashi's case even more fascinating is that he had very little formal schooling. Born only a year after Commodore Perry's first visit to Japan, and thus long before the establishment of the modern school system, Takahashi's primary marketable intellectual skill was his knowledge of the English language, developed outside of formal schools at an early age.

Takahashi was an autodidact who had many mentors in his learning process but few if any masters – in fact, one can argue that for the most part he was self-taught. This approach to learning set him off not only from his Western contemporaries in the bureaucratic world, most of whom were university graduates, but also from his Japanese counterparts, men like his more orthodox predecessor as finance minister, Inoue Junnosuke, who was one of the early graduates of Tokyo Imperial University. Takahashi's learning, aside from his early and idiosyncratic English-language study, came mostly on the job – in a variety of government agencies in a bureaucratic career that lasted for two-thirds of a century. One might say that Takahashi was a policy "artisan," except that his "workshop" was the civil service office, not the potter's or the weaver's atelier.

Takahashi was born on July 27, 1854, the son of a shogunal court painter and a family maid, the sixteen-year-old daughter of Edo fishmongers. As an infant, he was adopted into an *ashigaru* family – that is, one of the lowest levels of samurai – from Sendai domain. As Ronald Dore writes in his book on Tokugawa education, *ashigaru* had much more limited opportunities to attend school than did even moderately higher-ranking samurai youths (1965:75, 84, 226). And although Takahashi recounts many incidents from his childhood in his memoirs, he gives no evidence of having attended school as a youth. He tells us that at age seven, he went to the Sendai domain Zen Buddhist temple in Ōzaki in southern Edo as a page to wait on the chief priest. We can assume that he developed some ability to read and write Japanese while serving at Jushōji (Takahashi 1988:23–26).

At the temple, Takahashi came in contact with a Sendai domain official named Ōwaraya Shindayu, an acquaintance of Fukuzawa Yukichi, who thought Japan needed to rebuild its military using Western weapons. He believed that young men should learn French and English and that even clever *ashigaru* could play a role. Thus, in 1864, the young Takahashi was sent to study English in Yokohama with an American missionary's wife. He spent the next three years as a language student and then as a "boy" in a British bank in Yokohama. In July 1867, the thirteen-year-old Takahashi, who spent much of his last year in Yokohama drinking and gambling, almost lost the chance to continue his language studies in America when his domain lost confidence in his commitment to learning. Only after he took matters into his own hands and signed on an American whaling ship as a cabin boy did the Sendai domain officials relent and choose him for study abroad. In July 1867, wearing his first Western shoes (only women's shoes were small enough for him), Takahashi left for San Francisco, where he unwittingly sold himself into three years of bonded servitude. Having extricated himself, Takahashi returned to Japan in December 1868, shortly after the Meiji Restoration.

Because Sendai chose to resist the new Meiji government, the youthful Takahashi found himself a fugitive from justice. He was saved when the twenty-one-year-old Mori Arinori, a Westernizing official of the new government from Satsuma, one of the victorious domains in the Meiji Restoration, took Takahashi and two other young returnees under his wing and protected them – Mori believed their language skills were essential to the new Japan. For the next thirteen years, Takahashi either studied or taught English in various schools around the country or served as an interpreter in the Education Ministry. For example, in one of his few forays into formal education, the teenage Takahashi studied English briefly at Daigaku Nankō, and while not yet twenty, he served as an interpreter for David Murray, an American hired as a high-ranking advisor to the Education Ministry. One of Takahashi's teachers and patrons while still a teenager was the missionary/government advisor Guido Verbeck, who taught English, social sciences, and Western technology to major early Meiji governmental leaders like Itō Hirobumi, Ōkubo Toshimichi, and Ōkuma Shigenobu. Takahashi continued to face occasional difficulties because of his carousing in this period of his life.

It was Takahashi's English-language ability that made his career. In 1881, the twenty-six-year-old Takahashi was transferred to the Agriculture and Commerce Ministry and assigned the task of investigating copyrights and patents. Essentially, he was given the British and American laws and codes, told to translate them, and then to write Japan's laws. It took Takahashi two and one-half years, but finally in 1884, the government promulgated his code. At age thirty, he became the first head of Japan's Copyright Office in October 1884 and its first Patent Commissioner in April 1885.

Takahashi spent most of 1886 abroad, traveling to New York, Washington, London, Paris, and Berlin to study foreign patent and copyright laws and systems firsthand. On his return home, he drafted new laws that in December 1888 replaced his earlier efforts. He then became the first director of Japan's Patent Bureau under the newly revised bureaucratic system. The 1880s, Takahashi's first adult decade, clearly played an important role in his education (recall that most of that education came about through on-the-job experience, not from classroom learning: by translating codes, by interviewing foreign patent and copyright experts, etc., not by going to Tokyo University). His work in the 1880s also proved to the government's leaders that he was a young man who could undertake and complete complicated tasks.

While in the Agriculture and Commerce Ministry, Takahashi came in contact with Maeda Masana, a charismatic mentor who both furthered Takahashi's education and temporarily derailed his career. Maeda, like Mori a young samurai from Satsuma (Maeda was eighteen at the time of the Meiji Restoration), was committed to a grass-roots kind of economic development. Maeda believed that Japan's economy would grow more quickly and soundly if primary emphasis was placed on fostering traditional and traditional/modern hybrid light industries rather than on heavy transplant industry. Thus he thought that the government should invest more in modernizing sericulture and the raw silk industry, the producers of Japan's major export commodity from the 1870s to the 1930s, than in steel, chemicals, and shipbuilding. Takahashi helped Maeda edit his thirty-volume *Opinions on Promoting Industry* (Kōgyō iken), the work that provided the empirical evidence on which Maeda built his proposal, and served as part of the team that presented the Agriculture and Commerce Ministry's point of view to the government in 1885. The heavy industrializers, led by Finance Minister Matsukata Masayoshi, and their *zaibatsu* allies, won the debate; Maeda, in defeat, left the ministry (temporarily), and his protege Takahashi went abroad to study copyright and patent laws (Soda 1987:105–124).

In 1889, Takahashi's involvement with Maeda led to even greater difficulties than a policy defeat. Maeda believed that resource-poor Japan needed to develop Japanese-controlled sources of natural resources abroad. Thus, with Maeda's encouragement, Takahashi and a group of investors raised ¥500,000, and Takahashi resigned from government in 1889 to manage a silver mine they bought in Peru. It turned out, however, that Takahashi and his fellow investors had been duped – the mine's ore had been exhausted. Takahashi returned to Japan broke, humiliated, and out of a job. But his experiences with Maeda, even in failure, were not without educational value for Takahashi. He wrote years later that it was from Maeda that he, Takahashi, had developed his concept of the state. "The state is not a separate entity divided from the self because there is no reason to have a self vis-à-vis the state. Oneself and the state are the same thing" (Takahashi 1936a:270). Takahashi, a civil servant throughout almost all of his mature life, was committed to making Japan a rich country (*fukoku,* but I would argue, not necessarily *kyōhei,* a strong army) and to bettering the livelihoods of its people – clearly, Maeda helped him develop this view – and it was a short step from the importance of the state in enriching Japan to the importance of using fiscal and monetary policy for economic growth. One of his biographers, Ōshima Kiyoshi, thinks he learned another lesson from Maeda. Takahashi wrote in his diary at the time that one of Japan's problems was a dearth of capital. Ōshima thinks that this was the basis for Takahashi's Depression-era idea that low interest rates for capital were necessary to encourage investment.

Takahashi returned to government in 1892, when he joined the Bank of Japan – not as a banker, however, but to speed to completion the overdue and overbudget construction of the bank's new building in Nihonbashi. (The Institute for Monetary and Economic Studies, where much of the research for this paper was done, is in this beautiful building.) Only after the construction was back on track did Takahashi become a banker. Takahashi was manager of the bank's Western Japan branch in the spring of 1895, when the peace conference that ended the Sino-Japanese War and gained Japan the 350 million yen indemnity that allowed it to go on the gold standard was held there. His activities in Shimonoseki furthered his career by bringing Takahashi in contact with several of Japan's senior statesmen, who took part in the peace negotiations.

Just after the turn of the century, Takahashi's English played a crucial role in the event that made him a national hero, earned him an audience with the emperor, and won him a rank in Japan's nobility. In 1904, Takahashi, with another fascinating, English-speaking bureaucrat, Fukai Eigo, as his assistant, went to New York and London to sell Japanese war bonds during the Russo-Japanese War. In 1903, the Bank of Japan had only 133 million yen in specie holdings, and the central government's total annual revenue was 398 million yen. The war cost Japan over four times that annual budget, 1.7 billion yen, and 78 percent of the cost was borrowed. Eight hundred million yen, or half the total cost, was borrowed abroad. Not only did Takahashi's efforts make him a favorite of the great men who ruled Japan, but it also gave him an object lesson in the usefulness of deficit financing and borrowing in times of crisis.

But Takahashi was not just a borrow-and-spend man. When he became governor of the Bank of Japan in 1911, he called for control of government expenditures, budget restraint, and reduction of outstanding bonds, because Japan's economy was suffering from the costs of its wartime borrowing – debt service on the "colonial" high-interest 6 percent bonds of the war's first year was onerous. In other words, he was a financial bureaucrat willing to use fiscal and monetary policy both to expand *and* to contract the economy, depending on the needs of the time. Takahashi became finance minister for the first of seven times in the Yamamoto Cabinet in 1913, just after the Taishō Political Crisis, and he opposed the military's attempt to increase the size of the army by two divisions. After the cabinet fell in 1914, Takahashi opposed Prime Minister Ōkuma's entry into World War I and his Twenty-one Demands to China in 1915, because he feared that an aggressive foreign policy would lead to increased military spending.

Because of his commitment to financial reality, Takahashi reiterated his opposition to excessive, but not all, military spending and influence throughout his later career. In a 1916 article, for example, Takahashi wrote that Japan needed to defend itself but that its defense spending must not exceed its financial capacity. Thus Japan should maintain peace through diplomacy, avoid war whenever possible, and eschew aggression in China (Takahashi 1936b:655–662). In 1920, during the Siberian Intervention, Finance Minister Takahashi sent a memorandum to Prime Minister Hara calling for the abolition of the army's and navy's general staffs. Takahashi opposed the huge, wasteful cost of maintaining an army on the Asian mainland, feared the rise of militarism, and believed that the military should be subordinated to the political parties and their government (Shinobu 1958:601). In a speech to the Diet on January 21, 1933, Takahashi stated that "most of our increase in governmental spending is for Depression relief, the Manchurian Incident, and weapons improvement, which are all temporary appropriations and will be reduced in a few years" (Gotō 1977:134). It was his efforts to pursue these ends – that is, to control the military and its spending – that cost Takahashi his life.

Takahashi proved his ability to use governmental policy both to expand and to contract the economy when he became finance minister for the second and third time in the Hara Kei and Takahashi Cabinets of 1918–1922. When Hara and Takahashi took office after the Rice Riots in September 1918, Japan was nearing the end of its World War I economic boom. Japan, as is well known, moved during the war into the Asian export markets of the European combatants, prospered, and moved into the mainstream of industrialization. In fact, primary sector workers fell by 2 million people from 1912 to 1920, and manufacturing workers increased by 1.6 million, an increase of 54 percent. Finance Minister Takahashi ran budget deficits, much as he would fifteen years later during the Depression, and he spent heavily on education, transportation, communications, and the military. But this "positive" fiscal policy, born both of Takahashi's economic ideas and Hara's political objectives of building a regional electoral base for his party, could not be carried on indefinitely (Nakamura 1993:33–37). The war brought not only prosperity; it also brought inflation. Consumer prices increased by only 74 percent in the thirty-six years from 1879 (the first year CPI data are available) to 1915; they increased by 138 percent in the five years from 1915 to 1920.

Tentatively in 1919, but not in earnest until 1921, Takahashi turned to a contractive fiscal policy in an attempt to cool the economy and stop Japan's inflation – a task made particularly difficult by the drying up of demand for Japanese goods after the war. He was probably too late to guarantee a soft economic landing during this period of "stagflation." Consumer prices fell by 7.2 percent from their 1920 high, but GNP fell too, by 6.5 percent. Manufacturing workers declined in number by 105,000, the first decline since the 1913–1914 slump just before the war. In other words, Japan fell into a recession in 1921–1922. One can argue, as many have, that Takahashi mistimed his fiscal policy at the end of World War I. He should have abandoned the positive policy sooner and thus brought about a softer ending to the World War I boom. But from our point of view – that is, from the point of view of an analysis of Takahashi's education, and of his understanding of the uses of countercyclical fiscal and monetary policy – his actions in 1918–1922 foreshadow what he did a decade later.

In the 1920s, Takahashi's career came to what would seem like its fruition. He was promoted to viscount in 1920, became prime minister at age sixty-seven after Hara's assassination in 1921, turned his hereditary peerage over to his son in order to run for Hara's parliamentary seat in Morioka, served as Agriculture and Commerce Minister in 1925 at age seventy (when the ministry was divided into two), retired, returned as finance minister for six weeks to resolve the Financial Crisis of 1927, and then retired again. In 1927, "Daruma" (a roly-poly folk doll) Takahashi, an overwhelmingly popular septuagenerian, must have thought that his long and honorable service as a public official was over – all he needed to worry about were his *bonsai,* his Buddhist sculptures, his grandchildren, and his house next to the Canadian Embassy in Omote-machi. Little did he know that he would serve for five more years as finance minister before assassins would take his life.

I would like to make two more points before I leave this brief survey of Takahashi Korekiyo's "education." First, when he introduced countercyclical policies in 1931–1932, he did not hit on reflationary policies by sheer chance. His "education" had led him to these ideas, and he had articulated their efficacy over two years before he returned to the finance portfolio in December 1931. Keynes's student Richard Kahn began working on the article in which he first introduced the multiplier theory in the summer of 1930. That theory appears, albeit written in homelier language than Kahn's, in an article Takahashi published in November 1929 to criticize the decision of the current finance minister, Inoue Junnosuke, to deflate the economy by returning to the gold standard and cutting governmental spending. Let me quote extensively from Takahashi's article to make this point.

> If someone goes to a geisha house and calls a geisha, eats luxurious food, and spends 2,000 yen, we disapprove morally. But if we analyze how that money is used, we find that the part that paid for food helps support the chef's salary, and is used to pay for fish, meat, vegetables, and seasoning, or for the costs of transporting it. The farmers, fishermen, and merchants who receive that money then buy clothes, food, and shelter. And the geisha uses the money she receives to buy food, clothes, cosmetics, and to pay taxes. If this hypothetical man does not go to a geisha house and saves his 2,000 yen, bank deposits will grow but the efficacy of his money will be lessened.
>
> But he goes to a geisha house and his money is transferred to the hands of farmers, artisans, and fishermen. It goes in turn to various other producers and works twenty or

thirty times over. From the individual's point of view, it would be good to save his 2,000 yen, but when seen from the vantage point of the national economy, because the money works twenty or thirty times over, spending is better. (Takahashi 1936a:247–249)

Takahashi then went on to criticize Inoue for stopping work on major government construction projects including the new Diet building:

When work was stopped on these three buildings, contractors lost their jobs. They in turn laid off clerks, engineers, and construction workers, the victims of government frugality. The people who lost work lost disposable income. The workers' reduced buying power was passed on to their suppliers and to people not directly involved in this construction work. They too laid off workers and this led to further reductions in production. As a result, the government's policies invited general recession. (Takahashi 1936a:249)

Second, the gregarious Takahashi made friends and won followers easily, some of whom influenced him. Two men stand out in this regard. The first is Fukai Eigo, a graduate of Niijima Jō's Dōshisha University in the early 1890s, when it was truly a bilingual university. Fukai's memoirs, a major source for those who study the economic history of the 1920s and 1930s, report two conversations with Takahashi in December 1931, just before and just after Takahashi became finance minister, in which he urged Takahashi to prohibit the export of gold and thus, for all intents and purposes, to leave the gold standard (Takahashi did not need urging here) and to end convertibility – that is, the right of Japan's citizens to exchange paper money for gold at the Bank of Japan. (According to Fukai, Takahashi needed urging there.) Fukai, who had accompanied Takahashi to London and New York in 1904–1905, had long been one of his closest advisors, and I think we can assume that Fukai influenced him during the Depression years (Fukai 1941:259–263).

While Fukai, a career Bank of Japan bureaucrat, influenced Takahashi's monetary policy, his support for the fiscal stimuli that Takahashi applied was ambivalent. Fukai, the vice-governor of Japan's national bank, was a reluctant reflationist (Shima 1983:88–93). But Japan had an eminent economic journalist in the interwar years, Ishibashi Tanzan, who was not. Ishibashi introduced many of Keynes's books in the pages of the *Tōyō keizai shimpō,* the economic journal that he edited; he translated Keynes, and he advocated use of fiscal policy to "inflate" the economy. In fact, Ishibashi was far more committed to these ideas than Takahashi. Ishibashi criticized Takahashi in early 1932 for moving too slowly in increasing government spending, continually criticized him for spending too much on the military (easier for a critic to say than for a finance minister to avoid), and criticized him again in 1935–1936 when Takahashi tried to slow government spending, according to Ishibashi, too quickly (Jiang 1898:29–49).

In this discussion, I have posed briefly three possible educational sources for Takahashi's monetary and fiscal ideas: his own experience, his own reading of Western economics, and the influence on him of Japanese students of Western economics like Fukai and Ishibashi. Of the three, the first seems the most important: Takahashi's education as a financial bureaucrat and statesman. Each of his educational experiences, in a sense, prepared him for the next. As an English language student and specialist, as an author of copyright and patent laws, as a disciple of Maeda Masana, as a wartime fundraiser, and as a post–World War I finance minister who believed in using governmental policy to stimulate *and* cool the economy, Takahashi prepared himself through step-by-step experience to carry out countercyclical fiscal and monetary policies in the 1930s.

Of course, one should not ignore the possibility of the second and third influences: Western economic theory learned directly or indirectly. I have no proof that Takahashi, fluent as he was in English, read Keynes. But there is evidence that he knew the works of other Western economists who were moving toward the "Keynesian Revolution." According to Gotō Shin'ichi, in the spring of 1933, Finance Minister Takahashi translated and distributed articles by Irving Fisher of Yale (an economist who influenced Keynes), by the University of Chicago Research Group, and from the London *Times* that advocated using governmental spending for public works as a way of stimulating economic growth during the Depression. These Western economists believed, as did Takahashi, that one should not concern oneself with balancing the budget in any one year but rather over a number of years (Gotō 1977:136–137). Since Takahashi disseminated these articles after he began his countercyclical fiscal policies, we should probably conclude that he used the views of American and British economists to protect himself from critics who attacked him as an "inflationist" and for "reckless" spending; nevertheless, if Takahashi read such economists in the 1930s, he might have read them in the 1920s or earlier.

There is also evidence that Japanese Keynesians like Ishibashi Tanzan could have influenced him as well. Ishibashi published his views often and widely, and he met occasionally with Takahashi to talk about economic policy. Nevertheless, I have discovered no "smoking gun" – no written evidence to prove Ishibashi's influence on Takahashi. And yet, I think we should interpret influence in a broader sense than direct

Keynes–Takahashi or Ishibashi–Takahashi contact and not assume out of hand that Takahashi was unlikely to have been influenced by Keynes. Educated Japanese, by the interwar years, had moved into the mainstream of Western, or should we say, the world's, intellectual life, and given the brief "educational biography" offered here, we can see that Takahashi was no exception. There is no reason that a Japanese finance minister would be any less – or more – likely than a British, American, or Swedish finance minister to decide on a "Keynesian" solution to his nation's problems. Takahashi, a successful autodidact, was a modern finance minister, and as such, he chose a modern solution to the problems his country faced; ironically, he chose this route when many of his more formally educated Western and Japanese counterparts did not.

References

Bank of Japan, 1966, *Hompō shuyō keizai tōkei* [Hundred Year Statistics of the Japanese Economy], Tokyo: Statistics Department, Bank of Japan.

1986, *Nihon Ginkō Hyakunenshi* [Hundred Year History of the Bank of Japan], Tokyo: Bank of Japan, Volume 7.

Dore, Ronald, 1965, *Education in Tokugawa Japan,* London: Routledge and Kegan Paul.

Fukai Eigo, 1941, *Kaikō nanajūnen* [Memoirs of Seventy Years], Tokyo: Iwanami shoten.

Gotō Shin'ichi, 1977, *Takahashi Korekiyo: Nihon no keinzu* [Takahashi Korekiyo: Japan's Keynes], Tokyo: Nihon keizai shinbunsha.

Imamura Takeo, 1958, *Takahashi Korekiyo,* Tokyo: Jiji tsūshinsha.

Jiang Keshi, 1989, "Ishibashi Tanzan no sekkyoku zaiseiron: Takahashi zaisei to no kakawari" [Ishibashi Tanzan's Positive Fiscal Policy Theory: Its Connections with Takahashi's Fiscal Policy], in *Nihonshi kenkyū* [Research in Japanese History] *328*: 22–49.

Kindleberger, Charles P., 1986, *The World in Depression, 1929–1939,* Berkeley and Los Angeles: University of California Press.

Nakamura Takafusa, 1993, *Shōwashi* [A History of the Shōwa Era], Volume 1, Tokyo: Tōyō keizai shinpōsha.

Ohkawa, Kazushi, and Shinohara Miyohei, with Larry Meissner, 1979, *Patterns of Japanese Economic Development: A Quantitative Appraisal,* New Haven and London: Yale University Press.

Ōshima Kiyoshi, 1969, *Takahashi Korekiyo: zaiseika no sukina shōgai* [Takahashi Korekiyo: The Colorful Life of a Financier], Tokyo: Chūō kōronsha.

Shima Kinzō, 1983, "Iwayuru 'Takahashi Zaisei' ni Tsuite" [Concerning the So-called "Takahashi Fiscal Policies"], in *Kinyū Kenkyū* [Research in Finance], 2-2: 83–123.

Shinobu Seizaburō, 1958, *Taishō demokurashiishi* [The History of Taishō Democracy], Volume 2, Tokyo: Nihon hyōronsha.

Skidelsky, Robert, 1994, *John Maynard Keynes: The Economist as Savior, 1920–1937,* New York: Allen Lane.

Soda Osamu, 1987, *Maeda Masana,* Tokyo: Yoshikawa kōbunkan.

Takahashi Korekiyo, 1936a, *Zuisōroku* [Essays], Tokyo: Chikura shobō.
1936b, *Takahashi Korekiyo keizairon* [Takahashi Korekiyo's Economic Theories], Tokyo: Chikura shobō.
1988, *Takahashi Korekiyo Jiden* [The Autobiography of Takahashi Korekiyo], Volume 1, Tokyo: Chūkō bunko.

14 Learning at the public bathhouse

Scott Clark

This chapter examines the process through which learning takes place among children at a *sentō* (public bathhouse). Specifically, I use a concept that I refer to as "embedded tutoring" to analyze how children move from limited knowledge to full participation as adults in *sentō*. Embedded tutoring shares many features with the model of legitimate peripheral participation (Lave and Wenger 1991) from which it is derived and that I use as a basis for my discussion of learning at *sentō*.

The concept of Lave and Wenger developed out of studies of apprenticeship. As I show in this chapter, the model while generally applicable does not fit all aspects of learning at the more informal site of the bathhouse. Embedded tutoring implies a somewhat different kind of process. The word "tutoring" suggests a dynamic process of exchange of knowledge among participants of various expertise. To succeed, tutoring requires guidance by some and appropriations of knowledge by others. "Embedded" suggests that the tutoring exists within some community of practice. It also points to a process of knowledge transfer that occurs within practices and experience not specifically designed for education. Together the words "embedded" and "tutoring" do, however, presuppose that the education is recognized, that it is not submerged into unconsciousness.

Training at *sentō* is less specialized than that of apprenticeship. It is not directed at training a select few in specific skills. Rather, its aim is to make all community members full participants. The training does not take place in a setting that is primarily or even secondarily oriented toward teaching and learning. The *sentō* is an arena of mundane activity. No special terminology related to the learning process exists. The lessons of value learned at *sentō* – beyond simply how to take a bath – are also encountered elsewhere in the society. Indeed, those valued lessons are defined by the society of which the *sentō* is part. The *sentō* is merely one site, but an important one, of reproducing those behaviors.

I first discuss the learning that takes place at *sentō* and then examine how embedded tutoring relates to this learning. The data upon which the paper is based derives from personal experience at *sentō* since 1968 and extensive ethnographic research in 1987–1988 (Clark 1994).

At the bathhouse

Historically, the *sentō* has been an important center of local community interaction. Until the last two decades, most residents of urban neighborhoods visited *sentō* daily. In 1968, for instance, less than 46 percent of dwellings in Tokyo and 41 percent of dwellings in Osaka had a bath in them (Statistics Bureau 1985:161). Families bathed at nearby public facilities with their neighbors and friends. For many young children, the *sentō* was the first place where they came in regular contact with people other than their immediate family. Thus the *sentō* served as a site of learning, a place where children learned about their neighborhood, their roles, and social etiquette. Over a period of time, children acquired the knowledge necessary to interact successfully in their community and to develop into fully participating adult members.

A person who grew up going to the bathhouse typically does not remember when they first went to *sentō*. Most went as infants. Their mothers began to bathe them there as soon as it was deemed possible and proper to do so. At least until they were toddlers, it was the mother's responsibility to bathe the child. This was thought to be an important element in the bonding of the mother to the child. At the bath, the skin-to-skin contact enhanced the development of a normal and healthy child–mother relationship (Lebra 1976, 1984). This bond is the first thing that the older person at *sentō* hoped that the child would develop.

Greetings

As children grow and begin to be able to walk and speak, they learn how to interact with other children and adults. One of the important behaviors is to perform the proper greetings. Adults, of course, must exchange appropriate salutations when meeting or leaving other people, and Japanese children are also expected to greet neighbors, friends, and acquaintances even when in the presence of their parents. The daily trip to the *sentō* provides a regular opportunity to observe when, where, and how such greetings are offered. From the time of infancy, each child, carried on the mother's back, is in a position to observe who is greeted under what circumstances, hear what is said, and directly feel the mother's body movements as salutations are exchanged.

When children are considered old enough to participate in greetings, their care-takers will see to it that they perform their roles. I have observed mothers, fathers, and other children prompt toddlers with the appropriate salutation as they meet or part at the entrance to *sentō*. A bow seems to have already been learned by this time and appears to be automatic when the words are uttered. In some cases, however, the older person prompts or encourages the youngest children to speak.

Many children, of course, have other opportunities for such greetings while accompanying their mother on shopping trips. In many cases, however, children remain at home in the care of others. The obligatory trip to the *sentō* affords regular occasions for learning this important social behavior.

Getting along with others

Bathing has its own set of rules. The parent usually washes younger children. Despite frequent admonitions to foreigners that they should wash before entering the tub, Japanese typically merely rinse their bodies before soaking unless dirt is visible on the body.[1] Children, however, are often scrubbed with soap by the parent and then released to soak and play while the other family members finish their baths. The child stands in front of the parent (or sits in their lap or on the floor) and is washed from the head down with the exception of shampooing the hair. Washing the hair appears to be cognitively separated from washing the body and may occur before or after.

The feet and the groin area are considered to be more polluted than the rest of the body and typically washed last. I have observed a number of parents admonish their children to wash the groin and feet last. While learning this sequence to wash the body, the child is also learning about conceptions of the body – that all parts are not the same. They observe that even though the adults may enter the tub before scrubbing, the older people are careful to rinse at least the groin and feet before soaking.

Children also learn how to wash and rinse without splashing soap or water on nearby people. They learn to enter the tub without overly disturbing the water, to restrict touching others to specific contexts, and to control their towel so that it does not brush anyone else.

An important lesson taught to children is that for the *sentō* experience to be enjoyable, they must not interfere with others. Children learn the bounds of permissible behavior in a Japanese group. They learn what is considered offensive and what is acceptable. Children are allowed and even expected to play at *sentō*. They may blow soap bubbles off of their towels, slide around on the wet floor, take toys in the tub, capture air bubbles with their towels in the water, write or draw in the condensation on the mirrors and walls, and generally have an enjoyable time with their friends. A limiting aspect of this play is that they must not bother other people excessively. If children overstep their bounds in play, then older adults may scold them.

As elsewhere in Japan, young children are highly indulged at the bath. The requirements for more restricted behavior as one grows older also applies at *sentō*. Since people of all ages are present at *sentō*, the child observes how its own behavior differs from that of children of other ages as well as that of adults. Since the *sentō* is a public place, the children have companions of a similar age, as well as some older and younger. The other children through association, play, demonstration, and explanation also act as resources of knowledge for an individual child. Thus the student is also a master, passing on knowledge to other children.

Children of either sex are free to go to both the male and female sections of *sentō*. After they are walking freely, children often go with their father (if he is with the family), who accepts the responsibility of washing the child. Then the children may go back and forth through connecting doors until the parents are finished. This freedom of movement between the men's and women's sections continues until the age of ten or so. Children have the opportunity to observe both men and women, to learn about differences in their bodies, and to see differences and similarities in their actions. Thus children have the opportunity to see how they can expect to develop physically as adults and how that relates to behavior, body deportment, and social interaction. At the *sentō*, they learn their gender roles in an environment that allows immediate comparison.

The children observe how adults interact in *sentō*. They see the broader social context enacted at the bath, learning who gets what sorts of deference and respect. Japanese consider that people naked at the bath have removed their differences and are equal. This naked communalism is thought to make them closer. The conception of equality allows them to interact at the bath in ways that are very enjoyable and normally more relaxed than many other situations in their lives. Contrary to their common depictions of themselves as removing all difference at the bath, however, Japanese persist in maintaining some distinctions. People of higher status continue to be treated in a somewhat deferential way. An example of this treatment is with older people who are offered assistance when needed. Elders may be given their favorite spots to wash or soak. Sometimes a person who was occupying that particular space will apologize for even being there. Children, in particular, are taught to make way for the elderly.

Children are also expected to show filial devotion to their parents and grandparents at the bath. It is common to see children washing their parents' backs and lightly massaging their shoulders. I never observed this being done at the behest of a coercive parent. The child is gradually taught through observation and encouragement that to take care of the parent and older people is an enjoyable duty. Parents will point to an incident of this filial devotion and tell the children how wonderful it is, gently persuading them to imitate those acts.

In one instance that I observed, a young man carried his aged father across the slippery tiles in the bathing area, washed him, and then placed him in the tub. This attracted the attention of those present. Everyone stopped talking and watched discreetly. It was apparent that the young man was admired for his filial action, and no one missed the opportunity to point out to children how wonderful and how important this behavior was.

The sentō *as a site of education*

That latter incident occurred in 1987. The young man and his father did not come to *sentō* regularly. In previous years, I have seen many examples of this type that went largely unremarked but were nevertheless noticed. The fact that virtually all activity ceased as this young man was taking care of his father is indicative of at least two things: The decreased number of *sentō* in Japan today means that fewer people in any neighborhood see each other at the bath on a regular basis; therefore they may not observe the same sorts of behavior as frequently as in previous times. The second is the explicit acknowledgment of *sentō* as a site of education.

The *sentō* has long been thought of as a place for children to learn about life and becoming a member of a community. Shikitei Sanba wrote a famous piece about *sentō* called *Ukiyoburo* in the early nineteenth century. He discussed several of the things about society and humans that could be learned while bathing there. For many years in essays in newspapers and magazines, Japanese have discussed the importance of *sentō* as a social education center for young people. Recently, the decrease in numbers of *sentō* as a result of increased numbers of baths in dwellings has been connected to current social ills by a number of essayists, radio and television commentators, and many of the people that I interviewed. They attribute a perceived lack of care about community, the elderly, and others in general to the missed opportunities to develop those values at a neighborhood *sentō*. They associate the apparently increasing numbers of sex crimes to a lack of the special kind of sex and body education that was possible at *sentō*.

Today, middle-school teachers who accompany children on school trips comment about the different attitudes exhibited by the children who are often uncomfortable about bathing with others of the same sex. Those teachers cite this as indicative of a general trend toward lack of healthy attitudes about their own bodies. Clearly, for many people, the *sentō* is thought to have served in the past as an important place of social education.

In an effort to recapture some of that training, I have often encountered parents taking their children to a *sentō* despite the fact that they have a bath at home. They wanted their children to experience the things that they learned themselves as a child. When I visited with them, those parents said that they felt that children could really learn how to get along with others at *sentō* and then would do better in school, at work, and throughout life. *Sentō* operators also capitalized on this perception in some communities by having nights when children were admitted without charge. They advertised the event as a time when children could learn important lessons about Japanese society and history. I have also frequently seen groups of boys with little experience accompanying another who used *sentō* regularly. While engaged in a conversation with one of these groups, the boys informed me that while the idea had been their own, their parents had encouraged them to come and had given them the money in order that they would also learn the lessons that the parents had learned in their youth.

In a related incident, in 1988, I watched a television program that took a bus load of middle-school boys to a *sentō*. None of the boys had been before. The cameras captured the boys doing things that were considered amusing because of the naivete displayed. They also showed the boys interacting with the older people who were present at the *sentō* in the early afternoon. The commentators, all celebrities, talked of their own experiences going to *sentō* and the valuable lessons they had learned there; and, in the case of the one celebrity who had never been, they discussed what she had missed by not having this educational experience.

Curriculums of teaching and learning

While children who go to *sentō* daily still learn similar lessons as their parents before them, it seems for many people today that the *sentō* has sometimes been transformed from a site where learning took place in a daily activity to an institution where education of youth is an explicit goal. Among many other examples of this transformation are two children's books, *Ofuroya-san – A Japanese Public Bath* (Nishimura 1977) and *Grandpa's Town* (Nomura 1991). The former book consists entirely of illustrations of a family going to a *sentō.* No text occurs except on the title page, which tells us that Atchan, her father, mother, and the baby are going to the bath. The illustrations sketch the trip and include examples of several of the lessons already discussed in this chapter. The children and adults greet neighbors and friends, young people assist old people, children play, several young boys get bothersome, and an old gentleman reprimands them. The illustrations clearly show how proper behavior makes everyone happy. The atmosphere is, or should be, harmonious; the alternative only causes dissension and unhappiness.

Grandpa's Town is a more complex tale about culture change in Japan. A boy and his mother are visiting his grandfather to convince him to come and live with them in the city. They worry that Grandfather is all alone now that his wife has passed away. On a trip to the *sentō* with his grandfather, the boy's first such experience, the boy has many opportunities to greet his grandfather's friends and acquaintances. He also observes firsthand the lessons and consequences of acceptable and unacceptable behavior when a young playmate causes some problems. In addition, this visit to the bath teaches the boy that Grandfather has many friends and is not alone even though he is separated from his family.

Both books are nostalgic reflections on a Japan that is rapidly changing. They are idealized and stylized. The stories represent what some adults feel is important to learn from such experiences. Consequently, the books have become didactic instruments. The *sentō* in these books is no longer a site where embedded tutoring takes place; rather, the books are a means to instruct children in proper behavior and a nostalgic past. Although both the actual experience of visiting a *sentō* and the books about *sentō* teach similar things, it is instructive to contrast the two.

Many children today have not personally experienced *sentō,* and it has become an exotic activity for them. The books use a style of illustration meant to capture the child's attention and depict the various aspects of the public bath in which children are interested. The *sentō* is an institution that children are already familiar with through stories and television. The authors have explicitly made an attempt to use a subject that is known but has a wondrous quality that is meant to stimulate the child to think and learn – specifically, to learn or reinforce the moral lessons illustrated. One may safely suppose that an adult reading the book with a child might reinforce those lessons with stories of their own. The adult may even use the book not to teach about *sentō* per se but to teach and convince the child to take on the desirable social behaviors illustrated in the book.

This is a type of learning not so different from that found in most formalized educational situations. It is of the sort that Lave and Wenger refer to as a "teaching curriculum" (1991:97). The books supply the resources for the learning. A child engages them through the images and words in the books, not through direct participation in the acts. Obviously, the learning from the books cannot approach the extent, depth, and complexity of the learning that can occur through long-term participation at *sentō* or, in Lave and Wenger's words, a "learning curriculum."

The learning of the social, moral lessons (which the book attempts to impart) by a child while actually at the *sentō* is quite different from reading about it. The learning by doing is situated; it is embedded in an everyday activity. The purpose of the trip to *sentō* is not educational – neither teaching nor learning. Its purpose is primarily hygienic but also social and recreational. Learning takes place there as a part of this broader intention. The actors – at least, the "teachers" and, presumably, most of the "learners" as well – are aware that learning is or will take place. Nevertheless, learning is not the object of the activity. This is an example of "learning [as] an integral part of generative social practice in the lived-in world" (Lave and Wenger 1991:35).

In this context, it is useful to examine embedded tutoring as a means to analyze the learning that occurs at *sentō*. Lave and Wenger define legitimate peripheral participation as "the process by which newcomers become part of a community of practice. A person's intentions to learn are engaged, and the meaning of learning is configured through the process of becoming a full participant in a sociocultural practice" (1991:29). The concept clearly incorporates dynamism through time in an ongoing process of incorporation. It assumes that people through a process of becoming intend to learn those things necessary to take their places in the community of practice. Lave and Wenger assert that the concept is of general utility in understanding learning.

Lave and Wenger used examples of apprenticeship to illustrate this learning process. While an educational component has long been recognized and valued in the case of learning by children at *sentō,* in contrast to apprenticeship, the educational element is nowhere near the head of priorities for the activity. Daily bathing takes place as one act in a more generalized social community with more general social goals. It is truly an everyday sociocultural practice, and it is in these locations of "directed experience" (a phrase I borrow from Singleton) that the notion of embedded tutoring leads us to examine what is learned.

Relations of power and learning

Many of the chapters in this volume examine examples of individuals who are highly motivated to acquire knowledge and skills. Apprentice potters and painters certainly appear to be willing to submit themselves to a variety of onerous tasks and experiences in order to obtain the knowledge.

We can safely assume that children want to become adult members of the community of which they are part, that, in Lave and Wenger's terms, the "newcomers" intend to become "old-timers." As part of the process of growing up, these Japanese children have an interest in learning how to be socially mature human beings. The goals and rewards of adult status are already defined, enacted, and observable in the community. As actors in this milieu, children see the privileges and problems of maturity and, in any case, probably accept growth as inevitable and, therefore, something to be prepared for. The adults also have a vested interest in the children becoming adults.

Since what they learn is societal behavior, the social context in which they are learning is not merely the bath but within the broader community in which they live. Learning to become old-timers at the bath (i.e., learning how to bathe) is only a part of the knowledge acquisition necessary. They are becoming old-timers in a more general community. Thus their learning at *sentō* is also more generalized, reflecting the broader context. The *sentō* is not organized to train newcomers to become old-timers but serves as an important locus for such training because of its nature as a social entity. Children at *sentō* learn to bathe and also learn how to become old-timers in the neighborhood, in the community.

Learning at *sentō* requires knowledge and skill of action in a specific cultural context. Persons who have the knowledge – masters at various degrees of attainment – are present, and the newcomers acquire this knowledge over a period of time. The children learn skills and are expected to use them and teach them as they move through stages in their life cycle. The youngest are expected to act in a particular way and to modify their behavior as they reach other levels. Those levels are not defined by the activity in the *sentō*. They are defined in the wider society. Thus the children move through the stages not as they have mastered the necessary skills but as organized in a broader social context. They demonstrate mastery of the skills as they move through life-cycle stages.

One might well ask what would happen if a person does not master the skills. In apprenticeship, a person may presumably achieve a status by demonstrating the skills over an appropriate time period. At *sentō*, the status has already been achieved in the outside community. The expectations for behavior at the bath are based upon that status. In cases where the appropriate behaviors for the status were not engaged, I have seen old-timers correct and censure the offenders.

The old-timers have relatively higher status and power. The higher the status of the old-timer relative to the newcomer, the more authority exists over the novice. An old-timer has the responsibility to teach, guide, and correct the younger. This responsibility also is learned and accepted as a person grows. Each should impart their own knowledge to less experienced (usually younger) persons.

Unlike the discussions of power relationships by Lave and Wenger, differential power at *sentō* does not necessarily involve conflict between newcomers and old-timers. In examples of apprenticeship, the newcomers as acquirers of specialized economic skills are in a position to replace the old-timers. Increasing participation in the community of practice by children at *sentō*, however, does not threaten displacement of the old-timers. If anything, the acquisition of increased skills implies a more congenial, supportive environment for the old-timer. The application of power involves a desire to *add* fully participating members to the group without the potential problems that might occur if they were seen as replacing old-timers.

Indeed, the tensions introduced by differential power relationships are not those of a threat of replacement but of acceptance of particular ways of behaving. In 1987, at a *sentō* in Sapporo, I watched as a group of four young teenage boys came to a bathhouse for the first time. They were visibly nervous and obviously did not know what they were doing. One older man gently showed them where to undress and then indicated where the stools and basins were. The boys began to disrobe. Two of them quickly imitated those around them and stripped completely, then proceeded to the bathing area holding their towels casually in front of their genitals. The other two, however, were embarrassed about being completely nude in front of the men, the female *bandai-san* (attendant who takes the fees and watches over the bath), and a woman in her twenties who was cleaning the dressing area. These two boys removed their shirts, shoes, and socks. Then they wrapped the small towel around their waists before removing their pants and undershorts. Two older men quietly "harrumphed" about this unusual and unneedful display of modesty.[2] Meanwhile, the other two boys had begun a vigorous scrubbing. These quick learners then entered the tub to soak.

The other two visibly embarrassed boys could not bring themselves to remove the towels and scrub themselves. They began to wash with soap held in their hands without removing the towels. Typically, the small towel is lathered with soap and then used to scrub the body. As they finished and rose to enter the tub, an elderly gentleman stopped them. He berated them for attempting to enter the tub with their towels.[3] They were perplexed, not wanting to remove them. The old-timer then proceeded to what he and the other old-timers considered to be a more important issue. In their view, the boys while wearing the towels could not possibly have cleaned their groin areas sufficiently to enter the communal tub. He explained to them the importance of washing the groin and feet before entering the tub. He pointed to another young man who had just begun and was rinsing his groin and feet before soaking. This old-timer would not let these two into the tub before they returned to the faucets and washed properly. The two boys were too embarrassed to comply with the requirement to remove the towel and exited to the dressing area where they managed to dress without exposing themselves.

This incident caused them some public embarrassment and discomfort. It made the mood in the bath uncomfortable for everyone. The other men talked with the two boys who were better adjusted and attempted to explain the situation and asked them to convey their feelings to the boys who had left.

This is one example of how tensions can arise between the newcomers and old-timers. In this case, two boys did not (could not?) comply and left. Teaching and learning broke down. Everyone was uncomfortable. The old-timers, however, wanted the newcomers to participate fully in the *sentō*. Their concern was not about being replaced and therefore did not limit access to knowledge. Indeed, their own continued participation in a declining activity would be assured if more newcomers entered the scene. Even in the past, before the continuing existence of *sentō* was threatened, however, old-timers were not "replaced" by the newcomers.

The skills learned at the *sentō* need not be "stolen" (Singleton, Chapter 7, this volume) either. The masters are not privileged holders of secrets. Rather, those with the social skills and knowledge to impart to their younger companions hold only what is considered appropriate for the entire community. They do not have secret scrolls or techniques but rather a body of knowledge and experience held communally. Nor do the learners have a promise of obtaining something that will reward them with economic security or prestige. Diligence in learning at the bath will not secure them a higher place in the community. A lack of knowledge will, perhaps, result in some social ostracism. But because social skills are important within the broader community, they are shared freely with little apparent control to access.

In a broader examination of learning, I argue that differential power relationships have to be examined in more complex ways without assuming replacement as a constituent dynamic of the process. At *sentō,* because an additive model exists rather than a replacement one, and the expectations of level of performance are defined by a community exterior to the locale (the *sentō* is situated within that community), access to the knowledge is rarely limited. A child may be praised one moment for acting beyond the expectations of its age and then be allowed to violate willfully the same principle the next moment. The control is not directed toward restricting access to increasingly praiseworthy performance but rather to performing at an expected degree of competence befitting the person's current status.

Conclusion

Embedded tutoring has led me to think about the process of learning at *sentō* in a different way. Prior to applying it to write this chapter, I had only considered how children learn in a more traditional manner. In many, undoubtedly most, institutions and activities, learning takes place in complex ways. Thinking about learning in ways broadened from those developed by Lave and Wenger allows us to examine the various actors involved in the process and the dynamic ways in which knowledge and skills are transferred. Embedded tutoring is, I think, a useful perspective from which to analyze the learning of children as they become full participants in this particular community of practice. Clearly, the values and practices of the community are undergoing reproduction and change at the bath. Children are learning and practicing them as they develop into adults. The children are strongly motivated to learn because of their membership within the community. They are, to paraphrase Lave and Wenger, absorbing and absorbed in the community.

Embedded tutoring in this instance contrasts with the studies of craft, art, and occupation that, of course, emphasize the place of master and apprentice, of those with and without knowledge. The "apprentices" of the bath do not steal the knowledge from the masters. Indeed, the "masters" differ greatly from their counterparts in apprenticeship situations. At *sentō,* people with knowledge and skill are present; those people are the entire community of adults. They are not a select few who have acquired specialized learning available to limited individuals. Likewise, all children have access to that knowledge; they are all "apprentices" no less motivated to learn than those indicated by the traditional use of the word. By moving the focus away from the master–apprentice relationship to the structure of the community's learning resources, the concept of legitimate peripheral participation successfully illuminates the active participation of the apprentice in the acquisition of knowledge and skills. However, it leads to assumptions such as those about power relationships (i.e., a replacement model). As I have attempted to show, when all adults – indeed, anyone with some knowledge, including children – are the resources and all children are learners, replacement tensions do not necessarily exist. An additive model is in place, and the power tensions shift elsewhere.

Notes

1. The practice of rinsing or soaping may be changing. Impressionistically, I feel like more people use soap before soaking in the communal tub today than they did in the 1960s.
2. Longtime participants at *sentō* have numerous stories of the "silly" (*bakabakashii*) modesty of young people who do not have experience bathing with other people.
3. In the past, towels were commonly taken into the tub and used to scrub the body while soaking. Today, this is seen as unclean, and signs are prominently placed that tell people not to dip the towel in the water or scrub themselves while in the tub. Towels are left outside the tub, placed on the head, or otherwise held so that they do not touch the water.

References

Clark, Scott, 1994, *Japan, a View from the Bath,* Honolulu: University of Hawaii Press.

Lave, Jean, and Etienne Wenger, 1991, *Situated Learning: Legitimate Peripheral Participation,* Cambridge: Cambridge University Press.

Lebra, Takie Sugiyama, 1976, *Japanese Patterns of Behavior,* Honolulu: University Press of Hawaii.

1984, *Japanese Women, Constraint and Fulfillment,* Honolulu: University of Hawaii Press.

Nishimura Shigeo, 1977, *Ofuroya-san – A Japanese Public Bath,* Tokyo: Fukuinkan-Shoten.

Nomura Takaaki, 1991, *Grandpa's Town,* New York: Kane/Miller Book Publishers. Originally published in Japan in 1989 under the title *Ojiichan no Machi,* Tokyo: Kodansha, Ltd.

Statistics Bureau, 1985, *Statistical Indicators on Social Life of Japan,* Tokyo: Statistics Bureau, Management and Coordination Agency.

15 Growing up through *matsuri*: Children's establishment of self and community identities in festival participation

Saburo Morita

Japanese children in modern times are extremely busy. Most pupils attending elementary schools have at least two or three kinds of *juku* (private schools for afterschool classes and tutoring) appointments a week. And many *juku* require them to attend more than twice a week. Consequently, children are busy after school attending *juku* and preparing for them as well as for daily homework. Because each child has his or her own schedule, he or she has to call friends and arrange a suitable time to play. Children have to find a combination of friends who have different time zones of the day open for play. Eventually, it becomes harder and harder to find playmates in the neighborhood.

Festivals

One of the few chances for neighborhood kids to get together for fun is at *matsuri* (community festival) time. Most communities, even in newly constructed towns, have local festivals or their equivalents. Everybody, old and young, male and female, has a chance, sometimes felt as an obligation, to cooperate and become better acquainted. Usually, people gain familiarity with the community and affection for it especially through participation in the *matsuri* (Yoneyama 1986; Matsudaira 1990).

In my book on *matsuri* (1990), I argue that among the many community events in Japan, we should consider as *matsuri* only those that give participants a chance to express real inner feelings or pride, and only when they help the participants to establish their sense of connection to the community. *Matsuri* is an emic concept that should be judged by its participants. Event (*ibento* in Japanese), on the other hand, is an etic concept appropriate to planners. They can create a popular event, but they can't make a *matsuri* without voluntary cooperation by spontaneous participants.

Seemingly, *matsuri* and event are exclusive concepts. Many people tend to see *matsuri* as more religious, more traditional, and sometimes more obligatory and restrictive than modern, secular, functional, free events. But these are not exclusive distinctions.

The national high school baseball tournaments held in Japan every spring and summer, for example, are big events planned and supported by such organizations as the Japan High School Baseball Association, the Ministry of Education, the mass media, and so on. They are surely well designed and well organized. There is no doubt that they are most successful as popular events. But at the same time, they are *matsuri* for the young baseball players and other participants such as cheerleaders. We sometimes call them "festivals for the young" (*wakamono no saiten*). They are not religious events. Baseball has no relation with Japan's long tradition, though we can analyze the way of practice, the goals of players, or the human relationships in a team, and so forth in terms of that tradition. Nevertheless, we assume that the ball deity (*kyū-shin*) or the Goddess of Victory can sometimes affect the outcome of a game. And it is taken for granted that a high school should not participate in the tournament in Kōshien Stadium if anyone connected with the school's baseball team is accused of robbery, violence, or drunkenness. We have a kind of purification period before the national meet begins. In these senses, this event is very much like a traditional *matsuri*.

Events are planned for an explicit purpose. A business event may be created to advertise the company's name, to sell its products, to sample consumer reactions. Administrators may plan an event to stimulate the local economy, to lure tourists from outside, to appeal to the residents for cooperation in making their community more comfortable. To make an event successful, it is important for planners to have a clear goal. To have a successful *matsuri*, it is crucial for participants to spontaneously feel it as theirs. The formal goal can be as vague as serving the deity of community or just simply following tradition. Such formal goals are usually a cover for practical reasons, which, if acknowledged openly, might leave people feeling manipulated. Any *matsuri* was once an event: Somebody planned it, at least the first time. A *matsuri* is a mixed product of planning and history.

In this chapter, I compare a community in suburban Kyoto with one in downtown Nagasaki. Each covers about the same geographical area. Both are home to many busy children. But their histories are completely different. Sakaidani-Garden-House (people call it just Gāden) began its history in March 1984. It is the newest community in the Rakusai New Town located between the "western mountains" (so-called Nishiyama) and the Katsura River. Suwanomachi in downtown Nagasaki, on the other hand, has its origin around the middle of the seventeenth century. This district (*cho-nai*) is well known for its Jaodori (dragon dance) performed during the nationally famous Nagasaki Kunchi Festival. Located in the heart of a tradition-rich city, the Suwanomachi residents have been blessed with a variety of historied local events including the Shoro nagashi (*bon* festival), Peeron (the cutter-type boat-racing competition), Hata-age (kite fights), and the Kunchi festival.

Gāden residents have no such list. Rakusai New Town belongs administratively to the ancient capital of Kyoto. But it is physically and culturally detached from downtown Kyoto, so the New Town has had to find its own identity through sports and cultural events based on its four elementary school districts. Gāden residents have created several such new events as the Gāden Kodomo Natsu Matsuri (children's summer festival) and the Mochitsuki-taikai (rice-cake-making day).

In my judgment, the *natsu matsuri* in particular is an event on its way to becoming a full *matsuri*. Actually, they made a *taru mikoshi* (small portable *sake*-cask shrine) in 1991 but replaced it with a *kujira dashi* (whale float) in 1992. They are still inventing their tradition. The event could disappear before it gets to stable *matsuri* status.

What is the difference in the two *matsuri* when viewed through the eyes of children who participate in them? What do they encourage children to feel about their community? Do such festivals help children establish their self-images and community identities? These are the main questions I examine.

Gāden children's summer festival

The Gāden is a small community (93 households) within Rakusai New Town (10,000 households). Because it is a ready-made town designed by the Kyoto Municipal Bureau of Urban Planning, all the houses are very similar both in their appearance and interior structures. Every house has two stories. Most of them are duplexes occupied by two independent households. They were on sale in 1984 at the cost of about 30 to 40 million yen per single-family unit. It was affordable middle-class housing in a convenient location (very close to a mall with banks, post offices, a hotel, and a famous department store), with a good environment (between a park and bamboo forest that is a nature preserve).

The lucky winners of a lottery held on February 3, 1984, met for the first time at the end of that month to organize a *kanri kumiai* (management association). Actually, all the articles of incorporation including rules for membership, housing repair, common property management, and so on had already been prepared by the city housing bureau, which had informally appointed the first management committee. The residents had nothing to do but affirm the proposal, although they asked many questions on details.

Almost all residents moved in during the interval from late March to the end of the first week of April 1984. Their native communities were different, and they knew nothing about one another. But in terms of generation (mainly thirty-something married couples with young children) and economic stratum (young middle-class small business owners, teachers, municipal officers, etc.), they had much in common.

About a half-year later, some residents proposed that the community should have its own *jichikai* (or self-government board). There was little dispute over why the Gāden needed a *jichikai* when it already had a management committee. As most Japanese do, however, they decided to create the *jichikai* in order to affiliate with the larger, upper-level association self-government boards. Eventually, sports or entertainment events were assigned to the *jichikai,* while official relations with government agencies and informal negotiations among residents became the mission of the *kanri kumiai.*

The first Kodomo Natsu Matsuri was held on the Saturday after *bon* vacation in August 1985. Kyoto has a long Jizōbon tradition. In mid-August, the children of a neighborhood meet to play and to eat delicious foods at street corners where there are statues of Jizōbosatsu (the Buddhisattva who guards children). The custom is so popular in Kyoto that communities which have no *jizō* statue will rent one for the occasion.

Most of the Gāden residents came from areas outside Kyoto and have to return to their parental homes at *bon.* Few people remain in the community, which is why the *matsuri* is held just after the *bon* vacation. Parents of elementary schoolchildren must help prepare for the kids' festival, by hanging out lanterns on which each child's name is written, and by cooking and serving food. They also have to prepare for the Saturday evening party for adults, with *karaoke,* beer, and food. Childless residents also join in this evening version of the festival, which is held just before the children's one. So it has become an occasion for community-wide solidarity.

As time went on, the people were getting more familiar with one another. A few became noted as *matsuri-zuki* (festival freaks), eager to be involved. By 1991, the festival had been elaborated to include a *taru mikoshi* (small portable *sake*-cask shrine) for the children. People also made small *happi* (festival jackets) for the children. There is no Shinto guardian shrine or *jizō* in this community. So, obviously there is no relationship between the portable shrine and any religious organization. In 1992, the portable shrine was replaced by a *kujira-dashi* (whale float). Most of the children who take part in the kids' festival are in kindergarten or elementary school. They know each other very well because they played together in preschool and because most of them go to the same elementary school. They also get together at the park next to the Gāden for about ten to twenty minutes for radio gymnastics in the early mornings of summer vacation. But because they are very busy going to various kinds of *juku* – including kids' clubs for sports, music, calligraphy, fine arts, dance and the abacus, as well as those for learning English, math, science, and other intellectual subjects – children have few chances to play casually with one another on the streets or in their houses. Because the afterschool schedule of each child is different, they have to consult appointment books when arranging a time to play together. So the combinations of playmates vary depending on what day of the week it is. When by chance they have extra time and want to play, they use the telephone like businessmen or women scheduling a conference.

Therefore the summer festival offers the children of Gāden an unusual chance to play with kids in their neighborhood. It seems to remind them of their friendship in preschool times. The *jichikai* also encourages residents to participate in sports events such as softball tournaments for kids. Children between third and sixth grade practice at the park on early mornings in May. Parents (or elder siblings who are in college) serve as volunteer coaches. These kinds of cooperation seem to have reinforced community identity among children as well as adult residents. For the children, *matsuri* activities bring them not only joy but a feeling of home town belonging and safety.

Suwanomachi and dragon dance performances

Suwanomachi is one of fifty-eight districts offering performance services to the Suwa *jinja* (shrine) during the Kunchi, the shrine's autumn festival. The beginning of the Nagasaki Kunchi dates to 1634, and the construction of Dejima, a landfill island in Nagasaki Bay that was used as the international trade center during the Edo period. Nagasaki originally developed as an international port town owned by the Christian *daimyō*,

Ōmura Sumitada. He donated the port to the Jesuits from 1580 to 1587, and it became the central city of Japanese Christianity. After it was taken over by Toyotomi Hideyoshi, Nagasaki was ruled directly by the shogunate, and Christianity was suppressed. The Tokugawa *bakufu* tried to reconstruct the traditional religious order destroyed by the Christians. The reconstruction of Suwa *jinja* and the beginning of the Nagasaki Kunchi were strongly supported both financially and administratively by the Nagasaki governors. In this sense, the Kunchi started as a kind of political event, though religious in form.

At first, this festival was very simple. Farmers of suburban Nagasaki carried portable shrines and representatives from each district paraded with simple *kasaboko* (decorated umbrellas). Women from the two pleasure quarters danced in front of the shrine. But as the international trade city expanded and new landfills were constructed, the number of districts serving the community deity increased, and the festival became gorgeous. Eight years after the big fire of 1663, Nagasaki had seventy-seven *cho*'s; they were divided into seven groups with eleven *cho*'s in each group. Each group offers performance services to the Suwa *jinja* in an annual rotation. The two pleasure quarters perform in alternate years. In addition to these town districts (*machikata*), there are twelve rural districts (*gōkata*) divided into four groups of three *cho*'s each. Each district carries a *mikoshi* once every four years. In short, almost everyone living in Nagasaki and environs will be called on to play a role in the Kunchi at least once every seven years.

This now-traditional division of duties and complex combination of dance performances was established in the festival's first thirty to forty years. When a governor appointed by the Meiji state tried to reform the Kunchi into a simple and purely State-Shintoistic version, Nagasaki citizens resisted, and eventually, he was fired. People threw stones at the festival procession for the first time. It surely became a *matsuri* at that point. The basic structure of the Nagasaki Kunchi continued through World War II, which brought serious damage to the city and its residents especially by the atomic bomb.

Suwanomachi was reportedly established around 1636 and named after the Suwa shrine. In 1986, there were 330 households and 867 residents registered in this *cho*. But less than one-third of them are active in the festival. This is not an unusual phenomenon for the urban center in the modern city.

Mr. Makoto Yamashita (1918–), who has taken responsibility for producing the famous Jaodori ("dragon dance," but we might have said "snake dance," historically and literally), has to redouble his efforts in order to recruit powerful young *jakata* ("dragon dancers") whenever Suwanomachi offers service to the shrine outside his *cho.* Although recruiting the festival performers outside one's own *cho* is contrary to festival tradition, Mr. Yamashita had no alternative.

Mr. Yamashita is an excellent innovator of performances as well as a guardian of tradition. He created the *ko-ja* ("child dragon") and the *mago-ja* ("grandson of dragon") after the war. Young people of Suwanomachi who wish to participate in the Jaodori performance can do so as children, grandchildren, or musicians.

Suwanomachi has two adult dragons, *seiryuu* ("blue," actually green, "dragon") and *hakuryū* ("white dragon"). Each dragon needs ten carriers and one *tamatsukai,* who carries a golden ball that the dragon chases. Sometimes the dragons dance on a narrow stage at the same time. *Jakata*'s have to dance very hard carrying an oak pole weighing over forty pounds while moving in unison. One team of *jakata* needs to be relieved by another one, while they are dancing, before the members of the first one get exhausted. They need physical strength, stamina, and technique. It requires long and hard practice.

The purification ritual for all Kunchi participants of the year is held on June 1st. Practice for the dance performance begins early in July. In 1986, more than sixty physically powerful men of Suwanomachi or other districts gathered at a hotel in response to Mr. Yamashita's request to affirm their willingness to participate. Hard training started on an evening in mid-July. On the same evening, more than fifty children of Suwanomachi came to the athletic ground of an elementary school, where the adults (including some fathers) had gathered. Preschoolers, who carry the *mago-ja,* don't have to practice walking much. But first- and second-grade boys (*jakata* or *ko-ja*) must practice hard, and this is all the more true for boys and girls beyond third grade (*jabayashi*). Without practice, no dragon will dance.

Practice continued almost every evening from mid-July to September 9th. Mr. Yamashita conducted all the sessions both for adults and children. Because he often scolds children loudly and will sometimes beat them lightly on the head or hands, his way of training seemed old-fashioned. His attitude, however, was the same toward adults. Whenever he scolds, he stresses the importance of each member's precise movements to the whole performance. He did not hesitate to correct persons in high social position. It was his overriding concern to encourage a successful Jaodori performance. Many children complained about his severe attitude, but the majority were pleased to observe adult members practicing just as hard and being corrected just as thunderously.

It took time for some children to understand the significance of what they had done. Most of them are busy, and some really don't want to participate in the Jaodori. For kids who were pressured by their parents to participate, it took more time to get the whole picture. So Mr. Yamashita adopted a simple but powerful appeal, giving a 100-yen ticket to each child who came to a practice session; it seemed to work very well for some. But according to comments they wrote after a month and a half of practice, the experience of physical cooperation among neighborhood kids, and seeing directly that adults were making as much effort as the children, seemed to be a very positive influence.

To be able to participate in a festival like Kunchi is a privilege for a child living in downtown Nagasaki. A sixth-grade boy who played a big drum in the *takarabune* (treasure ship) dance of Nigiwaimachi was also learning jazz piano. He had to practice piano every day at home with his mother. So for him, he said, it was a joy to be able to practice with his friends in the summer of 1986.

The reward for weeks of long and hard practice is the attention and admiration of people on festival days, from the 7th to the 10th of October. Visitors came from various parts of Japan. TV cameramen and photographers from the big papers and magazines were there, as were their classmates. This was another reward.

Discussion

The social environment surrounding children in Gāden and Suwanomachi is not so different. The numbers attending *juku* are increasing, but the numbers of children per family, on the other hand, are decreasing. The fewer the number, the more their parents seem to take interest in their education, and the more they tend to lose interest in community activities outside the schools. In this circumstance, children also tend to lose the feeling of being connected to the community in which they live. If they felt indifferent to the community and to their neighbors, their efforts to establish their self-identities would be endangered. The love of and by their community is important for children to stabilize their souls and personalities.

In this regard, the cultural environment of these two communities is quite different. Both have their own festivals. Gāden's *matsuri* is easy to take part in. If friends or relatives were visiting there, they too could participate in the festival and enjoy its activities together with the Gāden children. But the access to the Nagasaki Kunchi is not so easy. A young adult male living outside of the *machikata* area of Nagasaki and wishing to participate in the dragon dance may have a chance to be recruited by Mr. Yamashita. It is almost impossible, however, for children outside Suwanomachi to be invited.

Nagasaki Kunchi has become established as a large, complex system with rules for when, who, what, where, and how. It also provides an answer to the question of why: Just repeat the religious ritual forms in order to express thanks to the Guardian God! Children in Suwanomachi are able to grow up step by step through performing roles based on their sex and age. Although some other criteria such as social and economic rank, household descent, or difference of gender were operative in the past, people ignore most of them these days. Tradition need not always mean structural rigidity: The system has to be restructured to keep pace with social change. That's why a community needs both tradition keepers and innovators. Mr. Yamashita is, in this sense, an ideal person not only for the *jaodori* of Suwanomachi but for the whole Kunchi festival.

Due to continuous reforms by Mr. Yamashita and other leaders, almost half of the fifty *jabayashi*'s in Suwanomachi were girls in 1986, though all the *jakata*'s still were male. Suwanomachi children had to bear long and hard training. Mr. Yamashita scolded them; he was different from their parents and teachers. In spite of it, the children seem to be satisfied with their experience. Love of the community and the joy of cooperation seem to be inculcated effectively in them. Their roles were peripheral. But they were taught repeatedly that those peripheral roles are connected to the vitally important core and are equally indispensable for the whole *jaodori*. So they gained pride as members of the famous *jaodori* performance.

Which *matsuri* impressed children more? It is obvious that the Kunchi did. Children in Suwanomachi are blessed with an active festival tradition. This cultural situation helps them find their positions in our society by connecting them to their community and to a human network made through long cooperative practice. Children living in an area that has a well-organized active *matsuri* have the advantage of being able more easily to establish stable self and community identities.

References

Matsudaira, Makoto, 1990, *Toshi-Shukusai No Shakaigaku* [Sociology of Urban Festivals], Tokyo: Yuhikaku.

Morita, Saburo, 1990, *Matsuri No Bunka-Jinruigaku* [Cultural Anthropology of Festivals], Kyoto: Sekaishiso-sha.

Yoneyama, Toshinao, 1986, *Toshi To Matsuri No Jinruigaku* [Anthropology of City and Festival], Tokyo: Kawadeshobo-shinsha.

Part IV

Appropriations of cultural practice

16 Learning to swing: Oh Sadaharu and the pedagogy and practice of Japanese baseball

William W. Kelly

Anatomy of a swing

Hitting a baseball at the professional level is one of the most difficult accomplishments in all of sports. A batter, standing just over sixty feet away from a pitcher, has about four-tenths of one second to focus on the ball coming out of the pitcher's hand at up to 100 miles per hour and to swing his bat at the precise speed and angle to get it to an exact position at just the moment when he can make contact and strike the ball such that it will elude the nine players positioned to field it.[1] Even the very best professional hitters can fail to hit safely seven out of ten times.

And of all hitting, the most dramatic, the most celebrated, the most difficult, is the home run – the long ball hit in fair territory between the two baselines far enough to carry over the distant outfielders and beyond the 300- to 400-foot fences. It requires great physical power, but that power must be applied with split-second timing and with the precise coordination of eyes, shoulders, arms, wrists, hip, and legs.

The world record for the most home runs in a professional career is held by the greatest Japanese power hitter of all time, Oh Sadaharu. Oh's career statistics show him to be fully the equal in talent and physical prowess to the greatest American hitters – Ty Cobb, Babe Ruth, Ted Williams, Mickey Mantle, Hank Aaron. In twenty-two professional seasons, Oh came to bat 9,250 times in 2,831 games. He hit safely 2,786 times for a .301 lifetime average. He will be most remembered, however, for his lifetime total of 868 home runs, a world professional record that far surpasses the American record, Hank Aaron's 755 career homers, which had itself replaced the long-standing record of the legendary Babe Ruth (714).

Oh accomplished this with one of the most distinctive swing styles in all of baseball history. In what fans and journalists tagged as the flamingo, or scarecrow, stance,[2] the left-handed hitting Oh would raise his front, right leg as the pitcher was winding up, and balance quietly on his back, left leg while awaiting the delivery. He would then step forward on to his front leg at the moment of ball release to swing the bat.

In principle, hitting a baseball requires a combination of translational and rotational energy. As the physicist Robert Adair explains, pushing off and stepping from the back leg to the forward leg translates power forward "into the pitch"; then, using the forward leg as a fixed pivot, the hitter transfers that momentum by rotating the arms, hips, and legs when swinging the bat off the shoulder and around to make contact (Adair 1994: 62–71). Over the years, however, individual hitters have enacted these principles in an enormous range of stances – for example, by planting the feet various widths apart and in different configurations in the batter's box, by stepping forward in distinctive timings, by bringing the bat across the plate with a downswing or with an upswing or with a level swing, and so forth.

Yet even among such a wide variety of hitting stances, well known to fans, Oh's flamingo perch was highly unusual. The great Mel Ott was among a very few American pros who also lifted the forward leg while awaiting the pitcher's delivery. Even here, however, there were two crucial differences that make Oh's case an instructive one for this volume on situated learning. The first was the spiritual idiom in which Oh cast his swing – in discourse, the way in which he talked about the elements and rationale of the swing; and in practice, the way in which he trained often by swinging a sword or a *kendō* stick in addition to a baseball bat. This would appear to mark his stance as distinctively "Orientalized." One might find support for this in the subtitle of his 1984 English-language autobiography, *A Zen Way of Baseball* (Oh and Falkner 1984).

Oh's swing was acquired through a long and difficult learning process. He was a powerful hitter from his earliest efforts on neighborhood and schoolboy teams. But on breaking into the pros, he fell into a prolonged slump that very nearly ended his career. It was only saved through the intervention of a mysterious baseball *sensei* named Arakawa Hiroshi, a coach–master who put him through an arduous three-year pursuit of a totally new hitting style – and a radically new spiritual philosophy of hitting, indeed, of playing baseball. It was only at this point in his career and through the sustained encounter with Arakawa-*sensei* that Oh learned and perfected his trademark flamingo stance. It was this physical and spiritual make-over by Arakawa that then carried Oh for almost two decades to a team success unparalleled in Japanese pro baseball history and to an individual accomplishment that will surely remain a world record for some time to come.

This chapter focuses on both of these extraordinary features of Oh's swing – the learning process and its representational form. My premise is that all levels and all kinds of sports are, centrally, sites of learning, instruction, practice, mastery, and judged performance. And the situated, instrumental, and physical nature of sports activities mark teaching and learning in settings quite different from more conventional classroom pedagogies. Playing sports requires much less transmission of abstract knowledge than the inculcation and embodiment of mind–body skills. Sports are practices, and learning sports is like learning pottery, carpentry, shamanic healing, or farming. Sports thus fall squarely within a notion of learning as situated activity – learning, as Lave and Wenger put it, as "legitimate peripheral participation in a community of practice." They comprise one more "likely place" in the topos of this volume.

Each of these elements of Oh's life – his unique swing, his struggle, and the world record it brought him – is well known and much celebrated by Japanese fans. Oh himself has written a number of autobiographical accounts, and a voluminous sports journalism, book-length commentaries, and television portraits have made his biography familiar to several generations of post–World War II Japan.[3] Not only is the framework of his life story conventional, but its themes are also familiar; it is a life story periodized as stages and dramatized as adversity overcome and success gained through relentless effort. Both the achievements and the disappointments are of properly heroic proportions. Indeed, it may be so familiar to a Western sports fan as to be surprising, given the common foreigners' image of Japanese baseball as a dull game of many ties played by faceless clones overtrained into mediocre performances. Perhaps the one element that would appear to mark Oh's story as stereotypically "Oriental" is that it pivots on his baseball swing and his guided pursuit of a perfect body dynamics through a singular spiritual attitude. But what I argue in this chapter is that this image is quite deceptive. Oh's learning to swing was paradoxically both more idiosyncratic and more generic than "Oriental." His was not a paradigmatically Japanese approach to baseball pedagogy and practice. In its particulars, his experience was highly unusual for Japanese baseball; in its more general features, it was not unlike the transmission and honing of skills throughout sports. First, however, let us place the swing within his career and within the community of practice that is Japanese baseball.

Oh's life within Japanese baseball

It is hard to exaggerate baseball's popularity in twentieth-century Japan. The sport has been played in Japan for 120 years, since its introduction by U.S. physical education teachers in the 1870s and its adoption as a club activity by the premier school of the time, the First Higher School. Baseball spread downward through the public school system and upward to universities in the first decades of this century. Only in the 1930s was the first professional league organized by a powerful newspaper owner, Shōriki Matsutarō, whose own team, the Yomiuri Giants, dominated the league for decades and recruited Oh when he turned professional in 1958.

Baseball is played by more Japanese than any other sport, in schools, colleges, company leagues, and adult community leagues, as well as the professional major leagues. The pro level is organized into two leagues of six teams each, the champions of which meet at the end of a 140-game season in the Japan Series. Eleven of the twelve teams are owned entirely by major corporations; each team has a twenty-five-man playing roster and a thirty-five-man reserve squad.[4] In its amateur and professional forms, it is watched by more Japanese than any other sport. I am tempted to add that more is probably written about baseball than any other sport in Japan, although I have no basis for this claim except many hours of browsing bookstores and newsstands.

The popularity of baseball, therefore, assures and is assured by its central place in the educational system, the corporate world, and the mass media. The life of one of its genuine superstars offers many lessons for understanding this sport and its manifold significance in twentieth-century Japan. Here I focus on those aspects of Oh's case that illuminate the nature of teaching and learning in sports.[5] Still, because his learning of the flamingo stance is so situated within the longer contours of his career in baseball, it is appropriate to approach that learning experience through a brief introduction to his life in baseball.

1940–1956: Sandlot days in Tokyo

Oh was born in Tokyo in 1940 and thus entered elementary school just as the war ended and the Allied Occupation was beginning.

The streets of Tokyo were bomb-ravaged but also baseball-crazy. This was a sports fever that extended well back to prewar days of school ball and tours by visiting American pros. Babe Ruth and other American greats had played exhibitions here in the 1930s, and they remained popular heroes. Kids like Oh roamed their neighborhoods, gathering in the open spaces for pickup games with whatever they could fashion into bats and balls.

However, Oh was not entirely like the other neighborhood kids; he was – and is – Chinese. That is, his father was from Taiwan and had Chinese citizenship. He married a Japanese woman and moved to Tokyo, where they operated a noodle shop in the old downtown ward of Sumida. He was imprisoned for a year during the war and, Oh later learned, tortured during that time on suspicion of being a Chinese agent.

Playing ball in the neighborhood, Oh showed considerable talent, and by his teen years he was sought after by ward teams, school teams, and even by adult leagues. He often highlights one particular memory as consequential, a practice game at dusk on a local riverbank field in late November 1954. A local resident stopped by to watch, well known to the kids as Arakawa Hiroshi, then playing for a pro team. After sizing up Oh's pitching and hitting, he called the boy over and suggested casually that Oh might hit better if he switched from a right-handed to left-handed stance. Oh did, and he promptly hit a long double off the outfield fence. Arakawa nodded approvingly, and Oh remained a left-handed hitter for the rest of his life.[6]

1956–1958: High school standout

Two years later, Oh entered Waseda Commercial High School, the private feeder school for the university of the same name and one of the premier baseball factory schools in Japan. This wasn't a straightforward matter of recruitment. It was a second chance for Oh; he had failed by one point the entrance examinations for the public school that his father intended for him. He was one of some 200 freshmen who showed up for the Waseda baseball team when the school year began in the spring of 1956. Almost all of them stood around the entire year raking the field, washing the uniforms of their upperclassmen, carrying their equipment, and chanting cheers nonstop. Few of them even got to touch a baseball, except when retrieving an errant foul. One of those exceptions was Oh, who was pulled from the freshman crowd and immediately won a place on the pitching staff. This, too, he later discovered, he owed to Arakawa, who had put in a word with the coach and manager; it turned out that Arakawa was an alumnus and unofficial scout for Waseda.

Within three months, he was living every schoolboy's dream of appearing with his team in the summer national baseball tournament at fabled Kōshien Stadium.[7] He had a wild up-and-down experience, pitching a no-hit, no-run game to get Waseda into the tournament, and then helping to win the opening game with a ninth-inning bunt, before his pitching fell apart in the second-round game, which eliminated the team.

His second season was even more turbulent. Waseda High was selected for the 1957 national invitational tournament, held in the late spring at Kōshien. Practicing frantically to get in shape for the tournament, which began soon after the start of the school year, Oh developed intensely painful blisters on his throwing hand. As he pitched the early games at Kōshien, the blisters became so infected he could barely grip the ball. Following the tournament by radio at home in Tokyo, his father learned of his son's ailment and left immediately for Osaka. That night, he came secretly to Oh's bedside in the team dormitory and quietly applied a special balm of ginseng root and Chinese wine; he left immediately afterward to return to Tokyo to open his noodle shop the next morning. That next day was the championship game, and Oh started as pitcher for the fourth game in as many days. The balm had the desired effect, and the pain subsided for much of the game. In trouble at the end, he gutted out the final inning for the victory – in front of 60,000 spectators and a nationwide broadcast audience.

But the thrill of victory was quickly replaced by the anger of discrimination and then, the following year, by the agony of defeat. That summer, the Waseda team was chosen to represent Tokyo in the National Athletic Games; Oh was soon informed that he would not be able to participate because he was not a Japanese citizen. The following year, 1958, was Oh's third and final season, and Waseda was again invited to the spring Kōshien tournament. Oh pitched and won the first game but lost the next game, and the team went home. That summer, they reached the final game of the Tokyo regionals, seeking to qualify again for the summer Kōshien tournament. On August 3rd, Oh found himself pitching against another powerhouse, Meiji High School, in fabled Jingu Stadium. The game went into extra innings, and an attack of nerves caused him to blow a 5–1 lead in the bottom of the twelfth inning. Oh later claimed that "In a lifetime of playing baseball, that was the toughest defeat I ever experienced" (Oh and Falkner 1984:60).

1959–1962: Disastrous early years with the Yomiuri Giants

Despite the Jingu fiasco, Oh was widely regarded as the top high school prospect, and that winter he was drafted by both the Hanshin Tigers and the Yomiuri Giants. Although they had just lost the Japan Series for the third time in a row, the Giants were still the preeminent professional team. Oh also preferred to play in Tokyo rather than in Osaka, the Tigers' home. Giants fans were delirious. Oh was joining the year following their signing of Nagashima Shigeo, the best college player in history, and the combination of the top high school player and the top college player on the same team electrified fans all across the country. The coup sold tickets, but as important to Yomiuri, it also greatly stimulated television and newspaper sales.

The pair burst onto the scene in one of the most memorable games in Japanese baseball history: the "Emperor's Game" on June 26 of Oh's first season.[8] It was so named because Emperor Hirohito, reputedly an avid baseball fan via print and broadcast media, was attending his very first baseball game. The contest pitted the Giants at home against their arch-rivals, the Hanshin Tigers. The early lead bounced back and forth, with Nagashima homering in the fifth inning. The Tigers regained the lead, but Oh hit a seventh-inning home run to tie the score. Then even more dramatically, Nagashima hit a bottom-of-the-ninth inning *sayonara* home run to win the game for the Giants. This was the first time Oh and Nagashima had homered in the same game, an *abekku* pair of home runs (from the French, *avec*) by a duo soon to be dubbed the "O–N cannon."

However, Oh's story continued to play unpredictably, and difficulties soon surfaced behind this early acclaim. The Giants had quickly decided that Oh should drop pitching to concentrate on hitting, but despite all the fanfare, his first years as a hitter were rough. He struck out often and went through one slump after another. His rookie season batting average was an abysmal .161. He quickly developed a taste for heavy drinking and late-night carousing at Ginza bars, which only compounded his downward fall. The fans were harsh, playing on his name (Oh, or Wan in Chinese, means king) to tag him *sanshin Oh,* the "strikeout king." The Giants were having serious reservations about keeping him.

1962–1965: From "strikeout king" to "home run king" under Arakawa

The boy wonder of high school baseball was spiraling downward toward disaster when fortune intervened in the spring of 1962, once again in the form of Arakawa-*sensei.* Without even knowing their past connections, the Giants hired Arakawa as the team's new batting coach, specifically charged with the "Oh problem." Over the next three years, Arakawa saved Oh's career with his quirky philosophical formulas. In Oh's story, Arakawa-*sensei* is Fate personified.

Arakawa had had an undistinguished career in the Pacific League, but he was a keen student of the game, especially batting. He developed a theory of batting that was based on down swinging, believing it to be the shortest and most efficient motion in moving the bat around and through the ball plane. Arakawa had also begun to study Zen as a player and became a devotee, although a somewhat bemused one.

He demanded of Oh at that first spring camp: "If you really want to make it as a pro, you will do exactly as I say for three years!" (Oh and Falkner 1984:115). Oh was amenable; he immediately realized that Arakawa's down-swinging style offered help toward his major problem, a "hitch." This was his habit of pulling his bat back momentarily, just at the instant of the pitcher's release; in so doing, he lost the fraction of a second necessary to swing fully and make contact.

Almost immediately, though, Arakawa went beyond his customary advice and proposed a radical solution to the hitch:

> Arakawa-san at that point assumed a batting position from the left side, then carefully raised his right leg so that he was standing on one foot. "You see," he said, "standing in this position, if you hitch, you will fall flat on your ass." (ibid. 117)

Oh thought he was joking, and it wasn't until much later that they returned to what became Oh's trademark, one-legged stance. In the meantime, though, Arakawa proceeded to lead Oh on a tour of Japanese spiritual Ways. "The real problem we were facing," Arakawa informed Oh, "was to apply the Japanese psyche to an American game" (ibid.).

Arakawa began to share with Oh some of the results of his study of Zen and quickly moved on to *nō* drama. Arakawa had pored over Zeami's fifteenth-century treatise, *Kadensho,* believing that its pronouncements on stage movements might offer some hints for baseball stances. Then, just as Oh himself was starting to study *Kadensho,* Arakawa abruptly announced that it was "time to move on" (ibid. 118). Now, it was *kabuki*:

The movements in it, he said, even though more exaggerated than those in *nō*, are delicately balanced on the transition from "motion" to "rest." I was to meditate on this constantly and seek to apply the image as best I could whenever I strode to the plate. Meanwhile, Arakawa-san said, he would delve into all the literature he could on *kabuki* in an effort to further this line of approach. (ibid. 119)

This Way-of-the-week was not whimsical but rather followed Arakawa's own peripatetic search for sources of inspiration. Arakawa's search for *kabuki* insights in fact led to a different path. Late one night, Arakawa showed up at Oh's rooms quite excited about a book he had just discovered by the great *kabuki* actor Kikugoro. In it, Kikugoro disclosed that he had found great inspiration in the martial art of *aikidō*, especially its stress on *ma*, the space in between. Kikugoro related his visit with the founder of *aikidō*, Ueshibe Morihei, at the latter's small *dōjō* training hall in the Shinjuku district of Tokyo. This is also what Arakawa and Oh did.

Arakawa told Oh that *aikidō* would be of immense value in learning to "eliminate *ma* and absorb the opponent," but he refused to let Oh actually practice it ("I can't afford to let you get hurt"). Instead, on their regular visits to the training hall, Oh would watch Arakawa get pounded in practice by Master Ueshibe, and he would then have to listen to Arakawa's lectures about the *aikidō* philosophical basis in "agape" or love and the need to strip oneself of opposition.

Oh was a dutiful student but did grow impatient with the seeming gap between *aikidō* and baseball, indeed, between all of these philosophical excursions and their application to his baseball difficulties.[9] And he continued to flounder as the season began in 1962. The down swinging compensated in part for his hitch, particularly for outside pitches, but pitchers around the league soon learned that they could get him on a tight inside pitch.

Matters reached a (perhaps apocryphal) peak one rainy day in late spring at the Giants coaches' meeting before a game with the Taiyō Whales at the Taiyō Stadium in Kawasaki. It was held to deal with the "Oh slump," and Arakawa faced loud criticism from the other coaches. He came out of the meeting and went directly to Oh, announcing that drastic measures were required. He ordered Oh to try the "flamingo" stance he had suggested some time before. The muddy field prevented practice, even in the warm-up circle, so when Oh came to bat and assumed the one-legged stance, the crowds were stunned – and then began hooting derisively. He proceeded to slap out a single, and then, two innings later, a home run. Returning to the Giants home park two days later, Oh belted another home run.

This was not a fluke; his hitting did improve dramatically, despite continued misgivings about Arakawa's explicit spiritualizing. He hit twenty-five homers after the mid-season All-Star Game break and finished the season with a league-leading thirty-eight home runs. It finally seemed as if Oh had broken the jinx and was ready to meet the team's expectations that had worn thin over his first three pro years. He even began to think about eventually breaking Babe Ruth's home run record.

Such optimism was premature. In retrospect, Oh came to see that 1962 season as simply the beginning of the next phase of his maturation as a hitter. In an important sense, the story of Oh's subsequent career was the struggle initially to understand the flamingo stance and then to perfect it.

For this, he found *aikidō* essential, particularly in its emphasis on centering one's balance on the body's "one point" and on waiting. *Aikidō* thus provided both the technique and the idiom for comprehending and formulating a batting stance and attitude toward hitting. A good example of this was Oh's adopting, from this time on, an unusual way of holding the bat – tipping it back toward the pitcher. But there was even more:

> It turned out that Arakawa-san had all the while been making his own plans. These had little to do with my having won a title or two. His mind was already in the future. "You are ready now," he said, "to really acquire the Body of a Rock." I suggested that this was what I had been striving to achieve all season, but he replied that there was far more to what we were doing than simply gaining balance. "Immovable Self-Discipline comes only when you master the use of *ki*. And this you have only just begun to do." To that end, he said, we were now going to turn to the use of the Japanese sword. (ibid. 151)

Thus they moved from *aikidō* to *kendō* and what was to be a two-year concentration in how sword handling could further improve his bat handling. They began with fifty straight days at a *kendō* practice hall in Tokyo during the 1962–1963 off-season. Once again, Arakawa practiced its techniques, which included numerous footwork and sword-handling patterns, several of particular relevance to the baseball swing. Of particular importance was *kendō*'s insight into hand and wrist actions at the moment of cutting. The conventional baseball view was that, for maximum power, the hitter twisted the wrists at the moment of ball contact. *Kendō* taught that the twist should come just *after* contact. Practicing with the sword on tubes of bound straw, Arakawa realized that rotating the wrists on initial entry caused the sword to move up through the straw; twisting the wrists just after entry produced a straight, smooth traverse. This coincided with his own thinking on down swinging, and he put Oh through interminable practices of this motion.

As always, Arakawa kept spiritualizing the act of hitting – framing it as an action of physical balance and inner poise, as a gathering of one's *ki* energy – but arduous repetition was at the core of *kendō* training. Throughout the accounts of this period of Oh's life, Arakawa appears as a psychologically acute coach, with a genius for understanding and manipulating the body and spirit of his student to extract maximum effort.

All the practice began to pay off. Oh had a solid season in 1963, and the Giants won the league title and the Japan Series. He did even better in 1964, finishing with fifty-five home runs, a single-season record that still stands today. Throughout this period, in the off-season, he continued his *kendō* training (although Arakawa always prohibited him from engaging in actual contact with *kendō* sticks), and by late 1964, his three-year apprenticeship was complete. He had emerged, in his own mind, as a Master Batsman:

> I had reached the point where I simply lived to hit. How can I say it without sounding foolish? I craved hitting a baseball the way a samurai craved following the Way of the Sword. It was my life. (ibid. 175)

Still, Oh did not hide his disappointment that his record was not well recognized by the public. In 1964, the Tokyo Olympic year, the Giants didn't win the league pennant, and, most disheartening to Oh, his teammate Nagashima's marriage was given much wider media coverage.[10] It was also at this moment that Arakawa brought his constant tutelage to an end. Again the rationale was cast in a spiritual idiom. He explained to Oh that Oh had now progressed through the first three of what are said to be the four stages in martial arts training: He had mastered the first stage of technique (*gi*), the second stage of skill (*jutsu*), and the third stage of art (*gei*). Only the fourth remained: *dō*, or the Way itself. And that was to be Oh's own day-to-day, season-to-season quest for batting excellence.

1965–1974: The Giants' V-9 glory years

Oh continued to consult with Arakawa throughout his career, but the focus of Oh's story shifted at this point to his place on the team – and what a team it was becoming! One couldn't construct a better sports gloss on national history than the Giants' nine-year reign as consecutive champions of Japanese baseball. In the aftermath of the Tokyo Olympics, during the boom years of Prime Minister Ikeda's "double-your-income" policies, through the national crises of the Nixon shocks, right up to the first oil crisis of 1974, the Giants were a lightning rod for national prestige and patriotic pride. They were Japan's Team.[11]

The Giants were led by their two stars, Oh and Nagashima, their popularity assured by the backing of the Yomiuri companies, by then the most powerful news and entertainment organization in the country. They were managed by Kawakami Tetsuharu, who had been known during his player years as the "god of hitting." As manager, Kawakami quickly became famous for a style of authoritarian leadership called "managed baseball" (*kanri yakyū*). He demanded iron discipline, arduous practices, stolid teamwork, a conservative playing strategy, and *no foreigners.* The Giants had been the first team in the early days of pro baseball to hire a foreigner, the famous White Russian pitcher from Hokkaido, Victor Starfin. Then, after World War II, they were the first team to again hire a foreigner, the Japanese-American from Hawaii, Wally Yonamine. Now, under Kawakami, they deliberately "purified" themselves, becoming the first team to proclaim itself all-Japanese.[12]

From 1965 through 1973, the Giants won nine consecutive Japan Series titles, totally dominating the league and thoroughly reshaping the image of professional baseball. With the enormous power of the parent media company behind them, they projected a player image and a playing style that was coordinated, committed, and relentlessly efficient. They were a resonant metonym for the Confucian capitalism that foreigners and Japanese themselves were then reevaluating in a new positive light as the culture's unique accomplishment.[13] The Giants emblemized Japanese baseball – or at least what most Japanese at the time wanted to imagine it to be – and in so doing condensed professional baseball into the Giants' image.

1974–1988: The later years of individual records and manager woes

One of the obvious ways in which a life story diverges from the life it narrates is the story's emphasis and pacing – its variable richness. To create coherence and causality, a narrative will attend carefully to some moments of a life while passing lightly over others. In a life story that pivots on a swing, it is no surprise that Oh's story lingers disproportionately over those years, especially the three years under Arakawa's tutelage, 1962–1965. This creates a tempo that reminds me of the characteristic *jo, ha, kyū* rhythms of *nō* drama (see Rimer, Chapter 2, this volume): the opening statement, the stately thematic presentation, and the fast wind-up. Thus, in Oh's story, what is fully the second half of a thirty-year professional career as player, coach, and manager is actually treated very briefly as an inevitable coda to the long struggle to find a unique, and uniquely successful, swing.

The watershed year for the Giants as a team was 1974. They failed to win the league pennant, and their championship streak came to an end. Nagashima retired after seventeen seasons to take over from Kawakami as the Giants manager. This, Yomiuri management hoped, would revive the team fortunes, but in fact the Giants never regained their dominance of the Central League. For Oh, however, it was the moment when he began to bear down on the American career home run records. He won the triple crown that year for the second season in a row (a remarkable feat that no American player has yet accomplished) and pushed his home run total to 634.

In the meantime, at the beginning of the season, Hank Aaron had finally surpassed Babe Ruth's career total, hitting his 715th on April 8th. The Yomiuri newspaper capitalized on the publicity by bringing Aaron over to Japan after the season for a home run derby between the American and Japanese champion. Aaron won, 10–9, but it marked the start of a long-distance friendship between the two players and drew further attention to Oh's race to overtake Babe Ruth and Hank Aaron.

Three years later, on September 3, 1977, the thirty-seven-year-old Oh finally surpassed Aaron's total, hitting an outside sinker into the Korakuen stands for his 756th homer.[14] Then, over the final three years of his career, with his reflexes slowing and the team floundering, he pushed his total up over the 800 mark. With little more to prove, and uncomfortable about his declining powers, he retired after the 1980 season. (Even his retirement press conference was upstaged by Nagashima, who chose the following day to announce his own retirement as manager.) Oh remained with the organization as coach and assistant manager.

It was in the early 1980s that a last wave of biographies, broadcast documentaries, and Oh's English-language autobiography appeared. Most therefore do not even address his final five years with the Giants, from 1983 to 1988, when he was elevated to manager.[15] Like Nagashima and Fujita Motoshi before him, he had little success in resurrecting the team's fortunes. The players and coaches were sharply factionalized into a small minority who supported his efforts and the majority who remained loyalists to Nagashima. Oh finished his five-year manager's contract in 1988 and assumed the role of a polite but rather diffident elder statesman of the game within Japan. Recently, however, he has been lured out of retirement to begin managing a brash upstart team in the Pacific League, the Fukuoka Daiei Hawks. With even greater media fanfare, Nagashima had been returned in 1993 as the Giants' manager, and the press and fans eagerly anticipate a Japan Series that will pit the former teammates against one another.

Pedagogy and practice

This essay is predicated on the proposition that sports are situated, instrumental, and physical practices. People learn sports as they learn most skills and dispositions in life outside of schools – through, as Lave and Wenger put it, "legitimate peripheral participation in a community of practice." Sports are indeed a "likely place" for practicing practice.

And yet part of the significance of Oh's case is the ways in which it fits within but also stretches this rubric of legitimate peripheral participation. Its distinctiveness is apparent in a number of elements of the pedagogical relationship of teacher-master and learner-student.

- Regarding the "master": The relationship of Arakawa-*sensei* ("master Arakawa") and Oh-*senshū* ("player Oh") was predictably asymmetric, with Oh showing continuing deference to and gratitude for the guidance of Arakawa. However, Arakawa was hardly a master in the sense of *aikidō* founder Ueshibe or the Zen monastery abbot who taught and disciplined Victor Sōgen Hori (1994) – or even the old naval quartermasters whom Edwin Hutchins describes (cited in Lave and Wenger 1991:73–76). As we have seen, Arakawa himself had been a rather mediocre player and could claim authority only by virtue of his personal insights into batting dynamics and training psychology. Moreover, as one of the Giants' batting coaches, he was not even particularly high in the team hierarchy.
- Regarding the "student": Oh was very much the student-learner in the relationship, putting himself under Arakawa's direction and guidance. He was, however, hardly a novice of the game when he did so but was already a nationally known professional in a prolonged and highly publicized slump. Oh did in fact become a master, but in the sense of becoming an accomplished star of hitting and not in the sense of himself becoming an effective teacher of hitting. He has had such ambitions, which he has attempted to fulfill, with little apparent success, as coach and manager after his playing days.

- Regarding the "teaching" and "learning" between them: Coaches do just that; they coach "from the sidelines" and are beyond performing. Thus Oh's training under Arakawa was not in the nature of an apprenticeship to a practicing swordsmith or potter or elementary school teacher or other position in which the teaching is in doing centrally and the learning is in watching and waiting to the side. There was some observing, especially when Arakawa forbid Oh to engage in actual *aikidō* or *kendō* mock combat. More frequently, though, the roles were reversed, and Arakawa coordinated and monitored the prolonged drills that he demanded Oh practice over the years. The content of the teaching and learning – batting – was itself contradictory; it is an absolutely fundamental baseball skill, but in Oh's case the aim was remedial and corrective. Furthermore, although swinging the bat is a basic, physical motion, Arakawa's teaching was rationalized in quite esoteric philosophical idioms. Indeed, there was a good bit more talk-teaching than one finds in many peripheral learning settings.
- Regarding the "community of practice": The prolonged (re)-training under Arakawa was under the auspices of the Giants team and went on in the midst of Oh's continuing to play at the center of the lineup during the three seasons. And yet, it was also a rather private training, usually done at sites apart from the Giants' ballpark or other team facilities – in Arakawa's home, at Ueshibe's training hall, and so forth. The team left Arakawa and Oh to their own devices and gave them considerable latitude in designing their routines. It was a most peripheral learning!

These and other features of Oh's case raise some intriguing questions about its significance for our appreciation of learning in sports settings. How unique were the features of Oh's arduous acquisition of swinging from the flamingo stance? How common were they to training in Japanese baseball? How common were they to the general learning experiences of baseball players and other sports performers?

To be sure, foreigners and Japanese alike most commonly take Oh's story at face value, as a condensation of a uniquely Japanese-style baseball. His career, as he and Arakawa put it, was the consummate application of "the Japanese psyche to an American game." By this understanding, Oh's has been a distinctively Japanese life struggle of overcoming adversity and accomplishing success only through sustained sacrifice, total dedication, and indigenous spirituality. He is a true warrior in the Way of Baseball. In fact, to Robert Whiting, Oh embodies what he calls the Code of Conduct for Samurai Baseball, whose articles include harmony, modesty, and self-effacement; loyalty to the team and absolute obedience to managers and coaches; and hard work, sacrifice, and fanatical training.

As I suggested at the outset, I find this image to be quite misleading.[16] Of course, *nō* drama, *aikidō,* and *kabuki* are indubitably Japanese religio-aesthetic ways, and there was an undeniable fanaticism to Oh's regime and his willingness to entrust his rehabilitation to the quirky formulas of Arakawa. However, Oh's story is quite unique in the biographical annals of Japanese baseball. Teams do occasionally employ Zen meditation techniques and the media love to cover the ceremonial blessing that many teams receive at a Shinto shrine or Buddhist temple at the start of a new season or before a final series. I have found nothing, though, in individual biographies or team histories that remotely approaches the Arakawa–Oh story.

Moreover, Arakawa's employment of such spiritual idioms and practices was complex. On the one hand, he appears to have been quite opportunistic. Arakawa led Oh down these well-trod paths to religious enlightenment, but from the outset, he warned Oh of his very pragmatic, irreverent, and instrumental ambitions:

> "The goal of Zen is to become void of desire," Arakawa told Oh, "but can a man attain such a high goal? What a baseball player looks for is how to get a base hit – how to smash the ball – and the farther the better. How can a pro ever be void of such a desire?" (Oh and Falkner 1984:113)

Arakawa had no intention of using the spiritual Ways to empty Oh of selfish desire. Quite the opposite, they were calculated means of *enhancing* that personal drive and individual accomplishment. And yet, however peripatetic and idiosyncratic, the spiritual journey was not entirely cynical and manipulative. Perhaps it might be best characterized as the pragmatic application of metaphysical principles and attitudes toward the perfection of physical form and mental concentration.

A second aspect of Oh's case also belies an easy characterization as "samurai baseball." I refer here to the difficulties of channeling self-actualization into the grooves of group objectives. Japanese organizations' suppression of individual initiative and selfless commitment to group objectives have always been stereotypic pieties mouthed by corporate flacks and accepted at face value by outside commentators and critics. In fact, however, postwar large organizations have always been defined by the continual tensions between the variable talents and motivations of individual members and the multiple (even inconsistent) aims of the hierarchically structured group. Group harmony, hierarchical authority, and individual motivation have always coexisted uneasily in Japanese organizations, like organizations everywhere.

This was certainly the case with the Yomiuri Giants, despite their carefully polished image of "managed baseball." Indeed, it was well known that despite that phrase, manager Kawakami actually stressed individual effort to the players. As Oh himself explained:

> "Kawakami baseball" was generally thought of as team-oriented rather than individual-oriented. But that really was not it. Of course Mr. Kawakami stressed harmony among us. He purified himself at a Buddhist retreat before he took over as manager. . . . But it was his approach to the game that distinguished him most. Play with greed for victory, he taught, and this he most peculiarly emphasized as an individual thing. One strove for the highest individual goals possible and did so relentlessly. . . . We had an obligation to the team, but this obligation was best fulfilled by learning to use ourselves individually to the limit.[17]

Self-sacrifice, one might say, is a rather more complex disposition than that of a cardboard samurai – and rather more like definitions of effort familiar to athletes in the United States and elsewhere. Part of the fascination of Oh's story is precisely the longstanding engagement between a player with one of the most unique perspectives on his own performance and a team with one of the most pronounced public images for regimented collective effort – and the drama of how the team and the player reconciled themselves to one another and were altered by the encounter.

In sum, there is much reason to question those interpretations of Oh's case that treat it as a synecdoche for Japanese spiritualized and selfless behavior. At the same time, it is equally unsatisfying to bracket it as a fascinating curiosity even for Japan, and so unique as to be uninstructive. Despite its obvious distinctiveness, there are several elements of Oh's case that do speak directly to the nature of learning in sport-as-situated-activity, and it is with this that I wish to conclude.

Learning-practice theorists are surely correct that there are obvious differences between formal classroom teaching and situated learning. However, they are also astute enough to realize that it is not helpful to map this distinction onto a contrast of talking and doing. There is a great deal of quite necessary and didactic talk in sports practice and performance. There are rules, techniques, and strategies that must be explained and tested and diagrammed as well as drilled and executed. There are playbooks and rule books to memorize, "skull sessions" to attend, and hours of video to watch and analyze. In this way, the forms and reasons for sports actions are made explicit – in order to become implicit. Indeed, much of sports performance would appear to fall into a gray zone between automatic action or reaction and calculated deliberations.[18]

Sports also have a capacious concept of preparation-as-practice. Oh was already the best known and most highly regarded high school athlete in Japan when he joined the Giants and fell into his slump. Yet his three years under Arakawa were spent on an absolute fundamental of the game. His (re)learning to swing was not without parallel to my eight-year-old daughter's learning to swing this year under her softball team coach. The physical and mental skills that enable sports activity must be continually honed and often reshaped. There is little useful distinction between learning and (re)learning, between training and (re)training.

Finally, learning (in) sports is generally a mix of the prescriptive and the novel. Repetitive drills and supervised practice give a highly managed character to sports routines, as we have certainly seen with the Yomiuri Giants. And yet the drive to survive and to win, to excel and to exceed current thresholds, puts equal value on experimenting, on taking risks, on a search for a new style. Oh, like athletes generally, tested limits by testing conventional wisdom and current techniques.

Sport performance in contemporary society is so public, so institutionally elaborated, so readily quantifiable, so easily critiqued and appreciated by athletes and spectators alike, that it is no wonder that it is carefully framed, rule-governed, and made predictably patterned. And yet the anxiety and the anticipation of what will happen in the next instant can never be allayed. The power of sports performance is precisely in the tension between the ever-suspenseful moment of uncertain outcome and the narrative and statistical webs of signification in which these moments are suspended. Oh's learning to swing in his irreplicable way only enhanced the pleasurable tensions in his performance for a generation of Japanese fans.

Notes

1. This is the time lapse of a fast ball thrown at an initial, "muzzle" velocity of ninety-eight miles per hour (see Adair 1994:28 and 35).
2. Oh's position was also tagged a scarecrow stance (scarecrows placed by Japanese farmers in their fields are one-legged, in the belief that they don't need to walk).
3. Written and broadcast material on Oh, like any Japanese baseball star, is voluminous and wildly variable in partisanship, reliability, and detail. My sources for this essay have included several Oh autobiographies, especially in English (Oh and Falkner 1984)

and Japanese (Oh 1981) (see also several Chinese versions, e.g., 1986, which I have not been able to use for this manuscript); a recent volume of Oh's essays and recollections (Oh 1993); a 1978 television documentary (NHK 1989); and commentary and journalism in English (Whiting 1977, 1989; Cromartie 1991) and Japanese (Arimoto 1992:169–245; Terauchi 1982; Nagashima and Oh 1993; Chiba 1993).

4. For further details, see Whiting (1977, 1989). The twelfth team, the Hiroshima Carp, is jointly owned by Mazda and the City of Hiroshima.
5. The larger topic of Japanese professional baseball is the subject of my ongoing research. For a rather different use of Oh's life story, see Kelly (in press).
6. This scene is dramatized in animation in the NHK documentary. See also Oh and Falkner (1984:27–29). Arakawa's advice was timely though not profound. As any baseball fan knows, the preponderance of right-handed pitchers, and the advantages of hitting left-handed against right-handed pitching, are obvious incentives to batting left-handed.
7. Rival newspaper companies had started separate national tournaments for middle school, and later, high school teams in the mid-1910s. They became immensely popular, and in 1925, both were moved to a huge new stadium, Kōshien, in the outskirts of Osaka. The Mainichi newspaper chain still sponsors the spring tournament, which is an invitational. The Asahi chain sponsors the summer tournament in August, which brings to Kōshien representative teams from every prefecture that have won regional knock-out tournaments earlier in the summer. In English, see Whiting (1989:239–262).
8. Whiting (1977:98–102) describes the game, although he places it in May.
9. After yet another poor start, Oh found himself walking the late-night streets of Tokyo drenched to the skin from a rainy season downpour, wondering to himself: "The objective of *aikidō* was to strip oneself of opposition, to reconcile oneself with the universe. The enlightened one merges with the universe. . . . In enlightenment, time ceases to exist. There is the universe, which is everything – sorrow and joy, gain and loss – and there is you. Unfortunately, here was also me, languishing in the rain, struggling hopelessly against myself" (Oh and Falkner 1984:129).
10. The Oh–Nagashima rivalry is much analyzed in Japanese journalism. From the start, though, their relative standing with the parent company and with fans was clear. Nagashima was and remains the most popular player in baseball history. He was anointed Mr. Giants, and Oh realized that as long as Nagashima was on the team, he would always be number one with spectators, fellow players, and the front office. Nagashima's marriage raises also the issue of gender – not only the male exclusivity of this, like most mass sports, but also the invisibility of home life and the marginalization of players' wives. The young Nagashima was touted as Japan's most eligible bachelor. In 1961, his fourth year with the Giants, he announced with great fanfare that he was not getting married until he was at least thirty. He declared he was a "sportsman" and that his muscles and reflexes (*undō shinkei*) would continue to grow until age thirty. He owed it to the team, he said, to channel all his growing energy to baseball until then. This was a sentiment that large corporations encouraged in their young managers (among other ways, by pay and benefit structures that made early marriage financially difficult). Oh, on the other hand, married quite early and very quietly, but as one might expect from a *sarariiman* of the era, his family is virtually invisible throughout his story. The Japanese sports press occasionally mentions his

wife as long-suffering and bitter and his three daughters as openly angry at Oh, but the only real personalities admitted into his narrative are Arakawa and his parents.

11. Matsuzono Hisami, when owner of the Yakult Swallows, once declared that the best possible outcome would be for the Giants to finish first and his own team to finish second! This was a matter of sentiment – he was a longstanding Giants fan – but also corporate business; Yakult yogurt drink sales were said to decline whenever the Swallows defeated the Giants! (Whiting 1989:7)
12. Oh's mixed parentage as well as the mixed ethnicities of several teammates complicated that claim, of course. This is related to the larger concerns of Japanese ethnicity and cultural nationalism in Kelly (in press).
13. Some sense of self-image is conveyed in "Nihonjin to Kyojin-gun," which appeared in 1984 on the occasion of the team's fifth anniversary (Iwakawa 1984a). It reports on a series of interviews with 102 former members of the Giants organization. A partial English translation appeared as "The Mystique of the Yomiuri Giants" (Iwakami 1984b).
14. Aaron had retired at the end of 1976 with 755. The reaction of the American baseball world was largely patronizing. Oh's record was dismissed as incommensurate because he played against inferior pitchers in smaller stadiums. Aaron himself was polite and congratulatory and has avoided belittling Oh's total. In part, this reflects his own struggle. As an African-American, he encountered enormous prejudice as he threatened Ruth's record, and he has remained outspoken about baseball's discriminatory practices in keeping African-Americans out of the front office and managerial positions. Oh has been equally conciliatory toward Aaron. He has always claimed that he would never have reached such a total if he had played in the United States: "But it was my record, and it was baseball's record nonetheless! It was the devotion of a professional's career" (Oh and Falkner 1984:244–245).
15. There was, of course, a voluminous sports journalism about the Giants during those years, dissecting the team woes and Oh's managerial difficulties. In English, the splendid autobiography of Warren Cromartie (Cromartie and Whiting 1991) is valuable on this and many other points because Cromartie played under Oh during those years and came to respect him enormously. Cromartie reports, for example, that Nakahata, the captain and a Nagashima loyalist, would sometimes refer to Oh as "*wan-ko.*" This was a play on the Chinese pronunciation of Oh, *Wan,* like Oh's longstanding nickname, Wan-chan, but *wan-ko* meant "dog." See also my essay on the notorious Randy Bass incident of October 1985, which involved Oh and the Giants, and Whiting's chapter, "Giant Headache," on the series of mutual difficulties between the Giants and the various American players they hired between 1974 and 1988 (1989:161–200).
16. It is also ironic, given Oh's mixed parentage and Chinese citizenship, but again that is taken up in my other essay.
17. Oh and Falkner (1984:196–197). See also Oh (1993:65–68). Kawakami, not surprisingly, represented all sides of the triangular tensions of harmony, hierarchy, and individual pursuit. Like many ex-managers, when Kawakami retired in 1974, he became a much sought-after speaker and writer on the corporate motivational circuit, dispensing such advice to executives as "Most players are lazy. It's a manager's responsibility to make them train hard" or "If your leading salesman opposed you, fire him. For if you allow individualism, it will surely fail!" (quoted in Whiting 1989:74)

18. It is also misleading to dismiss classroom instruction as abstract and disembodied. As any analyst of "hidden curricula" would insist, the lessons of school can be quite directly and physically connected with one's place(ment) in society – the time discipline of bells and periods, the dress codes that put ties and skirts on adult authorities, the desks that orient students away from one another and facing the standing authority, the prevalent grading and tracking, and so on.

References

Adair, Robert, 1994, *The Physics of Baseball,* Revised edition, New York: Harper Perennial.

Arimoto Yoshiaki, 1992, "ON to tomo ni," *Pro yakyū: sangoku-shi,* pp. 169–245, Tokyo: Mainichi shimbun-sha.

Chiba Isao, 1993, "Dāta de miru Oh Sadaharu & Nagashima Shigeo no kiseki," *Shukan Bēsubōru,* June 7, pp. 50–53.

Cromartie, Warren, with Robert Whiting, 1991, *Slugging It Out in Japan: An American Major Leaguer in the Tokyo Outfield,* Tokyo and New York: Kodansha International.

Hori, G. Victor Sōgen, 1994, "Teaching and Learning in the Rinzai Zen Monastery," *Journal of Japanese Studies 20*(1): 5–36.

Iwakawa Takashi, 1984a, "Nipponjin to Kyojin-gun" [parts one and two], *Bungei shunju 62*(6): 132–148 and *62*(9): 168–194.

1984b, "The Mystique of the Yomiuri Giants," *Japan Echo 11*(3): 60–64.

Kelly, William W., in press, "Blood and Guts in Japanese Professional Baseball," in Sepp Linhart and Sabine Frühstück (eds.), *The Culture of Japan as Seen through Its Leisure,* Albany: State University of New York Press.

Lave, Jean, and Etienne Wenger, 1991, *Situated Learning: Legitimate Peripheral Participation,* Cambridge: Cambridge University Press.

NHK, 1989, *Oh Sadaharu: 800-go e no michi* [Videotape of television documentary], Tokyo: Nippon hōsōkyōkai. (Original broadcast: 1978)

Nagashima Shigeo and Oh Sadaharu, 1993, "Taidan: Nagashima Shigeo VS. Oh Sadaharu," *Shukan Bēsubōru,* June 7, pp. 20–25.

Oh Sadaharu, 1981, *Kaiso,* Tokyo: Keibunsha.

1985, *Chiu hsing ti hui hsiang* [Chinese version of *Kaisō*], Wang Chen-chih, ed., Nan ching shih: Chiang-su jen min chu pan she.

1993, *Yume o oe: yakyū ni kaketa jinsei,* Tokyo: NHK shuppan.

Oh Sadaharu and David Falkner, 1984, *Sadaharu Oh: A Zen Way of Baseball,* New York: Random House.

Skolnick, Richard, 1994, *Baseball and the Pursuit of Innocence: A Fresh Look at the Old Ball Game,* College Station: Texas A&M University Press.

Terauchi Daikichi, 1982, "Sūpāhērō no jōken: Nagashima to Oo o anata wa gonin shite nai ka," in *"Nippon kabushikigaisha" shuppansu* (*Shogen no Shōwa-shi, 9*: 160–165), Tokyo: Gakken.

Whiting, Robert, 1977, *The Chrysanthemum and the Bat: Baseball Samurai Style,* New York: Dodd Mead.

1989, *You Gotta Have Wa: When Two Cultures Collide on the Baseball Diamond,* New York: Macmillan.

17 Good old boy into alcoholic: Danshukai and learning a new drinking role in Japan

Stephen R. Smith

Rudy (1986) and Cain (1991) have demonstrated how members of Alcoholics Anonymous (A.A.) come to understand themselves not simply as people who have problems with alcohol but as sufferers from a disease called "alcoholism." This diagnosis and reinterpretation of self does not happen precipitously, and it certainly does not occur simply because the drinker is told that he or she is an alcoholic. Rather, the process of learning is interactive, negotiated between the drinker and the significant others in a social context. It is a slow process of change that occurs primarily through the central ritual of A.A., the telling of experiences with alcohol. At A.A. meetings, beginners hear old-timers tell of alcohol's destructive effects on their lives. In time, newcomers take their turn at telling tales, copying the format that they have heard. Experienced members who follow the novice will pick up on those parts of the tale that express A.A. principles and weave them into their own narrative. Those elements that contradict A.A. principles are ignored. In time, as certain elements of their stories are reinforced, and as they become sensitive to the discursive style and content of the old-timers, the beginners modify their stories in ways that conform to A.A. orthodoxy. In the process of revamping their autobiographies, they internalize A.A. principles and come to identify themselves as alcoholics. They are also transformed from beginners into old-timers.

Lave and Wenger (1991) have referred to this process of learning as "legitimate peripheral participation." Not all education is didactic. Much learning goes on in the context of a community of shared knowledge and practice, where beginners are accepted as marginal members who incrementally become central participants by successfully recreating the behavior of full members.

In this chapter, I show a similar process of nondidactic education going on in Danshukai, a Japanese sobriety group modeled after A.A. I show how practices of some Danshukai groups exclude newcomers from peripheral participation – and thus prevent their full membership and deny them support in their quest for their sobriety.

The data for this chapter were gathered primarily during research in the Kansai region (Kyoto-Osaka-Kobe) in 1981–1983, and more recently during a follow-up study in fall 1992. My research included doing rounds with doctors at alcoholism hospitals, working in bars, and attending Danshukai meetings.

It should be noted that this chapter is concerned with men and alcohol in Japan, and the word *men* must be emphasized. Male and female drinking patterns in Japan are generally quite different. Any statements about "drinkers" refer to men and cannot be assumed true for women.

The Japanese meaning of alcohol

Interactive drinking or drinking in groups is a very important and public part of Japanese male life. Drinking in Japan is positively valued. Assuming that the social occasion is appropriate, it suffers from none of the ambivalence found associated with alcohol in America. Surveys show more than half of a Tokyo regional sample agreeing with a statement that drinking is essential to life, and more than one-third supporting the traditional adage that alcohol is the best of medicines (*Sake wa hyaku yaku no chō de aru*) (Kono, Nakagawa, Saito, Shimada, and Tanaka 1977:29).

Generally speaking, drunkenness receives the same positive evaluation as drinking. Being drunk (*yotte iru, horoyoi*) is a desirable condition. Many drinkers will be explicit in saying that they drink to get drunk (*you tame ni nomu*); after all, why else would one drink?

The working world of Japanese men is held to be very stressful, and drinking is recognized as the best relief from that stress. Observers, while recognizing that drunks can sometimes be tedious, usually see drunkenness as benign and show immense tolerance for the shenanigans of drinkers. A cliché that acknowledges cultural indulgence holds that Japan is paradise for children, foreigners, and drunks.

The stigma of alcoholism

Drinking and drunkenness are, however, not without their limits of social acceptability. A common Japanese term for deviant drinking and drunkenness, called *arukōru chūdoku* or *aruchū,* is ordinarily glossed as "alcoholism." The Japanese popular definition of alcoholism is far narrower than American alcoholism, in part because the range of acceptable drinking and drunkenness in Japan is much broader. Nightly drinking to the point of intoxication, including gross changes in comportment, is considered to be an acceptable – if not always pleasant – part of male life in Japan. It is a common reaction of Americans, upon seeing the frequency of Japanese drinking and the apparently extreme loss of control, to assume that they are seeing problem drinking and possibly alcoholism. Such is not the Japanese perception.

An older view of drinking in Japan (a view still found in some rural communities) limits the definition of alcoholism to compulsive drinking that regularly leads to violence. It is really only the irreparable breaching of human relations, because of constantly picking fights, that results in condemnation and labeling as "alcoholic." Men who get violent when they drink, yet persist in drinking, eventually exhaust the ability, or desire, of their families to make excuses for them. Under such conditions, the offender is disowned and banished from the family or is committed to a mental hospital. Forced commitment is arranged in conjunction with a doctor who diagnoses the alcoholic as psychotic.

Although violent drunkenness is the distinguishing trait of alcoholism in tightly knit communities, other criteria are important among the more general public. Surveys consistently show "hand tremor" to be the single most important identifying trait of an alcoholic (Tani, Haga, and Kato 1975; Horii, Tani, Haga, and Kato 1976; Tani, Haga, Horii, Fukui, and Kato 1977, 1978; Kawakami et al. 1982). Issues of drinking behavior – like "needs to drink every day," "works while drinking," and "drinks in the morning" – are noted but are moderate to poor runners-up as socially recognized symptoms. In Japan, frequent drinking and consuming large quantities are not synonymous with problem drinking, much less alcoholism.

The Japanese lay definition of alcoholism is not medical, and it certainly does not equate alcoholism with a disease (Terashima 1969). It is widely held that an alcoholic is one because he is weak-willed. The argument goes that people who become alcoholics a priori like alcohol. After all, if they did not like alcohol, they would not drink so much. And what's not to like? Some men become alcoholics because they enjoy drinking, but they do not have enough strength of character to delay gratification and wait for an appropriate occasion. Instead, they drink when the desire hits them. This definition of the alcoholic as weak-willed makes the act of drinking volitional and the alcoholic responsible for his own failings. In popular usage, the term "alcoholic" is thus a moral, rather than a medical, label.

Although all Japanese recognize that alcoholism can exist, laymen universally told me that alcoholism is rare, or nonexistent, in Japan. There is no question but that few Japanese perceive alcoholism as a pathology of any significant magnitude. An international Gallup poll (Gallup 1985: 69) asked the question, "In your country, today, how serious do you think alcoholism is?" Of the thirteen nations surveyed, the Japanese reported the lowest level of concern: 17 percent said very serious, 40 percent quite serious, 32 percent not very/not at all serious. By contrast, Americans (third, after the French and Italians) reported 71 percent very serious, 26 percent quite serious, 2 percent not very/not at all serious.

The stigma of abstention

Drinking may not be stigmatized in Japan, but *not* drinking certainly is. A teetotaler is called a *geko,* and the man who is a *geko* is the object of pity at best or derision at worst. A nondrinker is problematic, a social albatross. A man who does not drink does not partake appropriately in the rituals of drinking. Equally important, he does not share in the emotional warmth and camaraderie that goes with drinking and therefore inhibits others who do drink.

Drinking is also closely linked to Japanese gender roles. Generally, women do not drink; men do. A traditional adage about "real men" is that they "*nomu, utsu, kau*"; they "drink, gamble, and buy [women]." Being able to drink, and drink a lot, is widely considered manly and is good for one's reputation in both Japan and America.

Immense amounts of business, either the informal exchange of office information or the closing of deals, takes place in a drinking arena. Those who do not drink are at a distinct disadvantage. The concept is even crystallized in a Japanese adage, *geko no tateta kura wa nai,* "no teetotaler will ever get to be a millionaire" (Masuda 1974:324) or more literally, "there are no storehouses built by teetotalers."

Certainly Americans are familiar with the feeling of being an outsider when others are drinking and you are not, and the heavy social pressure to join in. But the social benefits of drinking and the potential costs of abstention in Japan exceed anything an American normally experiences.

Resistance to the identity of "alcoholic"

As indicated previously, some patterns of drinking behavior are unacceptable in Japan. But short of the most extreme cases, families collude – consciously or unconsciously – with the compulsive drinker in minimizing his problems. There are several good reasons. First, there is a general ignorance of the Western biomedical model of alcoholism and its behavioral symptoms. Although a person may suspect that he or she or a family member is an alcoholic, the popular definitions are too narrow and, in practice, ambiguous to give useful guidelines. The medical implications of alcoholism are not widely known or appreciated. Second, there is a cultural tolerance for drinking and drunkenness that can easily prevent recognition of dysfunction. Finally, there is a desire to avoid the stigmatizing label of "alcoholic" that may taint not just the drinker but the entire family.

It should be added that employers may not approve of the behavior of compulsive drinkers, but on-the-job drinking is an issue that is seldom confronted. Heavy-drinking, white-collar employees in lifetime-employment corporations may simply find themselves removed from responsibility and decision making. Drinking on the job may limit a career, but it does not necessarily result in dismissal.

The reasons for a Japanese man to think of himself as a heavy drinker, and not think of himself as an alcoholic, are numerous and persuasive. Occasionally, a man with drinking problems decides spontaneously that his life has become unmanageable and that he is an alcoholic. But most do not. How, then, did it come to pass that most self-acknowledged Japanese alcoholics learned this new identity?

Doctors, diagnoses, and didactics

As late as the early 1980s, most Japanese physicians had little knowledge of the disease model of alcoholism common in the West and promoted by Alcoholics Anonymous. The physician's view of the problem was informed by the popular conception of alcoholics as weak-willed as well as by older psychiatric models of alcoholics as psychotics, a product of Japanese medicine's roots in German medicine (Bowers 1965). Long-term heavy drinkers who suffered from alcohol-related disorders were treated for specific symptoms (e.g., gastritis, pancreatitis) and discharged without any recognition of the larger etiology. Those who persisted in drinking and getting in fights would be diagnosed as alcoholic and forcibly institutionalized in mental hospitals, where the intentions were more custodial than therapeutic.

Most acknowledged alcoholics in the Osaka region report that they had seen many doctors over the years and had been hospitalized several times with alcohol-related problems, but the first serious suggestion that they were alcoholic came when they were referred to one of the few specialty hospitals. At these institutions, doctors see alcoholism as a progressive, possibly fatal, disease that can be treated but not cured (rather like diabetes). The exact etiology remains unclear, but the alcoholic's self-destructive behavior is understood primarily as a consequence of the disease and the avoidance of withdrawal symptoms, not as a matter of choice. Alcoholism specialists therefore see their task as first restoring the patients to the best possible physical well-being, and then educating them about the disease nature of their affliction. Lacking the resources and the inclination to take lifelong responsibility for the alcoholics they treat, specialists also introduce them to the lay self-help groups, Alcoholics Anonymous and Danshukai.

The educational process at the specialty hospitals is both didactic and mimetic. There are regular lectures given by doctors on different aspects of alcoholism, but all emphasize its disease nature. Their weekly meetings held for the entire in-patient body look very similar to self-help meetings. And many times a week, patients attend group therapy sessions where they are expected to speak about their drinking histories. Each of these practices, beyond whatever direct benefit it may have to offer, also prepares the patients for participation in Alcoholics Anonymous or Danshukai.

Danshukai

During the 1950s, members of the Japan Temperance Union and a number of doctors began to look for humane and effective ways to treat alcoholics. The search led to Alcoholics Anonymous. A.A. is a fellowship of men and women who voluntarily come together to help each other attain and maintain sobriety. Founded in 1935 in Akron, Ohio, there are now about 500,000 A.A. members in the United States and Canada (A.A. General Service Office, no date–a:1), and over one million members worldwide (General Service Office, no date–b:1).

In Japan, a number of self-help groups for alcoholics were set up following the American A.A. model. Some of these groups were established as Alcoholics Anonymous, but these initial Japanese A.A. groups floundered. They proved to be ineffective and were dissolved. One explanation, widely held, for why those groups failed is that their founders were physicians and Temperance workers, not alcoholics, contrary to the American pattern. Furthermore, it is said that the founders tended to maintain personal control over the groups rather than allowing for egalitarian participation and spontaneous change. Not until Father John M., an American Maryknoll priest and A.A. member, established a group in Tokyo in 1976 did A.A. take root in Japan. Father John has consciously set about carrying A.A. first to those who are most needy, Japan's derelicts. There are Japanese A.A. centers in the skid-row districts of nine cities and an estimated membership of 500.

Whereas some of the first self-help groups identified themselves as being Alcoholics Anonymous, others were merely inspired by A.A. and took on different forms. In 1963, two of these latter Danshukai, or "Sobriety Groups," united to form Zennippon Danshu Renmei, the All Nippon Sobriety Association. This united front, which I refer to here as simply Danshukai, proceeded to incorporate other independent groups while establishing new ones around the country. By 1981, there were 293 Danshukai groups with 595 local meetings in 47 prefectures, with an official membership of 40,000.

Danshukai is, in fact, sometimes called Japan's A.A., and the gloss is informative, even if it is not quite correct. Superficially, they do seem very similar. Both programs hold regular meetings for small groups of alcoholics. In each case, people tell of their problems concerning alcohol. They seek support and give it in their ongoing struggle to abstain from drinking. Members are reassured that they have a disease. For both groups, the first objective is to help members achieve and maintain sobriety, and then to spread the message of hope to other alcoholics.

There are, however, numerous differences between Danshukai and Alcoholics Anonymous in principles and in practices, many of which those familiar with A.A. will find striking. Danshukai has no principle of anonymity. There are no closed meetings. Danshukai membership is not restricted to the alcoholic but assumes that a concerned family member serves as adjunct member and active participant. Although Danshukai is open to both men and women, women alcoholics seldom join. In practice, the organization functions with men as members and with wives, or mothers or (rarely) adult children, as adjuncts.

Ethnography of a Danshukai meeting

While there are major philosophical and organizational differences that separate Danshukai from A.A., those differences are not at issue here. Rather, the concern of this chapter is facets of Danshukai that socialize new members, introducing them into the Danshukai lifestyle and ethos. The essential event of Danshukai is the regular meeting (*rei-kai*) of the local branch (*shibu*). Such meetings are held once a week, usually in the evening (after normal working hours), and last for two hours. Following is a brief ethnographic description of a typical Osaka Danshukai meeting.

T. City Danshukai, Nishi Branch meetings take place in a community center on Thursday evening, from 7:00 to 9:00. People begin to trickle in around 6:45. Mr. and Mrs. O., in their late thirties, with their young son (about five) in tow, often are among the first to arrive. Children at meetings are exceptional, but this child has come on several occasions. No one objects. Mrs. O. puts her bag on a seat near the door in a rear corner of the room, and then takes the boy back down the hall with her to the kitchenette to make tea for the meeting. Her husband moves up to a seat near the front of the room. As other wives arrive, they take seats near Mrs. O. so they can talk and help with the tea. Men released from the local alcoholism hospital to attend the meeting also sit near the door. They have to leave early to catch the last bus back. The only reserved seats are places at the front of the table held for the moderator (*shikai*) and the president (*shibuchō*). There are no assigned seats, but people do tend to sit in the same section, week after week.

As the hour approaches 7:00 and more people show up, the room gets noisier. The atmosphere is warm and chatty. Most of these people have seen each other at several meetings a week for years and have gotten to know each other very well. Should the air of casual intimacy not occur spontaneously, however, it is supposed to be consciously cultivated by group leaders as a warm-up for the meeting to come.

When the moderator, Mr. C., arrives, he starts circulating attendance lists. Everyone is to sign in, giving full name and institutional affiliation. The affiliation might indicate that one is a visiting member of another Danshukai group (typical), a hospital in-patient (common), or a social worker just dropping in to pay respects and keep tabs on a few of his or her cases (exceptional but not irregular). The president, Mr. E., arrives and, first thing, hangs over the blackboard at the head of the room a large banner showing the Danshukai logo and giving the name of the branch. Every group has such a banner. Mr. E. then checks with Mr. C. to see if there are any visiting hospital in-patients. If there are, their attendance cards, supplied by the hospitals, will be collected and stamped. The cards prove that the patient has actually gone where he was supposed to and can be used to get reimbursement for transportation costs from the Social Welfare Office.

Promptly at 7:00, Mr. C. calls the meeting to order by announcing "Good evening, everyone" (*Minasan, konbanwa*). In unison, the gathering responds, "Good evening" (*Konbanwa*). As moderator, Mr. C.'s job is essentially administrative. It is his responsibility to see that the meeting runs according to schedule. With no more than the briefest words of salutation and necessary announcements, Mr. C. begins calling on speakers from the list.

Each person, as called upon in turn, is supposed to speak of his experiences with alcohol (*taiken happyō*). The content of one's monologue was not a matter of Zen Dan Ren national organization policy until 1991 (Zennippon Danshu Renmei 1991), and even now some groups permit people to speak of whatever they wish. In the Kyoto-Osaka region, however, one is supposed to hone close to the issue of alcohol. Meandering is indulged, especially among the inarticulate, but those who get too lost will be chided, and on rare occasions, those who persist in wandering will be cut off either by the president or the moderator.

Speeches have a number of formalized elements. A speaker usually opens with a salutation and self-identification. "Good evening. I'm Sato from the Minami branch" (*Konbanwa. Minami shibu no Sato desu*). There often follows a statement of how long it has been since he has had a drink. Ideally, at this point, a speaker launches into a long personal anecdote about the awful things he once did for a drink, but many speakers, especially those new to Danshukai, are at a loss to say anything more. Even among those who do speak up, many are inarticulate, giving a confused and rambling monologue. For some, the best that they can do is devise a list of the year they first drank, the years they entered hospitals, the year they first attended Danshukai, and so forth. They may repeat the chronology in identical form at every meeting. All speakers end with a pledge to try hard and with an expression of thanks (*Ganbatte ikimasu. Yoroshiku onegaishimasu*).

The order in which people are called upon, at least in the Nishi branch, is standard. Those first called are one or two regular members, unaccompanied, who are ordinarily not tongue-tied but are disinclined to speak at great length. They present an easy example to be imitated by inexperienced visitors, such as the hospital patients, who are called upon next. Newcomers are followed by experienced visitors from other groups (except for leaders, who may be saved for the end). Next, couples are called upon. Husbands always speak first, assuming they are in attendance. (If it is a mother rather than a wife who is affiliated with the alcoholic, she would also be called upon at this time.) The husband's speech follows the standard format, but a wife's is different. Typically, her presentation is shorter than his, often angry or tearful. She tells how awful it was when he drank, how he has greatly improved and everyone is much happier . . . and it is all owed to Danshukai, thank you. The best speakers, very often former leaders of the Nishi branch or visiting leaders from other groups, are saved until the end. They are the most articulate, entertaining, and influential; thus they raise the quality of the meeting at the end. In addition, these leaders will share responsibility for seeing that the meeting ends as scheduled. If it has been an unusually fast night, with no one else having had much to say, the roll completed and a half-hour remaining, these men will delve deep into their histories and tell long stories. Conversely, if everyone else has done a good job at speaking and time is running short, these senior members will forgo their chance to hold the floor and instead offer up the most perfunctory or obligatory salutations and thanks.

The final speaker of the evening is always Mr. E., the president. Up to this point, it is he, and he alone, who has entered into dialogue with the speakers. All others are expected to listen quietly. He consoles the wives and encourages patience. He commiserates with husbands and supports them in their pain. He teaches, again and again, that alcoholics suffer from a disease and that only through sobriety can their lives be saved. They are not weak-willed and self-indulgent. After all others have spoken, Mr. E. makes announcements, reminding members of special events like an anniversary party of the hospital Danshukai group that they should try to attend. In the final moments, Mr. E. summarizes the evening, weaving together the ideas and experiences that have been expressed. On a good evening – and he has many good evenings – he can be inspirational, reminding members how far they have come and exhorting them to keep up the never-ending struggle.

During the last moments, Mrs. O. or one of the other wives makes a quick sweep of the tables. First, the ashtrays are cleared. Almost all the men are smokers. From early on, the room has been filled with a gray haze, and by the end of the meeting ashtrays overflow. Teacups are also gathered. Cups are always distributed at the beginning, and two or three times a night one of the women will have quietly passed around the inside of the circle of tables with a mammoth teapot, offering refills. If candies or crackers (*senbei*) have been handed out, as is sometimes the case, the wrappers will need to be cleared. Finally the tables are wiped with a wet rag.

The last formal act of the evening is the recitation of the Sincerity Pledge and the Family Pledge. Everyone stands and faces the front, where large placards showing the pledges have been placed. Men go first, echoing the Sincerity Pledge read by someone designated that evening.

- I joined Danshukai and I stopped drinking.
- From this time forward, I will never behave like a coward, using alcohol to give me courage.
- Hereafter I will never drink alcohol.
- As long as my many fellow members have stopped drinking, there is no such excuse as "I can't stop."
- I too can completely abstain.
- I pledge from the bottom of my heart to stop drinking.
  —Today, and one day at a time, I will not drink.
  —With courage and pride, I will abstain.
  —I will abandon the selfishness of my past, to serve my family and society.
  —I will always attend Danshukai meetings.
  —I will regularly help others who, like me, suffer from alcoholism.

Next it is the women's turn, but rather than a responsive reading, the women simply read the Family Pledge in unison.

- My husband/my son joined Danshukai. Stopping drinking is truly hard. My husband/my son, who made the decision to abstain, is wonderful.
- My husband's/my son's drinking is an illness. Because it is an illness, it must be cured. Furthermore, it can be cured.
- My husband's/my son's affliction is my affliction.
- In order that my husband/my son stops drinking, I will suffer, too; I will be cured, too.
- I pledge to cooperate with everyone from Danshukai in my husband's/son's sobriety.

There follows a quick round of applause, and the meeting is over. Most people are in a hurry and leave quickly, waving good-bye. But a few linger, forming small groups where they can discuss their personal and immediate problems.

Danshukai lifestyle

Active attendance is essential in Danshukai. A man who must work late will call the group leader, or his wife will express his apologies.

If he misses often, leaders will seek him out to find out what is wrong. Although formally obligated to attend only their own group, good members are expected to visit other groups, too. Core members will attend four or five local meetings a week. They will also go to monthly "alumni" meetings at hospitals and annual commemorative meetings, as well as prefectural, regional, and national study groups and seminars. Furthermore, in any time left over, the same people get together socially to do things like go hiking, hold year-end parties (*bonenkai*), or sing (home *karaoke*).

Unlike the A.A. practice of freely associating with any group one wishes to, Danshukai – at least in Osaka – bases group membership on residence. One may attend meetings of other branches, is even expected to as an active member, but when one joins, one must be a member of the group with governance over one's own neighborhood. In fact, territoriality runs so strong that all the local branches of the T. City Danshukai agreed that if a member quit one branch he would not be allowed to join another. Such jealousy seems unfortunate because joining a group does not entitle one to anything: There is no voting; there are no exclusive publications. Joining is a declaration of commitment and receives the response of acceptance.

Restricted participation: Kantō Danshukai

Everyone agrees that Danshukai's function is to help alcoholics not drink. Some leaders feel that the means to this end is to spread the word to as many alcoholics as possible and to make sure that as many of them as possible are in meetings, where they hear others tell of their experiences in overcoming the seduction of alcohol. If a man is in a meeting, then at least for two hours he is not drinking. Danshukai leaders who hold this inclusive attitude, and many do, are inclined to believe in the importance of large meetings. Other Danshukai leaders take a more exclusive and more long-term view. These leaders see the act of telling one's experience (*taiken happyō*) as essential to the process by which an alcoholic can overcome his personal obsession with alcohol; without *taiken happyō*, there is no real change. Leaders who are of this opinion strongly favor small groups, where everyone is sure to get a chance to speak.

National policy now speaks to this question (Zennippon Danshu Renmei 1991) and underscores the centrality of the *taiken happyō* experience to successful participation in Danshukai, but regional tendencies continue to exist between Danshukai in Kansai (Kyoto-Osaka-Kobe) and in Kantō (Tokyo and environs). The reasons for the distinctions are first historical. The initial Danshukai groups in western Japan were the product of doctors' attempts to help patients. Their understanding of A.A. was informed by psychotherapeutic models of small-group interaction and catharsis through confession. To this day, Kansai Danshukai works closely in conjunction with the medical community and generally promotes small groups with lots of *taiken happyō,* explicitly limited to one's experience with alcohol.

The Danshukai movement in Tokyo was a product of the Temperance movement and was viewed with some hostility by doctors, who may well have seen it as a threat. Danshukai in Kantō now has a cordial relationship with the medical community, but it is not as close as that found in Kansai. When leaders of the early Danshukai movement in Kantō looked for models for social interaction within their experimental A.A.-like groups, they naturally turned to traditional relations of hierarchy and dependency (*amaeru/amayakasu*). Kantō Danshukai emphasizes the compliance of new members with the admonitions of seniors. Tokyo Danshukai groups are marked by their size (reportedly some are up to a hundred or more members) and an inclination toward sermonizing by leaders.

As Danshukai groups gain more members, it becomes difficult for everyone to participate. For this reason, sister branches often fission off. Among urban Danshukai groups, however, there is a tendency toward large meetings; this is particularly true in Tokyo. In rural areas, Danshukai meetings can be held in private farmhouses because they are large. In rural areas, members are so widely dispersed that the meeting site often rotates from house to house so that people can take turns commuting. In urban areas, on the other hand, there is a real shortage of places to meet. Private apartments are ordinarily too small, commercially available space (like a restaurant) is too expensive, and public meeting places are in short supply. Those public meeting halls that are available are often capable of accommodating extremely large groups. An endlessly expandable space and a dearth of alternatives exacerbate the Kantō Danshukai tendency toward growth without fissioning.

Kansai doctors say that the expansion versus fission question has definite therapeutic consequences. When a new group forms, whether by independent creation or by fission, the leaders are usually men who, though not necessarily chronologically young, are still young in their sobriety. They have been dry for no more than a few years; therefore they do not take their sobriety for granted, and they are enthusiastic about Danshukai. They want to devote their energy to the group, and their enthusiasm is contagious. Of equal importance is the fact that, because their days of hopelessness are not too far behind them, they still have a lot in common with struggling new members. The feeling of shared experience creates a strong bond of mutual trust and commitment among all members. Recidivism is relatively low among early members of a group.

As Danshukai groups age and expand, the differences in experience between the leadership and the newcomers becomes significant. Leaders, who may have ten or more years of sobriety, become less empathetic with feelings of newer members. New arrivals grow frustrated with the irrelevance of the leaders' *taiken happyō* to their own experience. Furthermore, in large Tokyo groups, the act of *taiken happyō* becomes less and less accessible to newcomers because it is the bailiwick of those with seniority. (In Kansai Danshukai, with its emphasis on *taiken happyō* and more egalitarian practice, large membership creates the problem that each speaker gets no more than two or three minutes, hardly time to develop an emotionally involving recollection.) While senior members reinforce their already secure sobriety, junior members are denied participation in the therapeutic confessional process and grow dissatisfied with their exclusion from the political action. Many slip off the wagon. The result is that many large Kantō Danshukai groups have an unexpected, "mushroom"-shaped membership structure: A disproportionately large body of entrenched old-timers dominate the meetings, and a large proportion of newcomers seek to stay dry, but a significant number of members of medium-length participation is missing. There are always new arrivals, but few of them succeed in staying very long.

Discussion

I have tried to indicate that Japanese men who become alcohol-dependent have many strong incentives to see themselves as merely heavy drinkers rather than alcoholics, despite the fact that they may have social and health problems that stem from their drinking behavior and which might be improved by altering their behavior in recognition of a new identity as alcoholic. Wives are unhappy with their husbands' behavior but often reinforce that behavior as they collude in avoiding the stigma of being called an alcoholic. Most Japanese physicians are ignorant of the disease model of alcoholism and its symptoms and thus may repeatedly treat the symptoms without advising the patient of the source of his problem.

In a world that reinforces male alcohol consumption and penalizes abstention, where do men learn to see themselves as abstemious alcoholics?

Education in the disease model of alcoholism comes to the heavy drinkers first from alcoholism specialists and primarily in the form of didactic lectures. I have no indication of how much of the manifest content of the lectures is actually absorbed. In truth, patients sit quietly but often look dazed. On the rare occasion when the lecturing doctor poses a question to some unsuspecting member of the audience, there commonly follows a moment of confusion as the patient tries to remember what is being talked about. This is not to say that nothing is learned at these lectures. The authority of the doctors' lectures – often accompanied with flip charts of metabolic pathways and slides of alcohol-damaged organs – establishes the legitimacy of the disease model.

Yet professional alcoholism therapists and acknowledged alcoholics in Japan recognize that the most effective – and only practical – way for alcoholics really to internalize the significance of their condition and to learn to alter their behavior is by going to Danshukai meetings. If a recently released patient is serious about stopping drinking – whether he sees himself as an alcoholic or not – he is supposed to *hyakkai reikai* (literally "one hundred times [attend] meetings"), a variant of the A.A. adage, "ninety days, ninety meetings." If one follows this prescription, one is repeatedly imbued with the same ideology and rituals as one interacts with the same local members. In most Kansai Danshukai meetings, everyone including beginners and anthropologists must speak, but the demands are not great. (The requirement to speak stands in striking contrast to A.A. policy, where all participation is voluntary.) The minimal response is highly formalized in standard phrases of salutation and thanks. Furthermore, a variety of models for alternative stories is presented at every meeting.

The opportunity to speak (*taiken happyō*) of the horrors of one's life as an alcoholic is important for a number of reasons. Psychologists see it as being therapeutic because it is a cathartic release of guilt. It also permits the alcoholic to vent his psychological obsession with drinking in a productive and socially approved forum.

But members of Danshukai learn that storytelling is important in other ways. *Taiken happyō* is the means to higher status within the community. Men who are earnestly trying to stay dry will devote most of their free time to meetings and other activities with regular members. With time, they may learn that Danshukai is a social community unto itself, one where – for the first time in their experience – it is prestigious and masculine *not* to drink. The usual indicators of social status are of minimal significance. Employment, wealth, schooling, class, and the like are replaced by Danshukai markers. The primary standard of prestige in

Danshukai is the progress one has made in controlling one's drinking. And one way to indicate how far one has gone is by establishing how bad one was. The greater one's past degradations, the more impressive one's present sobriety. And each day of sobriety, publicly announced in a story, is an incremental increase in status. When one's name is called within the sequence of speakers is not only indicative of what kind of story might be appropriate for one to tell but also a public recognition of one's progress in competence from a rank beginner to a regular or a leader. Committed members of Danshukai are thus motivated to develop their own archetypal narratives of their lives as a prisoner of alcohol.

Lave and Wenger (1991), in their study of situated learning, argue that we tend to recognize only didactics and overlook the importance of mimetics. Much learning, important learning, occurs not in the classroom dominated by the lecturer but in the arena of practice. Newcomers are granted a marginal position in a group that creates its identity through the control and enactment of special knowledge. The newcomers are allowed to first observe and then partake in increasingly demanding elements of community action. Through observation and mimicry, the newcomers learn the ways of the old-timers and show their understanding by behaving in ways that conform to community standards.

To be sure, lecturing occurs in Danshukai. It is part of the role of the president of the local branch to make explicit the values of Danshukai. As each member makes his speech and, in particular, during closing remarks, the president is empowered to criticize or instruct. But, in practice, the president seldom strikes a negative note or lectures an individual; rather, he is more likely to express support and reiterate points made by others to underscore their importance.

It is the process of doing, of copying, that transforms the members from newcomers into old-timers. At most Danshukai meetings, everyone in attendance is called upon. The expectations of beginners are modest. They are shown acceptable patterns of *taiken happyō* by those who precede them. Highly formulaic statements are acceptable. But each person is expected to speak. Through hearing the stories told by others and listening to their affirmations, through repeated recitation of pledges so that Danshukai ideas and jargon arise spontaneously in one's speech, and, most importantly, through the revision and expansion of one's own stories and incorporation of member comments, newcomers create new selves who behave as regular Danshukai members should.

To be transformed, the beginner needs a real – even if minor – way in which to participate and move from the margin to the center. New members are necessary to the continued existence of a corporate body; old members all must someday retire. Central, then, to the development of both the individual and the group is "legitimate peripheral learning" (Lave and Wenger 1991:29). Initiates need to be granted a role in the community of practice, with the understanding that, through mastery of the knowledge and skill required for full participation, they will become full-fledged members. And part of the acquisition of knowledge comes from practice. Lectures alone are insufficient. "For newcomers then the purpose is not to learn *from* talk as a substitute for legitimate peripheral participation; it is to learn *to* talk as a key to legitimate peripheral participation" (Lave and Wenger 1991:109).

The importance of access to the floor so that one can tell stories is confirmed by the problems that arise in urban Danshukai. The vagaries of local history and limited venue have tended to make Danshukai meetings expand rather than splinter. With too many members and too little time for everyone to speak at length, a response often found in Kantō is to limit *taiken happyō* to old-timers.

Lave and Wenger (1991:104) call such exclusion of newcomers from full participation "sequestering." The recruits in Kantō Danshukai can be said to be "legitimate" participants because they are recognized as belonging to the group, but they are treated as peripheral in that they are denied their turn to *taiken happyō*; "they are not given access to activity in the community of practice" (Lave and Wenger 1991:104). New recruits continue to enter Danshukai under these circumstances, yet many lose interest and leave the group. The tragedies of these conditions are twofold. While old-timers reinforce their already secure sobriety, alcoholics in need of support abandon Danshukai because the organization has not made a full commitment to them. Furthermore, the alienation between old-timers and newcomers is only exacerbated as junior members leave. It is an unfortunate fact that some Danshukai groups are confronted with the practical problem of where to meet, and that problem can have undesired side effects. As long as Danshukai groups accommodate these constraints by expansion, and fail to recognize the significance (one is tempted to use the medical term "efficacy") of situated, participant learning, they appear destined to undermine their most important goals.

Note

I would like to thank two institutions for their generous support of the research that led to this article. The initial research was underwritten by a Fulbright (IIE) Pre-Doctoral

Research Grant. Follow-up work was assisted by a Faculty Research Fund Board Grant from Wittenberg University.

References

A.A. General Service Office, No date–a, "The 1980 survey of Alcoholics Anonymous," General Service Office, Box 459, Grand Central Station, New York, New York.

A.A. General Service Office, No date–b, "A.A. at a Glance," General Service Office, Box 459, Grand Central Station, New York, New York.

Bowers, John, 1965, *Medical Education in Japan,* New York: Harper & Row.

Cain, Carole, 1991, "Personal Stories: Identity Acquisition and Self-Understanding in Alcoholics Anonymous," *Ethos 19*(2): 210–253.

Gallup, George, 1985, "Alcohol Use and Abuse in America," *Gallup Report,* No. 242, November.

Horii, T., Tani, N., Haga, H., and Kato, N., 1976, "Inshu ni kan suru Ishiki Chōsa, Dainihō: Kango Daigakusei," *Japanese Journal of Studies on Alcohol 11*(1, 2): 25–30.

Kawakami, F., Fukui, K., Kitabayashi, M., Haga, H., Tani, N., Nabekura, M., and Kato, N., 1982, "Inshu ni Kan Suru Ishiki Chōsa," *Japanese Journal of Alcohol and Drug Dependence 17*(4): 368–376.

Kono, H., Nakagawa, J., Saito, S., Shimada, S., and Tanaka, A., 1977, *Drinking Habits of the Japanese,* Tokyo: Leisure Development Center.

Lave, Jean, and Wenger, Etienne, 1991, *Situated Learning: Legitimate Peripheral Participation,* Cambridge: Cambridge University Press.

Masuda, K. (ed.), 1974, *New Japanese-English Dictionary,* Fourth Edition, Tokyo: Kenkyusha.

Rudy, David R., 1986, *Becoming Alcoholic: Alcoholics Anonymous and the Reality of Alcoholism,* Carbondale and Edwardsville: Southern Illinois University Press.

Tani, N., Haga, H., Horii, T., Fukui, K., and Kato, N., 1977, "Inshu ni Kan Suru Ishiki Chōsa," *Japanese Journal of Studies on Alcohol 12*(4): 213–222.

1978, "Inshu ni Kan Suru Ishiki Chōsa," *Japanese Journal of Studies on Alcohol 13*(2): 135–142.

Tani, N., Haga, H., and Kato, N., 1975, "Inshu ni Kan Suru Ishiki Chōsa," *Japanese Journal of Studies on Alcohol 10*(1, 2): 35–40.

Terashima, Shogo, 1969, "The Structure of Rejecting Attitudes toward the Mentally Ill in Japan," in W. Caudill and T. Lin (eds.), *Mental Health Research in Asia and the Pacific,* Honolulu: East-West Center, pp. 195–215.

Zennippon Danshu Renmei, 1991, *Shishin to Kihan,* Osaka: Osakafu Danshukai.

18 Did an ox wander by here recently? Learning Americanized Zen

Maureen W. McClure

John, Rudi, and rogue Zen

This is a firsthand account of learning Zen in the United States. I learned the spirit of Zen through Japanese sacred art, but the master was not Japanese, and the community in which I lived from 1976 to 1980 did not claim to have direct connections to Rinzai, Soto, or other traditions and temples in Japan. My practice, however, was closely tied to the Rinzai traditions, which assert that all work is art (Rinzai 1976). It was a small, intentional community of six to ten students living in one household with one of the finest Asian sacred art collections in the world. The core group consisted of about six longer-term students; the rest usually remained for less than a year. Many of the students were artists. All of the core students eventually left, and John Mann, our teacher, sold the house in 1983.

It was an authentic educational experience for me within a Japanese religious "aesthetic" mediated by American interpreters and my own American background. Within this setting, my experiential education in Zen principles was neither academic nor schooled. Even now, as an educational scholar, I have constructed my "story" from my experience as a learner. Anthropological discourses about apprenticeship learning, specifically "situated learning," helped me frame my experience and make educational sense of a part of my past (Lave and Wenger 1991). I had many teachers in our community at Livonia: John, the other students, the practice, the sacred art, and the ox-herding pictures. From them, I began to learn that success is compassion, and that a moment of it is priceless.

I grew up in Erie, Pennsylvania, the elder of two daughters. My father was a lawyer, my mother a school nurse. Encouraged to become a teacher, I eventually became a federal programs' coordinator for "disadvantaged youth" in the rural and working-class school districts of western Pennsylvania in the early seventies. Disenchanted with what I considered to be the stifling authoritarianism of the formal school programs, I began to read extensively about other pedagogical approaches, hoping to find something more consonant with my beliefs. Following up on a book I found particularly intriguing, *Learning to Be,* I visited its author, John Mann, in the summer of 1976 (Mann 1972). He was at the time a professor of sociology at the State University College at Geneseo, New York. I discovered that John was intensely interested in East Asian views of aesthetic consciousness. He had participated in the early work on comparative, creative religious experiences at the Esalen Institute in Big Sur, California, which resulted in works like *The Dancing Wu Li Masters* (Zukav 1979). In addition, John had worked with an American spiritual teacher in New York – Albert Rudolph, or Rudi.

John was teaching at New York University when he met Rudi in New York in the early sixties. They were both a part of Greenwich Village's "beat generation" of the fifties, with its zeal for Zen. Rudi was a notorious sacred art dealer who had no compunctions about smuggling art out of Tibet "to prevent its destruction at the hands of the Chinese communists." His students also told stories of his buying art before the Japanese government, which was tracking down national treasures, and American museums, interested in acquiring Asian masterpieces, realized what he was doing. In the sixties, Rudi became increasingly interested in Indian saints and became a swami. Then he died in a plane crash in 1973 at the age of forty-five.

John was a beneficiary of Rudi's sorties, and he invested most of his money in Rudi's art, including the money his wife thought was set aside for a house on the Hudson, designed by Frank Lloyd Wright as one of Wright's last projects. His wife never forgave him, and eventually John, divorce decree and sacred art in hand, landed in upstate New York. He bought a house and started teaching meditation classes; eventually, a small group of students, most of them artists, moved in. The students in the house served as a de facto security system for the art. John invited me to come and stay for a couple of weeks. I accepted and went prepared for a two-week stay, which lasted four years.

Backward into apprenticeship

I was sixteen years old when I had my first experience with what is called in Zen a "cleared mind," or *kenshō*.[1] I had recently received my driver's license and was driving my mother's Volkswagen "Beetle." There is a park near my high school with a windy road. I loved the feel of driving curves and often pretended I was a Grand Prix race car driver wending my way through the streets of Monaco. One day I was leaning heavily into the final turn when I noticed that the bark on the trees in front of me was still very wet from the rain. The deepness of the color, the texture of the bark, the outline of the trees against the sky, all converged into a naked, powerful beauty. The raw vitality of the scene in front of me was so overpoweringly complete that the world just stopped. There was no time, no history, no "me," no tree . . . only what I have no other word for . . . God. For a moment, heaven, earth, joy, and I were one.

I was deeply humbled by the beauty, majesty, and compassion of that moment. I was awestruck because I knew instantly that it was complete and eternal. As I finished the turn and headed toward home, my second reaction was to think that I was probably going to die soon. I was resigned. It was worth it. My third thought was that I was probably genetically deformed, and if I reported this to anyone, they would take me away and I would die in a mental institution. I decided the problem did not belong to the moment. It was so beautiful, healthy, and complete that I simply assumed that it was not "mine." I was grateful for it but terrified of telling anyone because I didn't want to be carried away in a straitjacket. I was silent also because I feared "losing" its memory.

As I look back, I mark that moment as the formal beginning of my apprenticeship. I wanted to be a saint. If this were a saint's experience, I thought . . . wow . . . then nothing else would ever matter in the same way again. I had seen Jesus' lilies, so Solomon's glory had less appeal.[2] Alas, there were no clearly defined career paths for apprentice saints in Erie, Pennsylvania, in 1964. There was no master with whom I could exchange commitment and ardor for skills, socialization, and cultural legitimacy. There was only a door of experience. It had opened for a brief moment, and I had hurled myself through it.

The house

My apprenticeship was situated in three communities of practice (Lave and Wenger 1991). The first and broadest for me were the Asian classical traditions that integrated religion, work, art, and modern speculations on human potential. In the late seventies, John and Rudi's other teachers moved away from traditions that focused on work, art, and community, giving rise to a refined, everyday consciousness (Zen) toward traditions that focused on techniques that triggered extraordinary states of consciousness (Himalayan forms of yoga). Everyday life became the means for sustaining ever rarer experiences. My interest was in the former; the quality of my everyday life was an end, not a means.

The second, more narrowly defined community consisted of about ten groups of Rudi's students, scattered all over the country. Livonia was one of the smallest groups. Bloomington, Indiana, and Big Indian, New York, each had more than fifty members at their height in the 1970s.

The third community was John's house in Livonia. The house had a relatively stable core of about six people; the rest "floated." Not all students lived in the house; some drove in for evening classes and dinner. Most of the students had connections with the college in nearby Geneseo. The house enabled the live-in studio artists to keep their expenses down, form small businesses to earn a living, and pursue their art in off-hours. For example, three of the "core students" – Bobby, Patrick, and Wayne – formed a painting company. They had a contract with a company that managed a prestigious apartment building in Rochester.

John's presence was central in class. In long classes, he would help us focus our attention by touching our foreheads or backs. He never hit us with a stick, as in other Zen practices. Outside of class, however, the everyday tasks of learning to live with each other fell to the core students: Donna, Jean, Linda, Patrick, and Wayne.[3] Donna was a dancer and choreographer from Brooklyn. She was a devout Roman Catholic and was interested in Asian and Native American ways of healing. Jean was a raku potter who had studied in the United States and Mexico. She was the plants' favorite. Linda was a photographer and librarian who worked in multimedia. She also designed and built her own furniture. Patrick was a potter and the restoration expert for the art. He helped oversee many of the house's endless projects. He wore Cheryl Tieg T-shirts, loved pizza, and was the best cook in the house. Dogs and children followed him home. Wayne was a certified medium and sci-fi addict who had worked in Fiji. His imagination was pungent with ideas about designing communities that were ecologically responsible. He pushed hard for us to think of ways to celebrate creative nonviolence over competitive acquisition.

Unlike highly formalized monastic traditions, we were expected to help create rituals to support current students. The ritual structure was quite flexible, depending on who lived in the house at the time. For example, if a student were interested in the effects of nutrition on creative awareness, the rest might join in for support. There was the "macrobiotic food and *shiatsu* period," the "herb period," and the "martial arts period." Each period was embraced with fervor to learn from the others in the house. We had no traditional program to learn, no "correct" way for making turnip soup or passing the master his dessert. As core students, we were a prudish lot about sex (monogamous, longer-term), smoking (quit), drinking (rare), and drugs (never saw).

John received no direct payment for his teaching. Rudi had expected his teachers to demonstrate work as mastered art. Students were expected to be economically self-reliant, working either in house businesses or on their own. Each person who lived in the house was expected to pay rent and contribute weekly for food. The rent was $125 a month in 1976, and $250 in 1983. Food and household supplies fees were $10 per week but could vary, depending on how much money we had. I remember some lean months when I had to cook for ten on a three-dollar daily budget. Each student, regardless of seniority, was expected to be responsible for one meal a week, including shopping and cooking. Other household chores were rotated so that everyone had to take turns doing less tasteful duties. These group efforts were intended to create more time for further meditation or for work in the art studio. Alas, endless group projects emerged – from installing insulation to fixing roof leaks in the house, at the cottage, and at other centers.

Newcomers were expected to work hard. There were two meditation classes a day, at six in the morning and at six in the evening. In the interim, time was to be spent at work or in school. We were expected to excel at everything. If we didn't, we were at least expected to have made a 110 percent effort. We were expected to live each day so fully that we were totally exhausted, physically, mentally, and creatively. A typical day for me meant getting up at 5:30, having class, running six miles, eating the latest healthy breakfast, and driving forty-five minutes to the university for morning classes. Evenings were spent listening to Rudi tapes, in advanced or specialized classes, or studying. The "core" students taught me a lot. They soon became my closest friends and colleagues. Together we learned to struggle in the world with fierce intensity and gently bizarre humor. If one didn't have time to listen, another did. We were bound together in the same common plight. We needed each other because much of our learning was painfully disorienting.

The apprenticeship: Principles and techniques

John's work consisted of a framework, essential principles, and techniques. The framework could be described as "All work as art. Intense observation. Practice. Surrender. Repeat." The principles were drawn from classic teachings, but their emphasis was based on John's personal experience. Among the essential principles were energy, light, flexibility, detachment, flow, quiet, center, heart, growth, no harm, and open. "Essential" to John did not mean generic in that the meaning was self-evident, like a standardized product. He taught us that "essential" meant connecting with the experiences of all those who have preceded and who will follow.

His techniques came from three sources: his own teacher, his research into art apprenticeships, especially theater arts, and his own constructions. Examples of classic techniques were intense observation and ruthless critical self-reflection on personal assumptions of meaning. John also drew from many sources in performance arts. He liked Moreno's work from the 1920s in the Theater of Spontaneity, because students could create improvisational role performances to identify with and to respond to familial, social, and ideological expectations (Mann 1972:100).

During my first class, and for many after, as soon as I would start to relax, a "jukebox" would start playing songs from the sixties in my head. The music was so loud, clear, and complete that at first I looked around for the radio. As a novice, I was tied to the techniques of John's practice. I needed tips on breathing, on centering, on visualization, on letting go of tensions. They didn't help because I didn't know how to think about them. I kept attaching a single meaning to a single term and a single behavior. At first, I thought "surrender" meant learning to turn off the jukebox. I thought that when I learned to do that, I would "know" how to surrender. Was I wrong! Every time I thought I had mastered the term, a new experience arose to be connected with it. Once the music quieted down, I noted that my jaw was painfully clenched. I realized it had been so for years, but I had "anesthetized" it so it seemed normal. The more I tried to "let go," the worse the pain got. I finally learned to go right "through" it by centering and not avoiding or provoking it. I was surprised to find the pain was often attached to disturbing emotions like anger, grief, or fear. John linked it to Wilhelm Reich's notion of "character armor."

The physical–emotional awareness practice was miserable. The cognitive self-reflection was even worse because it was so disorienting. For example, before I moved to Livonia, I didn't think much about cleaning toilets. At the house, cleaning became a major event. I would continuously ask myself questions like, "Do I care enough about this? Am I taking too long to complete this task? Where is my breath? Can I do my job and still feel the soles of my feet? Why am I thinking so much? Is this work or play?" The world became a far more primitive place. I didn't know where my words, my gestures, my tone of voice originated. I didn't know what I meant by what I said. My new-found "sight" was often, and still is, deeply isolating.

John did not use traditional Zen practices of koans and dialogue. He believed that the route past the rational mind was through attention to internal sensations. Quiet was more powerful to John than words. All, however, was not necessarily calm and beauty. Legitimate spiritual experiences, by John's definition, might be preceded by great terror or exhausting pain. I sometimes saw people weep or flail about uncontrollably, despite rigorous self-discipline.

Slowly I began to learn that if I weren't fretting about my latest slight, I could be more aware of the community of life around me. Instead of being heavy and self-absorbed, I could become quiet and feel the sunshine on my face or more keenly observe the utter uniqueness of a passer-by's face. I began to think of life as a giant Star Wars Bar, where each person came from a different solar system yet was connected by a single breath.

When John retired and left Geneseo, he placed the priceless sacred art in commercial drive-in storage lockers in Avon for years. A terrible fire damaged or destroyed much of it. I shall mourn this loss for the rest of my life, but I will always cherish the gifts of their memory.

Americanized Zen versus American Zen

John's strong emphasis on cooperative rather than collective identity won no friends either on the "spiritual circuit" or in the larger society. He never appropriated many of the traditional cultural symbols of Zen or other traditions, so his work was difficult to "recognize." We were American spiritual outlaws, a role we relished with verve.

Because we stuck out in the conservative little town of Livonia, we were marginalized but fortunately not bothered. We were also a disgrace in the eyes of many of the more mainstream spiritual communities, such as the Rochester Zen Center. Roshi Philip Kapleau, an ordained monk with legitimate Rinzai credentials from Japan, had settled in Rochester, New York, and started a center. Roshi Kapleau and John Mann had limited connections. I was told that neither recognized nor approved of the other. There were, however, occasional courtesy calls. We were invited to the Zen Center as a group one Sunday. The contrast between the two groups was jarring.

Kapleau's group had adopted many of the traditional cultural symbols that John ignored. A Japanese Zen monk would have found their center organized in ways that would have been familiar. Students wore black robes and sat *zazen* on grass *tatami* mats in spacious rooms with paper *shōji* screen walls. They ate simple vegetarian meals. Their gardens were elegant. In contrast, we lived in an American farmhouse and shopped at the Champion's outlet store. John showed up for the service in a loud, Hawaiian print shirt. We had meat on our breath. Our garden had statues across from the clothesline. It was Roger Rabbit and Toontown meet the Grown-ups.

The roshi, the meditation hall, and the students wore a studied serenity. We weren't serene; we were exuberant. We entered the sitting room first and were placed near large bronze bells. We plunked down with a sense of purpose. Kapleau's students marched in and sat down carefully with a mannered elegance. Later we quipped that we were the country mice visiting our city cousins.

We were annoyed that as guests, we were seated in the least desirable place in the room, because the sound next to the large bells was very loud, making it uncomfortable, even painful. We assumed it was an insult. I took it as a challenge and became intensely aware of the bell's energy, absorbing it as though the sound were fuel. The more I took in, the more alive I felt. I suddenly realized why some of the best students lived at the margins. I looked at Kapleau's students and John's and marveled at the difference. Kapleau's group seemed to be working hard to fit into a collective identity. They were trying to carry a heavy mantle of tradition. I wasn't sure it would support them. We were struggling hard enough to have our own identity; we couldn't carry a collective, too.

The Rochester Zen Center survived Roshi Kapleau's retirement and death but suffered in the struggles for succession. Ours did not survive John's retirement. We had our individual lives, but our community was lost.

Solace in other teachers: The art

The lightness, whimsy, and gentleness in the house belonged to its silent teachers in the house: the art. And what an art collection it was. It engulfed the house and all of those within. It attracted artists who just wanted to be near ancient, sacred pieces: bronzes, thankas, stone and wood carvings from all over Asia. In my first room on the back porch, for example, I chose a large, fierce Japanese plaster guardian. He sat on a three-foot stand with a large halo behind him. He was well weathered and had been consigned to the barn. I thought he was perfect for me, because I felt pretty weather-beaten at the time. I thought of Christian guardian angels and was smitten by the idea of having one who was short, stocky, and cranky.

John taught me to give the sacred art my truest self and yearn for the same in return. I thought this was a great trade because I didn't like most of what I had. I spent hours in front of the guardian, surrendering my pain and anguish, asking for anything God wanted to send. Over time, I imagined that the guardian had a very clear but complex "self" that I could recognize. I imagined I had to become a warrior myself in order to go "through" the internal pain I had. My guardian seemed to return my pain with compassion. I grew to be very fond of him.

Everywhere I looked, the message of the sacred art was clear: Life was art, life art, inseparable, complete, sufficient. Museum curators from places like the Metropolitan would come to visit and pay their respects. The curator of the Asian art collection for the Boston Museum, a Japanese shinto priest, came and taught us how to approach the art. His approach was highly ritualized and formal. We just couldn't make his ways work for us, so we invented our own. We instead treated the art with warmth and humor instead of distance and formal piety. We accepted the art both as formal teachers and as the closest members of our extended family. Don swore the back-porch guardian was "into" John Denver. We "knew" the art wanted us to be our authentic selves, not translations from another culture, so we treated it like we would our own relatives. In Livonia, my relatives just moved a little slower and looked a little different than most.

The boundaries between the art and my imagination became very thin and strengthened my ability to use nonrational sense making. My interaction with the art helped create feelings of gentleness and compassion that I could not have imagined developing on my own. The art, more than John, became a source of comfort. I thought of the art as gifts from the artists who had gone before me. The serenity I felt being with them was enough to return me to the beauty of the trees that I had seen when I was sixteen. This time, however, I learned that *kenshō* was only a beginning. The gifts from the past showed me my responsibilities to those here now and to those who waited in the future.

The Zen apprentice: Herding oxen

It may help the reader at this point to frame a model for apprenticeship of essential principles in a broader context. In Zen, the Way of the apprentice is framed through the classical ox-herding pictures. These ten pictures serve as guidelines for the person seeking enlightenment. Each picture represents a stage of development. They are also brilliant examples of the practice of essential principles because they require the experience of the viewer for interpretation. Unlike legal texts that try to codify behavior in concrete, self-evident language, the pictures are ambiguous. They reflect a way of personal experience, not a code of cultural expectations. I have shown these pictures to American students with no knowledge of Zen. When they hear the stories, some laugh spontaneously in sympathy with the struggles of the poor student.

At first, I thought the pictures were sequential, and they are, for the most part. Now, however, I think of my relation to them as Alice in Wonderland wandering around in adventuresome and scary mazes that turn endlessly in on themselves. For example, after an experience like the one I had as a teenager, it took me many years to get back to the first picture. Also, as I progressed through the stages, I humbly found that I could not hold fast to my learning and slipped back as often as I moved "ahead." Most unsettling, and the best joke of all, was to discover that the end was just the beginning, and I had been nowhere at all. To complicate the illusion, the pictures appeared gentle and benign, and fooled me. The struggles of awareness and self-reflection may have been gentle for some, but it was often a war zone for me.

The first eight pictures are Chinese in origin; the last two are Japanese additions. They are accompanied by text and poetry. It is a story of mastery and harmony. The first picture, "Seeking the Ox," shows a man alone on a road. The text reveals that he is driven by a deep yearning. In the second picture, he "Finds the Tracks." He cannot yet "see" the ox, but he has entered the periphery of its experience. In the third picture, the "First Glimpse of the Ox" is made. The student is instructed to learn to "see" the ox by practicing intense awareness of everyday experiences. The student finally participates in the fourth picture, "Catching the Ox," in which a small person struggles to harness a very large ox. In some pictures, only the ox is visible. It is an amusing image for students' ungainly attempts to harness their "attention." Commanding attention doesn't work, but caring for it does. "Taming the Ox," the fifth picture, shows the establishment of a sustained relationship. Both the apprentice and the ox must negotiate rights and responsibilities. Anyone who has negotiated contracts with pets understands the failure of the Western machine metaphor of command and control. The ox must consent to be tame, so the student must learn to "speak ox."

Now the apprentice can learn to "see" more creatively. The student in the sixth picture, "Riding the Ox Home," plays the flute on the back of the ox. Together they head home in playful harmony with each other and the rest of the world. Creativity requires playfulness, humor, and joy, not fear and intimidation. In the seventh picture, "Ox Forgotten, Self Alone," the apprentice has returned home. It is a small place in a large, beautiful world. He and the ox's spirit have become one. He can now turn from his own internal struggles and "see" the natural world around him more clearly. The eighth picture, "Both Ox and Self Forgotten," is represented as a single perfect circle, a test of Zen mastery. It is the experience of *satori,* when the experience of self falls away and there is a sense of complete oneness with the natural world. The artist and the art are one. The Chinese story ends here.

The Japanese, with social practicality, ask "Now what?" and "What about social relationships?" In the ninth picture, "Returning to the Source," one sees the simple but complete majesty of the universe in a fragment, say, a tree branch. The master releases his socially constructed view of the world and returns to his transcendent origins with their unconditional love. Thus *satori* becomes embedded in his everyday experience of the spirit of immanence. Life becomes an affirmation, an unshakable choice to forgive, celebrate, and engage it, with all of its pain and terrible beauty. The transcendent and the immanent are one. There is no need to strive for enlightenment because the rational mind – too slow, loud, and self-absorbed for compassionate action – has dissolved into quiet oneness. The master realizes that life has always been there, that his heroic efforts have been of no import. His enlightenment was always a gift of grace; his saintly practices were useless. Now they interfere with his sublime ordinariness.

> He has returned to the Origin, come back to the Source,
> but his steps have been in vain.
> It is though he were now blind and deaf.
> Seated in his hut, he hankers not for things outside.
> Streams meander on of themselves,
> red flowers naturally bloom red. (Kapleau 1972:310)

The individual may be personally one with the world, but that experience is not yet integrated into the social community. Experience requires expression. The master now must go home and just be himself. In the tenth and final picture, "Entering the Market with Helping Hands," the master is seen returning home. He is now older, rounder, and smiling. He is greatly relieved from the burden of being a saint. He greets daily life with a healthy exuberance, within an unshakable choice to affirm life as it is. Through compassionate language and actions, the master now guides others to an understanding that their angst can be overcome through grace. He creates his own life, he is no longer dependent on the experiences of other saints. The Japanese pictures complete the cycle of apprenticeship by showing the master's responsibilities to society. It is not enough to experience the creative spirit; it must be integrated into everyday life and shared with others. The master now carries a wine bottle in celebration. All work is now art.

> Barechested, barefooted, he comes into the marketplace.
> Muddied and dust-covered, how broadly he grins!
> Without recourse to mystic powers,
> withered trees he swiftly brings to bloom. (Kapleau 1972:311)

The experience

The spiritual experiences that occurred in my apprenticeship were highly distinctive and instantly recognizable. I have "felt the Spirit" in beautiful natural sttings, especially in the Four Corners area of the American southwest, in a Quaker meeting in Pittsburgh, and in an Assembly of God church service in Gilbert, West Virginia. I can best describe this experience for me as a tangible sensation of "tingling" often accompanied by a sensation of lightness and health, a feeling of great power, deep peace, or timeless community. The closest, consistent, physical natural experience I can relate it to is the feel of ozone-filled air just after lightning has struck. Sometimes it felt like I'd been hit by lightning, other times by gentle rain. For all John's tolerance, he never reached out to the Christian traditions of Pentecostalism that are so much a part of the religious heritage of the United States. Yet the preacher's wife in West Virginia in 1993 "opened" my heart as surely as John, though I doubt that the two would ever voluntarily get together to compare notes.

In Zen, the immanent spirit is so important that it is seen not as a visitation but as omnipresent in nature. It also brings creativity that can be expressed in everyday life. Creativity in Zen is not an immutable asset we acquire at birth; rather, it is deeply linked to a quiet but intense appreciation of natural beauty, and it emerges from our struggle to make sense of the world. Creativity does not begin with an act of natural talent, as in the West, but with a relationship – "sight" – first with self and then with others (Herrigel 1960; Suzuki 1964; Singleton 1989a). I am learning that Zen tranquility emerges from the excruciating pain of seeing and embracing life as it is and creating something beautiful in it one moment at a time. Art was John's way to transcend existential angst through creative experience. His metaphor was the artist dancing above the flames. The totality of Zen, however, is deeply embedded in Japanese culture and cannot be "appropriated." It can be courted and translated but never copied.

Its spirit already has deep roots in U.S. popular culture, some triumph and some trash. The spirit of Zen, what Vaclev Havel calls the "miracle of being," is as American as apple pie. Its amazing grace, however, is often more raucous than tranquil. European Zen is Bach and Mozart. American Zen in the Northeast is Thoreau, in the West is fly fishing, and in the South is gospel – rockabilly and down-and-dirty delta blues.

As a student, I learned to "see" beauty in nature and in the art of those who had struggled before me, and to feel their compassion within me as a gift, so that I wanted to contribute to the next generation ... and it only took twenty-five years to write this sentence. Today, at work, I am more aware of the simple sensual pleasures of breathing, tasting simple food, or watching the flutter of a bluejay's wing. The smallest things, like the "line" of a tree branch or the play of light on a garbage can, have become sources of insight and pleasure. These pleasures remain after the "great experiences" have gone. Even as I write this, I notice with delight the erratic rhythms of a squirrel's tail.

Notes

1. According to Roshi Kapleau (1972), "*kenshō* (literally, seeing into one's own nature): Semantically, *kenshō* and *satori* [spiritual awakening] have virtually the same meaning, and they are often used interchangeably. In describing the enlightenment of the Buddha and the Patriarchs, however, it is customary to use the word *satori* rather than *kenshō,* the term *satori* implying a deeper experience" (p. 335).
2. Lilies tie Christianity to Zen Buddhism. Gasan, a famous Zen master, was asked if he had read the Bible. When he said no, the student read the lilies passage from St. Matthew. The master replied, "Whoever uttered these words, consider an enlightened man" (Sohl and Carr 1970:i).
3. There were other important students whose time overlapped less with mine or who were there for shorter time periods: Celeste, Cheryl, Diane, Debbie, and Don.

References

Herrigel, Eugen, 1953, *Zen in the Art of Archery,* Boston: Routledge & Kegan Paul.

Kapleau, P., ed., 1972, *The Three Pillars of Zen: Teaching, Practice, Enlightenment,* Boston, MA: Beacon Press.

Lave, Jean, and Wenger, Etienne, 1991, *Situated Learning: Legitimate Peripheral Participation,* Cambridge: Cambridge University Press.

Mann, J., 1972, *Learning to Be: The Education of Human Potential,* New York: The Free Press.

Rudrananda, S., 1984, *Behind the Cosmic Curtain: The Further Writings of Swami Rudrananda,* John Mann, ed., Arlington, MA: Neolog Publishing.

Rinzai, 1976, *The Zen Teaching of Rinzai,* I. Schoegl, trans., Berkeley: Shambala Publications.

Singleton, John, 1989a, "Japanese Folkcraft Pottery Apprenticeship: Cultural Assumptions in Educational Practice," in Michael Coy, ed., *Apprenticeship: From Theory to Method and Back Again,* Albany: State University of New York Press, pp. 13–30.

Sohl, R., and Carr, A., eds., 1970, *The Gospel According to Zen,* New York: Mentor Books.

Suzuki, D. T., 1964, *An Introduction to Zen Buddhism,* New York: Grove Press.

Zukav, G., 1979, *The Dancing Wu Li Masters: An Overview of the New Physics,* Toronto: Bantam Books.

19 Learning to be learners: Americans working for a Japanese boss

Jill Kleinberg

This chapter looks at cultural transmission and acquisition of knowledge from an intercultural perspective. It focuses on one work group – the Printer Group – in a U.S.-based subsidiary of a Japanese company. It describes the process by which Americans in the Japanese-managed group learn to be learners in a way far more "Japanese" than "American." The "doings and sayings" (Frake 1983) of both the Japanese boss and his American subordinates reflect an approach to bringing the uninitiated (i.e., the Americans) into a community of practice similar to that gleaned from observations of traditional pottery enterprises (Kleinberg 1979, 1983; Philip 1989; Singleton, Chapter 7, and Haase, Chapter 6, this volume) as well as observations of modern enterprise in Japan (Rohlen 1974; Yoshino and Lifson 1986).

Responses of American employees in the "binational" organization lend particular support to a cultural theory of learning illuminated by students of situated learning in various Japanese settings. These American participants not only are unencumbered by the baggage of existing social science interpretations of Japan, but the intercultural work situation makes the Americans keenly aware of behavior they perceive to be different. One of the interesting issues surrounding the case study of the Printer Group is how a Japanese model of learning came to be accepted by work group members whose societal culture and past work experience are decidedly unlike the Japanese.

A cultural theory of learning

Accounts of pottery workshops and modern business organizations reflect certain broad principles that are commonly embedded in the learning process for newcomers. A culturally specific notion of membership serves as an overarching principle. It may be symbolically expressed both officially and informally in the metaphor of "family" (*kazoku,* or *ie*), and through other concepts that imperfectly translate as unity (*danketsu*) or fellowship (*wa*) or a feeling of oneness (*ittaikan*). Membership, therefore, implies a sense of belongingness and the reciprocal obligation between the organization and employee encompassed by that belongingness (Lebra 1976). It implies, moreover, connection within an elongated time frame. Learning work skills cannot be separated from learning to be a member of the organization and work unit: Work is a vehicle for instilling a sense of membership; membership is a vehicle for ensuring the accomplishment of work.

Supporting principles involve the organization's concern for the spiritual (*seishin*) or character-building dimension of learning. Ideal personal qualities include self-sacrificing and self-disciplined persistence and effort. Hardship (*kurō*), in particular, leads to the desired consciousness. Effort should be aimed at achieving group goals and exercised in a spirit of cooperativeness. *Kyōchōsei,* a cooperative attitude toward fellow workers and the organization as a whole, perhaps is the root of what Western commentators often talk about as the dedication of the Japanese to their company.

Ideally, spiritualism and technical ability simultaneously evolve within the framework of small-group solidarity and commitment, focused on the "master" (*sensei*), in the case of pottery workshops, or the section chief (*kachō*) in a large organization. Prominent among the leader's responsibilities is facilitating the development of persons in subordinated status (Yoshino and Lifson 1986). As noted elsewhere in this volume, the leader accomplishes this less through direct guidance than by providing opportunities for learners to master skills (and proper attitudes) by trial and error and by watching their workshop or office seniors. In fact, group members other than the formal leader share responsibility for developing learners. The acquisition of character, work skills, and membership occurs gradually and incrementally, often through repetitive and mundane activity. Even in larger organizations that have formalized training programs, individual progression largely reflects the leader's intuitive understanding that the newcomer is spiritually and technically prepared to move on to a new level of endeavor.

The model of learning sketched earlier takes shape through patterns of social interaction guided by Confucian-influenced assumptions (Rohlen 1974). The building blocks are found in fundamental social constructs like those that Lebra (1976) identifies as belongingness, empathy, occupying the proper place in a vertically graded social order, reciprocity, and dependence. My impression of learning in settings I have observed is of an inexorable process of conscious and unconscious molding, both by and to these normative patterns. Sometimes members themselves sense the force of such molding. For example, when I was doing participant observation in a medium-sized Tokyo firm, a sister subsidiary to the company analyzed here, a "freshman" clerical worker who was influenced by a high school year in the United States said of her work experience, "It's like having your individuality worn away."

In my role as ethnographer, I too have experienced shaping. A precondition to gaining confidences is to achieve at least quasi-membership in the community being examined. Community members enable that transformation through continuous coaching. While doing research in a pottery-making village, for instance, queries couched in terms like "I hear that Yamato [pseudonymous workshop name] invited you to dinner last night. You'll stop by to thank them?" drew me into the unending chain of ritualized reciprocal exchange that is one aspect of membership.[1] Resistance to the constant scrutiny and (usually indirect) lessons in situationally appropriate behavior erupts on occasion. Overall, however, resistance turns to acceptance and even gratitude for being embraced by the community and thus given the opportunity to do one's work. As Rohlen (1974) shows in his study of a Japanese bank, the transition from resistance to acceptance and, eventually, gratitude is a culturally appropriate trajectory for learners, facilitated, but only in part, by calculated managerial practice.

An interpretive perspective

This analysis of the Printer Group adopts an interpretive perspective on the interrelated processes of teaching and learning (hereafter referred to simply as "learning"). The ethnographer's goal is cultural description, where description means to represent and contextually explain those "webs of significance" that humans create for themselves through their social interaction (Geertz 1973:5). Interpretation, therefore, aims at "gaining access to the conceptual world in which our subjects live so that we can, in some extended sense of the term, converse with them" (Geertz 1973:24). Relevant data derive from more than one year of participant observation in the company, including informal conversations and unstructured interviews with most of the employees. Data analysis emphasizes identifying recurrent themes through content analysis of employees' words and actions (Kleinberg 1989).

Reconstruction of the conceptual world of the Printer Group organizes around three interrelated foci: (1) the meaning of membership, (2) shaping the learner, and (3) the social relations of learning. Understandings about learning form part of a wider culture of the Printer Group. This culture has been described elsewhere (Kleinberg 1994a), but, while the earlier description touches on the points made here, it does not specifically distill meanings that relate to learning.[2]

To identify sense making as a group phenomenon implies that the Japanese boss and the American subordinates share the same understandings. This is with some qualification. For the group manager, these understandings reflect mainly tacit knowledge about proper ways of thinking and behaving in a work context, influenced by his societal culture and acquired through his long participation as a member of the parent organization. For the Americans, they reflect tacit and explicit knowledge of being a learner in this particular work group, acquired through social interaction among members.

The organizational setting

The focal organization was a Los Angeles-based subsidiary of the American arm of a major Japanese trading company (TC America), and called here by the acronym LASCO (Los Angeles Subsidiary Company). LASCO's business focused on the development and distribution of computer peripherals. The company was entwined in an intricate web of organizational relationships: primary business communication flowed between LASCO, trading company headquarters in Tokyo (TC Japan), a sister subsidiary in Tokyo (TOSCO), and various independent manufacturers in Japan. Tension existed between LASCO and "Tokyo" (the headquarters *and* the sister subsidiary) over who controlled the computer peripherals business, and between LASCO and the subcontracting manufacturers over such matters as scheduling.

LASCO was unquestionably a Japanese-dominated organization despite the fact that *chūzaiin* – men sent from the headquarters for an extended tour of duty – constituted only about 13 percent of the company's roughly 130 employees. *Chūzaiin* occupied key positions, from president down through most of the middle-management posts.

Organizational cultures

Both Japanese and Americans working in LASCO shared the understanding that "we are a company divided." The distinctive we–they dichotomy that separated "Japanese" (i.e., the *chūzaiin*) and "Americans" (i.e., all locally hired employees regardless of country of origin) recognized differences in their respective status in terms of position, tasks, information, and influence; differences in their respective relationships to the firm with regard to pay and benefits; and general differences in their way of thinking about work, interpersonal relations, family, and so forth. Also shared at the organization-wide level were cultural assumptions about LASCO's uniqueness and about change being a constant phenomenon, as reflected in the company's frequent structural reorganizations.

Prominent American and Japanese subcultures existed. Americans understood LASCO as very different from companies they were familiar with from past experience in the way positions were defined (or not defined) and the way work was organized. Missing was a clear demarcation of job parameters and the "proper" correspondence among job title, job responsibilities, authority, and pay. Americans' subgroup cultural knowledge, moreover, included the understanding that they were out of the flow of information, decision making, and influence and that they had little opportunity for advancement.

The Japanese subgroup culture was far more elaborated than the American. It encompassed understandings about the (close) relationship between LASCO and other subunits involved in the computer peripherals business as well as understandings about how to manage LASCO. Among the latter was the cultural knowledge that Americans were a problem to manage. In particular, Americans tended to interpret their jobs too narrowly and inflexibly. This contrasted to the more organic view that the Japanese subgroup culture took of both structure and responsibility (i.e., both should be determined largely by the capabilities of individuals and needs of the organization). Furthermore, Americans tended to be too much concerned with self-interests and too little focused on the interests of the work group or organization.[3]

The Printer Group

During fieldwork in LASCO, I observed each of the company's work groups. I concentrated on the Printer Group for roughly two months, spending most of each day watching and participating in its activities. This group handled several models of printers, which it moved through two channels, known as the "OEM" and "distribution" channels. It worked with OEMs (original equipment manufacturers) such as IBM or Apple to supply printers for their brand-name systems, and it worked through exclusive distributors in the United States and Canada to sell LASCO brand-name printers to retailers. The group included thirteen people. Nine resided in Los Angeles, two in New York, and two in Chicago. "Ken" Sasaki, the group manager, was the only *chūzaiin.* Men occupied all the formal managerial positions. Except for one woman, Ellen, women were attached to men in a purely secretarial capacity.

Seven of the group – Ken and six "Americans" – can be considered core members. These were persons who held line positions, who had managerial or supervisory responsibilities, who regularly dealt with customers, and whose work was very interdependent. The issue of approaches to learning most clearly concerns core personnel.

Ken Sasaki had been a *chūzaiin* employee with LASCO for almost two years. He became head of the Printer Group when it was formed in one of LASCO's reorganizations eight months before I began studying the company. During this tenure, this group became LASCO's most profitable business unit. Forty-two years old at the time of my fieldwork, Ken had joined the trading company when he was twenty-two and a fresh university graduate. LASCO was his second U.S. assignment. The first posting, a five-year stint, occurred when he was in his early thirties. Ken's English was difficult for someone unaccustomed to native Japanese speakers of the language. He spoke rapidly and, often, in monologue form with many incomplete sentences. Americans understood him from context and because of the energy and the emotion he communicated. Largely due to Ken's personality and behavior, deep emotional ties bound members of the Printer Group.

All but one of the core Americans (Dennis) also had an extended history with LASCO. Two years was the shortest tenure, while most of the Americans had worked there for five to eight years. Given their long association, the binational firm no longer was strange, unfathomable terrain. The individual personalities of the core Americans contributed to their adaptability. None of them were stridently individualistic, and on the whole, they were people more concerned with interesting and challenging work than with visible symbols of advancement. The "old-timer" members had been working together as part of the Printer Group since its inception.

It is important for understanding the dynamic of the Printer Group to note that two of the "Americans" were intimately familiar with Japanese culture. Daniel was of Chinese descent but grew up and attended university in Japan. Despite his fluency in English, some Americans saw Daniel as "Japanese" or, at least, "100 percent trading company oriented." He was well versed in trading company politics and lore, and he often accompanied the *chūzaiin* to lunch or dinner. Ellen, officially "Administrative Assistant" to Ken though her work involved various line responsibilities, also grew up in Japan and graduated from a Japanese university. Her father was Japanese, and her mother was of Chinese-English descent.

Ken took charge of subordinates who had, individually, extensive work experience. Core Americans ranged in age from thirty-six to fifty-seven, with the exception of the twenty-two-year-old Dennis, who will be discussed as a special case for understanding Ken's approach to learning. The seasoned North Americans each had held several jobs in the U.S. electronics industry before joining LASCO. LASCO constituted Daniel's only U.S. work experience, but Ellen had worked for another Japanese firm in the area.

I observed the Printer Group in what many organizational analysts would consider the total integration stage of its formation. It was a mature and well-functioning group able to deal with complex tasks and handle membership disagreements in creative ways; members were motivated by group goals and were generally satisfied (Schermerhorn, Hunt, and Osborn 1991). A substantial body of shared cultural knowledge that helped group members smoothly navigate their social setting had already emerged. Interestingly, this group alone, of all LASCO's Japanese-managed units, achieved such cohesion. Other work groups were unable to transcend the effects of American and Japanese differences in assumptions about work that contributed to the pronounced we–they dichotomy.

The Printer Group culture, for example, emphasized the integrating theme that the group is unlike any other work group in LASCO. Two broad understandings defined the group's uniqueness. For one, members considered themselves to be like a "family." Their version of family encompassed the notions that each person is an important part of the group and that everyone's ideas should be respected. Second, uniqueness was reflected in the idea that the Printer Group was the best group, a sentiment shared by many persons throughout LASCO. Not only was it the friendliness group; it was also "the crazy group," where everyone laughed and joked and had fun while, nevertheless, working hard. It was best, furthermore, because of its success (Kleinberg 1994a).

Enacting a Japanese theory of learning

It is noteworthy that, despite their experience and existing knowledge of the industry, as participants in the Printer Group, core subordinates relived the role of "newcomer" or learner. Equally noteworthy, the assumptions and behaviors required of persons in this role evoked a decidedly Japanese style. The following section of the chapter examines both the operative assumptions and the process by which Ken's subordinates learned the role of learner.

The meaning of membership

One set of assumptions, as mentioned, concerned "the meaning of membership." This phrase is not one that group participants used or would even feel comfortable with. Rather, it is a term that captures shared understandings regarding the work group.

Membership in the Printer Group meant a kind of emotional, and time, investment unfamiliar to most Americans. Ken often used the term "family" to represent the feeling of involvement and oneness he associated with membership. The Americans occasionally used this term but, more typically, simply talked about the group with a frequency, an excitement, and a warmth that demonstrated their understanding of involvement and belongingness.

The concept of membership also encompassed behavior directly related to work. Basic technical skill or knowledge naturally was expected. Just as importantly, membership meant expressing – through words, through actions – proper attitudes. Evident attitudes that reflected membership were: willingness (in Ken's words, a "spirit") to work hard, and to work until a task was completed; a flexible conceptualization of one's job; eagerness to master new skills and knowledge or to bring in new business; a willingness to help one's co-workers; and, finally, caring about the work group – as both a work and social unit. As has been noted for other, Japanese, work contexts (Rohlen 1974; Sumihara 1992), these attitudes often assume the force of morality.

In Ken's thinking, a critical task for the newcomer was to internalize the appropriate understanding of membership. Core workers also talked about the group in a way that indicated they too understood the necessity of *becoming* a member. Thus an important aspect of membership was the knowledge that understandings embedded in the concept were something to be acquired over time. Formal position, by itself, did not signify membership in the group. Membership was learned and earned.

The meanings attached to membership are reflected in the utterances of group members excerpted in the cultural description that follows. Reference to one particular participant, known here as Steve, and his brief (roughly three-month) sojourn in LASCO threads through the cultural description. Steve's presence sparked a situation in which Ken's teaching failed, eliciting responses that revealed much about Ken's understandings regarding learning.

Steve was hired by Ken into a new position of product marketing manager just before I focused on the Printer Group. From the first, he had difficulty. Steve's concept of the job contributed to his inability to mesh with the work group "family." He was, essentially, unable to accept the role of learner by which one acquired membership. In his American cultural experience, an incoming manager's success hinged on quickly making one's presence felt. Steve also had an industry-specific idea of what it meant to be a product marketing manager in terms of responsibilities and authority. Nevertheless, he entered the Printer Group without a job description and, in his view, without a clear mandate. He found, moreover, that various members of the group had responsibility for areas he believed were legitimately his responsibility, given his position. He aggressively attempted to alter the work setting to match his expectations.

Ken's reaction to Steve revealed, for one thing, the way he linked concepts of family, trust, and the process of getting a job done. One conversation, for instance, concerned Ken's hiring of Dennis, fresh out of college and comparatively unformed, to be the sales manager in the New York office. The choice reflected Ken's wish to bring in a person more amenable to the role of learner than Steve. Implicitly comparing Dennis to Steve, who had not yet left LASCO, Ken explained that a family feeling cannot be maintained if an employee is too "professional" in an American sense.

> Some are just too professional. I can't trust. Always like inside game with those people. And, as you may feel, in this area [the group], I want to bring it like a family. Once I trust men, I trust. And success or failure, I want to share with everybody. And for that purpose, and long-range target, I pick Dennis.

In Ken's mind, Steve's actions indicated he was in too much of a hurry to grab responsibility, besides being too territorial and too centered on self-interest. The job title by itself meant nothing to Ken. Rather, he assumed that a new person works into the group gradually, allowing time to see how his or her talents can best be utilized. He felt that he tried to convey to Steve this perspective on the gradual development of one's role. The following excerpt from a later conversation with Ken, after Steve was fired, reveals his moral outrage over Steve's failure to be a conforming, cooperative member of the group.

Judging from experience, I see his [Steve's] character better. He is into a political issue – to sell his name rather than doing the dirty job. . . . It is hard to adjust himself to the organization, yet he has a strong inside ambition to be regarded as a big shot. . . . He always spends more time on expanding his own responsibilities than on doing the job.

Other members of the group, especially the Americans whose responsibilities included some claimed by Steve, shared Ken's discomfort. As the group evolved, jobs took on a diffuse character, with tasks added as individuals showed both interest and capability. Members enjoyed the opportunity to develop on the job. Furthermore, work was structured in such a way that carrying out one's individual job required a good deal of cooperation among co-workers. Acceptance of diffuseness, overlap, ambiguity, and mutual aid – adding up to a general flexibility in one's job – constituted a primary attitude necessary for membership in the work group community.[4]

Ellen, for example, gained ever wider responsibility in scheduling product from Japan and interfacing with LASCO's Administration Group for billing and credit matters. Where her work had once involved just sales administration for accounts directly managed by Ken, increasingly she helped with accounts managed by American co-workers as well. Irving, whose job originally and formally centered on the Printer Group's technical support activities, expanded his responsibilities into new product development. John, in addition to his normal duties as a sales manager, gradually assumed responsibility for gathering current market information and supplying it to others in the group, especially to Irving and Ken.

With the proper attitude about flexibility, the group could maintain a healthy balance of self and group interests, where the primacy of group welfare need not be questioned. Steve's emphasis on clearly demarcating his responsibilities and authority vis-à-vis that of others threatened to destroy this balance. It promised also to destroy the dependencies built into work arrangements that helped hold the group together.

Another mark against Steve was his perceived reluctance to participate fully in the social life of the group. For example, after an intense two-day sales meeting, Steve declined to join the others for a late-night foray into Little Tokyo's bar scene. John later talked mainly about Steve's missed opportunity to build understanding with Ken. In fact, the core workers shared a tacit understanding that socializing was an important aspect of broader membership, of "fitting in" generally. In John's words:

I think he [Steve] made an error by not being there. A certain amount of personal time here to spend getting to know, by going there [Little Tokyo], we were getting to know his [Ken's] world. It's very beneficial to understanding him, one more item. It's a two-way street.

The Americans were reluctant to articulate their feelings about Steve but communicated their discomfort as much by what they left unsaid. One summed it up: "One of two things will happen. Either Steve will adjust to the situation and perform, or Steve will find himself a job elsewhere." Ken's and their attempts at molding, however, failed to bring Steve into group membership.

The social relations of learning

In this environment of interdependency, much of the cooperation directly related to learning reflected the willingness of seniors, or at least persons with more experience or knowledge, to help their juniors, or members who are less knowledgeable. This of course fits the model of *senpai–kōhai* relations, which play a key role in traditional craft and modern industrial settings (Rohlen 1974). Ellen and Daniel, the core members who shared Japanese cultural literacy with Ken, in particular performed the role of *senpai* to the other Americans. They did so, for instance, by serving as intermediaries in communications with Japan and by helping co-workers learn to communicate themselves by fax or phone with Japanese counterparts. Before Ken and the North Americans became comfortable with one another, Ellen and Daniel facilitated their communication as well, translating both words and intentions. North Americans also played the *senpai* role. John, Irving, and Harry, for example, were generous with their advice and offers of aid to Dennis.

Not surprisingly, Ken was the ultimate *senpai* for each of his subordinates. His relationship with other group members approximated in fact the traditional *oyabun–kobun* or patron–client pattern (Lebra 1976), with the accompanying assumptions of dependency and reciprocity. A later quote shows that Harry actually characterized the relationship with Ken as "a parent–child type thing" and described Ken as "almost like a protector." Ellen also cast Ken in the role of parent-protector, although she didn't use those terms. Despite being passed over for official promotion to manager (a circumstance she attributed to Ken not fighting hard enough for her with the president because of her gender), Ellen still considered him a mentor and felt a deep emotional attachment to him.

> But the reason I like this work, and I stay here, is I get the recognition from Ken. He understands me. And then he has good consideration for me. That's a big help. So I work hard on behalf of him, and my time is his time. So it's all right. But I need some kind of good recognition and consideration from him. And he's giving me, so . . . but I am happy if he can give me *better* [i.e., formal promotion].

Subordinates perceived that Ken established a very personal relationship with each individual. His ability to do this facilitated his role as parent or protector. Harry articulated at some length what makes Ken special, giving insight into how he cultivated respect and loyalty. (Harry cautioned: "Don't get me wrong, he's not God.")

He has a leadership quality that he just knows how to interact with people in group situations, one-to-one situations. I don't think it's something that's learned. I think it's an instinctive personality trait that he has which sets him apart from the rest of us and other managers inside the company. I think Ken's approach will vary to the individual, will vary to the person. I think he has a capability of having people want to work for him. He also has that unique capability of being able to, at least in my case, get my respect – and Ken and I do not agree on everything; he'll be the first to tell you we have many disagreements. [*Harry laughs.*] But I respect him, and I wouldn't want to work for anyone else [i.e., *chūzaiin*] inside this company other than Ken.

Ken has a way of getting his point across in such a manner that you know where he's coming from but, at the other end, he lets you know that you're a human being. He makes you feel like an entity and unique. But at the other end, you know and understand that he has a job to do. He has goals to meet, and he intends to meet them. And you have an option: Either together we can go forward and meet the goals, or we can go our different paths.

He is able to blend in, fit in. He's able to, at the end of work, become one of the guys. But yet you know he's not one of the guys. . . . Everybody I've spoken to, whether they agree philosophically with some of his positions, has the same type of feeling. So that's a uniqueness.

Clearly the relationship with Ken was the most significant one for core workers. Ken's actions, largely within the patron–client model, provided the main context for learning and for playing out the role of member. The North Americans' response to Steve is partly understood in this context. If, as Steve hoped, he eventually rose to be national sales manager, he would represent a hierarchical link between Ken and the American sales managers. Their sense of membership primarily hinged on the direct and close relationship with Ken. As Harry, the sales manager situated in Chicago, reflected:

I don't think he [Steve] understood the feeling that we as a group have about not being terribly anxious to have a national sales manager. . . . We want to maintain that – that accessibility [to Ken] . . . it's the type of thing where, if you will go back to the parent–child type thing, it's almost like a protector. I mean, he's there, and he does take care of his people. He'll tell *you* that you didn't do this or you should do this; but to the rest of the world, no way.

Shaping the learner

Ken molded subordinates to membership over time. For example, he made many occasions for social gatherings, initiating such rituals as lunches or dinners to celebrate birthdays, the arrival of a new worker, the departure of an old one. On these occasions, Ken usually made a short speech or said something funny or nice about each person. He laced his talk with references to "our unique group" and the "unique individuals" in it and publicly utilized the metaphor of family. The frequent extra-work activity with its face-to-face interaction and rich vocabulary expressing the group's specialness helped foster a sense of belongingness among members qualitatively different from what most American managers aim for.

North Americans sensed both the process of shaping and the, for them, elongated time frame. As they perceived it, shaping occurred in large part through task activity, notably with regard to access to information and responsibility. They enjoyed scant access to either until they had, as they understood it, won Ken's trust. John offered the following interpretation:

> I think that, at least within this organization, you have to earn your position. You are not given responsibility. You earn your responsibility. Therefore, you must display your trust[worthiness], your willingness to work, your devotion to the company and, once you have accomplished that, then the information and the amount of information you get just keeps going up.
>
> When I first came into the group with Ken, it was very difficult getting anything from him. It was almost a black-and-white, cut-and-dried type approach to the business. And, as we progressed, over the last six months – it's a total contrast now, where I can get almost any information that I require, you know. I think it's: number one, asking the right question; number two, asking at the right time; and the other thing is that he will trust you with the information when he gives it to you.

Harry echoed John's developmental perspective on the relationship with Ken. Ken created a particular relationship with each subordinate. The following excerpt reveals Ken, too, as a learner.

> What happened when he became my boss, his attitude was very stringent, not flexible ... and I think as his own personal responsibilities started to grow, and as the program became more successful and he built up the trust level with those people that worked for him, he started, little by little, to let the real Ken Sasaki come out. . . .
>
> I think he's to a degree conscious or feels – it might not be true – that he doesn't comprehend the language as well as he would like. So I think he feels insecure in that area. I think because of his own self-image that he wanted to maintain, initially he came on like he was concerned and very forceful. But later on, when he was able to understand the personalities – I think he deals with each of us differently, as individuals and separately, ... the two things were trust and success, which allowed him to loosen up and be more what I think he feels comfortable with.

In John's opinion, he earned Ken's trust because his work style was compatible with Ken's expectations. John talked enthusiastically about "finishing a job, developing a business from ground zero, and carrying it to success." Rigid conceptions of appropriate work hours or appropriate job responsibilities did not constrain him. As John described himself:

> I look at it like: I have a job to do, and if it means that I work til 8:00 at night, I'll work til 8:00 at night to get the job done. . . . I would rather complete the job and do a good job than worry about, you know, personal time. I do expect my weekends – that's my family time, and only if it's required for shows or whatever do I spend time out of town. But I think that they [the Japanese] have seen that – that I'll go to other groups, I'll do anything to solve the problem. Like I tell M. R. [secretary], "I don't have problems, I have challenges."

As John noted, people who proved to Ken that they were hard working, flexible, capable, loyal, *and* patient – in other words, that they satisfied Ken's notion of membership – gradually acquired greater responsibility and more challenging work. Such work was, in essence, reward for surviving the rigors of one's learner status; it was reinforcement for learning the proper way of thinking and behaving.

A vivid example of Ken shaping a proper understanding of responsibility among subordinates comes from the two-day sales meeting mentioned earlier. It was the group's first formal sales meeting, initiated and organized by the recently hired Steve. All the managers attended, including Harry and Dennis from out of town. (Daniel called Ellen in for the discussion of new products, as she had asked to be present for this.) Steve attempted to establish his position as marketing expert with a "philosophy" for the future success of the group. He also asked each person to outline their view of his (Steve's) job in his continuing effort to sort out and demarcate who was responsible for what in the group.

Not long into the meeting, however, it became clear that Ken, rather than Steve, controlled it. For example, he would interject with comments such as: "I don't want to disturb, but, just my suggestion: Presentation first. Questions so we understand. Later on we can fight or yell." Ken's agenda included, for one thing, guiding actual newcomers – that is, Steve and Dennis – toward an understanding of how they should approach their job. Several times, for instance, he directed Steve to work in cooperation with the head of the Marketing Group. (Ken was aware of friction between the two, again over ambiguities concerning respective responsibilities.)

> Steve, some suggestion from me. These days LASCO is regarded as a printer manufacturer, a new vendor. So a lot of people come here to visit Mr. Tateishi [the president]. They come with the new technology. They call Matt [Tateishi] or write to him. Because he is busy, I am busy, all that information goes to C. B. [Marketing Group Manager] . . . .

So you should keep good communication with him . . . and you feed back information to us. . . . But the corporate marketing, as I said before, he is responsible for the time being . . . so then we give Matt and C. B. [corporate marketing] contacts, right?

To Dennis, Ken gave guidance like:

You are new – just out of the university, fresh with LASCO. . . . In order to be a leader, from now on we need different information or idea. So I want your good comment. . . . Even if you have same idea as discussed by other, tell in your words. Exchange your own ideas and philosophy. In our group, everyone should say something. Don't hestitate.

One of Ken's main methods of molding subordinates was to reveal his thoughts to them. The principle was the same as in Japan, where subordinates learn indirectly through their *kachō*'s verbal and nonverbal behavior what his intentions or desires are. Working with North Americans, however, Ken was consciously more direct. The outcome should be the same: understanding and appropriate action. The nuance in both contexts is different from simply telling people what they should do; revealing one's thoughts concerns empathy between superior and subordinates. The following excerpt from a conversation with Ken gives a feeling for this process. The corollary, of course, is that the followers should be intent on trying to grasp the leader's thoughts.[5]

I feel comfortable to communicate here in the U.S., rather than in Japan. . . . Americans are very straight and easy to communicate. Sometimes with raw emotion, I speak myself. In Japan, very little chance to speak out myself. If I did, everyone thinks I'm crazy. My people [Printer Group] say I'm crazy anyway.

My nature is to be direct and say what I think. I show myself to anybody [in the group], and I think that all of them understand what I am thinking and want to do. . . . I don't care shouting or yelling. The next time we should laugh and smile. That's good.

Ken's behavior in the sales meeting demonstrated how he revealed his thoughts and built empathy by sharing information of a nature normally not accessible to LASCO's American employees. For example, he used the meeting to indicate the future direction of the company and the Printer Group. In doing so, he talked specifically about the troubled relationship between LASCO and Japan, intimating the proper response of group members:

Please remember next year is very important. Don't rely on TC Japan – very busy. So we make our own product specification. . . . If we are unhappy with TC Japan or SEC [the printer manufacturer], then we can find someone else to make. Very political. Of course, this is just philosophy. But if you have this philosophy, then your words to Japan will be effective. Not to fight against Japan, but to do the best business here – for TC Japan and TC America, too.

This sales meeting succeeded from Ken's perspective in that it furthered group identity and unity of purpose. It failed, however, from Steve's perspective, as it did not solidify his position in the group. During his remaining time with LASCO, he never learned to share responsibility and (properly) cooperate with others. While Steve thought at one point he had officially negotiated a satisfactory job description for his position, he was even more frustrated when it did not change anyone's behavior. Ken recalled everyone discussing the fact that "people get into the other's area" and that "he [Steve] didn't understand that way," but Ken did not indicate that he felt it was an issue that had been or needed to be resolved.

The formal break between Steve and LASCO came after information about a contemplated spin-off of the Printer Group as a new sales subsidiary prematurely leaked to the press, with Steve mentioned as the source. Ken justified firing Steve by the fact that "his philosophy does not meet with my requirements" and that Steve did not try to "fit in." He keenly felt his failure to bring Steve around, concluding "I didn't review his record and character and personality well enough."

We saw when he hired a sales manager for the Eastern region, he gave careful thought to the candidate's character and malleability. Ken interviewed four people in New York, deciding on twenty-two-year-old Dennis because he sensed desired qualities.

He is young, very capable, intelligent, nice looking, and very aggressive – but aggressiveness is inside. Inside aggressive. And very soft touch approach to other people . . . he would work well with OEMs.

This was the first time Ken had hired a subordinate whom he consciously planned to nurture Japanese style. He described his hopes for Dennis:

I have some ambition and hope to bring him and educate him – train him to be a very good member of LASCO. . . . I explain to him I am not interested in a short-range or typical American business relationship, between Dennis and LASCO and between Dennis and myself. I explain that it will be 80 percent Japanese way and 20 percent American way.

Ken said he would train Dennis much as he would train a successor to a job in Japan. Apparently he did not realize that the process outlined differed little from his mode of interaction with other core group members.

I talk to him. And occasionally I go, or I bring him to L.A. I have him sit down beside me [when representatives from OEMs visit]. I explain to him and ask him to comment on the conversation. This is the typical way of training the successor. So my know-how, learned through about twenty years, and I feel I should give away everything that I have to him.

Dennis joined LASCO fully cognizant that Ken had in mind a long-term mutual commitment. He viewed his present role as that of trainee and proved himself eager to learn. This hiring strategy was an experiment supported by LASCO's top management. Matt Tateishi talked often about the need to initiate American employees into the intricacies of the larger trading company organization; he considered, for example, sending people like Dennis to Tokyo for a year or two of training. If Dennis worked out well in the Printer Group, this kind of Japanese-style hiring would be tried more widely in the future.

Summary and discussion

Ken's approach to teaching his subordinates to be good Printer Group members resembled in significant ways my observations in rural pottery workshops and in the Tokyo subsidiary of the same Japanese trading company. Admittedly, certain details differed. Ken did not emphasize the philosophy of spiritualism or character building to the degree it was stressed in the other settings, although he did show awareness of character as both an objective of and fundamental precondition for learning. Nor did Ken have a notion, however abstract, of any particular sequence of stages for learning the work of production; he had only the idea that newcomers prove themselves through performance centered, initially, on basic and mundane tasks.

In all three contexts, however, the concept of membership was paramount; socialization into the work of production was inseparable from socialization into the status of member. And similar principles and methods underlay teaching this concept. Overarching was the principle of molding. Teachers and learners shared a whole set of understandings around recognition that people must be shaped to conform to the requirements of membership. They understood, for example, that shaping takes place over time, that rituals of social interaction contribute to the acquisition of membership, that task assignment is both a vehicle and a reward for learning, that task performance and attitude are linked, and that much of the learning revolves around intuitively grasping the thoughts and intentions of the teacher.

The intercultural setting described here, nonetheless, raises important questions. An obvious one is why the Printer Group exemplified a "Japanese" cultural theory of learning that resulted in a cohesive work group culture, when other Japanese-managed units in LASCO generally suffered from intercultural miscommunication and conflict. I have emphasized elsewhere (Kleinberg 1994a) that various factors contributed toward both the positive outcome and the "Japanese" flavor of it. These include the personalities, cultural background, and particular work experiences of group members, as well as the favorable market conditions for the work group's product.

The core Americans, on the whole, were not aspiring fast-trackers. Either they were innately more interested in the content of work than position and power, or their work history led them to expect few formal trappings of advancement. The rapid expansion in printer sales at the time of fieldwork nevertheless enabled group members to expand their work roles. As individuals, members tended to exhibit those personal qualities, like flexibility and cooperativeness, that some Japanese firms operating in the United States have learned consciously to seek when hiring local personnel (Sumihara 1992). Moreover, we have seen that Ellen and Daniel, somewhere between insider and outsider with respect to Japanese society, played a critical role of cultural intermediary.

Certain other Japanese group managers enjoyed a close relationship with one or two of the Americans in their work unit, normally where the American was predisposed to accept the status of learner. The explanation for the lack of groupwide cohesion built around Japanese cultural patterns in other groups is complex and different for each group. I briefly comment on two work groups to show the kinds of factors to consider.

One administrative support group, for instance, was perhaps too large to expect the same unity. Furthermore, the work itself engaged participants less in the sense of excitement or mission that helped unify the Printer Group. Because of its size, most people had as immediate "boss" a locally hired manager rather than the *chūzaiin* group manager who might embody a Japanese theory of learning. This particular *chūzaiin* manager indeed liked to talk about his theories of management and to contrast Japanese and American ways of doing things. Nevertheless, his intercultural skills were less developed than Ken's. His response to the difficulties of communication presented by language and cultural gaps was to withdraw from interaction with American subordinates, except the few he felt comfortable with or with whom communication was essential.

In another sales group, American subordinates constantly complained about their Japanese boss and about the group. Their complaints reflected general American subgroup cultural understandings: "We don't know what we are supposed to be doing; Pete [the boss] doesn't tell us what is going on; there is no place for me to advance."

Possibly a strong sense of membership would have emerged if the sales group included more LASCO old-timers and fewer individuals who were keenly concerned about career, and if the group were not constantly adding new members. But the personality of the Japanese manager again looms large as an explanatory variable. Pete was less patient than Ken. Moreover, he clearly had more interest in making sales than in the details of managing and educating subordinates – especially in the intercultural setting. Pete tended to interpret perceived differences in Japanese and American approaches to work as evidence of American inferiority. (This is not an uncommon perception among Japanese managers; see Sumihara [1992].) He did not avoid interaction with American subordinates, but he expected so little from them that he rarely tried to shape their thinking or behavior. It is my impression that, in an all-Japanese setting, Pete would manage within a theory of learning described in this chapter, although co-workers might well consider his version of the theory more oriented toward task than people. If he proved unable to manage in appropriately Japanese manner, he would not advance far in the organization (Rohlen 1974; Yoshino and Lifson 1986).

In all of this cultural description, have I actually described something that is uniquely Japanese? We know that some U.S. firms – IBM before its present restructuring being a prime example – strongly emphasize the selection of appropriate people and their systematic socialization into acceptance of well-articulated organizational values. Cross-cultural parallels always can be found. Nonetheless, if we look at situated learning holistically, the parallels become less obvious. A Japanese theory of learning, at least as I have observed it in practice, rests on ideas about relationships among people, and about the relationship of the individual to the group, neither of which are predominant normative patterns for most Americans. The case study of the Printer Group nevertheless shows that, under the right circumstances, Americans may begin to internalize these patterns. They may begin to spin new webs of significance markedly different from ones spun in the past.

Notes

1. Philip's (1989) tale of apprenticeship in a hinterland pottery making community offers an evocative portrayal of the way a learner is molded – to the master's mode of

conveying knowledge of the craft, as well as to the unwritten rules of membership in both workshop and community.

2. The analysis of meanings regarding learning largely rests on the same utterances and observed actions that provide data for uncovering other shared understandings of the Printer Group described in Kleinberg (1994a). This illustrates an important point about the complexity of the process of sorting out culture. The same utterance or string of utterances, or the same action, may simultaneously reflect different meanings or, in terms of ethnoscience ethnography, different categories of cultural knowledge (Spradley 1980).

   Revisiting the same data yields new levels of comprehension and some new interpretations. I quote Van Maanen (1988:118) on this point: "Coming to understand a culture in a way even remotely similar to that of those that live within it is a continuous and, if the fieldworker is careful, a deepening interpretive process. . . . Events and conversations of the past are forever being reinterpreted in the light of new understandings and continuing dialogue with the studied."
3. See Kleinberg (1994b) for a fuller description of organization-wide and Japanese and American subgroup cultures in LASCO, and for discussion of how these emergent cultures are influenced by nation-specific cultural assumptions regarding work, described in Kleinberg (1989).
4. Perhaps this is an assumption about work especially characteristic of a trading company; see Yoshino and Lifson (1986).
5. Silin (1976: chapter 2), in a study of leadership and values in large Taiwanese enterprise, discusses the importance of followers grasping the not always clearly revealed thoughts of the leader: "The prevention of disorder caused by egocentric behavior is a focal concern of leaders. The inculcation of personal loyalty through the perpetuation of the leader's thoughts is the main method by which he attempts to achieve this goal. Loyalty is thus largely conceived as a rationally determined subscription to the leader's thoughts" (57).

   In the Printer Group, grasping and acting upon Ken's thoughts also expresses loyalty and ensures order. In contrast to the Taiwanese case, however, the emotional element is important. In Taiwan, the concept of loyalty denies the emotional component, emphasizing instead a rational commitment that is dependent on the leader's success. "Emotionalism or appeals to emotional considerations as a means of achieving solidarity are associated with lower-class groups of dubious intent" (Silin 1976:58). We have then perhaps two different societal interpretations of Confucian-influenced organizational ideologies (e.g., Rohlen 1974; Silin 1976).

References

Frake, Charles O., 1983, "Ethnography," in Robert M. Emerson, ed., 1983, *Contemporary Field Research: A Collection of Readings,* Boston: Little, Brown, pp. 60–67.

Geertz, Clifford, 1973, *The Interpretation of Cultures,* New York: Basic Books.

Kleinberg, Jill, 1979, *Kinship and Economic Growth: Pottery Production in a Japanese Village,* Ann Arbor, MI: University Microfilms International.

1983, "Where Work and Family Are Almost One: The Lives of Folkcraft Potters," in David W. Plath, ed., *Work and Lifecourse in Japan,* Albany: State University of New York Press.

1989, "Cultural Clash between Managers: America's Japanese Firms," in *Advances in International Comparative Management,* Vol. 4, ed. Benjamin S. Prasad, Greenwich, CT: JAI Press, 221–243.

1994a, "The Crazy Group: Emergent Culture in a Japanese–American Binational Work Group," in *Research in International Business and International Relations,* 6: 1–45.

1994b, "Practical Implications of Organizational Culture Where Japanese and Americans Work Together," *NAPA Bulletin 14,* National Association of Practicing Anthropologists.

Lebra, Takie Sugiyama, 1976, *Japanese Patterns of Behavior,* Honolulu: The University Press of Hawaii.

Philip, Leila, 1989, *The Road through Miyama,* New York: Vintage Books.

Rohlen, Thomas P., *For Harmony and Strength: Japanese White Collar Organization in Anthropological Perspective,* Berkeley: University of California Press.

Schermerhorn, John R., J. G. Hunt, and R. N. Osborn, 1991, *Managing Organizational Behavior* (4th edition), New York: John Wiley & Sons, Inc.

Silin, Robert H., 1976, *Leadership and Values: The Organization of Large-Scale Taiwanese Enterprises,* Cambridge, MA: East Asian Research Center, Harvard University.

Spradley, James P., 1980, *Participant Observation,* New York: Holt, Rinehart & Winston.

Sumihara, Noriya, 1992, *A Case Study of Structuration in a Bicultural Work Organization: A Study of a Japanese-Owned and -Managed Corporation in the U.S.A.* Ann Arbor, MI: University Microfilms International.

Van Maanen, John, 1988, *Tales of the Field: On Writing Ethnography,* Chicago: University of Chicago Press.

Yoshino, Michael, and Thomas B. Lifson, 1986, *The Invisible Link: Japan's* Sogo Shosha *and the Organization of Trade,* Cambridge, MA: The MIT Press.

Epilogue

Calluses: When culture gets under your skin

David W. Plath

> I hold my right hand up to the light and look at it slowly. The skin is cracked in places, wrinkled and dry from daily contact with clay, the nails filed down past the fleshy tip. It looks more like a tool than a hand. I flex the fingers, watching the tendons pull over the knuckles in long lines. What did this hand look like a year ago? The fingers are thinner now; the muscles at the base of the thumb are thick and flexible. A long band of muscle running from my wrist up my forearm bulges slightly. Fall spent on teacups, winter repeating rice bowls, then spring concentrating on plates, and finally summer months of small-necked bottles and flower holders – my hands have been molded too.
>
> Leila Philip (1989:255–256)

A story that went around some years ago had to do with plans for a new dormitory for official visitors to the Vatican. Sketches for the building were sent up to the Pope for his approval, but many days passed without a response. The staff architects were troubled because His Holiness ordinarily returned papers promptly. When the sketches reappeared, they triggered a second worry: The Pope had not, as was his usual practice, covered the sheets with comments and suggestions. There was only one remark, in the margin of one of the drawings:

Suntni angeli?

Which means, as you all know from high school Latin, "Are they angels?" Only after careful study of the drawings did the architects get the message: They had forgotten to allow space for the toilets.

Are they *angels*? Some of us have been asking that question lately about a certain species of clever primate and how it goes around trying to humanize itself. We suspect that the late twentieth-century's reigning theories about learning and culture have become relentlessly cerebral. Such theories foreground the ways that knowledge is taken into the head. Or they point up cultural meaning as a process of conscription, a collective "writing on the body" as though it were a naked statue needing to be clothed in graffiti. But those who are constructing theory seem to have forgotten the toilets. It is as though the human body has been checked at the door and then left in the coat closet of scholarly attention. The result is a head model in which people acquire knowledge by some process of immaculate perception.

Or are *they* angels? If "they" are Japanese, it might seem so when we listen to our education presidents and governors, who portray "them" as citizens of an oriental Lake Wobegon, where all the children are above average. The media, as usual, go a step further and extrapolate this logic to the plane of cultural nightmare, announcing that just as "they" have been outproducing us on the assembly line, so "they" soon will be outthinking us in the classroom.

Earlier in the century, by contrast, when the media were less prissy about the human body, the nightmare of choice was the fear that "they" were beginning to outperform us physically, as evidenced by Japanese swimming medals in the 1932 Los Angeles Olympic Games. And then, as now, the explanation hinted at unfair competition: Japanese athletes were being given whiffs of oxygen just before leaving the locker room (Hoberman 1992:103).

The nightmare has a long pedigree; perhaps it arose as a byproduct of the Industrial Revolution a century earlier. Euro-Americans were uneasy about the possibility that mechanization was turning "civilized" people into couch potatoes. Savages and peasants (farmers without tractors) on the other hand remained capable of astonishing feats of strength and endurance. After Japan's victory in the Russo-Japanese War, the foremost French physiologist of the day, Philippe Tissie, made a field trip to Japan to examine bodies. On return, he reported that the Japanese may have had an "anthropological advantage." Their small stature and habits of sobriety enabled them to endure fatigue – a finding that may tell us more about French national anxieties than about Japanese actualities (Hoberman 1992:70).

If Patricia Steinhoff is right when she says that Japan Studies is confronting a "loss of irrelevance" (Steinhoff 1993), we all may be drawn inexorably into the forums of Western public discourse, where a favored trick is to play the Japan card. But unless we borrow a few ideas from forensic anthropology, we may have little to say about the salient issue of the fate of the human body in a postindustrial world. Or have Nintendo and the information superhighway rendered the wisdom of the body irrelevant?

I am not referring to our efforts to report information about the Japanese body so much as to our habits of underconceptualizing it. When we describe conduct in particular situations, we discover interesting things that happen below the cranium. If our subject is the arts, martial or graphic, we gaze down into the *kokoro* ("heart") or even below the belt into the *hara* ("guts"). But when we offer general sketches of Japanese character or self, the body fades. The robustly Japanese features, we say, are spiritual qualities such as *ki* or *seishin* (both translatable variously by words such as "spirit" or "soul" or "life-force," etc.) or social sensitivities such as *amae* ("hunger to be cared for") and *omoiyari* ("attentiveness to another's needs"). We feel compelled to explain how the Japanese self is embedded socially in Confucian duos of human relations, but we finesse the issue of how that self is embodied culturally – how it is flesh transformed, or what John Donne called "a province wrapped up in two yards of skin."

Dumb bodies

Shyness toward the carnality of knowledge is no property unique to the Japan researcher. All across late twentieth-century scholarship on the human condition, one sees a propensity to investigate symbolic inscription with more enthusiasm than is shown toward fleshly incorporation. The analytic activity of choice is to strip open the sociologic of signs and categories in the mind while leaving the body decorously clothed in its local "social construction."

Trend-setting thinkers have, to be sure, urged that we pay attention to the "live-ware" of the body as well as to the software of the mind. To take just one instance by way of illustration: Clifford Geertz (1973) sermonizes on the "danger that cultural analysis . . . will lose touch with the hard surfaces of life . . . and with the biological and physical necessities on which those surfaces rest" (30). He names the hard surfaces (for him they are the politico-economic substructures) but says nothing about the still-lower biological and physical necessities; perhaps he regards them as self-evident or invariant.

So one has to infer these necessities from his practice of cultural interpretation, and in his practice, culture equates with public meaning, which equates with traffic in symbols. Geertz offers the example – which many others have parroted over the last twenty years – of winks versus blinks. Winks can mean something and are open to interpretation; blinks cannot mean but only be. The body is outer habitat, a resource for possible meanings, but not inner habit, a generator of them. To use Geertz's famous phrase, culture is "local knowledge," by which he means it is localized in a particular place and time interval. In studies such as *Agricultural Involution* (Geertz 1963), he deftly demonstrates how such knowledge can take on physical form in the built environment. The human body is not included as part of the built environment.

But neither winks nor blinks help us apprehend the sedimentations of experience within the body. A callus, for example, is neither wink nor blink. It has inertial force, but it is not autonomic: These little trained insensitivities (petty bureaucrats of the flesh) develop only as a result of volition. We have to force ourselves to go on abrading the skin, to endure discomfort, often pain, until the flesh firms and hardens. On the other hand, a callus is not a communicable wink, though meanings might be read upon it and turn it into a badge of office or an emblem of effort sustained.

In short, the Geertzian approach, for all its achievements, does not help us bring the body out of the closet. It does not challenge our legacy of hypodermic models of learning, as do Jean Lave and others (including many authors in this volume), who start by situating learning within a community of practitioners. For them, knowledge becomes a property of activity, not a substance to be injected. From this perspective, we can begin to view the body as a mode of learning, not simply a repository of it. "If the body is not a thing," writes Simone de Beauvoir in *The Second Sex*, "it is a situation ... it is the instrument of our grasp upon the world, a limiting factor for our projects" (Murphy 1987:9). And this is the lesson I draw from the book I call Murphy's Testament.

Robert F. Murphy was a talented social anthropologist. During the time we were colleagues in the same department at Berkeley, I came to treasure his perceptiveness about human relations and his wit in describing them. A decade later, Murphy felt the first spasms of what turned out to be a degenerative tumor of the spine. Slowly, inexorably over several years, he lost all capabilities of movement. His mind remained quick, however, and by will and effort he was able to record in plain prose what happens to those afflicted in midlife by paralysis, persons "who have to become reembodied to their impairments" (ibid. 10).

Don't think of my book as autobiography, says Murphy, "but the history of the impact of a quite remarkable illness upon my status as a member of society, for it has visited upon me a disease of social relations no less real than the paralysis of the body" (ibid. 4). Disability of this magnitude, he explains, is not just an encumbrance on living but an ontology, a condition for being-in-the-world.

The body is not just an implement, Murphy adds, not just some quintet of sense organs orchestrated and conducted by a mind. "The landscape of the body is, explicitly or implicitly, the means and the perspective by which we place ourselves in environments and experience their dimensions ... the body is not a thing, an entity separate from the mind and from the rest of the world in which it is situated. The body is also a set of relationships that link the outer world and the mind into a system" (ibid. 99). Murphy sums up his personal situation-in-the-world by giving his book the title *The Body Silent.*

Smart bodies

Some of us are beginning to rephrase Freud's question and ask if all knowledge needs to be reexamined as a form of carnal knowledge. Setting aside those themes of sexuality or libido that Freudians seem compelled to discover everywhere, we are asking rather literally how knowledge gets under our skin (Strauss 1992:1) or, like calluses, into it. (For a brief and lively essay, see Kensinger [1991]; for discursive overviews, see Lock [1993] and Worthman [1992].)

Likely places for learning, a key theme in the chapters of this volume, are a convenient beachhead from which to launch inquiry because the conduct of apprentices has to be seen as involving the "live-ware" of the body (the potter's molded hands) and the hardware of things (properties of tools and clays) as much as the software of the mind (inherited ideas about what pots should look like and be good for).

Freud's ideas about body modalities were a promising step toward conceptualizing human physiology as a system of learning and not just a receptacle for learning. The modalities offer a view of early infancy as a period of apprenticeship that all of us must pass through – we must discover how to become situated within a human body just as later we must discover the sounds and meanings of the local language. Long before we even can walk, much less talk, we are incorporating routines for dealing with the world around us: ways of breathing, ingesting, excreting. Shaped by local custom and personal peculiarities, we "in-form" our body as a house of habits, psychosomatic calluses that both facilitate and frustrate our projects.

As most of you are aware, the idea of body modalities fell into scorn at least among social scientists after enthusiasts propelled it beyond the brink of explanatory overkill. The approach has been denounced so often that I need not add another voice to the chorus. I will only note that the early Freudians' weakness was the reverse of the Vatican architects: They could not forget about the toilets. And they made an array of assumptions, central to theory, that empirical research has yet to confirm – assumptions such as that in any society the mothers of infants make up a community of practitioners that is homogeneous.

Applied to our apprenticeships that erupt after infancy, Freudian pedagogical thinking must be modified in other ways as well. It is primarily a torso psychology, fascinated by orifices but indifferent to the extremities or to humanity's astonishing talents for mobility. Also, the approach bypasses the question of how the modalities connect up as a system. In many kinds of situated learning, however, the big challenge is not that of polishing particular motions so much as it is getting one's whole act together.

Before I began to train students in the use of cameras for ethnographic field research, I expected their main difficulty would be acquiring hand–eye coordination. As it turns out, some of them need more time than others do for this, but there are only a few congenital klutzes who never seem to master the task. The great hurdle for most people comes in learning to blend the camera – which means its operator as well – into the impromptu and often very subtle choreographies of reverberating movements that occur in any ordinary scene of human action this side of catatonia.

This involves software issues in the mind: All of us are shy some of the time. And some students, shy or not, have absorbed postmodernist dogma about the camera as Intrusive Tool of the Oppressive Colonialist Gaze. But the veteran camera operator learns that people are just as likely to welcome as to resent the presence of the camera *as long as* it is not being used to peer in some voyeuristic way. This requires the right "live-ware" of the body. Camera and operator must become participants in the action, moving unobtrusively in synch with the ensemble. In the hyperverbal milieu of our graduate schools, it is not easy for students to take the plunge into whole-body learning.

The documentary films of Robert Flaherty go in and out of favor with shifting fashions among the critics. But Robert Flaherty the camerman continues to evoke admiration from the community of practitioners. For example, Basil Wright, himself a master, remarked forty years later about Flaherty's 1933 film *Industrial Britain*: "I still think it's a marvelous film. I still do. I think the shooting is marvelous: the magic with which that old boy Flaherty could anticipate a movement, start to move his camera just before the potter was going to move his hands ... " (Sussex 1975: 27). Leila Philip's master told her many times, "Your mind may forget, but your hands, never" (Philip 1989:255).

The *ama,* the shellfish divers that Jacquetta Hill and I have been studying for some years (see Chapter 12, this volume), are a particularly instructive example of whole-body learning. They very literally must engage in total immersion as the first requisite for practicing their craft. It is not just an encumbrance but a state of being in the world.

The divers work in a hostile environment around rocky reefs, in tidal waters. Few humans can remain submerged for more than about two minutes without an artificial source of air, which the divers are forbidden to use. No primate has adapted to full-time existence in that environment, and not even the most selfish primate gene appears to covet it. One survives there only by keeping a complex battery of psychophysical skills and sensibilities in smooth, ongoing coordination. One can thrive there as a huntress only by continuing to reimmerse while carrying on advanced studies of the seascape, of the habits of abalone in it, and of the behavior of one's rivals who are just as eagerly pursuing those same abalone.

Focusing the self, centering, "becoming one-pointed" is a key concern in *aikidō* and other martial arts, in Zen and other modes of meditation, in *sumō* and other sports. But all such forms of practice are terrestrial. The body in zero position is planted against the deck and held to it by gravitation. Posture is upright most of the time. And except for during a tornado or typhoon, ambient air pressure against eardrums, eyeballs, lungs, and kidneys will vary so little that it can be disregarded as constant.

Out in the tidewater, the *ama* have few such luxuries. Buoyancy pulls against gravitation so that a diver must exert herself just to remain submerged and continue her mission. Ambient water pressure increases with depth; more than a few feet below the surface, it is strong enough that she must be attentive to the dangers of tissue rupture. She would prefer to work upright, or at least horizontal, but much of the time she will be working in a head-down mode. This is because body fat accumulates around the hips and makes them more buoyant than the head and thorax, an encumbrance that worsens with age. She is immersed in a brine that pickles the skin and that is in motion continuously, often erratically. Reefs and sea bottom are stable compared to the waters, and yet much of the time they *appear to be* moving because the diver sees them through relentlessly swirling fronds of vegetation.

In other words, the tidewater environment multiplies the problem of keeping one's body modalities harmonized. Vertigo is an ever-present threat. *Ama* will never be postmodernist because a "de-centered" diver is soon going to be a dead diver. De-centering translates into vertigo, and vertigo can trigger panic: One loses coordination or sense of location and direction; one gulps seawater instead of air. Or at the extreme, one goes out-of-body in the "ecstasy of the deep" (more likely by far to afflict an amateur sport diver than a professional *ama*) – plunging deeper and deeper in the mistaken conviction that one is no longer at the mercy of ambient water pressure or the entropy of respiration.

Many *ama* take Dramamine to dampen the potential for motion sickness, which can encourage vertigo. And when the divers invite a visitor to ride to sea with them, the inevitable first question is, Do you get seasick? When I heard the question for the first time, I thought it was a matter of polite concern for a guest, perhaps backed by the experience of having had to collect the flowers of someone else's motion sickness. Having spent two of my Navy years riding amphibious landing craft, I am prepared to testify that of all of mankind's schemes for inducing motion sickness, the prize should go to small craft bobbing in the tidal zone. But I am wondering if the divers' attention to others' susceptibilities might also be reflexive evidence of their own deep-seated worries over becoming de-centered. To collapse this dynamic of centering into the static concept of body *image,* or into the passive concept of the body as turf for symbolic "contesting," is once more to render the body silent.

Reembodiment

Submerged in tidal surges of bioelectronic technology, our species is now obliged to reembody itself as part of a new phase of being-in-the-world. We need new psychophysical calluses so that we will be more effective, and maybe a little more comfortable, using all the new hardware and software that the twentieth century has thrust into our everyday environments.

We are caught in a crossfire of possibles. On the one hand, electronic delivery systems, which promise out-of-body raptures in virtual reality, seem to be shrinking and stunting our capacity for immediate sensory experience. On the other hand, the new biotechnologies – organ transplants, mechanical implants, steroid injections, and so on – seem to be extending our ranges of physiological performance and endurance way beyond what could have been predicted even a generation ago. Human genes were not programmed to deal with this situation "naturally" – we are obliged to cultivate ourselves for the task. Nowadays many of us in many of our daily activities feel like apprentices struggling to steal the secrets of a shopful of new tools.

The challenge is not just to acquire new skills but also to acquire poise, at-home-ness while using them on this new landscape of carnality, a landscape still cut by the old rift valley of mortality. Listening to the rhetoric of the techno-missionaries (for whom paradise is a globally integrated virtual reality), there are times when I feel like paraphrasing the Pope's query and asking if anybody is designing pit stops for the information highway.

To put it into anthropological terms, we have been given a new agenda for domestication. Much as our Neolithic ancestors had to tame the raw powers of plants, animals, and fires, we need to make the new technologies user-friendly, servants to our projects.

Or to borrow a phrase from Japanese English, the issue is not high-tech so much as "my-tech." A lexicon of "my" words erupted into Japanese speech about thirty years ago. As incomes doubled with prosperity, people could upgrade their kits of personal machinery – trade motorbikes for automobiles, radios for televisions. *Maikā* (my-car) is allegedly the earliest of these locutions, supposedly coined by a Toyota marketing executive. But soon there were other terms as well, ones such as *maikarā* (my-color, i.e., my television) and *maikūrā* (my-cooler, i.e., room air conditioner) (Plath 1990).

What is so intriguing about these little words is that in ordinary Japanese speech, each of them functions as a unit, a noun. *Mai-* and *-kā* can be parsed into two morphemes, but they fuse in a single word. And this word has to be rendered in American English as two words, as "private car" or "personal automobile," without the first-person possessive. In Japanese, *maikā* can belong to anybody. One can refer to his, her, your, our, even to my *maikā*.

"My-tech" is repopulating the world with new models of selfhood. And the received ideologies, the established systems of prestige and status, will have to come to terms with these biomechanically magnified hominoids. In one direction, the "my-tech" self, oriented to biomechanical others as well as to human ones, complicates and weakens those traditional systems of morality that try to control persons by binding them in human relationships. The primal scene (played recurrently in the United States in comic strips) is encapsulated in the utterance, "Dad, can I have the car keys tonight?"

In another direction, "my-tech" rivals the gateway to liberation that the modern state opens with its promise to guarantee personal civil rights. This promise of hard-individualism-by-force-of-law is cross-cut by "my-tech's" premise of a hardware individualism based on equal access to the open road. All models of cars are created equal on the Interstate – at least in the ideal – and so are all modems on the Internet. And you are in the driver's seat.

The Freudian concept of body modalities addressed the issue of embodiment as a universal and recurrent process that all of us undergo singly in order to be recruited into the species. But the Freudians have been indifferent, even hostile, to the historical problem of collectively reembodying a new wave of technologies. Credit the Freudians with helping people shake off some forms of surplus bodily repression, but when it comes to "my-tech," the Freudians are flaming reactionaries.

As the one discipline in the humanities and social sciences that claims to take species incarnation seriously, anthropology has got to give more attention not only to reembodiment in technology's environments but also to the body as an environment for technology. I'd like to think that this is beginning to happen, that as a discipline we will revitalize the sense of mission that Franz Boas set for us a century ago – to understand how our species transforms the landscapes of our habited bodies every bit as much as the social and physical terrain we inhabit.

Zeami put it this way, in his instructions to practitioners of *nō* drama: "The mind of a master is a mind able to understand its own body's capabilities."

Note

The name Kōhara Yukinari does not appear in the text nor are any of his many books and articles cited, but this chapter ultimately derives from the many long conversations, over more than thirty years, in which he has patiently tutored me in his unique vision of an "anthropology of the body." Very little of his work has been translated into English; I hope that somebody out there with the appropriate language skills will get the message. It was Professor Kōhara who persuaded my wife and me to get acquainted with the shellfish divers of the Shima Peninsula.

References

Geertz, C., 1963, *Agricultural Involution,* Berkeley: University of California Press.

1973, *The Interpretation of Cultures,* New York: Basic Books.

Hoberman, J., 1992, *Mortal Engines: The Science of Performance and the Dehumanization of Sport,* New York: The Free Press.

Kensinger, K. M., 1991, "A Body of Knowledge, or the Body Knows," *Expeditions 33*: 3, 37–45.

Lock, M., 1993, "Cultivating the Body: Anthropology and Epistemologies of Bodily Practice and Knowledge," *Annual Review of Anthropology 22*: 133–155.

Murphy, R. F., 1987, *The Body Silent,* New York: Henry Holt and Company.
Philip, L., 1989, *The Road through Miyama,* New York: Vintage Books.
Plath, D. W., 1990, "My-Car-Isma: Motorizing the *Showa* Self," *Daedalus 119*: 3, 229–244.
Steinhoff, P., 1993, "Japanese Studies in the United States: The Loss of Irrelevance," in *The Postwar Development of Japanese Studies in the U.S. – Historical Review and Prospects for the Future,* Tokyo: International House of Japan.
Strauss, C., 1992, "Models and Motives," in R. D'Andrade and C. Strauss, *Human Motives and Cultural Models,* Cambridge: Cambridge University Press, pp. 1–20.
Sussex, E., 1975, *The Rise and Fall of British Documentary: The Story of the Film Movement Founded by John Grierson,* Berkeley: University of California Press.
Worthman, C. M., 1992, "Cupid and Psyche: Investigative Syncretism in Biological and Psychosocial Anthropology," in T. Schwartz, G. M. White, and C. A. Lutz, *New Directions in Psychological Anthropology,* Cambridge: Cambridge University Press, pp. 150–178.

Selected glossary

aburamushi: cockroach; literally grease beetle; auto mechanic
aikidō: art of self-defense (martial art)
aikyōgen: interlude in a *nō* play
ama: female diver; literally woman of the sea; e.g., shellfish divers (Chapter 12)
amae: dependency; hunger to be cared for
amaeru: to actively seek dependence on another
amayakasu: to be indulgent
arubaito: side job; moonlighting work
aruchū (or *arukōru chūdoku*): alcoholism
arukōru: alcohol
ashigaru: samurai of the lowest rank
atama de oboeru: head learning (cf. *karada de oboeru*)
bakabakashii: silly, ridiculous
bandai-san: attendant at a public bath
biwa: Japanese lute
bon: Buddhist summer festival of the ancestors
bōnenkai: year-end party
bugaku: court dance and music
bunjin: scholar; literary man
burikko: one who coyly feigns helplessness in order to dodge responsibility
buyō: Japanese dance
chadō: tea ceremony; the way of Tea
chūzaiin: employees delegated from headquarters to branch offices of a Japanese corporation (Chapter 19)
daidō: proper course of action; a great cause; literally main road
daimyō: lord of a fief
daisenpai: superior seniors; literally a big senior
dandori: stages of work; an order of tasks for a particular job (Chapter 8)
danketsu: unity
Danshukai: Japanese sobriety group modeled in part after Alcoholics Anonymous (Chapter 17)
dashi: parade float
dentō: tradition; traditional
deshi: apprentice; literally disciple
deshi gashira: head students (e.g., in the Kanō school atelier, Chapter 3)

detchibōkō: apprenticeship in commercial families and family shops
dō: a traditional art; the Way; the fourth stage of martial arts training (alternative reading for *michi*)
dōjō: training hall
dōzoku: organization of households linked by real or fictive genealogical ties
edokoro: studio, workshop
ehon kata: senior students in charge of the copybooks in the Kanō school atelier (Chapter 3)
enryo: restraint; reserve
fukoku kyōhei: rich country, strong army
funado: boater divers, skilled *ama* who work with boatmen for maximum catches (Chapter 12)
funpon: copy, painting reproduced for reference
funponshugi: copybook method of teaching art; literally doctrine of *funpon*
Gāden: literally garden; name of a new community (Chapter 15)
gagaku: court music and dance
gakuga: paintings that display innate talent of the painter (Chapter 3)
ganbaru: persistence; hold on; perseverance
gei: art; the third stage of martial arts training
geko: one who cannot tolerate alcohol; teetotaler
genzai: the present time
gi: technique; the first stage of martial arts training
gofun: white paint (used for tracing a painting)
gōkata: rural district
guinomi: large sake cup
haiku: seventeen-syllable Japanese poetry form
hakobu: walking style in *nō*
hama: beach
hamon: expulsion
han: team, group; feudal domain
hana: flower; used by Zeami to describe dramatic accomplishments of an actor
hansei: reflection, self-examination, introspection
hara: belly, "guts"
hatsubutai: first stage appearance (in *kyōgen,* Chapter 5)
hatsuen: first performance (in *kyōgen,* Chapter 5)
hatsuyaku: first role (in *kyōgen,* Chapter 5)
hiden: secrets; secret transmission
hiragana: cursive characters of a Japanese syllabary (for words of domestic origin)
hiraki: opening performances for an actor that lead to a new stage of their career (in *kyōgen,* Chapter 5)
hōchō no ie: house of the slicing knife; an *iemoto* of fish slicers (Chapter 1)
hyakkai reikai: attend a hundred meetings (e.g., in Danshukai, Chapter 17)
ibento: (public) event
ichiba: marketplace, market
ichimai mono: single sheet compositions, paintings
ichininmae: fully formed; full-fledged
ie: family; household

iemoto: lineage schools of fine arts; head of such a school
ieomto seido: the *iemoto* system
ieryū: art or style of a household (e.g., in *iemoto* arts)
igaku hakase: medical doctorate, M.D. degree
ikebana: flower arranging art
ikyoku: medical office, department
ippuku: a break; rest; a tea break
iso: tidal zone; seashore, beach
ittaikan: feeling of oneness, unification
jabayashi: dragon band member (in the dragon festival, Chapter 15)
jakata: dragon dancer (in the dragon festival, Chapter 15)
jaodori: dragon dance (in the dragon festival, Chapter 15)
jichikai: self-government board
jizō: guardian deity of children (often represented by simple stone statues)
jo, ha, kyū: stages of rhythmical process from slow to fast (e.g., in *nō* drama, Chapter 2)
jō: upper rank
jōruri: ballad narration for the puppet theater
Jubokushō: a treatise on calligraphy (Chapter 4)
juku: private schools for after-school classes, tutoring, sports, arts, etc.
jutsu: skill; the second stage of martial arts training
kabuki: classical Japanese drama form, a popular form of theater
kachō: section chief (family head – when written with a different Chinese character)
kangeiko: training and exercises in the middle of winter
kanji: Chinese characters used in Japanese writing and names
kanri kumiai: management association
kanri yakyū: managed baseball (Chapter 16)
karada de oboeru: learning by the body (cf. *atama de oboeru*)
kasaboko: decorated umbrella used in festivals
kata: precise practice exercise forms (often associated with the martial arts)
kazoku: family
keiko: lesson; practice
keikoba: practice room, hall
keikogaki: drawing practice
kendō: Japanese-style fencing (a martial art)
kenkyūsei: research student; apprentice teacher (e.g., in Suzuki's Talent Education Institute, Chapter 9)
kenshō: a cleared mind; literally seeing into one's own nature (Zen, Chapter 18)
ki: spirit; energy
kibishii: severe
kisozukuri: craft skills; foundational skills for making something (e.g., pottery)
koan: riddle (Zen, American adaptation, *kōan* in Japanese)
kobun: junior (in paternalistic relationship)
kōhai: junior (in hierarchical relationship)
kokoro: spirit; heart; heart and mind
koshi: hips
koto: long Japanese harplike instrument

koya: clubhouse, hut
kuden: secret oral transmission
kuge: noble; nobility
kurikaeshi: repetition
kurō: hardship
kyōchōsei: cooperative attitude
kyōgen: classical comic drama, usually performed in association with *nō* drama (Chapter 5)
ma: the space in-between (in *aikidō*)
maikā: personal car (Epilogue)
maikārā: personal color television (Epilogue)
maikūrā: personal cooler, air conditioner (Epilogue)
manzai: comic stage dialogue
matsuri: community festival
michi: road; way; journey; duty (used in relation to the intensive learning of art, religion, morality)
mikoshi: portable shrine used in community festivals
minarai: apprentice; novice who learns by observation
mingei: folk art; folkcraft (word invented by Yanagi Sōetsu)
mohon: copybook; paintings copied as models for one's future studies (Chapter 3)
monomane: the imitation of things; role playing (Zeami uses the term to mean an actor's essentialization of a role, Chapter 2)
mosha: copy, reproduction
mukuchi: taciturn; literally having no mouth
nagauta: epic songs
naginata: halberd; shafted weapon with axlike cutting blade
natori: accredited master (in Japanese dance)
ningyō jōruri: puppet theater
nō: Japanese medieval lyrical drama (English spelling Noh)
nusumi keiko: surreptitious learning; stolen lessons
okedo: bucket divers, *ama* who use floating tubs to collect their catch (Chapter 12)
oku eshi: high-ranking official painters (of the Kanō school, Chapter 3)
omoiyari: sympathy, compassion; attention to another's needs
omote eshi: second-rank official painters (of the Kanō school, Chapter 3)
Oomoto: a new religion (Chapter 4, official spelling in roman characters)
ōrai: copybook, e.g., for practicing calligraphy
oyabun: senior (in paternalistic relationship)
oyabun-kobun: paternalistic relationship (literally parent-role and child-role, but referring to bosses and followers)
oyogido: swimmer divers; beginning stage in an *ama* career (Chapter 12)
rakugo: comic story telling performance
roshi: American adaptation of *rōshi* to mean Zen priest (Chapter 18, in Japanese *rōshi* means an old teacher or priest)
ryū: style; art
ryūgi: school; system; method
sadō: the Way of Tea
sainō: ability; talent

Sainō Kyōiku: development of ability; Talent Education (official translation for Suzuki violin teaching method, Chapter 9)
sakazuki: small sake cup
sakka: artist
samisen (or *shamisen*): Japanese three-stringed guitar
sashimi: sliced raw fish
satorasaseru: to lead one to realization (i.e., teaching without teaching); leading to spiritual enlightenment
satori: spiritual awakening (Zen)
seishin: spirit; spiritual
seishin tōitsu: mental concentration
seiza: sit straight upright
senpai: senior
senpai-kōhai: senior–junior relationship
sensei: teacher; master; general term of respect
senshu: player
sentō: public bathhouse
setoyasan: potter, literally plate maker; craftsman (Chapter 7)
shakuhachi: Japanese flute
shamisen (or *samisen*): Japanese three-stringed guitar
shasei: sketching or painting directly from nature (Chapter 3)
shiatsu: a Japanese medical massage therapy
shishō: master, teacher (in relation to an apprentice)
shitsuga: paintings that display systematic training, i.e., learned skills (Chapter 3)
shitsuke: discipline, manners (acquired through upbringing)
shogakai: painting and calligraphy gatherings
shōji: sliding door frames covered with paper
shōka dōzoku: entrepreneurial families; linked commercial household organizations
shū, ha, ri: observance, break away, detachment (e.g., in learning tea practice)
shūdan seikatsu: group life
shūgyō: course of learning
shujū kankei: master–pupil relationship
sōgō: high rank of Buddhist priest, also applied to some artists in the Tokugawa era (Chapter 3)
sumō: Japanese traditional wrestling
sunao: docile; obedient; gentle
taiken happyō: public announcement of one's experience (e.g., in Danshukai meeting for alcoholics, Chapter 17)
tarento: radio and television performers, "talent"
taru mikoshi: small portable sake-cask shrine
tatami: thick straw floor mat
tehon: a model or pattern for practice
tejun: order of hand movements
te-tsumugi: hand spinning and weaving (Chapter 11)
tōban: monitor; person on duty; person temporarily responsible for a particular duty
totei: apprentice
totei seido: apprenticeship system

uchi: insiders' group (e.g., family, work group)
uchi deshi: live-in apprentice
ukiyoe: pictures of the floating world (actors, courtesans, and townspeople), a style of popular prints and paintings based on everyday reality
wa: harmony; fellowship
yakifude: charcoal brush for drawing
yakimono: pottery
yakyū: baseball
yamatoe: paintings done in medieval native Japanese styles and themes
yūgen: deep, dim, mysterious (Zeami used this term to describe an actor's grace, Chapter 2)
zaibatsu: monopolistic business corporate groups
zazen: religious meditation (Zen)

General bibliography

Anderson, Jennifer L., 1991, *An Introduction to Japanese Tea Ritual,* Albany: State University of New York Press.

Becker, Howard S., 1982, *Art Worlds,* Berkeley: University of California Press.

Coy, Michael, ed., 1989, *Apprenticeship: From Theory to Method and Back Again,* Albany: State University of New York Press.

von Durckheim, Karlfried Graf, 1962, *Hara, The Vital Centre of Man,* London: G. Allen & Unwin.

Goody, Esther, 1989, "Learning, Apprenticeship, and the Division of Labour," in Coy, ed., pp. 233–257.

Herrigel, Eugen, 1953, *Zen in the Art of Archery,* Boston: Routledge and Kegan Paul.

Hori, G. Victor Sōgen, 1994, "Teaching and Learning in the Rinzai Zen Monastery," *The Journal of Japanese Studies,* 20: 5–35.

Hsu, Francis L. K., 1975, *Iemoto: The Heart of Japan,* Cambridge: Schenkman.

Irie, Hiroshi, 1988, "Apprenticeship Training in Tokugawa Japan," *Acta Asiatica,* 54: 1–23.

Isabella Stewart Gardner Museum, 1993, *Fenway Court 1992* (Special issue, John R. Rosenfield, ed., "Competition and Collaboration: Hereditary Schools in Japanese Culture"), Boston: Isabella Stewart Gardner Museum.

Kondo, Dorinne, 1990, *Crafting Selves: Power, Gender, and Discourses of Identity in a Japanese Workplace,* Chicago: University of Chicago Press.

Lave, Jean, and Etienne Wenger, 1991, *Situated Learning: Legitimate Peripheral Participation,* Cambridge: Cambridge University Press.

(Peak), Lois Taniuchi, 1986, "Cultural Continuity in an Educational Institution: A Case Study of the Suzuki Method of Music Instruction," in Merry I. White and Susan Pollack, eds., *The Cultural Transition: Human Experience and Social Transformation in the Third World and Japan,* Boston: Routledge and Kegan Paul, pp. 113–140.

Philip, Leila, 1989, *The Road through Miyama,* New York: Vintage Books.

Pirsig, Robert M., 1974, *Zen and the Art of Motorcycle Maintenance: An Inquiry into Values,* New York: Morrow.

Plath, David W., and Jacquetta Hill, 1987, "The Reefs of Rivalry: Expertness and Competition among Japanese Shellfish Divers," *Ethnology,* 26: 151–163.

Rimer, J. Thomas, and Yamazaki Masakazu, 1984, *On the Art of the Nō Drama: The Major Treatises of Zeami,* Princeton: Princeton University Press.

Rohlen, Thomas P., 1973, " 'Spiritual Education' in a Japanese Bank," *American Anthropologist* (October), 75: 1542–1562.

1974, *For Harmony and Strength: Japanese White Collar Organization in Anthropological Perspective,* Berkeley: University of California Press.

Rosenberger, Nancy R., ed., 1992, *Japanese Sense of Self,* Cambridge: Cambridge University Press.

Singleton, John, 1989a, "Japanese Folkcraft Pottery Apprenticeship: Cultural Assumptions in Educational Practice," in Coy, ed., pp. 13–30.

1989b, "*Gambaru:* A Japanese Cultural Theory of Learning," in James J. Shields, Jr., ed., *Japanese Education: Patterns, Problems, and Prospects,* University Park: Pennsylvania State University Press, pp. 8–15.

1992, "Deconstructing Apprenticeship Models in Folkcraft Pottery: Traditional Arts and Alternative Careers in Mashiko Workshops," in Paul Greenough, ed., *Redefining the Artisan: Traditional Technicians in Changing Societies,* Center for International and Comparative Studies, University of Iowa, pp. 101–118.

Yanagi Sōetsu (adapted by Bernard Leach), 1972, *The Unknown Craftsman: A Japanese Insight into Beauty,* Tokyo: Kodansha International, Ltd.

Index